SOUP THROUGH
THE AGES

SOUP THROUGH THE AGES

A Culinary History with Period Recipes

Victoria R. Rumble

Foreword by Sandra Oliver

McFarland & Company, Inc., Publishers
Jefferson, North Carolina, and London

Frontispiece: Mother feeds her daughter from a bowl of hot porridge, one of the most basic forms of soup, and often the main source of nourishment for children, especially in Scotland. Chromolithograph A. & C. Kaufmann, ca. 1873 (Library of Congress, Prints and Photographs Division, Reproduction Number LC-DIG-pga-01725).

LIBRARY OF CONGRESS CATALOGUING-IN-PUBLICATION DATA

Rumble, Victoria R., 1957–
Soup through the ages : a culinary history with period recipes / Victoria R. Rumble ; foreword by Sandra Oliver.
p.   cm.
Includes bibliographical references and index.

ISBN 978-0-7864-3961-4
softcover : 50# alkaline paper ∞

1. Soups—History.   2. Food habits—History.   I. Title.
TX757.R86   2009   641.8'13 — dc22   2009011893

British Library cataloguing data are available

Cover photographs ©2009 Pictures Now

Manufactured in the United States of America

McFarland & Company, Inc., Publishers
Box 611, Jefferson, North Carolina 28640
www.mcfarlandpub.com

With love to my sons,
Joshua and Matthew

Acknowledgments

I am thankful for everyone who offered sources, critiqued a chapter, or offered other assistance. He Who Stands Firm and Jim Sawgrass, your verification of facts in the American Indian chapter is appreciated, and thanks are due to both Archie Matuck of the Hualapai Nation for verifying information on native foods of Arizona, and Ned Jenkins, archaeologist.

I am very grateful to Andrew Smith, food historian and author, for his invaluable advice on organization of materials and words of praise and encouragement, and to Mrs. Peter Rose, author and food historian, for her additional input and recipe for the medieval chapter.

I am grateful to Steve Abolt and Tim Pickles, military historians, for their critique of the military chapter, and to Barbara Leucke for contributing the seed lists in the military chapter.

The interlibrary loan staff at the Florence-Lauderdale Public Library has been immensely helpful in obtaining books from remote locations. Appreciation is expressed for help from the staff at the Auburn University Library, the University of North Carolina at Chapel Hill library, the Strathclyde University and Mitchell Libraries in Glasgow, the Oban (Scotland) Public Library, and a private library on the Isle of Lismore, Scotland.

I thank the Old Foodie website for permission to reprint "Soup as a Weapon," and appreciate input from curator Rachel Chisholm of the Highland Folk Museum, Kingusee, Scotland.

I appreciate Ken Wolf of Temple B'nai Israel and his critique of the biblical and modern Jewish chapters.

I am grateful to Jeff Bridgers at the Library of Congress for help in eliminating any copyright concerns on the prints and photographs used in the book from the holdings at the LOC.

I appreciate German translations from Kay Gnagey, and each of my reviewers deserves my gratitude. A special thanks goes to Liz Williams of the Southern Food and Beverage Museum for assistance with the Cajun/Creole chapter, and to my daughter-in-law, Jennifer, for proofreading the manuscript.

Table of Contents

Foreword
by Sandra Oliver

In quiet corners all around the country one can find earnest food historians rooting around in very old cookbooks, looking for recipes and information about all kinds of dishes from the past. *Soup Through the Ages* is for the benefit of those people who want to know and can appreciate not having to do the research themselves.

In this volume assembled by Victoria Rumble, you will find just such a collection of recipes and references about that most universal of dishes, soup. With an eye to recreating and telling the story of these dishes, Victoria Rumble has extracted material from many primary and a few secondary sources from very early times to the modern age, drawing from cookbooks, newspapers, magazines, and travel records and descriptions. She examines soups from ancient times, through the Renaissance and colonial eras, and on to the modern era of soup.

Readers will no doubt be glad to have a volume to carry with them into a primitive camp where the Internet never reaches, to pull off a shelf when a question arises, or to set by the bedside to peruse before sleep. Some will be grateful for a review of early sources and bibliography suggesting where else to look for answers to their questions. Anyone will be glad to see the documentation provided by the notes.

Even if you have only the most cursory interest in historic food, even if you never intend to cook a thing from this book, surely you will enjoy reading it.

SANDRA OLIVER, editor of *Food History News* and author of *Saltwater Foodways: New Englanders and Their Food at Sea and Ashore in the 19th Century,* was the recipient of the 1996 Jane Grigson Award for Scholarship in the Julia Child Cookbook Awards. She founded the fireplace cooking program at Mystic Seaport Museum in 1971.

Preface

By examining cultural changes throughout history we can see how various cuisines developed, and by exploring the wide range of textures and flavors we can arm ourselves with sufficient knowledge to produce a soup designed to suit our own palate.

This volume is primarily a history book, secondly a cookbook. Enough recipes are given in the appendix to allow every cook to prepare dishes in keeping with any era of history or any setting. Some readers will find it excellent armchair reading while others will turn straight to the recipe section and head for the kitchen.

It is meant as a one-volume overview of the development and changes in this most basic dish, and the author makes no claim to being an expert on Roman or Greek cooking. However, it is important that early information be provided in order to understand the changes to and additions in recipes through the years and the eras in which various ingredients became available.

Methods of making soup evolved similarly from one culture to another. They began with the most basic porridge or pottages made from grains and pot herbs and progressed to include peas or beans, pasta-like products such as vermicelli or macaroni, and meat or fish. The quality of the pottage improved in sync with the advancement of agricultural practices, improvement in the quality of vegetables and herbs, and the availability of durable cookery vessels.

Most cultures developed some version of a fruit soup, either fruits added to the grain-based pottage or wholly fruit soups flavored with various spices. The soups were made from whatever native fruit was ready for harvest at the time of preparation or from dried fruit.

Soups improved simultaneously with advancements in the quality of cookery vessels. By the medieval era earthen pots had replaced troughs or animal hides used for boiling, which was done, sometimes by the addition of hot stones to liquid, a process that evolved similarly in almost every culture. At that time, even the earthen vessels were beginning to be replaced with those of metal to the extent that almost every household had a brass pot or cauldron as well as earthen ones.[1]

Cooking is a prime example of progress going awry between the Roman era and the medieval era in that as more and more spices became available, it was almost a race to see how many could be put into any one dish. During the next decades cooks realized that soups and other dishes were in fact more flavorful without such extravagance. At that point, cookery began to evolve into the refined, artfully, and sometimes subtly, seasoned dishes we know today.

Partly due to the cost of fuel, during the Renaissance roasting was often left to the nobles while the lower classes lived primarily on soup. Thus, given the great extent to which they were prepared, it stands to reason that many of the pottages and soups of that period remain popular today. Although households continued to eat from the soup cauldrons which remained constantly at the hearth with new ingredients added as portions were taken out, soup was also prepared quickly, as evident from this description penned in 1789.

> The bread is all ready in a big wooden dish, with a little knob of butter, and then the boiling water is poured over it. Voila! That's the soup. A clove of garlic and a raw onion grated by the cook and sprinkled over the soup — that's the seasoning...[2]

Readers may ask why the early cultural history is important when this book is written primarily for Americans. The answer is simple, really: No other nation in the world is home to as many different cultures as the United States. To write a culinary history for Americans is to explore the origins of food history from those many cultures. While we can't explore every culture in one volume we can concentrate on the ones which had the greatest influence in the early colonization of the United States.

It wasn't the major events, movements, and "isms" that most shaped history; it was the masses of common people who worked hard, fought hard, loved hard, and died young. Wars are fought by individuals. Crops were improved one farmer at a time sharing his successes and documenting his failures. Dishes were created for the elite, but through hard work and toil, the peasant often rose above his poverty and took his place among the innovators.

How many seasons did John Evelyn spend eating various sallets before he knew which were the tastiest and put this information into book form? Did the miserable African captive know when he planted the first okra in the New World that he would influence a regional cuisine that would be appreciated the world over? Did the metalsmith who made the first trade kettles bound for the New World have any idea that once the Native American accepted one, the loss of his culture was inevitable? Would he have cared?

Some may wonder what circumstances dictated the contents of soup cauldrons in the many nations of the world. There is no one answer, but we can explore some possibilities. Season largely influenced the soups of the past. While meats and vegetables could be potted, salted, dried, pickled, smoked, and so on to preserve them for winter, those who ate them day after day surely found them monotonous and somewhat bland. Summer brought a plethora of wild plant foods, cultivated vegetables, and grains. These were awaited with much anticipation, so much so that many cultures celebrated with festivals of the harvest.

By first harvesting a wide array of wild plant foods, then staggering plantings and planting multiple varieties as they became available, fresh foods could be dug or harvested for most of the summer and fall, and many remained in their nearly fresh state quite some time afterward if stored away in underground pits.

Season dictated when animals were slaughtered. When it was certain piglets would be forthcoming, a boar might be killed for food without fear of not having another to take its place. As chicks hatched and grew, an old hen or cock might be transformed into a tempting cock-a-leekie, and the farmer slept soundly knowing the production cycle would remain unbroken.

Crop failures, weather extremes, financial panics, widespread illness, discovery of new vegetables and grains, better means of transporting and preserving foods, and other factors that influenced the ingredients of the soup kettle will be explored in the coming chapters.

The purpose of this book is to define soup, to define the period of its creation and the circumstances of the day, and to enlighten readers (in this day of instant foods) about the importance of soup in culinary history and the relative ease with which it can be prepared. We will explore the first dark days of discovery and follow the development of soup through the decades, providing a quick reference to inspire the creation of new dishes and hone the skills needed to prepare old favorites. The information in the preface and in early chapters is given to show the development and progression of soup through the ages and to set the stage for preparation of soup and cooking techniques that had developed by the 17th century and which remain in use today.

The chapters are arranged chronologically in so far as possible, however, because some practices and recipes existed over the course of several centuries and evolved through several cultures, there is some overlap, and key information may be found in multiple chapters.

Living history museums and historical interpreters will find this book indispensable in planning and presenting historic foodways programs, while authors and filmmakers may add historical accuracy to novels and films through the use of correct foods, utensils, and cooking techniques for the era in which their work is set. Chefs and instructors will find inspiration from the past. Scouts and outdoors enthusiasts need look no further for ideas for an outdoor feast. And for the home cook equipped with minimal ingredients and a single pot, a meal worthy of any restaurant is within your grasp. Whether you are an amateur cook preparing dishes for the family table or a cook creating a signature dish for a restaurant, this book will provide the information necessary to make a steaming soup or stew in which flavors are so harmoniously blended that the palate is conscious of only the finished product.

Whatever your approach, it is my fervent wish that readers will be entertained as well as educated while enjoying the endless variety of soups. It is also my hope that families will rediscover the magic of the kitchen. In times past, it was where skinned knees were kissed and bandaged, where lessons were learned amid the heavenly aromas wafting from the pots, where the scriptures provided guidance, and where a child knew a loving embrace was within arm's reach. Back door guests knew a cup of tea and a friendly chat were always waiting at the table, and neighbors dropped by to share the bounty of their gardens or the kindness of their heart when times were poor.

In recent decades, as fast foods replaced home-cooked meals, it seems that family activities that were the backbone of moral decency have been replaced by video games and television. What better way to rediscover that warmth and comfort than in the kitchen, where tempting aromas and enjoyment of family heighten our anticipation of the meal that will soon be enjoyed?

Soup is easily prepared and of endless variety. With the aid of packaged stocks, canned beans, and fresh vegetables and herbs available in markets, a delicious and nutritious home-cooked meal can be ready in the time it takes to go for take-out.

I used primary sources in the research of this book, many of them decades or centuries old. A few secondary sources were consulted for verification when in question.

Quotes from diaries, magazines, newspapers, and other sources is left as it was found. Any term which may seem antiquated by today's standards, such as Indian vs. Native American, will be understood to remain as sentiment governed in the time in which it was originally written.

The word *receipt* is correct through the 19th century to refer to a recipe. In this book I used both.

Please see my other titles and culinary articles at www.thistledewbooks.com. I leave you with wishes for blissful meals, joy, and happiness.

PART ONE : THE OLD WORLD

1. Soup — The World's First Prepared Dish

From the earliest days of the bronze and iron ages came the discovery of prepared dishes. Man advanced from simply eating wild grains, seeds, or meat placed in or near a fire to preparing rudimentary dishes that followed some vague notion of food as a pleasing experience rather than the simple necessity of fueling the body. Soup has been at the forefront of filling and nutritious meals since that time.

Few recipes are given for the ancient Roman and Greek soups. Other than Renaissance fair and history enthusiasts who have studied the cuisines, modern palates disdain many of the earliest dishes due in part to the frequent use of offal and organ meats and the liberal use of spices in ways unfamiliar today. Soup in various forms, however, is perhaps the one dish where early examples are still enjoyable, and thus the importance of tracing it from its earliest days.

Civilizations throughout the world used animal hides (placed over a fire or heated with hot stones) or a cauldron of some sort (earthen or metal), fire, and whatever ingredients could be harvested or killed to develop amazing one-pot-wonders which remain in a perpetual state of evolution. How this technique evolved in various cultures remains a continuous theme throughout the following chapters.

Soup has been defined in slightly different ways during various periods of time. While it is very difficult to determine the liquidity of a dish from reading the earliest recipes, it should be understood that a great many dishes should be considered soup in some form. Broths have the greatest amount of liquid, followed by soup, chowder, stew or ragout; and pasta dishes contain the least amount of liquid. *Le Viandier de Taillevert* defined soup as: "semi-liquid food, mostly with soaked bread. Also **sop, soppys:** a bit of bread for dipping in a liquid, such as a soup or wine." And the 1856 edition of Webster's dictionary said "Fr. Soupe; Lt. zuppa, sop; Sp. Sopa, sop, or soup; G. suppe; D. soep; Ice. Saup. Strong broth; a decoction of flesh for food, highly seasoned. To sop."

Legend and folklore surround early foods. An old fable relays the story of a peddler who, being unable to procure a meal, drew from a velvet pouch a stone which he placed into a pot of boiling water under the guise of "stone soup." He told inquisitive locals that stone soup with cabbage was most excellent at which point one of the residents contributed a cabbage for the soup pot. One ingredient after another, villagers made a contribution until a delicious pot of soup was simmering away to be enjoyed by all.

The concept of stone soup[1] is not just the stuff of fables. In Tyler's *History of Mankind*,[2] he discussed a method of making soup in which meat and water were added to a hide and heated stones were dropped in to provide heat to cook the soup. As the stones cooled, they were replaced with hot ones. Both Native Americans and early Europeans used this technique.

The word *soup* evolves from *sop*, referring to chunks of bread used to soak up juices from meat. The broth-laden bread was then consumed as well. Historians agree that around the 12th century people realized this *sop* was as good as the meat itself, and by the 13th century soup making was becoming an art form.

Ancient Roman cuisine indicates evidence that soup making had evolved to the point that peasants and soldiers[3] relied on it for basic sustenance, while well before that time wealthy, eccentric gourmands prepared it as either a precursor to a banquet or a highly seasoned substantial dish served in its own right.

The Bible is a surprisingly informative document regarding early foods. Although it doesn't record recipes, it does leave a list of foods and utensils from which logic dictates soup, or as the Bible phrases it, *pottage*, was made.

In medieval kitchens, especially during the earliest decades, the cauldron was rarely emptied. Bits and pieces were instead added daily to what was already in the pot. This meant the soup never tasted the same twice. Since flavors lingered, ingredients strong in flavor such as colworts may have been the dominant flavor for days to come. This form of food preparation required no skill, and except when the pot was emptied in preparation for a fasting (meatless) day, practically no cleanup.

"Soop" recipes and printed cookery books were being printed in late medieval Europe, and by 1742 a printer and newspaperman, William Parks, printed the first cookery book in America in Williamsburg, Virginia. His *Compleat Housewife; Or, Accomplished Gentlewoman's Companion* was an edited and reprinted version of Eliza Smith's book, which was first printed in London.[4]

Parks' accomplishment was soon eclipsed by Amelia Simmons when she finished the first cookery book actually written in the United States.[5] She relied heavily on previously published sources for much of her information. Her first edition did not contain soup recipes, but she did note that parsley was good for soup. Subsequent editions did contain soup recipes and a recipe for chowder.

Compleat Housewife contained several soup recipes including those of peas, crawfish, Sante (French for health), "teel" (teal, a kind of duck), broth and bisques, and subsequent writers added to this repertoire. Susannah Carter dedicated an entire chapter to soup in her *Frugal Housewife*.[6]

Mary Randolph's 1824 book[7] contained sixteen soup recipes, but that was eclipsed by N. M. K. Lee's[8] eighty-seven recipes for soups, broths, and consommés.

The first book published solely about soup, *Soups and Soup Making*, appeared in 1882 and is credited to Emma Ewing.[9] The recipes in this book were common throughout the 18th and 19th century. Published cookery books contained recipes for soups, many of which were recorded verbatim from one volume to the next making it difficult to document them to one source. Some books recorded practically the same selection of recipes in almost the same order.

Cooking is an art, not a science. The difference between a cook and a master is the ability to comprehend the nature of the ingredients and manipulate the amount used to produce a finished dish that is pleasing to the palate. Use the recipes as a guide, follow your heart in creating the dish, and make it uniquely your own.

Soup that is traditionally served hot can be served chilled, and if you prefer pureed soup there is no reason not to puree a soup which is traditionally served with chunks of meat and vegetable. Soup can be served at breakfast as easily as at dinner, and it can steal the show as a fruity dessert rather than being a starter or main course.

Americans agreed with this philosophy by the 19th century, as evidenced by the following passage penned in 1901.

> Without a thorough knowledge of proportions an inexperienced cook should not attempt to alter recipes in their important points. When it is expedient to reduce or increase the amount given, the accomplishment is not difficult; but when you are short in the given and necessary quantity of one of the principals, you must be careful to reduce others in the same proportion. For example, in making a soup stock, you find the quantity of meat on hand less than the weight called for in recipe given, which directs you to use a little less than a quart of water to each pound of bone and meat. Unless your stock meat is rich in gelatinous substance, you must reduce the quantity of water and every other ingredient to correspond, otherwise you will have a poor [weak] stock and soup.[10]

Changing ingredients depended on the importance of the proposed ingredient in the recipe — anything on which flavor was dependent could not be left out or substituted without altering the characteristic flavor of the prepared soup or dish.

> Wine is usually considered optional, but if you wish to make wine soup, wine jelly, or lobster Newburg, and disapprove of the use of wines in cooking, some other flavoring will not do just as well, for the wine gives the distinctive character to the dish.... If ... the recipe is for a sauce and directs you to use cream, milk will answer as well and the sauce can be enriched by an extra addition of butter, washed and stirred into the sauce just before removing from the fire, but not allowed to cook.[11]

The common phrase "in the soup" is said to be of German origin dating to about 1887. "He sits in the soup" meant a place of misfortune through one's own fault, and "He has made a nice soup for himself" meant a ludicrous or ridiculous position in which one had placed oneself.[12]

By studying the information in this book one can avoid "sitting in the soup," and a delicious and enjoyable meal will be the reward.

2. Social Culture and Emerging Cuisines

In order to understand the cultures in which various soups were initially prepared, and the effect on later cultures, we must examine the significant periods of world history.[1]

Prehistory (Mesopotamia) (9000–500 B.C.E.)

Egypt (3200–3230 B.C.E.)

Old Testament — Biblical Foods

Greece (1200–300 B.C.E.)

New Testament

Rome (753–476 C.E.)

Medieval (c. 400–1450 C.E.)

Renaissance (c. 1450–1650 C.E.)

Reformation (1517–1650)

Enlightenment (1650–1800)

Romanticism (1798–1832)

Victorian (1835–1901)

Modern (1900–1945)

Mesopotamia refers to lands now called Iraq, southeastern Turkey, eastern Syria, and southwestern Iran. The area around the Euphrates and Tigris rivers is often referred to as the "Cradle of Civilization" because the first groups to share a common culture appeared here in the late 4th millennium B.C.[2]

Ancient Egyptians built a civilization in northeastern Africa which included, at various times, the areas of the southern Levant, the Eastern Desert and the Red Sea coastline, the Sinai Peninsula, and the area focused on the several oases. Egypt is bordered by Libya, Sudan, the Red Sea and the Mediterranean Sea. Scientists believe parts of Egypt near Sudan have been inhabited by man since approximately 8000 B.C. Those peoples evolved from simple hunter-gatherers to successful agriculturalists though their endeavors depended a great deal on the waters of the Nile River.[3]

Small communities flourished between 5500 and 3100 B.C., as evidenced by tomb and cave drawings and pottery shards. Those people were among the first to develop a method of recording information known as hieroglyphs, and it is from this era that our first historical writings began.[4]

Ancient Egypt is best known as the land of mummies, pharaohs, and pyramids; how-

Primitive cooking. High Bear, a Brulé Sioux man, cooking by putting heated stones into a beef-stomach container on the Rosebud Indian Reservation. This method of boiling and preparing food, especially soup, evolved similarly in various cultures (J. A. Anderson, photographer, 1911. Library of Congress, Prints and Photographs Division, Reproduction Number LC-USZ62-101274).

ever, its history is much more complicated and fascinating.[5] The lands of ancient Greece were quite extensive, and its economic status at the height of the period was unrivaled anywhere. Written records from ancient Greece start about 800 B.C. Notable writers include Herodotus, Thucydides, Xenophon, Demosthenes, Plato, and Aristotle. Athens was the center of wealth and power and seemed to draw talented and educated people.[6]

Greek cuisine has at its heart the three foods that grew best there — grain, olives (and olive oil), and fruit for wine.[7] Citizens in the wealthier locales enjoyed a wider array of foods than did the lower classes, who relied solely on what grew nearby.

Ancient Rome was a place of overindulgence and cruelty. However, the technology available then is amazing. After the fall of the Roman Empire it took hundreds of years for some of that technology to be rediscovered. Diet was reflective of both what was native and what could be brought in from lands under the extensive Roman rule.[8]

The biblical era was recorded in documents other than the Bible, such as the writings of historians like Josephus. It was the dawn of Christianity and a time of upheaval as radically different philosophies spread into various cultures. Jewish food laws had a great impact on developing cuisines.

In about the 3rd century A.D. the Roman Empire was losing ground as a dominant world power and various tribes infiltrated the lands, some intent on following Roman examples, others just as determined to reject the Roman way of life.[9] Various European peoples began to move about, absorbing from and adding to the cultural stew that would come to be known as the medieval era.

The medieval era was characterized by the feudal system in England supported by William the Conqueror. A feudal system had been used by the Normans since they settled in France about A.D. 900. In essence it refers to the way of life whereby the king owned lands, reserving a part for himself, providing a part for the Church, and the remainder utilized by others under the king's control. Comprising the social class underneath the king were barons, knights, and peasants, also known as villeins.[10]

The barons were wealthy and powerful. They leased land from the king and in return pledged their loyalty to the king. They could establish their own justice system, mint money, and establish taxes for the property (manor), but were obligated to provide knights to defend the king and kingdom in time of danger. They were also obligated to extend hospitality and provide food for the king and his entourage when they traveled around the countryside.[11]

Knights tendered military service in exchange for land bestowed upon them by the barons. Knights were obligated to defend the baron, his family, and holdings. The knights, though not as wealthy as the barons, enjoyed a prosperity that remained out of the reach of the peasants. Any land left over after the knights took their share was divided among the peasantry.[12]

Villeins had no rights,[13] no wealth, and usually no hope of a comfortable life. They married only with permission, and were required to work the land for the knights — without pay. In return for their labor they were allowed to live on the land, though they ate poorly and their homes were devoid of any luxury. The feudal system allowed the wealthy to get wealthier while those on the bottom of the economic ladder lived miserable existences with no hope of a brighter future. To hunt the forests or fish the streams was considered poaching, a crime often punishable by death.[14] Peasant diets consisted of coarse fare rarely worth recording, but a multitude of cookery books emerged through the Renaissance era for the nobility.

People throughout Europe and the Americas utilized similar methods of constructing shelter, building fires, fashioning the quintessential cook pot (often of clay), and using a variety of natural ingredients to sustain life prior to the availability of wrought iron or cast iron kettles and brass, copper, tin, or bronze cauldrons and pans.

While indigenous ingredients varied from one continent to another, cooking techniques and basic dishes evolved quite similarly in the centuries preceding the industrial revolution. When ships began to transport fruits and vegetables from one part of the world to another, prepared dishes began to utilize the new ingredients to the extent that in later centuries it is sometimes difficult to isolate distinct cuisines.

3. Ancient Egypt

Modern civilization has been traced from about 5500 B.C. in the valley of the Nile in Egypt.[1] With that civilization came social culture, though cuisine is often treated as being of little significance in discussions of Egyptian history, failing in the shadow of the importance of the pyramids and other wonders.

From the writings of Herodotus evolved the notion of Egyptians, Colchins, and Ethiopians having features recognized today as African which, when combined with geographic location, explains the similarity in early diet. In approximately 6000 B.C., humans in African regions began harvesting grains and tubers, which remain at the heart of the African diet today.[2] Soups and stews are popular African dishes, and the stew pot is one of the most important utensils in food preparation.

Herodotus tells us that the ancient Egyptians favored a form of millet, *doora,* for making bread, and 19th century writers discussed various aspects of Egyptian culinary history. Lentil pottage was "not an unusual dish":[3]

> The dishes consisted of soup, fish, meat, — boiled, roasted, and dressed in various other ways, — game poultry, a profusion of vegetables and fruit, with pastry and confectionary.... The poorer classes ate but little meat, and lived chiefly, as in all other countries, excepting this, upon vegetables, among which lentils for soup, doora for bread, with cucumbers, onions, cabbages, and radishes, held a principal place. The onions of Egypt were uncommonly good, and were freely used by persons of all classes. In general the onion was more highly valued among the ancients, than it is with us, although the effect of eating it upon the breath did not escape attention.[4]

Citizens of Thebes, the city memorialized in *The Iliad,* did not eat mutton. Lycopolites were said by Plutarch to be the only Egyptians to eat sheep flesh, though multitudes of sheep were raised for wool. A 19th-century historian noted, "Beef and goose constituted the principal part of the animal food throughout Egypt," along with ducks, quails, and teal. Cows were thought sacred; however, oxen were bred for table and for work.[5]

By the 19th century vermicelli makers in Cairo began to mix flour and water. On a thin griddle the size of a cartwheel, heated by a few shavings, they placed a colander with hollow pipes the size of knitting needles set in the bottom. They poured pasty fluid in a circular stream till the griddle was covered, then raked the cooked vermicelli into a pile. A "favorite stew of the Arabs" was made of green turnips, fresh onions, radishes, and, "heaps of nameless greens with the refuse bits of meat" in a common pot.[6]

4. Biblical Fare

Christ was born after the worst of the gluttony of ancient Greece and Rome, and perhaps Christianity played a part in modifying those diets. How did the foods Jesus and his followers ate differ from that of the Romans? The difference probably wasn't significant from that of the poorer classes of Rome, but it was vastly different from the wealthier classes in that they practiced moderation in food and drink where the Romans went merrily down in history as a race of gluttons prone to excess and greed.

Some scholars interpret various biblical passages to be metaphors. However, in order for a reader to understand the metaphor the subject being commented upon has to first be understood by the person being addressed. For example, when in I Samuel 8:13 the comment is made, "And he will take your daughters to be confectionaries, and to be cooks, and to be bakers," we know that these are actual culinary tasks recognized during biblical times even if the writer didn't mean the passage literally.[1] The passage makes it clear that cooking was primarily a woman's task. Even women of some rank were not above preparing foods if we take heed of II Samuel 13:8, which discussed Tamar preparing cakes of flour and meat. Deuteronomy 8:8 described a land of "wheat, and barley, and vines, and fig trees, and pomegranates; a land of oil olive and honey," and II Kings 18:32 reiterates most of those foods.

One difference in dietary practices was the use of butter. Ancient Hebrews' typical morning repast was bread with butter or cheese and perhaps honey, yet butter seems to have been used medicinally by the Romans. The consumption of cheese, however, is classic in both groups.

Foods found in ancient Palestine included almonds, antelope, anise, apples, beans (used as both a vegetable and ground for flour by the Jews), honey, pigeon, partridge, quail, wild ducks, boars, sheep (and ewe's milk), goats (and goat milk), cumin, dill, deer, lamb, figs, fish, hares, lentils, peas, mallow, millet, rye, saffron, mint, basil, coriander, thyme, bay, fennel, sage, capers, mulberries, mustard, olives (and olive oil), dates, onions, leeks, garlic, cucumbers, and pomegranate.

Saffron is taken from the pistils of the crocus, and has for most of history been the most expensive spice available. Its name can be traced back to the Arabic word for yellow. It is native to Southwest Asia and was first cultivated in or around Greece.[2] In Solomon 4:14 we read:

> Spikenard and saffron; calamus and cinnamon, with all the trees of frankincense; myrrh and aloes, with all the chief spices.

Pliny wrote of the importance of anise in seasoning meat and other foods. Fennel and dill were of equal importance. The presence of bay leaf is evidenced by Psalms 37:35: "I have seen the wicked in great power, and spreading himself like a green bay tree."

Salted or sun-dried fish were available in fish markets, and fish brought to market from Egypt were at times salted in Palestine.[3]

A peasant woman from the Bible lands preparing soup in an earthen pot over a fire made from thorns, ca. 1898. Additional containers are seen in the foreground. Library of Congress, Prints and Photographs Division, Reproduction Number LC-DIG-matpc05924.

In Numbers 11:5 we find documentation of the consumption of fish, cucumbers, melons, leeks, garlic, and onions. All of these were also eaten by the Romans, but unlike Roman scholars Biblical scholars did not leave accounts of specific ways in which these foods were prepared.

Many of the ingredients discussed in the Bible were prepared as a soup; although in the absence of actual directions for preparation, the reader is usually left to wonder exactly how foods were cooked. Those of limited means and with few utensils primarily boiled grains, herbs, vegetables, fish, and meats for soup in order to stretch the quantities of available food and limit the number of utensils needed to prepare the ingredients separately. The Bible doesn't use the word *soup*, but it does use the word *pottage* numerous times: "Esau asked for red pottage which was most likely a stew of lentils," From Genesis 15:29, is only one example.

In II Kings 4:38, a servant was instructed to put on a great pot and seethe (boil) pottage for the sons of the prophets. Into that pot went a wild vine and wild gourds, after herbs which were decreed "death in the pot." Meal was then cast into the pot, after which the stew was safe to eat.

We gain some idea of the combination of foods prepared for a large gathering from I Samuel 25:18: "Then Abigail made haste, and took two hundred loaves, and two bottles of wine, and five sheep ready dressed, and five measures of parched corn, and an hundred clusters of raisins, and two hundred cakes of figs, and laid them on asses."

Ezekiel 4:3 makes reference to an iron pan, and 4:9 describes how bread was baked during this time. Leviticus 2:3 uses the term "frying pan," but uses the word "baken" with regard to the meat prepared in it.

Bread was used to capture every drop of broth. In John 13:26, "Jesus answered, 'He it is, to whom I shall give a sop, when I have dipped it.' And when he had dipped the sop, he gave it to Judas Iscariot, the son of Simon"; and Ezekiel 4:9 says, "Take thou also unto thee wheat, and barley, and beans, and lentils, and millet and fitches [vetch, a legume], and put them in one vessel, and make thee bread thereof."[4]

Fitches also refers to *Nigella sativa*, an herbaceous annual plant of the natural order Ranunculaceoe (the buttercup family), which grows in the south of Europe and the north of Africa. It produces black seeds that are used like pepper, and which have a similarly pungent taste. In Syria, bakers sprinkle the seeds over flat cakes before baking them.[5] (The bread was most likely flatbread baked on a heated stone.)

Meat was roasted, as evidenced in I Samuel 2:15, and according to Exodus 12:8 it was roasted on or near an open fire. Game was much appreciated, according to Genesis 27:7, where a request is made for venison, "and make it savoury meat." Verse 9 discusses making kids "savoury" meat. We find in John 21:9, "As soon as they were come to land, they saw a fire of coals there, and fish laid thereon, and bread," which tells us fish was roasted directly over the coals.

Although forks for eating were not available yet, I Samuel 2:13 describes a large fork-like instrument with three tines used for lifting meat from a pot. Further explaining the array of kitchen utensils available at the time is Mark 7:4:

And many other things there be which they have received to hold, as the washing of cups and pots, brasen vessels, and of tables.

"Brasen vessel" referred to an *aenum* or *ahenum*. It was a vessel hung over the fire in which water was boiled for drinking or food was cooked.

Jeremiah 18:6 mentions clay in the potter's hands, and Romans 9:21 went so far as to convey the idea of the potter forming vessels from clay. Either of these passages may have referred to clay cook pots or storage jars. I Samuel 2:13 enlightened the reader on the array of cook pots in use in the biblical kitchen. He mentions that when flesh was seething [simmering] the priest's servant took a portion from the "pan, or kettle, or cauldron, or pot." *Cauldron* referred to any number of vessels which hung from a bail over the fire.

Exodus 16:3 spoke of a "flesh pot," however, there is no indication whether this refers to a metal or earthenware pot. Likewise Zechariah 14:20 speaks of pots for seething, though no distinction is made as to their type.

In Ezekiel 24:3, the Lord referred to "good pieces," thigh and shoulder, seething in a pot.

Only in the wealthiest of homes was a certain room or area, such as a courtyard, set aside for the preparation of food. The masses cooked, as other cultures cooked for centuries to come, over a fire built on the floor, often in the center of the dwelling so that heat radiated throughout. There was no fireplace as such, and smoke escaped through cracks and crevices in the walls and ceiling or the opening in a tent.

It is difficult to say at what point more adequate hearths began to emerge. Zechariah 12:6 refers to a hearth, but for centuries afterward *hearth* simply meant a pit for fire. Leviticus 11:35 spoke of an oven and "ranges for pots," the latter of which referred to some sort of portable stove, probably heated with charcoal.

Beans, lentils, and grains formed the base of soups, potages, or stews, which were often the only meal of the day for poorer citizens. Only the wealthier households would have been able to afford seasonings, even pepper, so the dishes were filling but bland in flavor. Salt may have been within reach of most households.

Salt, in fact, is considered by some scholars to have brought about the settling of Rome. The Via Salaria is an ancient road used to transport salt from the salt marshes at the mouth of the Tiber River.[6] The word *salary* comes from *salarium* which meant to pay someone such as a soldier with a supply of salt. Herodotus wrote extensively of the Libyan salt oases.

There were ample ingredients available for making wine, including pomegranates, figs, and dates. Much of the fruit, such as peaches, apricots, cherries, and plums, originated in Persia and Mesopotamia (now Iraq), but these were soon cultivated upon introduction. Wine was likely used to flavor the pottages.

Water was stored in large earthenware jugs or pitchers (see Genesis 24:15). I Kings 17:12 spoke of meal stored in a barrel. Other storage containers include goatskins, earthenware or metal jugs for honey and oil, and baskets for fruits, pastries, and the like.

Herbs and wild plants were eaten in salads to accompany the bread and soup.

Several passages in Joel discussed food and the importance placed on particular items. Joel 2:22 refers to the beasts of the field, trees that bore fruit, and vines that yielded strength. Joel 2:19 says, "Yea, the Lord will answer and say unto his people, Behold, I will send you corn, and wine, and oil, and ye shall be satisfied therewith"; and Joel 2:24 says, "And the floors shall be full of wheat, and the fats shall overflow with wine and oil."

In addition to wheat the Bible documented the other grains that grew well in the region, including emmer, spelt, einkorn, and barley.

Mortars and pestles were commonly used for grinding grain and spices.

"Meal" and "corn" were most likely references to wheat and barley. For many centuries the word *corn* was used to describe any number of types of grain. Maize was not native to biblical countries, and the word *corn* did not refer to maize until the discovery of America.

In Judges 6:19, when Gideon went in to make ready a kid and unleavened cakes of *ephah* flour, the flesh he put in a basket, and the broth he put in a pot. (An ephah was a Hebrew measurement of dry ingredients, about one bushel.)

Samuel I and II mention honey, butter, and cheese, which were probably consumed with bread, but the passage also states sheep were for David and his people to eat. We must rely on the cooking techniques we know existed at the time to hazard a guess as to how this meat might have been prepared.

Perhaps the most important aspect of biblical foods predates the birth of Jesus and the New Testament writers by several years. Moses was born c. 1525 or 1526 B.C. and is thought to have lived 120 years, dying c. 1405 or 1406 B.C. He lived during the earliest days of the Roman era and authored a divine accounting of foods which were acceptable and unacceptable for the Jewish people. According to Leviticus 11:1–22:

> And the Lord spake unto Moses and to Aaron, saying unto them, Speak unto the children of Israel, saying, These are the beasts which ye shall eat among all the beasts that are on earth.
>
> Whatsoever parteth the hoof, and is clovenfooted, and cheweth the cud, among the beasts, that shall ye eat.
>
> Nevertheless these shall ye not eat of them that chew the cud, or of them that divide the hoof; as the camel, because he cheweth the cud, but divideth not the hoof; he is unclean unto you.
>
> And the swine, though he divide the hoof, and be clovenfooted, yet he cheweth not the cud; he is unclean to you.
>
> Of their flesh shall ye not eat, and their carcase shall ye not touch; they are unclean to you.
>
> These shall ye eat of all that are in the waters: whatsoever hath fins and scales in the waters, in the seas, and in the rivers, them shall ye eat. And all that have not fins and scales in the seas, and in the rivers, of all that move in the waters, and of any living thing which is in the waters, they shall be an abomination unto you:

They shall be even an abomination unto you; ye shall not eat of their flesh, but ye shall have their carcases in abomination.

Whatsoever hath no fins nor scales in the waters, that shall be an abomination unto you.

And these are they which ye shall have in abomination among the fowls;

they shall not be eaten, they are an abomination: the eagle, and the ossifrage, and the ospray.

And the vulture, and the kite after his kind;

Every raven after his kind;

And the owl, and the night hawk, and the cuckow, and the hawk after his kind, And the little owl, and the cormorant, and the great owl,

And the swan, and the pelican, and the gier eagle,

And the stork, the heron, after her kind, and the lapwing, and the bat.

All fowls that creep, going upon all four, shall be an abomination unto you.

Yet these may ye eat of every flying creeping thing that goeth upon all four, which have legs above their feet, to leap withal upon the earth;

Even these of them ye may eat; the locust after his kind, and the bald locust after his kind, and the beetle after his kind, and the grasshopper after his kind.

The next passages included in the list of unclean creatures the weasel, mouse, tortoise, ferret, chameleon, lizard, snail, and mole.

In Deuteronomy 14 this prohibition includes the hare and coney (rabbit), which had not a divided hoof but chewed cud and therefore were unclean.

The abolishment of food laws for the masses came about at the hand of Constantine who, after assuming power in A.D. 306, forbade the persecution of Christianity, at which time the pope set about enforcing St. Paul's revelation and abolishing the Judaic food laws.

Popes, monks, missionaries, and others continued to debate dietary laws throughout the Dark Ages. As each faction seemingly swayed support for one theory the pendulum invariably swung in the other direction.

5. Ancient Greece

As the decades passed, the Greek poets sung, the philosophers wrote, the musicians played, the artists painted, and through it all a social culture evolved in a myriad of ways, not the least of which was the culinary offerings of the chefs. Dinners, the beloved picnics, and festivals benefited from a combination of all the social graces— luxurious dishes served amidst flowers and lotus petals beneath brightly colored mosaics and stately arches.[1]

Before the time of Christ, ancient Greeks had seen many years of warfare. The Persian wars ended in 469 B.C., the Pelopennesian Wars had lasted almost 30 years, and subjugation of Greece at the hand of Philip of Macedone in 338 B.C. was almost overshadowed by the subsequent conquests of Alexander, the Achaean League, and the Roman conquest in 146 B.C., which intertwined Greek and Roman history for the next several centuries.

Greece was raided by Alaric the Goth in A.D. 400, by Genserie and Zaber Kahn in the 6th and 7th centuries, and by the Normans in the 11th century. After the capture of Constantinople in 1204 by the Crusaders, Greece was divided into feudal principalities ruled by a variety of Norman, Venetian, and Frankish nobles until 1718 when it fell to the Turks who held it until the revolution of 1821.[2] Because of the many years under Roman rule and regionally indigenous foodstuffs there are similarities in cuisine.[3]

In the early days little attention was paid to the enjoyment of eating. A sparse and wholesome diet satisfied wants and assuaged appetites, but after the Greeks invaded Persia and were exposed to luxurious living their manners and customs underwent a process of emulation, and moderation and frugality were soon forgotten. Cooks and hosts of eating establishments rose in importance until their importance surpassed that of statesmen, warriors, and patriots.[4]

Greeks were fond of picnics, as evidenced by the writings of such ancients as Plutarch who once said invitations were issued to ladies a year ahead of time so that they might have their toilets suitably prepared when the feasting day came around.[5] He wrote at length on the propriety of bringing guests along for those meals.

In the writings of Athenaeus he substantiated the use of spoons, but he admitted more often than not that a hollow piece of bread served to convey food, even soup, to the mouth.[6]

Many of the foods listed here are taken from the fourteen books of *Deipnosophists* by Athenaeus,[7] and from the treatises of such notables as Plato, Xenophon, and Aristophanes. In Aristotle's *History of Animals* the list of fish grew to several hundred.

Fish and other water-loving animals commonly eaten included pike, bream, porpoise, seal, turbot, frogs, perch, roach, gudgeons, plaice, flounder, ray, mullet, and sturgeon. Molluscous animals harvested for culinary purposes included ink fish, periwinkle, whelk, shrimp, cuttlefish, mussels, cockles, snails, lobster, crabs, and oysters.[8]

Birds served on Greek and Roman tables included peacock, quail, geese, capons, plovers, mallards, teal, larks, martinets, cranes, chickens, pigeons, partridges, woodcocks, nightingale, sparrow, pelican, stork, finches, and flamingo.[9]

Vegetables used in Greek food included cabbage, leeks, lettuce, garlic, pulse, beans, vetches, wheat, nuts, barley groats, parsley, olives, fennel, lentils, sesame, and most likely all those used by the Romans.

Athenaeus described some 50 types of loaves, and 19th century historians traced the word *mess,* meaning a group of soldiers who prepared meals together, to the Latin *massa* and its Greek equivalent which referred to any sort of paste or dough made from barley, wheat, or spelt.[10]

Bread for *sop* was clearly plentiful in Greece. The custom was to eat with one hand while reclining propped on the other arm, a position not particularly conducive to eating dripping liquids — though according to Athenaeus they managed quite well.[11] This pose is seen on various vases and artifacts throughout the period. Athenaeus wrote:

> Every torrent ran with wine, and barley-pastes fought with wheaten loaves to be first to men's lips.... A river of soup swirling along hot pieces of meat would flow by the couches.[12]

Greek soup and early methods of preparing it were briefly described by Herodotus in the 5th century B.C. (c. 440 B.C.). His account documents the preparation of soup before pots were available in which to prepare it:

> As Scythia, however, is utterly barren of firewood, a plan has had to be contrived for boiling the flesh, which is the following. After flaying the beasts, they take out all the bones, and (if they possess such gear) put the flesh into boilers made in the country, which are very like the cauldrons of the Lesbians, except that they are of a much larger size; then placing the bones of the animals beneath the cauldron, they set them alight, and so boil the meat. If they do not happen to possess a cauldron, they make the animal's paunch hold the flesh, and pouring in at the same time a little water, lay the bones under and light them. The bones burn beautifully; and the paunch easily contains all the flesh when it is stript from the bones, so that by this plan your ox is made to boil himself, and other victims also to do the like.[13]

In Herodotus' method, the animal skin was heated externally, and care was taken not to burn a hole through the hide spilling its contents. The smell must have been less than appetizing as the hair burned off the hide. This method was used in many cultures, and Rachael Feild documented its use in remote areas of Scotland through 1720.[14]

Another ancient method of boiling meat and soup was used by the ancients, as proven by M. J. O'Kelly in 1954 at Ballyvourney.[15] Archaeologists reconstructed a site previously known for ancient deer-roasting from the mid-second millennium B.C. The team built a wooden hut which contained a meat rack and table, a boiling trough dug into the peat and surrounded by two large hearths, and a roasting pit. They used dampened wooden shovels to slip heated stones into the liquid and were thus able to boil to perfection a 10-pound joint of mutton in less than four hours. O'Kelly wrote:

> The trough, dug into the peat below the water-line, held 100 gallons of water, which was brought to the boil quickly by potboilers from the adjacent hearths, only thirty minutes being required to heat the water; few stones were needed to keep the water hot once the joint was placed in the trough. After nearly four hours, a leg of mutton was cooked to perfection, and was consumed by the archaeologists.

Some scholars document pit cooking of this nature since approximately 5000 B.C. O'Kelly may have gotten the idea for this experiment from a passage in an early Irish text, *Romance of Mils and Dubh Ruis:*

> He cut the deer's throat and then skinned it. Then he made a large fire of dead wood from the forest and he gathered a heap of granite stones and put them into the fire. He made a pit, square all round in the ground, and he filled it with water. He cut up his meat and he wrapped it in marsh grass and he put it in the hole ... he was supplying and continuously putting the well reddened long heated stones in the water, and he kept it constantly boiling until his meat was cooked.

Rachael Feild further described the method, saying a dug pit was divided in half with the fire in one half and the food to be cooked in the other after it was lined with stone and mortared with clay.

Reay Tannahill indicates that boiling was taking place long before earthenware pottery came into use (around 6,000 B.C.). It is thought that sections of bamboo lined with clay were the precursors of pottery vessels.[16]

Methods aside, what basic ingredients did the first soups contain? From the earliest times grains were grown in ancient Europe and Asia and made into porridge, which was the precursor of soup and bread.

Since no one who ate the soups of the ancients is around to describe them, and since many of the recipes list ingredients but give no amounts, it is necessary to peruse numerous sources to determine the strongest flavors that were likely featured in their dishes. These seem to have been honey, spices, herbs, and sauces containing wine or vinegar. Fish sauce was as common to the early Greeks as the Romans.

Early Greek foods probably achieved a harmonious blend of flavors from perhaps three or four spices or herbs, but the Romans, after adopting some of the cuisine, doubled or tripled the spices in a single dish.

Archestratus mentions stewing various fish in salt water with a few green leaves. Depending on the size of the fish, it was sometimes baked. Cheese and oil were frequently used with it.

While the ancient cooks used asafetida as a seasoning, it is unlikely many would appreciate it today due to its noxious odor. Lovage was prevalent though it can be bitter. Celery leaves could be used as a substitute. Coriander leaf is common cilantro. Rue is an evergreen spice best used fresh, but dried versions can be found.

Cultivated emmer wheat dates to c. 7000 B.C.[17] It produced small grains and was closely related to the modern durum wheat used in pasta. Emmer wheat and barley have been found at the pyramids in Egypt and scattered through most of the Near East and Europe from that era.

Barley grains have been found dating to 8000 B.C. in Syria and in Mesopotamia, Palestine, and Asia Minor, and Pliny the Elder wrote of roasting barley grains before making porridge.[18]

Millet has been found dating back as far as 4500 B.C. in China, and written instructions for growing it were found dating to 2800 B.C. Varieties are thought to have originated in Africa and Asia, and it was taken from Africa to India about 3,000 years ago. The hanging gardens of Babylon are said to have contained millet.[19]

Fava beans inevitably found their way into porridges despite the dictates of Pythagoreans regarding avoiding them, apparently due to the flatulence they produced.[20] Bean soup is such a ubiquitous dish that it would be difficult to find a culture that did not make it.

A few of the bean soups from around the world include: *feijoada*, a stew of beans and beef or pork, prepared slowly in a clay pot in Brazil and Portugal, which is served with accompaniments such as collard greens, cassava, and bananas; *sopa de frijol*, Mexican black bean soup with bacon, onion, rosemary, and oregano; *maarka bel lubia*, Moroccan bean soup made from white beans, cumin, paprika, saffron, garlic, and eggs; *fassoulada*, Greek bean soup with celery, tomato, onion, carrot, and herbs; *sopa del frijol negro*, Cuban black bean soup; *oshiruko*, Japanese azuki bean soup; and *supa de fasole*, Romanian bean soup.

> There is more nourishment in one barrel of good white beans than five bushels of potatoes; and what is better than bean soup or more palatable than good old fashioned bean porridge?[21]

The Iranian word for soup is *ash*, thought named for the kitchen, or *ash-paz-khaneh*, and the ever-present noodle soup tops the list of favorites. *Ash-e reshteh* is an ancient noodle soup which originally contained spinach and sweet fresh clover thickened with a flour-and-water paste. That paste became dumplings over time and, according to Persian literature, by A.D. 500 the dumplings had become noodles. Today it is a mixture of beans, greens, and noodles.

Greek bean soup, sometimes spelled *fasolatha*, has been dated by most culinary historians from ancient Greece. However, the recipe has changed somewhat over the years as evidenced by the addition of tomato in recent centuries.

A Danish traveler noted that Greenlanders made soup from seal blood boiled with other ingredients,[22] and Plutarch noted the cherished soup of the Spartan warriors of Greece made from blood, vinegar, and pork:

> A thing that met with especial approval among them was their so-called black broth [zomos], so much that the older men did not require a bit of meat, but gave up all of it to the young men. It is said that Dionysius, the tyrant of Sicily, for the sake of this bought a slave who had been a Spartan cook, and ordered him to prepare the broth for him, sparing no expense. But when the king tasted it, he spat it out in disgust, whereupon the cook said, "O King, it is necessary to have exercised in the Spartan manner, and to have bathed in the Eurotas, in order to relish this broth."[23]

Aristophanes, a Greek satirist, indirectly attested to the prevalence of soup in the Greek diet by these lines penned in the play *The Frogs*:

> DIONYSUS: "Did you ever feel a sudden urge for soup?"
> HERACLES: "Soup? Ten thousand times so far."

6. Ancient Rome

Biblical scholars agree that Jesus' birth date cannot be identified precisely. Most agree with the dating system established in A.D. 532, which places the birth in approximately the year 4 B.C.,[1] some 750 years after the founding of Rome.

The exact date and circumstance of the founding of Rome have swirled through the black mists of time, a mixture of fact and myth, however legend credits its beginning to 21 April, 753 B.C.[2] Archaeologists have uncovered artifacts which coincide with this date.[3]

As early as 1500 B.C., Roman citizens lived scattered in crude huts where they raised pigs and herded sheep, goats, and cattle. It wasn't until 753 B.C. that these inhabitants came together to form a town by uniting Palatine Hill and Quirinal, which became known as Rome.[4]

Tarquinius Priscus, from Etruria, was elected king of Rome around 616 B.C.[5] and, partly because of his wealth, the Etruscans became known as a race of gourmets, as evidenced by the many Etruscan tomb frescoes of feasts. In addition, they were skilled at bronze casting and especially so of cookery vessels and tripods.

In 147 B.C. the Romans left Carthage[7] in Northern Africa in ruins, and soon their plundering and waste included Egypt. Plants were gathered to extinction and animals were taken back to Rome for the entertainment of the citizens. Unfortunately, this was no petting zoo— many of the animals ended up on the dinner table after their performances.[8]

> The Romans began, of course, as simple feeders, but in process of time became such gourmets as the world has not seen since. Pulse, bread, fruit, vegetables, and only a few meats with wine and water, were the staple food of the early Romans; then came beer; and then, as the conquest of the world brought them more and more into contact with various customs, the list of articles and the modes of preparation became longer and more various.
>
> Then came the search after rarities. The livers of nightingales, the brains of flamingos, the tender parts of peacocks, wild boar, oysters, blackbirds, deer, hares, spices from all countries, and ingenious forms of pastry — these were dressed up in a thousand different ways, so that Apicius could leave ten books of receipts.[9]

Apicius and others have been credited with eating unbelievable amounts of food in a single sitting, some accounts so fantastic as to be physically impossible:

> And what did you think of those people who, mad for boar and stag, eat the wild beast from the arena? The boar is drenched in the [human] blood that is has shed. The deer lies in the blood of gladiators. Of the bear even the stomach is considered a delicacy, full as it is with undigested human flesh.[10]

Cato the Elder (234–149 B.C.) did not approve of such extravagance, and wrote of the virtues of a more reasonable diet of vegetables, fruits, and pulses.[11] Athenaeus[12] and Pliny[13] were among those who wrote about the dietary restrictions governing lavish banquets and the extremes resorted to in consuming the most exotic ingredients the world had to offer.

The Roman Empire along with the majority of its technology came crashing down roughly around A.D. 400–500. After Rome was sacked in 410 by Alaric,[14] Spain was shortly taken by the Visigoths, and by 450, Atilla the Hun entered Gaul (modern France) and proceeded to invade what is now modern Italy. (Italy as we know it today dates from the 1860s.) After Romulus Augustulus was deposed in 476, a new era was born.[15]

The eastern empire evolved into the Byzantine Empire until the fall of Constantinople, first to the Crusaders in 1204, and then to the Turks in 1453. During the 15th century, Rome became the world center of Catholicism.

Scholars and historians of note include Pliny the Elder (servant and student of natural history), Pliny the Younger, Tacitus, Cato the Elder, Aufidius Bassus, Josephus, and others. Pliny's historical writings included documenting the Roman physician Crateuas (author of a first-century B.C. herbal), and Hippocrates. Josephus wrote much on Roman history, including the occupation and conquering of the city of Jerusalem in 66.

Of food, Josephus wrote in *Antiquities of the Jews*:

> Helena, queen of Adiabene [queen A.D. 66–70, during the time of] Claudius Caesar.... Now her coming was of very great advantage to the people of Jerusalem; for whereas a famine did oppress them at that time, and many people died for want of what was necessary to procure food withal, queen Helena sent some of her servants to Alexandria with money to buy a great quantity of corn [grain], and others of them to Cypress, to bring a cargo of dried figs; and as soon as they were come back, and brought those provisions, which was done very quickly, she distributed food to those that were in want of it ... and when her son Izates was informed of this famine, he sent great sums of money to the principal men in Jerusalem.[16]

And in *Life of Pythagoras*, Porphyry wrote:

> As to food, his breakfast was chiefly honey; at dinner he used bread made of millet, barley or herbs, raw and boiled. To quiet hunger he made a mixture of poppy seed and sesame, the skin of a sea-onion, well washed until entirely drained of all outward juices, of the flowers of the daffodil, and the leaves of mallows, of paste of barley and chick-peas, taking an equal weight of which, and chopping it small, with honey of Hymettus he made it into a mass. Against thirst he took the seed of cucumbers, and the best dried raisins, extracting the seeds, and coriander flowers, and the seeds of mallows, purslane ... wheat meal ..., all of which he mixed up with wild honey.[17]

For his part, Diogenes Laertius wrote in his own *Life of Pythagoras*:

> Some authors assert that he himself used to be contented with honey, honey-comb and bread, and that he never drank wine during the day. He usually ate vegetables, either boiled or raw.[18]

The reach of the Roman rulers had grown steadily by conquest, and Roman provinces came to include what are now Sicily, Spain, Greece, Asia Minor, Syria, Judea, Egypt, North Africa, and all of modern France. It was this Roman influence which ultimately laid the groundwork for Europe's social and cultural values.

The first Roman homes were simple thatched huts, but after the burning, during Nero's time, the homes began an upward spiral of improvements which continued to escalate for the wealthy. Roman villas were being discovered and excavated by 1811.

> In the warmest part of the court the kitchen is to be located and adjoining thereto the ox-house with the stables turned toward the fire ... the bath also is to be adjoined to the kitchen for thus the place of bathing will not be far from those of the husbandry occupations.[19]

There is some bit of question as to whether Romans excelled in making sausages or obtained them elsewhere, but the Romans were fond of them.[20] They also liked fish and seafood, as evidenced through historical writings. Claudius Aelianus wrote about fly fishing[21] as early as the 5th century A.D., and Pliny documented catching mullet in nets, catfish in the Nile, pike in the Rhine, and sturgeon in the River Padus.[22]

Sergius Orata developed artificial oyster beds so that oysters were always available, and Lininius Murena was the first to raise fish in artificial ponds. Lucullus furthered this technology by digging channels whereby these fish ponds could be fed with salt water. Ovid (43 B.C. to A.D. 17) referred to oysters as, "a delicacy for our tables."[23]

The historian and writer Athenaeus wrote about the gastronomical observances of other authors. Most of these accounts have been lost, but a 19th-century writer observed:

> Athenaeus, in fourteen books, entitled "Deipnosophists," is, to a considerable extent, a treatise on gastronomy. Regular essays on the art of cookery existed in both languages [Roman and Greek]. Athenaeus enumerates no fewer than eighteen authors of cookery-books, some of which were in verse.[24]

Caelius Apicius is credited with having written *Apicius*, a collection of recipes favored by the Romans, at about the end of the 4th century or early in the 5th. It has sometimes been mistakenly accredited to Marcus Gavius Apicius due to the latter's distinction as an early gourmet. *Apicius* was published in 1498 in Milan and in 1500 in Venice. It has since undergone several translations and reprintings. C. T. Schuch's edition was printed in Heidelberg in 1867 and remained in print through the Victorian years. Vehling's English translation followed in 1936.

Countless books and poems throughout history quote *Apicius* or make reference to it, testifying to its widespread circulation. Apicius is said to have spent an exorbitant amount of money on "debauchery and gluttony." He was so addicted to food that he feared he might someday go hungry and, rather than face that dark possibility, he drank poison and killed himself.[25] The recipes include from the garden various peas, beans, lentils, chickpeas, and so forth, and meats including fowl, quadrupeds, and seafood. Apicius kept enslaved cooks to prepare food, and is one of the first to have done so. He once sold a cook for an amount equivalent to £772.[26]

Pliny, Plutarch, Petronius, and others were not gourmets, but their writing is almost equally important in that they provide knowledge of the types of food eaten. Cato documented recipes, including cakes, in his *De Agricultura*. Plutarch was one of several writers who favored a meatless diet. There were several reasons for following a vegetarian diet, not the least of which may have been valuing cows more as beasts of burden than as food.[27]

Apicius does not shed much light on the foods consumed by common people in that it was written for professional chefs working throughout Rome. Pliny and Plutarch, through their writings on natural history, may paint a more accurate picture of the diet of those of modest means. Grain, which formed the bulk of the peasantry's diet, could be made available for distribution to the poor by farmers in lieu of taxes, thus ancient Rome became the first culture to distribute food to those in need.[28] It was thought if the peasants had full bellies they'd be more likely to live peaceably. As grain was imported from Roman colonies, the philosophy was that Rome had conquered the world so the world should feed Rome.

The book instructed that broth which had taken on a bad odor could be placed in a vessel first turned upside down and fumigated with laurel and cypress. Before ventilating it, the broth was poured into the vessel. If that failed to refresh it, honey and fresh spikenard (a flowering plant from the Valerian family found in China, India, Nepal, and the Himalayas) were added. Ancient Greeks called lavender *nard*, and given lavender's use in cookery it may be what was referred to here.

The Romans used pot herbs liberally in their cookery, and the notation regarding keeping them in a pitched vessel attests to their importance. Oxygarum, for example, referred to a mixture of pepper, leaves (interpreted as parsley or lovage and mint), cardamom, and caraway mixed with honey after which broth and vinegar were added.

Ingredients found in *Apicius* include vinegar, ham, lamb, fish, sorrel, shellfish, garlic, leeks, almonds, sweet marjoram, thyme, bay leaf, fennel, hyssop, rue, ginger, dill, cinnamon, cumin, olive oil, cheese, flour, duck, anchovies, eel, anise, sausages, celery, parsley, apples, rice, mint, asparagus, grapes (wine), game birds, hazelnuts, filberts, bacon, chicken, basil, cabbage, beans, beets, spinach, boars, mushrooms, kale, turnips, barley, onions, cress, capers, purslane, cardamom, nasturtium, cardoon, caraway, figs, dates, carrot, cloves, chestnuts, cauliflower, caviar, cherries, chick-peas, artichokes, citron, snails, quail, parsnips, saffron, cucumbers, pumpkins, gourds, rabbits, hares, deer, plums or prunes, eggs, elderberries, endives, horseradish, peas, milk, lentils, lettuce, honey, pepper, garlic, olives, sardines, peaches, pomegranates, pears, truffles, dock, squash, and squirrel. According to the *History of English Gardening* (1829), other early writers (Palladius, Cato, Columella, Varro, Pliny, Virgil, and Martial) left important documentation on some of these foods as well.

The ruins at Pompeii preserved food being prepared and eaten in A.D. 79. Searchers found egg shells, bread, bones of fish and chicken, vases of olives in oil, fruit, figs, raisins, chestnuts, wine, and pastry.[29]

Paintings thought destined to decorate Roman banquet halls showed pullets, geese, ducks, partridges, fowls, game of all kinds, fruits, eggs, amphorae, loaves of bread, cakes, hams, and more. Goods found in the remains of shops or taverns included bottles, goblets, raisins, figs, chestnuts, lentils, scales for bakers, and pastry-cooks' molds.[30]

The Romans were the first to leave records of soup ingredients which were improved through cultivation over the next few centuries.

Carrots are thought native to Afghanistan. They were cultivated to produce a less woody and tastier version in the Mediterranean area before the Christian era. A near relative is Queen Anne's Lace which is typical of any variety allowed to return to the wild.[31] The modern version of the carrot was introduced into Europe between the 8th and 10th centuries. Carrots were purple, white, or yellow.

Cucumbers are thought native to the East Indies,[32] and they were cultivated for at least 3,000 years. They were available in Egypt when the pyramids were built, were known in biblical times, and were much appreciated by the ancient Romans. Scholars think they were introduced by the Romans throughout their holdings.

Leeks have been dated to the 2nd millennium B.C. and documented in Egyptian tombs. Nero's favorite vegetable was the leek, and he preferred it made into soup.[33]

Cress was traced to Persia. The origin of asparagus has been credited to Europe and Asia, which put it at the ready disposal of the Romans.

Any combination of these and other items could have comprised the soups of the working class. Ancient Romans sometimes perceived soup and broth as both food and a medicinal remedy which might increase fertility, cause the bowels to move, or settle "burning of the urine."

> Sausages, black puddings, broth, force-meat for stuffing, haggis, tripe, porridge, or hasty-pudding, pastry of almost infinite variety, with sauces and seasonings of many sorts, with fish or game, appear to have been the most favorite fare.[34]

Pliny wrote that *liquamen* or *garum* was made from salted fish and fish guts. He thought the finished sauce looked similar to honey. The process of making it was probably quite odoriferous. It might be replaced today with a strong fish stock flavored with anchovies. It was mentioned often in *Apicius*. Foods were highly seasoned in the Roman kitchen and sauces accompanied most dishes.

Soups and stews comprise a small percentage of the recipes from *Apicius*, however, poorer households prepared primarily porridges (gruel made from stone-ground grain), soups, broths, and perhaps stews that could be prepared in a single cook pot with basic ingredients. Even the wealthy consumed such soups when there were no guests to impress.

Clay pots (earthenware) were used, as were terra-cotta, stone, and lead. Some were designed to rest on a tripod. The Romans covered their food with a *testa*,[35] or domed earthenware cover, to seal in flavor while it cooked.

Chicken broth contained chicken meat, crushed peppercorns, stock, *must* (new wine before fermentation), and water.

A recipe for dumplings of pheasant instructs the cook to mince roasted pheasant meat with the fat and trimmings, season it with pepper and wine, shape it into croquettes or dumplings and poach it in seasoned water.

It could be said that fish stews are rooted in ancient Roman cookery in that *Apicius* recorded a method for preparing a fish stew by placing raw fish into a saucepan with oil, broth, reduced wine, leeks and green coriander and, while that cooked, adding crushed pepper, lovage, and oregano. The dish was thickened with egg yolks before serving. The stew didn't make use of the potatoes and onions found in subsequent versions.

Lamb stew was made of pieces of kid or lamb, chopped onion, coriander, crushed pepper, lovage, and cumin placed in a stew pot and cooked with broth, oil, and wine. The method of making stew was to remove the meat, skim any impurities, and return the meat to the broth. Another entry instructed adding raw herbs to parboiled meat then simmering it, and goat meat was suggested to be as good as lamb for such a stew.

Romans were fond of their native cumin and used it liberally. Predating the Roman Empire is this passage from Isaiah 28:27:

> For the fitches are not threshed with a threshing instrument, neither is a card wheel turned about upon the cumin; but the fitches are beaten out with a staff, and the cumin with a rod.

Seafood stew was made with minced oysters, mussels, and sea nettles combined with toasted nuts, rue, celery, pepper, coriander, cumin, raisin wine, broth, reduced wine and oil. This dish is similar to modern bouillabaisse or cioppini.

Cioppini is a classic Italian fish stew, the origins of which are not clearly traceable. It became a classic for Mediterranean fishermen who wanted to produce a tasty meal from their daily catch, and Italian immigrants introduced the soup to American cooks sometime between 1900 and 1920.

Apician minutal was a Roman soup made from oil, broth, wine, leeks, mint, small fish, small tidbits (forcemeat), cock's fries or capon's kidneys, pork, crushed pepper, lovage, green coriander or seeds, and honey.

A capon is an emasculated bird. The procedure is said to have first been performed in ancient Rome. Under Fannian law, there were restrictions on serving anything other than a hen, but after performing this procedure, the fowl was lawful to eat.

Minutal à la Matius was made from chopped leeks, coriander, bits of cooked pork shoulder, peeled and cored Matian apples, pepper, cumin, green coriander or seeds, mint, laser root, a little vinegar, honey, broth, and reduced must.

Sweet minutal is similar to the above recipe except for the addition of some sort of diced melon or squash. The cook was instructed to hollow out the shell of the fruit, indicating the dish might have been a sort of ragout stuffed into the hollow shell.

Apicius also includes recipes for *Minutal of Fruit*, *Minutal of Hare's Livers*, and *Red Apple Minutal.*

Soups of green pot herbs along with dishes of beans and pasta were the basis of Roman soldiers' diets. They also ate gruels like those eaten by the peasant class, such as barley broth (pap and porridge).[36]

The ruins of Pompeii shed light on the methods of food preparation through the utensils and vessels salvaged from the ash. These include wine dippers, colanders, strainers, frying pans, stew pots, knives, ladles, choppers, and a dinner gong to summon diners to table. Technology from the bronze and iron ages likely gave rise to the cooking pots and vessels.[37]

> Pollux gives a list of forty-two names which include pots, ladles, trays, choppers, braziers, mortars, skewers, spits, etc.[38]

Museum holdings show a wider range of kitchen pieces, including serving dishes and pitchers. The ruins at Pompeii contain raised hearths and ovens similar to a beehive. This is remarkable given that after the fall of the Roman Empire it would be many centuries before raised hearths and ovens became standard kitchen features.

Forks were unknown except as cooking utensils, and knives and spoons were usually in limited supply. Therefore, even upper class citizens usually ate with the forefingers of the right hand. Soups and broths were drunk from vessels, and large pieces of meat or vegetables were scooped out with the fingers and placed into the mouth. Table manners were described thusly:

> The Greeks ate without a fork or spoon. Soup they managed to drink out of bowls, as impatient juveniles have been known to drink it in our own time; or else they sopped bread in it.[39]

And preparations for cooking included:

> The processes of cooking ... are, singeing (hair and feathers), cleansing, chopping, cutting up, cutting across, cutting down the back, boiling, roasting, broiling, kneading, straining, sifting, stewing, pounding in a mortar, toasting, sweetening, seasoning, trussing, stuffing, and perhaps, we may add smoking.[40]

Heartier soups and the wide array of sauces which are recorded in *Apicius* were mopped up with chunks of bread which varied in texture and flavor according to the resources available to the baker.

Porray, or *porry*, was a thick porridge or soup made of green leaves, and sometimes other ingredients such as bread or onions. The greens often consisted of some combination of orach, swiss chard, borage, Good King Henry, watercress, spinach, and leeks.

A classic traditional soup made of broth and chopped greens, often wild greens such as chicory and borage, likely evolved into minestra or minestrone. Minestrone is basically a hodgepodge of ingredients thrown into a soup pot to produce a sustaining hot meal. There was no particular recipe for minestrone, and some believe it often contained bits of whatever was left from previous meals until the 1600s or 1700s when it emerged as a dish in its own right.

Soups did not contain tomato before about 1550 when the Italians began growing them, but by the 18th century tomatoes were firmly established as a main ingredient in Italian cuisine.

On the Right Pleasure and Good Health (1475), translated by Mary Ella Milham, includes a recipe for *minutal.* Green vegetables were plunged into boiling water, removed at once and cut up finely. When cut they were pounded in a mortar and boiled with sugar until cooked. This book also contained recipes for soups made from broad beans, gourds, herbs, and red chick peas. Antonius the Herbalist wrote on the use of pulse and was quoted often by Galen.[41]

Italian words which initially translated into the English word *soup* include *zuppa* (tomato soup or fish soup), *minestra* (a more substantial, often vegetable soup), and minestrone (a really hearty or large soup).

Soup survived in the Byzantine Empire after the fall of the western Roman Empire. After its fall to the Ottoman Turks in 1454, soups from Central Asia were assimilated into Europe's culinary traditions. The Turks were apt to consume soup at any time of day. Vegetables were used extensively in Turkish soups,[42] as was the tomato in later centuries.

By the 19th century, soups were an important part of the Italian diet for all social classes, and many of the soups we readily identify as Italian in origin were firmly established. These included soups made from pasta, eggs, bread crumbs, meats, vegetables, and legumes.

> The numerous pottages in which the Latin epicures delighted were made chiefly of prepared grain and pot-herbs, seasoned with wine and sauces to the taste. Barley, wheat, rice, peas, beans, gourds, were all used for the manufacture of the highly nutritive soups, which were often enriched with pulp of pounded meat, and morsels of tenderly stewed flesh.... Often these porridges were sweetened with honey, and sharpened with liquamen. Some of the lighter Roman pottages resembled closely the thin vegetable soups of the modern Lenten table. But none of them are comparable with the clear gravy soups of the nineteenth century. The Roman cared little for the pure flavour of meat-juice, though he employed it sparingly in his meretricious sauces.[43]

7. The Medieval Period

The Middle Ages were a time of discovery and rediscovery. After the fall of the Roman Empire many citizens lived in abject poverty in the shadow of unbelievably advanced technology such as the Roman aqueducts. Roads and sewers fell into disrepair as people lived in mere hovels, and food reverted, for a time, almost to the stage it had been when man lived on wild grains and seeds. The Black Death, or bubonic plague, claimed thousands of lives and left the survivors to rebuild a society that had completely deteriorated.

Almost any seeds, roots, nuts, berries, and leaves of wild plants were likely to find their way into the pottages. Examples of those early greens include plantain, mallow, dock, and nettles. During times of scarcity, the roots of plants such as wild leeks, carrots, parsnips, and turnips bulked up the pottages. However, it would be years before those tubers were any more than skinny, woody roots. Some of the seeds produced oils, which made the pottages richer, and fruits and berries were little more than pottage ingredients.

Gervase Markham used lettuce, strawberry and violet leaves, spinach, endive, and succory as pot herbs, and Sir Kenelm Digby's writings add sorrel, borage, bugloss, purslane, chervil, and beet leaves. Some used turnip tops (greens) in pottages.

Pilgrims from England also ate strawberry leaves in the New World. In an effort to aid a sick Indian chief, men from Plymouth prepared a "mock chicken" soup for him: "It was corn gruel, seasoned with green strawberry leaves and slices of sassafras root. He strained it through his pocket handkerchief." The chief recovered and asked the men to administer the same care to some of his people who were also sick.[1]

Remains of a village at Skara Brae on Orkney, assessed by radiocarbon dating at between 3200 and 2000 B.C., prove that at that early date the inhabitants were farmers. By examining trash and other remains archaeologists discovered their diet was primarily beef, sheep, fish, shellfish, barley and wheat, supplemented by deer, boar, seal, and shorebirds and their eggs.[2]

Examination of the stomach contents of Tollund man (discovered in a peat bog in Denmark) revealed he had eaten pottage made from both wild and cultivated grains not unlike the meals consumed at Skara Brae.[3] Similar testing revealed that another bog body, Haraldskaer woman, had eaten grain and blackberries. These discoveries show a remarkable similarity of diet in the early people.

Later, as farmers began to cultivate grains and vegetables, distinct cuisines began to emerge and "made" dishes took on varying degrees of refinement. As missionaries like St. Columba spread Christianity throughout Europe, vegetables and spices previously unknown began to emerge, sometimes initially more as curiosities than actual foodstuffs.

Pottages of cereals and seeds slowly improved with the addition of meat or fish, vegetables, peas, rice, seaweed, and others. Emmer and einkorn, barley, rye, and oats were important contributions to soup cauldrons and were of much better quality than their wild predecessors.

Studying medieval cookery books indicates several basic types of food. They included plain, relatively dry, roasted meat, pastries and pies; heavily sauced foods such as pudding; simple soups which were basically liquid, but sometimes with the addition of meat and/or bread; and a brewet of meat, poultry, or fish in sauce.

> Like Roman cuisine medieval cookery had a vegetable base. Of its half-hundred or so of soups, several consisted altogether of water thickened with boiled frumenty, rice, or pulse, flavored with pot-herbs and seasoned with common spices. In this way also, the medievalists concocted bean-soup, pea-soup, turnip-soup, cabbage-soup, parsnips soup, skirret soup, herb soup, gourd pottage, rice pottage. These thinner broths were sometimes enriched with the liquor of stewed meat or minced viands, but the vegetables dominated over all other ingredients. So also their thicker brewets and stews, messes less substantial than hotch potches, and more satisfying than the lighter soups—were thickened with bread, frumenty, oatmeal, prepared barley, rice, and products of the garden. The men of feudal England were copious takers of soup; and whilst some of their soups were meat and drink for the ravenous bellies of famished soldiers, others were delicate enough to please a modern epicure. Their humble-soup, and pig-soup, and roe-broth may be named as examples of the former sort. Their egg-soup and lark-soup were favourable specimens of the daintier preparations. Courtiers could appreciate a pottage of small birds boiled in almond broth, flavored with onions, pellitory, and salt, enriched with lard. Yeomen smacked their lips over steaming bowls of strongly seasoned "perrey of peson," i.e. the puree of the modern family table. But the medieval chefs were even happier in their fish soups than their flesh pottages. Skillfully prepared their eel-broths and sole-broths would extort praise from the most fastidious gourmets of the present day. Nor should their muscle-broths and oyster-soups be passed over without commendation. One of their oyster-pottages was execrably overcharged with ginger, sugar, and mace. Oysters in Cynee, on the contrary, was a preparation of high merit, if not of genius. But the grand fault of most of their soups was a multifariousness of materials and seasonings, resulting in confusion of flavor and torpor of palate. The same objection must be made against their more elaborate mortrews and hotch potches.
>
> The pot, as we have seen, was their commonest cooking utensil, and pottage was their commonest diet. Some of their richest soup contained so much meat or fish that the culinary historian doubts whether he should not rank them with broths or hashes. These same pottages were thickened with grain and meal.[4]

Jefferson thought the thinnest soups were herb-pottages, commended by the Church as fit diet for meager (meatless) days.

Martin Martin described the process of separating the grain from the stalks. A woman took a handful of grain in her left hand and set fire to it. With a stick in her right hand she beat the grain as the husk burned away to remove it from the stalk. That grain could be baked into bread within an hour of cutting it.[5]

Though ancient to our minds, saddle querns and later rotary querns greatly simplified the process of milling grains. After large mills were established, it was decreed that grinding grain in a hand mill defrauded the manorial lord and miller from a share of the grain milled for each customer.[6]

Dumplings have been added to soups to stretch the quantity for centuries, and almost every culture had their version of this ubiquitous morsel of dough. Early versions were fruit or meat wrapped in dough while later versions were simply pieces of dough dropped into soups. During the Great Depression of the 1930s, chicken and dumplings became more of an American southern eat-with-a-fork meal than the soup they were initially.

Dumplings seem to have been liked by many but despised by a few. In 1841 Sarah Hale said of soup, "Crackers, toasted or hard bread may be added a short time before the soup is wanted; but do not put in those libels on civilized cookery, called *dumplings*. One might as well eat, with the hope of digesting a brick from the ruins of Babylon, as one of the hard, heavy masses of boiled dough which usually pass under this name." Others liked them to the extent that whole recipes centered around the dumplings, and at some point during the late Victorian era Southern cooks fortified this soup to the point it was considered a main dish rather than a soup.

In 1832 Eliza Leslie instructed making pigeon dumplings by stuffing pigeons with oysters, wrapping each bird in dough, encasing that in a cloth and boiling until done — much the same way as apple dumplings were made. Other recipes from the l830s to the l860s called for stuffing the dumpling crust with peppered bacon or minced ham and boiling them. *Webster's* (1856) defined a dumpling as paste, usually with a filling inside. Fillings also included calf's liver, lemon, and fruits of all sorts.

James Sanderson published a cookery book in 1843 which was later combined with another prominent cookery book and sold as a double volume. It underwent several printings during the 1860s. Sanderson advised adding suet dumplings to mutton broth along with chopped parsley and marigold blossoms, which puts this form of dumpling in use during the early 1840s.

Dumplings have been part of European and Asian culture for many years, and were part of American Indian cuisine by the time Europeans arrived. Stuffed dumplings include Asian wontons, Italian ravioli, Russian pelmeni, and Jewish kreplach.

Sometime around 1300 a new starch found its way into English soup cauldrons. Sago was a thickener, and some say it was documented in Asian literature as early as the 12th century. Sago and other crops were exported from South America and the Natuna Islands.[7]

To process sago, the palm was felled and cut into lengths from five to six feet in length. The pulp was extracted, and the flour processed. The flour was moistened, pressed through a sieve, and heated to compact it into granulated form. In the 19th century a writer observed, "We seldom see sago in Europe except in its granulated form."[8]

It is not known exactly when arrowroot, a flavorless white powder, found its way into European soup cauldrons, but studies show it was being used in the Americas some 7,000 years ago.[9] Much like cornstarch, it is used as a thickener. Christopher Columbus encountered arrowroot powder when he made contact with the Arawak people of South America.

Vermicelli and pasta-like products, dating to the 14th century (possibly earlier), thickened soup or pottage as well as dumplings with the advantage that they could be made beforehand and kept until ready for use. Various noodles and pastas originated in Asia, Italy, and other parts of the world.

In a translation of Platina, there is a recipe for hollow pasta made from flour, egg white, and rosewater. The mixture was rolled thin and the middle hollowed out with a metal stylus. When dried it kept for two or three years, probably longer. It was cooked in rich juice (stock or broth) with herbs, butter, and grated cheese.

In 1868, the *Brooklyn Eagle* asked, "In those dark, those pitch dark ages, before side-dishes were invented, and when the majority of the half savage chasers of the mammoth lived on fullers' earth and cold lizard, what would not a tyrant of Central Asia have given for a French cook — a Ude, a Francatelli, or a Careme?" The article acknowledged that the first prepared dishes were soups, refined at varying speeds from one part of Europe to another. The English were said to "over-spice and under-vegetablize" their soups in an attempt to reduce the time spent on preparation, while the French had an unhurried approach to cooking, "so that the different ingredients of the extract may unite with each other easily and thoroughly."

The quality of prepared dishes was actually cruder in early medieval Europe than it had been during the days of Roman rule.

> The Iberians were almost exclusively animal feeders. Of cookery they had but the simplest ideas; raw or roasted meat, with wine and mulsum, summed up their notions of a banquet. The Lusithanians only drank water, and ate scarcely any flesh but that of goats. The Gauls were equally indifferent to vegetable food. They preferred swine's flesh, roasted, salted, or smoked. They drank wine, milk, and a barley drink; but wine was their especial favorite, because it intoxicated them. Maidens and youths waited at meals. The men sat on the skins of wild beasts. The ancient Germans were likewise mainly animal feeders and huge feeders. Wild boar, hare, deer, aurochs, black-cock, wild-goose, duck, pigeon, sheep, pigs, oxen, and horses with some fishes, were eaten raw as well as roasted. When the flesh was eaten raw, it was generally kneaded by hand and feet, in the skin, until it was tolerably soft. They drank must, meth [metheglin, a liquor made from fermented honey], beer, and wine, and drank it unstintingly.[10]

The type of dishes later served, at least to the upper classes, can be documented through ancient cookery books. One of the earliest written in English, *The Forme of Cury*, was compiled in about 1390 and contained 196 recipes.

Dishes were established during this period which remain favorites. Pea soup has been one of the most common soups throughout history, an almost compulsory addition in cookery books from the medieval era to present. It was made from fresh or dried peas, sometimes with mint, and with or without the meat from which the stock was made. Shredded lettuce, onion, leek, carrot, and the like were added at the discretion of the cook. The peas were usually pressed through a sieve or mashed with a spoon to thicken the soup so that it was similar in consistency to a cream soup. Because any sort of meat or fowl could be used to make stock and dried peas were light in weight, nonperishable, inexpensive, and easy to carry, pea soup was often prepared outdoors.

Unlike beans, which require soaking, dried peas could be put directly to cook which saved time in preparation and added to the popularity of pea soup in the outdoor kitchen. It was a popular Lenten dish.

Peas found in Spirit Cave, on the border between Burma and Thailand,[11] have been carbon dated to between 9000 and 6000 B.C. Several cultures have used peas since antiquity, including those of Iraq, Switzerland, China, and Egypt. Apicius included nine recipes for peas, some cooked with vegetables and herbs, others with meat or poultry, in his book. Pease porridge was a well-established dish by that time. The Greek dramatist Aristophanes (c. 446–c. 388 B.C.) wrote of pea soup in *The Birds*. Anne Blencowe included "Peas soope, gravy soop, and hodg podg" in her 1690s receipt book.[12]

Pulses dry easily and tend to absorb the flavor of whatever they are combined with to produce excellent pottage. The drawback was that dried legumes tended to sprout, and subsequently spoil, if exposed to dampness. By the Middle Ages, sprouting was prevented by making canebyns, or frizzled beans. The beans were soaked until they began to swell and burst through the hulls. Then they were dried again, the hulls discarded, and the beans chopped and toasted before being stored away. The beans kept better, and the flavor of the pottage was increased with the toasting.[13]

The method of cooking was to seethe (simmer) cuts of meat in cauldrons. The meat was taken out of the cauldrons with flesh forks after which it was often served separately. The broth was served with or without additional ingredients.

Rich meat soups were made of brawns (pieces of flesh) cut into gobbets (size of two thumbs) and dices, floated in hot broth thickened with meal and pounded flesh. In 1875, John Jefferson wrote:

When they have boiled meat, there is sometimes one in the company that will have the broth; this is a kind of soup with a little thin oatmeal in it and some leaves of thyme and sage, or other such small herbs. They bring this up in as many porringers as there are people that desire it; those that please crumble a little bread into it, and this makes a kind of pottage.[14]

Besides seething in a cauldron, fish or fowl could be encased in mud and placed in an ash bed with hot coals. When the hardened clay was cracked open, the feathers of birds or scales and skin of fish came away with it, leaving only the tender cooked flesh. This method of cooking continued through the 19th century, and was also commonly used in the United States.[15]

Foods and cooking techniques improved for many reasons during the medieval era. Some cultures made contributions significant enough to bear scrutiny on their own, but perhaps the most important improvement was the emergence of chimneys that brought the cook from a crouched position, trying to escape the worst of his or her smoke-filled existence, into the light of day. Woodcuts such as those of Bartolomeo Scappi show medieval manor kitchens with ventilated fireplaces and chimneys to draw out smoke, and kitchens were often separated from the rest of the structure for protection from fire, especially those in France and England.

Scappi illustrated the extent of personnel needed in lavish kitchens: the *hateur* was in charge of roasting, the *potier* oversaw the pots and "made" dishes, the *saucier* prepared the sauces to go with various dishes, the *broyeur* utilized the mortar, the *souffleur* maintained the fires, and the *potagier* prepared the various soups or potages.

And for this there should be provided large, fair, and proper cauldrons for cooking large meats, and other medium ones in great abundance for making potages and doing other things necessary for cookery, and great hanging pans for cooking fish and other necessary things, and large common pots in great abundance for making soups and other things, and a dozen fair large mortars; and check the space for making sauces; and there should be twenty large frying pans, a dozen large casks, fifty small casks, sixty cornues [bowls with handles], one hundred wooden bowls, a dozen grills, six large graters, one hundred wooden spoons, twenty-five slotted spoons both large and small, six hooks, twenty iron shovels, twenty rotisseries, with turning mechanisms and irons for holding the spits. And one should definitely not trust wooden spits, because they will rot and you could lose all your meat, but you should have one hundred and twenty iron spits which are strong and are thirteen feet in length; and there should be other spits, three dozen which are of the aforesaid length but not so thick, to roast poultry, little piglets, and river fowl: [Latin proverb]. And also, four dozen little spits to do endoring and act as skewers.[16]

Chiquart said a kitchen should contain two large two-handed knives, a dozen dressing knives, two dozen knives for chopping ingredients for pottages and stuffing, half a dozen scrubbers, and a hundred baskets for carrying and storage. His recipes are rich in pottages and bruets, and his kitchen was amply supplied with vessels for making them.

Equipment is similar in Italian and German kitchens though the space may seem smaller and more cluttered in some of the woodcuts. The kitchens of kings and nobles were places for the cooks to impress and amaze, but the kitchens or cooking areas of the working class were so basic as to defy comparison.

Rachael Feild[17] indicated the Greeks used metal cauldrons before most of Europe, and although they often brought cauldrons to trade with the English and Irish as early as the 8th or 7th century B.C., the cauldrons remained out of the reach of anyone too poor to possess anything worthy of bartering. Metal cauldrons became more prevalent after they were copied by Irish tinkers and peddlers.

The Forme of Cury contains recipes for soups, broths, caudles, brewets, soppes, ragouts, hashes, and pottages containing ingredients such as cabbage, rape, beans, herbs, gourds, rice, mushrooms (fungus), venison, bread, veal, chicken, rabbit, hare, oysters, mussels, saffron, onions, almonds, and so on. *Hoggepot*, an early recipe for hodgepodge, was made from geese, onions, wine, water, and bread.

The following recipe is typical. "Fenkel Soppes. take blades of Fenkel [fennel]. shrede hem not to smale, do hem to seep in water and oile and oynouns mynced perwith. do perto safroun and salt and powdour douce, serue it forth, take brede tosted and lay the sewe onoward." A similar recipe for soppes was made from leeks.

Little, if any, rice was cultivated in medieval England, so it may not have been common among the lower classes.

Pliny claimed the Romans were fond of pepper and that it came from the East Indies, making its way to England in about the 14th century.

Bartolomeo Scappi's cookery book, printed in 1485, was one of the first to show improvement in prepared dishes during the Renaissance era. Europe has known great upheaval and drastic change over the centuries as countries emerged and revolts transferred power. Food remained the one constant, although ingredients and methods of preparing it have been in continual evolution.

Don't discount soups from the Middle Ages as relics of the past. Appulmoy, made from almonds, milk, honey, and apples, and "snow pottage," made of rice and milk, saw resurgence in appeal throughout England in the 1700s.

The recipe for appulmoy in *The Forme of Cury* instructs the cook to take apples and "seethe hem in water, drawe hem through a straynour. take almaunde mylke & hony and flour of Rys, safroun and powdour fort and salt."[18]

Modern versions instruct us to peel, core, and cook apples until soft, mash them, add almond milk, honey, salt, perhaps cloves, mace, and galingale[19] or ginger and thicken with rice flour. It can be flavored with saffron. Almond milk was made from steeping ground almonds in water, broth, or wine, and it was used to thicken the soup.

De Guoy stated that cooks in India had used apples in making soup for over 1,000 years.[20] Other cultures known to have enjoyed hot or cold fruit soups include England, France, Poland, Russia, Switzerland, Germany, Austria, Brazil, Finland, Sweden, Norway, Scandinavia, Portugal, Mexico, Santo Domingo, Havana, and the United States.

Fruit soups have been made from coconut, oranges, cherries, plums, strawberries, peaches, passion fruit, avocado, blackberries, blueberries, boysenberries, huckleberries, melons, lemons, papaya, pineapple, raspberries, rhubarb, and rose hips.

The Crusaders brought plums back to France from Syria in the 12th century where they were crossed with local varieties to produce Ente plums. The French introduced them to California in 1856. The same French monks realized that by drying them they kept a year without spoilage, thus the prune, one of the lesser-known soup ingredients, became popular.[21]

The Crusades were the culminated attempts of Christianity to seize Jerusalem from Muslim control beginning in 1095 and continuing through 1291. Soldiers from throughout Europe found themselves exposed to spices and dishes quite foreign to them, and many may have returned home with herbs or spices to share with family and friends.[22]

Using spices in the amounts called for in early recipes may produce such a strong flavor the dish will be inedible. There is no comparison between modern spices and those of the ancients, which were often carried great distances in cloth bags and exposed to extreme heat, dampness, and exposure, to the point where they had already lost a great deal of their strength by the time they were purchased.

Food was prepared anywhere there was a hearth or fire, as in the case of students who could purchase bundles of fuel and prepare grain gruels, peas or bean pottage, roasted collops (slices) of meat, or bread such as oatcakes in their quarters. There was, as yet, little notion of going to a restaurant to be served a meal.

Lavish meals served in noble homes did not come without sacrifice on the part of the cooks, particularly those under the tutelage of the master cook, whose job it was to actually slice and dice, feed the fires, and stir the massive cauldrons. The heat was insufferable and the work back-breaking.

> The kitchen is his hell, and he the devil in it, where his meat and he fry together. His revenues are showered down from the fat of the land, and he interlards his own grease among, to help the drippings.... His weapons ofter offensive are a mess of hot broth and scalding water, and woe be to him that comes in his way. In the kitchen he will domineer and rule the roast in spite of his master, and curses in the very dialect of his calling. His labour is more blustering and fury, and his speech like that of sailors in a storm, a thousand businesses at once; yet, in all this tumult, he does not love combustion, but will be the first man that shall go and quench it. He is never a good Christian till a hissing pot of ale has slacked him, like water cast on a firebrand, and for that time he is tame and dispossessed. His cunning is not small in architecture, for he builds strange fabrics in paste, towers and castles, which are offered to the assault of valiant teeth, and like Darius' palace in one banquet demolished. He is a pitiless murderer of innocents, and he mangles poor fowls with unheard-of tortures, and it is thought the martyrs' persecutions were devised from hence: sure we are, St. Lawrence's gridiron came out of his kitchen. His best faculty is at the dresser, where he seems to have great skill in the tactics, ranging his dishes in order military, and placing with great discretion in the fore-front meats more strong and hardy, and the more cold and cowardly in the rear; as quaking tarts and quivering custards, and such milk-sop dishes, which scape many times the fury of the encounter. But now the second course is gone up and he down in the cellar, where he drinks and sleeps till four o'clock in the afternoon, and then returns again to his regiment.[23]

Galen and Moses Maimonides were among the physicians who wrote regarding the medicinal qualities of chicken soup. Maimonides was a rabbi and physician who lived from 1135 to 1204. He included chicken soup in a treatise he wrote on the treatment of asthma. He relied heavily on previous writings by Galen.[24]

During the Middle Ages Hungarian goulash, or *gulyas*, was created by herdsmen tending cattle who needed a simple one-pot hearty meal to provide basic sustenance. At the end of the 18th century it began to transform from mere trail food to something that would eventually define a nation.

The ingredient that gives *gulyas* its character is paprika. This spice has been a part of the Hungarian diet since the 18th century when it was introduced by the Turks.[25] Basic *gulyas* contains beef, onions, pepper, tomato, and paprika. Some cooks add potato or noodles and sour cream. There is no "official" recipe or method of preparation.

Ancient Hungarian cuisine included many soups and stews that utilized plentiful fish and game. Preparation was heavily influenced by the Turks and Bulgarians. Large cauldrons, called *bogrács*, were the main cookery vessels of ancient Hungary.

Popular Hungarian soups include *halászlé* (fish soup with paprika), *húsleves* (meat soup), *hideg meggyleves* (chilled cream-based sour cherry soup), and *jókai bableves* (bean soup). *Halászlé* was first prepared by fishermen from their catch. It contains onions, hot paprika, pepper, tomato, wine, and any combination of whole fish. *Lecsó* is a vegetable stew made from peppers, tomato, wine, spices, onion, and garlic. The Hungarian version of pea soup is called *sargaborsoleves*.

Documentation of Hungarian cuisine began in the 15th century after Beatrice, wife of King Matthias Corvinus, influenced food preparation with the addition of garlic, turkey, pasta, and other items. In 1526, Hungary fell under Turkish rule, and it was during that time that the use of paprika originated. The king and queen not only created dishes but also kept meticulous records which have been of great value to historians.[26]

Literature, Science, and Art on September 25, 1869 carried an article regarding the controversy of northern European nations of eating horseflesh. "An old book" inspired a reader to say that in the early days these people used horses as sacrificial beasts, and their importance was so great that a species of white horse was bred for that purpose and never subjected to work of any kind. Controversy erupted when King Haquin refused to eat this meat after becoming a Christian, and in an effort to put the matter to rest, made a public pretense of eating soup made of horseflesh.

Also a Christian, King Ingon of Sweden, was reportedly dethroned because he refused to eat horse flesh and when his successor was elected, he publicly abjured Christianity while sprinkling the people with horse's blood. The controversy caused Pope Gregory III (pope 731 to A.D. 741, Syrian by birth) and others to instruct missionaries not to allow, on any account, the eating of horseflesh.[27]

While controversies rose and abated, through it all various cuisines and cooking techniques were beginning to emerge which would remain constant, although refined over the coming years.

8. The Renaissance Era and Beyond

By the early Renaissance era, the groundwork had been laid for the world's cuisines, but there remained much work to do in refining and improving the dishes. Of equal importance was the advancement of agricultural practices and improving the quality of cultivated vegetables. A large selection of cookery books can be consulted for the former, and Thomas Tusser's *Five Hundred Pointes of Good Husbandrie* (1580), Nicholas Culpepper's *The Complete Herbal* (1653), and John Reid's *Gard'ners Kalendar* (1683) are excellent sources for the latter.

By knowing when a vegetable or pot herb became a garden staple, we can determine at what era of cookery it is correct to reproduce it today. For example, we can approximate the cultivation of potatoes in England by comparing two of these volumes. Culpepper did not list them in 1653, but Reid did in 1683.

Some say the Dutch King William brought potatoes with him into England, while others credit their introduction to Sir Francis Drake in about 1570 or John Hawkins in 1565. The peasantry soon began consuming them, and at that time potatoes began to replace dumplings in the soup cauldrons.[1]

Renaissance cookery books from various parts of Europe tend to show a similar progression of soup or pottage recipes from the medieval era through the Renaissance and beyond. Anne Blencowe's 1690 recipe for "peas soope" is more complex than the one in *The Forme of Cury* from 1390.

The earlier recipe contained peas, onions, sugar, salt, and saffron. In comparison, Anne's recipe was more complex:

> Take about two Quarts of peas & boyl them down till they are thick; then put to them a leeke & a little slice of bacon & a little bunch of sweet herbs, & let them boyl till they are broke. Then work them with ye back of a ladle thro a coarse hair sieve; then take about 3 pints of your peas & mix with about 3 quarts of very strong broth & work them very well together. Then sett them over a Stove & let them boyl very easily. Then as for your herbs, take to the quantity of a gallon of soope; take a large handful of spinage & one third of sorrill & one cabbage, Lettice; & a little Charvell & Creases & a head or two of sallery & Indive & ye heart of a Savoy & a litle mint, but mince ye herbs with one leeke very small, & put them into a brass dish or sauspan with half a pound of butter, & let ym stove till they begin to be tender. Then put to them a quart of good gravy or strong broth, but gravy is best, & when you have mix't it well then putt it into ye pott to ye peas & a little beaten cloves and mace. So let it stove.

Opposite: Kitchen woodcut, B. Scappi, 1574. An elaborate Renaissance-era kitchen in which seven workers attend to various duties. A pair of hares hang from a peg on the back wall, most likely bound for the soup pots. Cauldrons are seen on each side wall and various utensils and supplies are stored on the shelves. The high ceiling would have kept the work area bearable in hot weather as the heat rose. Library of Congress, Prints and Photographs Division, Reproduction Number LC-USZ62-110347.

about half an hour, then have a French roll, either dry'd in an oven or tosted by ye fire, in thin slices, then season ye soope to your palate & so serve it up. If you please you may put forcd meat balls into it, or any other thing, as palates & sweetbreads or Combs.[2]

Though there were few soup recipes in her book, we should not assume these were the only soups she prepared, but merely the ones she saw a need to record. Others varied according to availability of meat and fresh vegetables.

The rhyme "Peas-porridge hot, peas-porridge cold; peas-porridge in a pot, nine days old" is a reference to the practice of keeping the soup cauldron going constantly, adding to it as portions were taken out.[3] Green peas soup was also sometimes served cold.[4]

In 1736, Mrs. McLintock included in Scotland's first cookery book five recipes for soup, and one of them was for pease soup. The broth she used was apparently a stock made from beef and veal, mace, onions, cloves, and sweet herbs.

> Make your Broth after the Manner of the brown Soup; then take a lib. And a half of White Pease, boil them in Water till the skins come off them, then bruise them with a Spoon, strain them thro' a callandar, put them into the Soup, let them all soke together, put in a little Spearmint and Marygold, and serve them up.[5]

Mrs. McIver, in her 1787 Scottish cookery book, instructed the addition of a large parsnip or carrot with split peas and, if extra green color was desired, some freshly squeezed spinach juice. Acceptable herbs to add included thyme, winter savory, and mint. She approved the addition of a red herring or piece of pork, hung bacon, or a piece of beef for those who chose it. Her soup was served dished onto fried bread.

Mrs. Dalgairns, in 1829, used peas quite liberally, including six recipes for pea soup in her Scottish cookery book, and she also included them in additional soups bearing different names.

Potatoes in pea soup stretched the quantity, but added little, if any, additional flavor. Many agreed with Mrs. Colman (1870) that pea soup, "which is so great a favorite at many of our restaurant and public tables," was best when "there is literally no flavoring put into it but a little salt."

Other common soups of the Renaissance era include forms of almond milk, crayfish, bruets (slightly more liquid than stew) of chicken, kid, veal, venison, or similar meat, gruels such as frumenty, leeks, and other vegetables.

Sabina Welserin's German cookbook of 1553 added to that list recipes for goose soup (milk and toasted bread added to goose drippings) and blancmange. A Book of Cookrye (1591) contributed broth, capon in white broth, hodgepodge, broth of neat's (beef) tongue, pomage of apple, and almond milk.

9. Open Hearth Development

During the medieval era, cooking facilities began to emerge into what we recognize today, and because they developed at an amazingly similar rate throughout the world, it is imperative to understand the similarity in cooking techniques before examining the peculiarities of individual cuisines.

It is safe to say that every culture utilized a central fire at one time or another. While Europeans were building fires in the center of their floors, the Indians of North America were doing exactly the same. The technology seems to have evolved along the same path regardless of country of origin. According to the Illinois State Historical Society:

> During the winter season, the houses [of the Illinois Indians] were made of poles covered with closely woven matts of rushes, which were fairly watertight, particularly when they were two or three layers thick. There was a single low door, and a single smoke hole in the middle of the roof, so that one unaccustomed to the establishment had often to travel on hands and knees and keep his face close to the floor for the sake of air.[1]

Open hearth cooking techniques have varied little from antiquity through present. Earthenware pots and metal pots (usually bronze) and skillets were placed on tripods or gridirons, and lidded cauldrons slowly simmered away in Roman Britain just as they continue to do well into the 21st century.

The word *hearth* conjures up a vision of an open fireplace with an area paved in stone, concrete, or brick in front on which food can be prepared, and which poses some degree of safety should embers or a burning log roll out of the fire. It was not always so.

Webster's 1857 dictionary describes "hearth" as a paved area on which a fire is built and from which there is a passage for the smoke to ascend. This includes the entire area from the back wall of the fireplace forward to the front edge of the paving, extending out from the front opening of the fireplace.

In archaeology, *hearth* refers to a fire pit or fireplace from any era. Hearths are identifiable in an excavated area by the presence of fire-cracked rock linings or the presence of bones, charcoal, ash, and by-products.

Up until the 11th century, European hearths were in the center of the room, built on a slab of stone on the earth floor. They were surrounded by a ring of stones, perhaps with a large stone in back against which the fire could be banked at night. The smoke simply rose and exited through the thatched roof. This central fire provided even heating for the home.

Sometimes a provision was made for the smoke to exit through a small hole in the roof. Because smoke rises, the clearest air in the cottages was near the floor so chairs often sat particularly low allowing the cook and other inhabitants to escape breathing the worst of the smoke.[2]

41

Around the 11th century, medieval hearths began to move from the center of the room towards a wall. Hearths placed against a wall were referred to in some areas as down hearths. The next step in hearth evolution was to move the hearth into the wall by extending the wall to make a firebox and leaving an opening through which the smoke could escape — a chimney. With the chimney came loss of heat as a portion of the heat rose up and out with the smoke.

When the fireplace moved against a wall, an overhanging structure was placed over it to channel the smoke out. In Scotland this wooden hanging chimney was called a *similear crochaidh*.[3] In Ireland and Scotland, these structures were first made of wattle and daub. (Lengths of small branch, willow being a good variety, were woven in and out of uprights and then the whole was plastered over with clay and whitewashed.)

Some fireplaces were so large the back wall of the firebox was often damaged from the heat. To prevent this, cast iron or stone was sometimes placed against the back wall. These fire-backs not only protected the wall but more effectively radiated the heat back towards the fire where it more efficiently heated cooking vessels.

Laplanders used "a stone for a hearth with an iron pot upon it, a hole for the escape of the smoke,"[4] and in Norway such chimney-less rooms were called *rögstuer*.[5]

Many European homes continued to use the central fire and allowed the smoke to exit through the thatched roof into the 20th century. There are still people who remember and can talk about this method of heating and cooking used within their lifetime. The Isle of Lewis was one of the last Scottish territories to abandon that type of hearth.

It is highly likely that the English hearth tax[6] put into effect on 19 May, 1662 perpetuated the use of the central fires in regions where the tax was levied. Heads of household were troubled to pay two shillings per annum per hearth. These fees were collected half on Michaelmas and half on Lady Day. Those who received relief for the poor and whose property was valued at less than the established scale were exempt from paying the hearth tax. Schools, almshouses, and industrial endeavors were also exempt, though this exemption did not include blacksmith's forges or bakers' ovens.[7] The tax was collected by the Clerk of the Peace until 1688. It was revised in 1664, requiring everyone with more than two chimneys to pay the tax. In 1689 the tax was abolished by William II in England. The abolishment of the tax occurred a year later in Scotland in 1690.

While the central hearth was abandoned early in the United States, it was used through the colonial era. Native cultures used it in a way that was practically identical to that of early Europeans, and it is not certain whether the Native Americans or the European immigrants had more influence on the use of central hearths in the United States.

> Few [houses] except in their villages, were larger than sufficient to hold one or two dozen persons closely crowded, with a small space in the center for the fire over which their game was roasted or their corn was cooked.[8]

Archaeological digs in Iowa have shown that the Indians used the central fire in their lodges as early as 1200–1500.[9]

Roman homes were described as having "a great, smoke-blackened ceiling," and a few stools and benches with a movable brazier on the central hearth.[10]

British homes built prior to the 13th century were described similarly to those timber dwellings in London:[11]

> Not more than 16 feet in height, built of wood, and covered with reeds and straw. The general plan seems to have been that of a parallelogram ... the lower story was vaulted and lighted by small windows; but there does not appear to have been any convenience for warming except in the upper floor where there is a hearth in the middle of the floor with smoke-hole above.[12]

During the 14th century, fireplaces were in the center of the hall. Logs of wood were supported on "dogs," the smoke being left to find its way as best it could through an opening in the roof usually covered with a turret. Chimneys are found in the 12th-century Whitwall House, castles at Rochester and Hedingham, Conway Castle built by Edward I, and Kenilworth, but these are rare and exceptional examples. By the 15th century chimneys became common and several fireplaces often connected into one shaft.[13]

During the Middle Ages, baking was usually done on the side of the hearth when using the central fire, or else it was done outdoors. When fires moved to the walls, the oven was, sometimes built into the wall of larger homes and smoke exited through the same chimney. This design continued in use until kitchen stoves brought the next big evolution in kitchen design during the 19th century. The ovens were closed by means of a wooden door which later gave way to iron doors. The use of these "built-in" ovens was not prevalent in every culture. Scottish Highland kitchens did not contain such ovens.

To use the oven, a fire was built inside small models and maintained until the oven was of a high enough temperature for the day's baking, at which time the ashes were raked out and the food or dough put in. Larger ovens sometimes had a separate section where the fire was built underneath the oven, eliminating the need to rake out the embers and ash before putting in the food.

Dough, pies, or cakes were placed into the oven using a wooden peel and removed in the same manner. Sprinkling the peel with flour or meal prevented dough from sticking to the peel.

Some of the essential parts of a modern working fireplace:

1. Foundation. The base or foundation of the firebox is usually separate from the foundation of the house itself. It should be constructed of fire-resistant materials.
2. Ash pit. Ashes can be removed from the outside if a door is installed through which they can be removed.
3. Inner and Outer Hearth. The inner hearth is the area on which the fire is built. The outer hearth is the area that extends outward in front of the fireplace.
4. Supporting Walls. These walls extend from the inner hearth to the bottom of the flue where the chimney begins
5. Firebox. Fireboxes are generally lined in firebrick and are enclosed on three sides. Only the front is left open. Through this opening, wood is put onto the fire, ashes can be removed, and cooking can be done inside the firebox or in front of it.
6. Smoke shelf. This shelf projects from the butt walls and deflects downdrafts that can sweep down the chimney.
7. Damper. This device regulates how much air is allowed through the opening and helps regulate how much heat is generated.
8. Lintel. This is a metal support to hold up the masonry as it is laid.
9. Smoke Chamber. The smoke chamber reaches from the throat to the bottom of the flue. This is where smoke and gases are collected and exit the fireplace.
10. Flue. The flue extends from the smoke chamber to the top of the chimney. Its purpose is to create draft and discharge smoke.
11. Chimney. The chimney usually has a liner of fireproof blocks as a protective feature.
12. Chimney top or cap. Building codes regulate the height. This cap should extend beyond the roof. Most chimneys are capped to prevent birds from nesting inside.

Breaking camp, Brandy Station, Virginia. An African American man stands beside a chimney in the deserted quarters of General Jacob Hunter Sharp. Parts of the fireplace are seen. Photographer: James Gardner. From Gardner's photographic sketchbook of the war, published ca. 1866. Library of Congress, Prints and Photographs Division, Reproduction Number LC-DIG-ppmsca-12584.

By the 18th century, British households were becoming more adept at roasting on turn-spits, grilling on gridirons over or in front of the fire, and boiling and stewing in vessels suspended from cranes (called *swey* in Scotland), over the fire or placed on tripods over the heat.

Cooking cranes often pivoted from an attachment on the left out into the room, a holdover from days when it was thought good luck for activities leading to the preparation of food to follow the direction of the sun as it rose in the sky.

Pots hung from chains suspended from within the chimney, and in Scotland these chains were known as *slabhraidh*. The *slabhraidh* was hung from a wooden beam suspended high up in the chimney in homes that had one, and for those using the central fire, the chain or rope was hung from the roof.

Blacksmiths used a great deal of artistry in making the chains. Iron was expensive, and some homes used a wooden ladder type device to hold the pots.[14]

The cooking fires of Britain were usually fueled with wood through the second half of the 17th century, though some homes used coal or peat.[15]

So many medieval homes and other buildings were built of wood that entire cities could burn in the event a fire ever escaped its hearth. The word *curfew*, meaning to be home by a given time, evolved from *couvre-feu,* a device for covering the embers of a fire once it was banked for the night.[16]

Burt wrote that into the early 18th century many Scots were still in the habit of boiling beef in a hide and by other methods: "Being destitute of vessels of metal or earth, they put water into a block of wood, made hollow by the help of the Dirk and burning, and then with pretty large stones heated red-hot, and successively quenched in that vessel, they keep the water boiling till they have dressed their food."[17] Sir Walter Scott described a 14th-century Highland feast in his novel *The Fair Maid of Perth*:

> At a distance were to be seen piles of glowing charcoal or blazing wood, around which countless cooks toiled, bustled, and fretted, like so many demons working in their native element. Pits wrought in the hillside and lined with heated stones, served for stewing immense quantities of beef, mutton, and venison; wooden spits supported sheep and goats, which were roasted entire, others were cut into joints and seethed in cauldrons made from the animals' own skins, sewed hastily together and filled with water; while huge quantities of pike, trout, salmon, and char were broiled with more ceremony on glowing embers.[18]

Scott may have found inspiration for this passage in the actual account of the poet John Taylor, who described cooking methods used in a hunting trip he took in 1618:

> The kitchin was always on the side of a banke, many kettles and pots boyling, and many spits turning and winding, with great variety of cheere, as venison, bak't, sodden, rost, and steu'de beefe, mutton, goates, kids, hares, fresh salmon, pidgeons, hens, capons, chickens, partridges, moore-cootes, heath-cocks, capperkellies (capercailzie), and termagents (ptarmigan).... Thus a company of about fourteen hundred was most amptly fed.[19]

For some cultures the fire held an almost magical importance, never being allowed to go out if at all possible. This was partly due to culture and partly due to the difficulty in rebuilding it before matches were prevalent. In climates with a heavy rainfall, the fire was needed to dry the air within the cottage and the sods or thatch without.

In 1860, John Timbs wrote that on the college hall (Oxford or Cambridge) roof, "a small louver rises above the central hearth, upon which in winter a wood or charcoal fire used to burn until the year 1850."[20]

The central hearth was documented in Asia used by a group of southwestern Chinese people known as *Lolos* who prepared simple meals of boiled corn, oatmeal cakes, and dried meat.[21]

Hungarian Gypsies were travelers, rarely staying very long in one location. An 1854 source described their huts: "The huts are partly dug into the earth and thatched with turf, leaving a hole in the roof for the smoke to escape."[22] (Gypsies, once thought native to Egypt, live in many parts of the world, and are actually of East Indian descent.) Gypsy food, it was said, consisted mainly of meat and bread, "the latter his wife prepares in the eastern fashion in flat cakes baked in red hot ashes." The first of very few possessions to go into the hut was the soup kettle.[23]

> [Gypsy] Food is often common and scarce, and their cooking utensils are but few in number, and of the commonest kinds.[24]

A newspaper account in 1937 stated that the ancient methods of building in Germany and England were essentially the product of the same culture, because the Germanic-speaking people who colonized Britain started from that part of the mainland. The article outlined the restoration of two ancient homes in Luebeck, Germany.

> The restoration of the older of the two houses, showing a New Stone Age farmstead of about 2000 B.C. is a rectangular building with a steeply pitched roof of thatch. The ridgepole of the roof is supported on two stout upright posts and projects at either end.

The framework of the house is of stout, rough, unsquared timbers, and the spaces between are filled in with panels of "wattle-and-daub," that is, coarse wicker work plastered with clay. The windows are square and quite small.

Within, there is a central hearth of stones, with a hole in the roof to let the smoke escape. There is no chimney. Shelves against the wall and strings from the beams support the cooking and table utensils-well-shaped and neatly decorated pottery vessels of assorted shapes and sizes.

The second house, dated about the beginning of the Christian era ... is still rectangular with a straw-thatched, steep-pitched roof, but it is larger and built entirely of logs. Indeed, it resembles rather strongly the log cabins of pioneer America.

The central open fireplace still lacks a chimney, although there is a kind of flue supported on the rafters, that helps to lead the smoke toward the smokehole in the roof. Over the fire, a big bronze kettle is suspended on iron chains.[25]

In 1880 the style of great Italian palaces was credited to the early Romans.

In the earliest times, when the family lived entirely in the atrium, the only permanent furniture which it contained consisted of a few stools and benches, together with the movable brazier on the central hearth.[26]

The introduction of metal cooking vessels was as important to the advancement of the culinary art as the reformation of the hearth.

Queen Elizabeth I demanded that merchants report on advanced crafts so the techniques could be incorporated into the English way of life. Through endeavors of merchants like the East India Company and the Virginia Company, the advancements slowly became standard.[27]

The first pots made in England were made of sheet copper or brass. The sheets were shaped into sections which were riveted together making somewhat watertight cauldrons. Bell metal (a mixture of 80 parts copper to 20 parts tin) and cast brass followed. Wrought iron cleared the way for cast iron. Tin and copper were being made into cooking pots, tools, and other items by the Bronze Age (2500–700 B.C.).[28]

Traveling with Sir Walter Raleigh, Arthur Barlow wrote in 1584 that they swapped American Indians a copper kettle for 50 skins, apparently the first metal pot the Indians had encountered, and the account firmly establishes the common use of such pots at that time.[29]

Each metal lent particular attributes and faults to the cookery vessels made from it. Iron is an excellent heat conductor, but in parts of Europe where fuel was scarce the time it took to preheat iron vessels made them less desirable.

Brass (copper and zinc alloy) was a poor heat conductor, but because it did not retain as much heat, handles remained cooler and easier to handle.

Copper had a lower melting point, and if pots were heated too much the metal could warp or the handle bend. Copper, and to a lesser extent brass, could react with acids from fruits and vinegar creating poisonous verdigris. To eliminate this risk, many copper and brass pots were lined with tin. This was applied by melting tin in the vessel and swirling it around to coat the inside of the pot.

Not all cauldrons and pots were made with attached handles for hanging. Many were meant to be used with detachable pot-hangers. The hangers were made with a hook at the top, one on each end of the swiveling arms, so that the top hook hung from a crane, and the two on the ends attached through the lugs on both sides at the top of the pots.

Pots were made with and without legs, and in the case of the latter, tripods, sometimes called brandeths, were used to set the pot on so that it did not sit directly on the heat and cause the foods in it to scorch and burn. Early English pots tended to have sag-bottoms whether they had legs or not.

Medieval woodcuts show pots (generally a flat-bottomed vessel like a saucepan) and cauldrons that were flat-sided, flat-bottomed, bell-shaped with a lip or neck, with and without legs, with what appear to be flat lids or domed lids, and without lids. Lids were sometimes fashioned out of wood.

No pot is going to boil unless it is near enough to the heat source, and when using different size pots it is necessary to lower a smaller pot farther than a larger one. Trammels, which ratcheted up and down a distance of several inches, made it possible to shorten or extend the hook from which the pot was hung.

Vegetables and fruits were sometimes put into bags and hung on the inside of the cauldrons and meat was put onto hooks and lowered into the cauldrons where it simmered without touching the bottom of the pot. The foods could be removed and served separately from the soup that remained in the cauldron.

So many people have lovely and functional fireplaces in their homes it is a shame not to understand the advantages of using them to prepare meals. Often the only stumbling block to doing so is lack of knowledge regarding fire building, fire maintenance, and techniques of cooking with flame and embers.

Food cooks from the heat of the flames, from the heat of embers, and even from the insulative properties of ash. Once an understanding of the amount of heat produced by any one or any combination of these heat sources is reached, then food preparation on the hearth is similar to that done in the kitchen.

Grilling, roasting, baking, and frying are done over hot coals, and sometimes with more hot coals on top of the lid. Soup is as easily prepared as hanging a pot over the heat. Cranes from which to hang a pot or kettle may be obtained from a blacksmith or commercially. They are easily installed, and require little training to use successfully.

When hanging a pot from the crane it is desirable to use heat from embers more than heat from flame. To accomplish this, build the fire at least two hours before you wish to begin making your soup so that there is sufficient time to build a bed of coals. To begin, swing the crane out into the room and hang your pot from it. If you wish it to hang lower use an extra pot hook over the crane and hang the pot from it. After all ingredients are added, adjust the lid and swing the crane back near the flame. The temperature of the pot can be raised or lowered by moving the pot closer or farther away from the heat source.

When a fire is first built, the only heat generated is from the flames. After approximately an hour to an hour and a half the bricks of the fireplace begin to heat up and a small bed of coals collects underneath the logs, which are usually suspended on andirons. At this point, dishes requiring a minimal to modest heat source may be prepared.

For a cooking fire, it is best to remove the andirons or fire grate and build the fire directly on top of two fireplace logs. This will allow enough ash to accumulate to keep the embers red hot and ready to be removed and used. A fireplace in which the fire does not burn well will benefit from this technique.

After approximately one to two hours, the first wood placed on the fire should be reduced to embers and new pieces added to fuel the fire. Only now can the cook consider preparation of foods requiring medium to substantial heat in order to cook through.

At this point, it is possible to remove enough embers to place under a pot and on top for baking. Heat should radiate from the brick or stone in the fireplace, from the coals, and from the flames, and you should be able to hold your hand near the opening of the fireplace for only a few seconds.

The longer the fire burns, and the more embers that collect, the better for cooking. After a fire has burned for three hours or longer, there should be enough embers to prepare multiple dishes without worry the fire will go out.

Making stock is as simple as adding ingredients to a pot, hanging it on the crane, and positioning it for a gentle simmer. After the stock has been prepared and strained, ingredients may be added to make soup, simmering it to fragrant golden perfection.

Such a fire has adequate coals for baking bread to accompany the soup as well. Breads which do not require time for yeast to mature to leaven the bread require the least skill on the part of the cook, however, with a bit of practice anything that can be baked in your oven can be successfully made in a bake kettle placed over embers, with the lipped lid holding additional embers.

> The old rule of roasting and boiling is about twenty minutes to the pound; fifteen minutes is scarcely enough especially in cold weather, in a draughty kitchen, or at a slack fire. The fire for roasting should burn up gradually, and not attain its full power until the joint is approaching perfection. Boiled meat cannot boil too slowly. Boiling wastes less of the meat than roasting. Beef, by boiling, loses twenty-six and a half per cent; boiling is also, though less savory, a more economical way of cooking, as the water used receives the juice of the meat and makes an excellent basis for soup, which it is mad extravagance to throw away. The charm of a roast joint is the beautiful pale-brown color. The sign of a roast joint being thoroughly done (saturated with heat) is when the steam rising from it draws towards the fire.[30]

Good choices when the baker's skills are still developing include biscuits, cornbread, Irish soda bread, scones, and oat cakes.

Fire-building is simple and can be accomplished without adding unhealthy substances to ignite it. Avoiding the use of toxic chemicals to start the fire is especially important when foods are to be prepared in the ashes.

To start a fire, use a small amount of paper or dry tinder upon which lie small twigs followed by successively larger twigs and kindling. Build up from the tinder in the center, teepee fashion, so that when the tinder is lit the fire is fed by the smaller twigs and kindling first which will ignite the outer layers.

It is preferable not to use wood larger than three to four inches around, at least not until the fire has burned long enough to build a bed of embers and sustain itself when some of the embers are removed for cooking.

Successful fireplace cooking depends on using the right type of wood. Hardwoods burn hotter and last longer than softer woods, therefore they produce more, and hotter, embers for cooking. Wood to be used for cooking is best when aged six months to a year. Rotting wood will not make embers and is useless for cooking. Pine and cedar give an unpleasant taste and odor to food, and can produce intense heat if enough pitch remains in the wood. Treated wood should never be used in a fireplace because it can release toxic chemicals as it burns.

For outdoors enthusiasts, the same general guidelines for cooking fires hold true for outdoor cooking. The same heat sources remain in play, allowing much the same methods of preparation.

10. Ireland

Ireland is slightly larger than the state of South Carolina. It was settled very early, and remnants of forts and villages have been preserved dating to approximately 7,000 B.C. Northern Ireland is part of the United Kingdom, and the remainder became a republic in 1948.

Christianity spread to Scotland from Ireland with St. Columba in A.D. 563. As missionaries spread Christianity, they inadvertently left an indelible footprint on the cuisine of countries through which they traveled.[1]

The Celtic countries of Europe were opposed to the feudal system, following instead the patriarchal governmental system. The failure of the Scots, Irish, and Welsh to abide by the feudal system was a part of the conflict between them and their Saxon invaders, yet the Scots remained loyal to their clan chiefs until the English attempted to disband the clans in 1748.[2]

After its introduction in the mid–17th century the potato was such an integral part of Irish culture that Irish food can be broken down into three categories: before, during, and after the famine of the 1840s.

Oats and barley are thought to have been the first cultivated crops, and they may have first been grown at the Ceide fields in County Mayo.[3] Ceide fields are the oldest known field systems in the world. Plants along with a hearth and remains of a plow were found that were carbon-dated at 5,000 years old. The grains were used to make porridge or soup with fish, shellfish, seaweed, vegetables, and small game. Andrew Agnew wrote, "The larger game, such as the hart and hind, the roebuck and the boar, were sought for the pot."[4] The seafood soups and stews included salmon, trout, eels, lobster, periwinkle, mussels, crabs, prawns, limpets, oysters, cockles, and clams. In essence, anything was used that could be taken from the land or sea with an expenditure of labor but requiring no money.

Foods on the baron's table included savory broth, red fish, oysters, beef, mutton, venison, boar, grouse, partrek, duck, plover, game of every sort, haggis, harvest brose, porpoises, sturgeon, cormorants, coots, hedgehogs, cranes, swans, and peacock, while coarser fare such as smelts, salmon, moorfowl, and mallard may have been left to those of lesser means. During the medieval era badgers were "much esteemed for food."[5]

Where plates were insufficient, thick slices of bread did duty. The practice of guests being obliged to bring their own knives gave rise to the saying, "Bring no knyves unscoured to the table." Forks were as yet for carving and serving.[6]

> A crowd of a more youthful description of the peasantry are collected every spring-tide to gather cockles ... quantities of these shellfish thus procured would almost exceed belief; and I have frequently seen more than would load a donkey collected during one tide by the children of a single cabin ... the scallop, which here is indeed of very superior size and ... besides these other shell-fishes greatly prized by the peasantry, but which I never had the curiosity to eat, such as razor-fish, clams, and various kinds of mussels.[7]

Traditional cockle soup is similar to chowder. It was thickened with a butter and flour mixture added to cockle stock, milk, parsley, cream, and seasoned with salt and pepper.[8]

The same writer stated that "oysters found in the bays and estuaries along this coast are of very superior quality, and their quantity may be inferred from the fact that on the shores where they are bedded, a turf-basket large enough to contain six or seven hundred can be filled for a sixpence. A couple of men will easily, and in a few hours, lift a horse-load."

Along the coast, seaweed was used in soups. Wild plants replaced seaweed in inland soup cauldrons in the form of cress, wild garlic, wood sorrel, nettles, mushrooms, and so on.

Any game, meat, or offal, including sheep's heads, found its way into the cauldrons. Venison became scarce in about the 8th century through over-hunting. At that time the main types of meat used became beef, pork, and mutton. Rabbit was consumed after it was introduced by the Normans, though some sources say it was not eaten except out of necessity.[9] Several sources credit the introduction of the fallow deer to the Normans as well.[10]

> Their marshes and rivers (of which they have plenty) are visited by multitudes of wild fowl in the winter season ... their hills are stored with woodcock, grouse, heathcock, etc. Nor are they a little stored with red-deer, hares, and rabbits.[11]

Large quantities of chickens, geese, and turkeys were common on Irish farms, and game birds were plentiful and varied.[12]

Charles Kickham wrote of life in 19th-century Tipperary and of goose with dumplings, a "very savoury dish." It is interesting that in the American South, where there were concentrated numbers of Celtic emigrants, dumplings became a well-loved dish.[13]

Sheep's head soup was common on Irish and Scottish tables, and usually contained a good quantity of cultivated or wild vegetables and grains— usually oats or pearl barley. When served whole at table the sheep's head presented a macabre enough image to try the patience of even the strongest willed.

Families relied heavily on milk and cheese in providing meals, often preserving cheeses by coating them in the residue from burned seaweed rather than salting them.[14] Butter has been recovered after being buried for many years in bogs.

After the potatoes were harvested and the fall crop planted, Irish women and children took cows and moved to the booleys. Here, the cows produced the best-quality milk because they fed on a diet of fresh green grass. The milk was made into butter and cheese and carried with them when they left the booleys and herded the cows toward home.[15]

The king taxed families in food, namely cattle, pigs, or sheep, collected in summer. In the 5th century, the Church began to impose tithes of the first-born male of every milk-bearing animal. The Irish family, generally consisting of four generations born to a common great-grandfather, bore a heavy burden retaining adequate food.[16] Cows were valued by the average family more for dairy products than for beef.

Athenaeus quoted Posidonius, a Syrian Greek philosopher (131–53 B.C.), regarding the eating habits of the Celts. They spread straw or hides on the ground near the cooking area where meats roasted on spits and soups or pottages bubbled in the cauldrons, and sat at short tables to eat.[17]

Seaweed went into the soup cauldrons, as did eggs from ducks, geese, and wild shore birds. Seaweed consumed in Scotland and Ireland included carrageen moss, red-ware or tangle, dulce (tangle and dulce were once sold in the markets of Great Britain), and hen-ware.[18]

Henware formed an important article of food for the poorer classes of inhabitants on the coasts of Scotland and Ireland. An English naturalist, Reverend Johns, gave the following account of its edible qualities: "While walking round the coast near the Giants' Causeway, I once observed a number of men and women busily employed near the water's edge, and on inquiring of my guide, found that they were providing themselves with food for their next meal." Upon tasting it he declared it a very sorry substitute for raw carrot, with the fishy and coppery flavor of an oyster.[19]

Much use was made of fish, including salmon, trout, pike, perch, roach, and eel.[20] A favorite stew was prepared from whatever fish was at hand, with seaweed, vegetables, and pot-herbs.[21]

Early soup vegetables included celery, watercress, nettles, wild cabbage or kale, dandelion leaf, wild garlic, onion, chives or leeks, beans, and what are thought to have been onions, carrots, and parsnips. The Normans introduced peas and beans in about 1169 and turnips were added to the list sometime in the 12th century. Grains included oats, corn, barley, spelt, and wheat.

Colcannon, a thick stew of cooked cabbage or kale and mashed potato, has been a staple since the introduction of the potato.[22] Early references spelled the dish *Kohl-kenny* after the German *kohl*, or cabbage.[23]

Children under fosterage were fed common porridge of varying quality and amounts according to their station in life:[24]

> The children of inferior grades are to be fed on porridge or stirabout made of oatmeal on buttermilk or water taken with stale butter and are to be given a bare sufficiency; the sons of chieftains are to be fed to satiety on porridge made of barley meal upon new milk, taken with fresh butter, while the sons of kings and princes are to be fed on porridge made of wheaten meal, upon new milk, taken with honey.[25]

Legend has it that St. Patrick introduced the leek to Ireland. Given that St. Patrick was an escaped Roman slave who converted the Irish to Christianity,[26] and taking into account the ancient Roman love of leeks, this is highly likely. A traditional Irish leek soup made from oatmeal and leeks simmered in a base of milk is supposedly a reminder of St. Patrick.[27]

Some believe potatoes first came to Ireland with the Spanish, who are thought to have found them in South America and brought them to Europe in 1570. By 1590, they were grown in the British Isles and quickly went from a curiosity to a staple crop. Before the end of the 17th century, they had become known as the Irish potato. Rarely has any one food become so important a part of diet as the potato to the Irish. By the late 1700s, it is estimated that Irish males consumed as much as 14 pounds of potatoes per day with little else other than milk and occasional salted herrings.

Estimates are that a third of the population subsisted on the potato by 1840. More food could be harvested from available acreage when planted in potatoes than oats, and growing potatoes meant enough food to eat with some left over to sell for cash. But soon blight wiped out the potato crop, and estimates are that a million people died between 1845 and 1848. Another 2 million emigrated to the United States, Australia, and Canada.[28] In 1851, the Census of Irish Commissioners documented 24 previous potato crop failures beginning in 1728 that coincided with the years of the Little Ice Age.[29]

In 1846, the turnip crop was very good, and it was recommended that turnips along with carrots, parsnips, mangelwurzel (a root from the beet family grown for animal food), peas and oatmeal should be used in the absence of potatoes.[30]

Potato soup, leek and potato soup, nettle soup, and Irish stew are typical traditional soups, and a contemporary record notes, "Excellent broth made of beef, groats and oatmeal, leeks, and cabbage is a favourite and comfortable dish."[31]

An old Irish song says, "She fed them on potatoes and a soup made out of nettles/and a lump of hairy bacon that she boiled up in a kettle." Nettle soup is tasty, but contact between the skin and the hairlike protuberances on the nettle leaves produces a painful stinging sensation. Wearing gloves and long sleeves during the harvesting and washing of the young tender leaves is essential. Stinging is not an issue after the nettles are cooked.[32]

To prepare it, put a chopped onion and a small bag of nettle leaves (4 to 6 cups) into the soup pot with butter and sweat to wilt them. Add a couple of chopped potatoes, salt and pepper with a pint of good stock and a half pint of milk. Simmer until the vegetables are tender, then puree before serving.

Old folks at home in an Irish cottage with their canine friend. A soup cauldron hangs from a hook in front of the fireplace where a peat fire is laid. The large mantle was the driest place in the cottage and was where items required to be kept absolutely dry were kept. Stereocard ca. 1902. Library of Congress, Prints and Photographs Division, Reproduction Number LC-USZ62-59321.

The Scots would argue, and rightfully so, that *cal dheanntag* (nettle broth) is a traditional Scottish soup. Through the years, it has been more the product of frugality than of geography, each culture using what was available for harvesting. Traditional Scottish nettle soup contained oatmeal; most others did not. Nettle soup was also eaten in early Germany, Russia, and Poland.[33] In the United States there are six varieties of nettles, and they were made into soup and also cooked for greens.[34]

In 1995, Mike Corbishley conducted demonstrations of Bronze Age cooking in Europe based on archaeological evidence, and stated that people of the islands off the northern coast of Scotland continued to prepare many of the same foods, including nettle soup, into the 20th century.[35]

Brotchan is the Irish word for broth. *Brotchan foltchep* was made from leeks and oatmeal, and nettle brotchan contained young nettle leaves.

Modern Irish cuisine evolved slowly, many people unable to acquaint food with a pleasant experience after the death and destruction of the famine. Nevertheless, food cannot be separated from Irish culture. Even funerals and wakes were occasions for serving soup and stew. Author Leon Uris included the following passage regarding funeral food after the passing of Kilty Larkin in his epic novel *Trinity*:

> Three lambs had been slaughtered and an immense stew boiled in the great pot and a dozen loaves of fadge, a potato bread, browned on the baking boards.

Irish fare was generally coarse into the 20th century. One writer claimed that Ireland was "the least creative of countries," and that the servants "lived in huts, ate potatoes and oatmeal, and never saw any utensil but an iron kettle."

The Irish did, apparently, have their own sort of prejudices with regard to food.

> We were to have had "white soup of the Channel Islands"; made of the conger eel — a creature so despised that the starving Irish have refused to add flavor and nutriment to their potatoes by boiling them with a salted steak of the conger; and yet it is adduced, as a curious illustration of national prejudice, that while starving Paddy rejects the conger, large quantities of the fish are boiled down into stock, to be used in the making of turtle-soup in London.[36]

The famous showman P. T. Barnum once told the story of a restaurant owner who was in a quandary about being short one waiter for dinner. He convinced an Irishman to fill in and instructed him on his duties, telling him to first set before each diner a plate of soup, and when they finished that to ask what they would have next. Of the first two gentlemen Pat waited on, one ate his soup and the other did not, though he proceeded to place his order for the next course. Pat informed him he must first eat his soup.[37]

For many Irish Americans the epitome of traditional Irish food is corned beef and cabbage, but this was no more likely to have been served on St. Patrick's Day or any other day than any of the soups or other traditional foods.

11. Scotland

The universal food of Scots and Irish peasantry was oatmeal. It was made into soup or *brose*, porridge, stirabout, puddings, and bread, and eaten daily. The porridge was often made of barley. Though rarely used in America and Great Britain to make bread, barley was used in soups, and was imported to the United States from Scotland.[1] Peas and beans were common porridge ingredients, and the love of it crossed the ocean with the emigrants. "The English, [in New Hampshire] by boiling beans very soft with their boiled dish, and thickening the liquor, made bean-porridge which was a common and favorite dish."[2]

Writing of 18th-century Scotland, Graham stated that simple fare of hen broth, black beans, haggis, and crab pie was served in Scottish taverns for the well-to-do and the common tradesman alike.

In 1852, Hugh Murray described the Scots as being temperate with regard to food. Even the rich attached less importance to food than the English. Until about 1820, he stated, they were content with "the hardest fare," the bulk of which was oatmeal. He mentioned standard dishes of barley broth with greens, "kail, the chief produce of their little gardens," hotchpotch, "other soups," and haggis.[3]

The Scots have always been able to turn the most basic ingredients into a tempting pottage by softly (slowly) coaxing every bit of essence from the meat, bones, vegetables, and grains in the pot. Sir John Sinclair once said, "The greatest heroes of antiquity lived on broth."[4] An old adage agreed. "Where everything that every soldier got, Fowl, bacon, cabbage, mutton, and what not, was thrown into one bank and went to pot."

Scottish cooks changed hotchpotch from the original French recipe, using their abundant mutton. This soup was also referred to as *hairst bree* (harvest broth). In 1819 J. G. Lockhart called it "a truly delicious soup, quite peculiar to Scotland." There was no hard and fast rule or recipe for making the soup in early Scotland, other than using ingredients as fresh as possible. Cabbage was often used in place of the cauliflower, and on some of the islands, especially Lewis and Harris, wild greens were often harvested to use in the soup. Nettle tops, wild carrot, wild garlic, wild spinach, and a sort of wild lovage were commonly used.

To understand what may have gone into these soup cauldrons it is necessary to know what was available at various times and contrast the plenty of the lairds with the scarcity of the commoners.

Anyone who has ever seen the remains of a Scottish "lazy bed" has no doubt been struck with the severity of life in such terrain. There was nothing lazy about the practice. In the highlands where soil was sometimes only mere inches deep, potatoes or seed were put into the ground and covered with seaweed gathered and carried in a basket on the back great distances, often uphill.

A Victorian writer defined a Highland repast as "black-grouse-soup, red-grouse-soup, partridge-soup, hare-soup, rabbit-soup, potato-soup, pease-soup, brown-soup, white-soup, hotch-potch, cocky-leeky, sheep's-head-broth, kail, and rumbledethumps" which fairly aptly describes the tasty soups served from Scottish cauldrons, with the exception of those made from fish and shellfish.[5]

Scotland has approximately the same area as the state of Maine, and much of it remains rural. At its nearest point, it is a mere 12 miles across the sea to Ireland, which explains why so much of the culture and folkways are very similar. The sea is no more than 40 or so miles from anywhere in the country, making seafood a staple.[6]

The earliest foods consumed included dulse, nettle, pignut (truffle), wild parsnips and carrots, thistle, sorrel, ramsons (wild onions or wild garlic), mint, burnet, juniper berries, dandelion, and silverweed. As with the Romans, carrots were initially purple or yellow, and the wild Highland carrot was white.

John Reid left an excellent record of vegetables cultivated in Scotland in the 1600s in his *Gard'ners Kalendar*, published in Edinburgh in 1683. Most of them found their way into the soup cauldrons regularly, and the list is quite extensive compared to the writings of Murray in 1860.

Reid listed cabbage, carrots, turnips, skirret, potatoes, parsnips, asparagus, artichokes, cauliflower, onions, leeks, shallots, celery, purslain, beet, scorzonera, parsley, fennel, colewort, cucumbers, barberries, peas, beans (most sources agree peas and beans were grown by the 13th century), spinach, marigold, garlic, lettuce, cress, radish, sage, rosemary, thyme, rue, savory, marjoram, basil, chervil, corn salad, endive, and various pot herbs.

Given the difficulty of planting in the Highlands other than in lazy beds, perhaps the availability of seeds did not mean the vegetables were commonly grown in all regions. Graham stated that at the turn of the 18th century onions were imported from Holland or Flanders, neeps (turnips) were found in only a few gardens, and only the "rich and enterprising gentlemen" grew potatoes.

Highland women tucked their petticoats up to their knees and hauled heavy baskets of wet seaweed or dung to cover a patch of kail, colworts, barley, or potatoes. When there was no sea tangle near enough, brachen (fern) was cut in about July and spread on the ground. Ditches were then made on the brachen to make a covering of dirt some six or eight inches deep. The beds were then left to decay till spring, when holes were made in the beds and seed potatoes were dropped into the holes.

In 1634, hunger was so widespread that the bishops of Caithness and Orkney appealed to the Privy Council of Edinburgh for relief. In *The Crofting Years*, Francis Thompson wrote:

> Multitudes die in the open fields and there is none to bury them.... The ground yields them no corn ... and the sea no fishes.... Some devour the sea-ware, some eat dogs, some steal fowls ... some have desperately run in the sea and drowned themselves.

In her household book, Lady Grisell Baillie listed the following items as soup cauldron staples: barley, almonds, corn flower (cornstarch), lemons, pepper, prunes, salt, sago, vinegar, beef, mutton, pork, capons, chickens, turkeys, geese, plovers, ducks, teal, wild fowl, fish, salt cod, dried fish, oats, and spices. Pertinent kitchen utensils included a large copper pot, retinned pans and pots, brass ladles, skimmers, grates, and so forth.

Early on, households had a kail-yard (kitchen garden), and kail came to be known as a broth or an entire meal, as in the phrase "staying to take kail."[7]

Potatoes were mentioned in the duchess of Buccleugh's *Household Book* of 1701 and in several sources by 1730. Many claimed to have been the first to grow potatoes, but the mention in Reid seems to be one of the earliest.

Vegetables underwent drastic improvement following the formation of the Royal Highland and Agricultural Society in 1784. Meg Dods stated in 1826 that "where a turnip, cabbage, or a leek was fifty years ago the only vegetable luxury found on a country gentleman's table, we now see a regular succession of not merely broccoli, cauliflower, and pease, but of the more recondite asparagus, seakale, endive, and artichoke, with an abundance of early small saladings."

Silverweed (wild tansy)[8] tubers were dried and pounded and the resulting flour used to make bannock. The roots are long and thin and usually white or cream-color. They were easily stored.[9]

Available fruits included plums, cherries, apples, strawberries, pears, raspberries, gooseberries, currants, and crabapples. Like oranges, these were sold by street vendors in cities.

Of Scottish food Martin Martin wrote:

> Their ordinary food is barly and some oat-bread with water; they eat all the fowls, already described, being dried in their stone-houses, without any salt or spice to preserve them; and all their beef and mutton is eaten fresh, after the same manner they use the giben, or fat of their fowls; ... they boil the sea-plants, dulse, and slake, melting the giben upon them instead of butter, and upon the roots of silver-weed and dock boiled, and also with their scurvy-grass stoved, which is very purgative, and here it is of an extraordinary breadth. They use this giben with their fish, and it is become the common vehicle that conveys all their food down their throats. They are undone for want of salt, of which as yet they are but little sensible; they use no set times for their meals, but are determined purely by their appetites.
>
> They use only the ashes of sea-ware for salting their cheese, and the shortest (which grows in the rocks) is only used by them, that being reckoned the mildest.
>
> Their drink is water, or whey, commonly; they brew ale but rarely using the juice of nettle-roots, which they put in a dish with a little barley-meal dough; these sowens being blended together, produce good yest, which puts their wort into a ferment, and makes good ale, so that when they drink plentifully of it, it disposes them to dance merrily.[10]

Captain Cook made use of scurvy grass and cabbage palm on his voyages,[11] and sailors routinely put ashore to gather them and other wild plants to combat scurvy.[12]

We don't know all the ways in which scurvy grass was prepared, but one source indicated it was dressed as a salad, eaten raw,[13] and its young tender leaves were eaten like cress.[14] It was native to Europe and Arctic America.[15]

Samuel Johnson left numerous notes pertaining to Scottish food. He said the stranger found no shortage of plenty or delicacy.[16]

> The moorgame is everywhere to be had. That the sea abounds with fish, needs not be told, for it supplies a great part of Europe. The Isle of Sky has stags and roebucks, but no hares ... cannot be supposed to want beef at home. Sheep and goats are in great numbers, and they have the common domestick fowl....
>
> Their native bread is made of oats, or barley. Of oatmeal they spread very thin cakes, coarse and hard, to which unaccustomed palates are not easily reconciled. The barley cakes are thicker and softer.... As neither yeast nor leaven are used among them, their bread of every kind is unfermented. They make only cakes, and never mould a loaf.

He thought the geese a cross between the wild and domestic goose and fishy-tasting compared to those of England. He also stated that due to the shortage of markets, when a Scot had meat it was killed from his own herd. He stated that though the Scots had not long known potatoes they had become a vital part of their diet by 1773.

Johnson dined on cold mutton, bread, and cheese several times, and likely kept a supply of portable soup which was advertised in the *London Chronicle* as early as 22 September, 1761. He wrote in his journal about beef collops, fricassee of fowl, fried chicken, ham or tongue, haddocks, herrings, milk, and bread pudding with raisins and citrus peel. Collops (from the French *escalop*) were either slices of meat or rolls of meat prepared in various ways and so often served in Scotland that they were universally referred to as Scotch collops in cookery books.

Other suppers of merit included a roast turkey, curlew, tongue, fowl, greens, cuddies and oysters cooked in butter, and roasted potatoes.

The first cookery book published in Scotland was that of Mrs. McLintock in 1736. It was followed by *Mrs. Dalgairns' Practice of Cookery* in 1829. Elizabeth Cleland's book of cookery was published in 1755 and included several recipes for soup—cucumber, asparagus, pease (pea), turnip, and a broth of roots. In 1804, the *Farmer's Magazine* stated turnips were introduced to Scotland from Holland about 1725.

Mrs. Dalgairns' cookery book stated:

> In boiling soup less water is wasted in a digester than in a common pot, as in the digester no steam can escape. To extract strength from meat long and slow boiling is required, but care must be taken that the pot is never off the boil. All soups are the better for being made the day before they are to be used, and they should then be strained into earthenware pots. When soup has jellied in the pan, it should not be removed into another, as breaking it will occasion its becoming sour sooner than it would otherwise do; when in danger of not keeping it should be boiled up. It never keeps long with many vegetables in it. The meat used for soups and broths cannot be too fresh. When any animal food is plain boiled, the liquor, with the addition of the trimmings of meat and poultry makes good soups and gravies, as do also the bones of roasted or broiled meat. The gravies left in the dishes answer for hashes, and the liquor in which veal has been boiled may be made into a glaze by boiling it with a ham bone until reduced by a third or fourth part and seasoning it with the necessary herbs or spices.
>
> In boiling weak soups the pan should be uncovered in that the watery particles may escape. Cow-heel jelly improves every sort of rich soup; and for thickening truffles, morels, and dried mushrooms may be used with advantage.

She instructed the cook to thicken soup with flour and butter or cream and eggs, and not to boil it after adding the cream and eggs.[17]

Reflective of the changes in perception of soured or spoiled food through the generations, she instructed that brown gravy or mock turtle soup that had soured could be refreshed by boiling it with a bag containing pulverized charcoal.

She was quite liberal with her soup recipes, which included four for mulligatawny (curry broth), four for calf's head or mock turtle, two for brown gravy (curry), two for cressy, two for Scotch hare, hare, French hare, jugged hare, venison, brown venison, six for white soup, moor-fowl, two for pigeon, giblet, kidney, two for ox-cheek, Scotch barley, Scots kale, leek soup (which in Scotland is called cocky leeky), beef *brose*, rice veal broth, thick beef, beef or mutton, rice, veal, two for soup *maigre*, soup vermicelli, three for old peas, three for green peas, spring, cucumber, beet root, herb, tomato, two for vegetable, two for winter vegetable, two for onion, two for carrot, two for hotchpotch, winter hotchpotch, soup Lorraine, vermicelli, vermicelli *à la reine*, two for macaroni, soup *à la reine*, potage *à la reine*, potage *à la vierge*, simple soup, Prussian, stove or spinach, potato, potato flour, oyster, lobster, crappet heads or fish, water souchy, pepper pot, soup for the poor, soup for an invalid, chicken panada, rice and milk, cream of rice, two for friars' chicken, portable, ox-tail, rabbit, Meg Merrilies', and turtle.

A Gypsy mother in about 1920 cooking the meal. Soup was an important part of the Gypsy diet due to its ease of preparation and the fact it could be made with a minimum of cooking vessels and utensils. Library of Congress, Prints and Photographs Division, Reproduction Number LC-DIG-ppmsca-17418-00012.

Potage à la Meg Merrilies de Derncleugh, she wrote, "is a soup of gipsy invention composed of many kinds of game and poultry boiled together." In a time when Scotland was divided into districts, each of which was the domain of a particular tribe, Sir Walter Scott's father once found a Gypsy party on the moor with, "all the varieties of game, poultry, pigs, and so forth."[18]

Cullen skink is a traditional soup similar to chowder. Mrs. Dalgairn did not give a recipe for it, but she did include crappet heads. It differed from chowder in that it contained no potatoes or milk, but it did contain crushed hard biscuit like chowder. Crappet head was made of fish stock, haddock, onions, parsley, shortbread or hard biscuit crumbs, mushroom and walnut catsups, and white wine thickened with butter and flour. Forcemeat balls made from the fish used to make the stock, with onion, crumbs, salt, pepper, nutmeg, and egg whites, were placed into the fish heads and boiled in the broth before thickening it.

Skink means "essence" in Gaelic, referring to the broth which is the soup's base. According to Jamieson, it also referred to strong soup made from a shin of beef. The village of Cullen, which is credited with creating Cullen skink, was established in 1189 and relied on the textile industry for its main support until the 1800s when herring fishing emerged as its main industry. The soup was developed during the 1800s when fishing became the main trade. Cullen skink is made from fish stock, potatoes, onions salt and pepper, and milk or cream.

The Scottish word for broth is *brose*. It is commonly made from any combination of mutton, peas, barley, oatmeal, salt, turnip, carrot, leek or onion, or cabbage. Mrs. Cleland's 1750s recipe instructed the cook to use beef, fowl, carrots, barley, celery, sweet herbs, onions, parsley and marigold (some varieties are edible).

The distinguishable difference between *brose* and porridge was the way it was cooked. In *brose*, the oatmeal or other grain was placed into a bowl and boiling water or broth (either meat or vegetable) was poured over it.

The leek, native to the shores of the Mediterranean, was early naturalized throughout Europe. Through the 19th century, leeks and celery were kept during the winter by burying them in trenches.

Sir Walter Scott mentioned cock-a-leekie three times in his *Waverly novels*. It has remained a favorite of the Scots for centuries, and was discussed in Meg Dods' cookery book (1826), which Scott is thought to have contributed to.

Meg Dods stated that the soup "must be very thick of leeks, and the first part of them must be boiled down into the soup until it become a lubricous compound." She called leeks one of the most honorable and ancient pot herbs.

Legend has it that losers in cockfights were sometimes found in pots of fine cock-a-leekie.

Adelaide Keen wrote in 1910 that "cocka leekie" was the oldest known soup, dating to the 14th century, and *Murray's Modern Cookery* stated it was a favorite of King James I. Sheep's-head soup is at least as old.

Sheep's heads were singed over the fire with a hot poker to remove all the wool before boiling. This was a smelly job usually entrusted to the village blacksmith. An Englishman, George Saintsbury, wrote that haggis and sheep's head were "things that the lips should not allow to enter them," though households of all incomes served them.

The meat might be picked from the head or not, and the head and trotters served separately from the soup or not, per the discretion of the cook. The head was sometimes split, the brains removed and fried separately before putting the head to soak overnight for making soup the next day.[19] In *The Antiquary* (1816), Scott wrote:

> This national preparation was wont to be a favourite Sunday dinner dish in many comfortable Scottish families. Where gentlemen "killed their own mutton," the head was reserved for the Sunday's broth; and to good family customers, and to "victuallers," a prime tup's head was a common Saturday gift from the butchers with whom they dealt.

Meg Dods used the head and trotters, barley, peas, carrots, turnips, onions, parsley, salt and pepper to make *powsowdie* (sheep's head broth).[20]

A 19th-century treatise advised,

> A poor man can seldom afford to purchase even the coarsest joint of mutton; but if he lives near a town, he can often get the sheep's head and pluck for less than 1s 6d, indeed very frequently for a shilling; and with these his wife can make up four hot meals.[21]

Though it was considered by the English to be an indispensable part of Scotland's national character, the following passage seems to negate the use of sheep's heads by the English. "In

Scotland sheep's head and trotters are much used in soup; and English private families would do well to make more use of them, as they afford strong jelly, and the proper flavor may be given by the judicious addition of beef, game, ham, and anchovy."[22]

In 1806, an English physician wrote of the Grecian black broth of Lacedaemon and stated it was probably the same as sheep's head broth.[23] The same source referred to the Scottish version as "a national dish of great antiquity":

> The head must be singed at the blacksmith's with a red hot iron, till not a single particle of wool remain. This operation requires much attention, as the iron must not be allowed to make any impression on the skin. When singed put the head into a tub of soft water for a whole night. After being well scraped and washed, split it asunder and take out the brains.

Deer heads "chopped in pieces" were stewed down to jelly and added to soup by the Scots to enrich it.[24]

The eating of sheep's head broth did not end when Scots and the Irish landed on American soil. The following account of a meal which included "sheep's head kail" (kail was a common term for soup) was written by a guest in the American home of a Mr. McDonald in 1861:

> Clarence had seen, when he was standing by the fire, the nose of some animal pushing itself up among the vegetables in the pot like a black hippopotamus among the reeds of the Nile; but he did not expect to make his dinner of the mess. However, now like a good soldier, he sat down with a ready appetite for whatever was coming, asking no questions. To his agreeable surprise, the soup was white as milk, though the head — it might be of a ram from its size — was there in a large platter, on the centre, without the horns, and the wool singed all off. Garden stuffs of all kinds, known, and some only known to Janet, had been boiled for two full hours with the head among them; so that it would have defied a French cook to tell the prevailing flavor of what McDonald called this dish of hotch potch. Barley bread, unleavened, baked upon a griddle, thin and tough as leather, was eaten to this soup; when at the close Janet put down a square bottle and a basket of oatmeal cakes alongside of a skim-milk cheese; all of which were intended as a dessert.[25]

Fynes Morison described what was probably cock-a-leekie in his 1598 *Travels*. Although he does not mention leeks, they were so basic their use was taken for granted.

> Mysel, he says, was at a knight's house, who had many servants to attend him, that brought in his meat with their heads covered with blue caps, the table being more than half furnished with great platters of porridge each having a little piece of sodden meat. And when the table was served, the servants did sit down with us; but the upper mess, instead of porridge, had a pullet, with some prunes in the broth.[26]

Morison went on to say the Scots regularly ate oatcakes (inevitably the companion to soups), but in the cities wheat bread was available for purchase. A physician, Andrew Borde, also paired the Scots with their "oten" cakes (1542), saying they had plenty of "fysh and flesh."[27]

William Hazlitt stated the "Scotch" were long poor and that only their fish, oatmeal, and whiskey kept them alive, quoting a remark from 1590 that the English could profit by consuming more fish if it were available.

Burt wrote in 1730[28] that the Scots weren't big meat eaters, and that for the poorer classes their meat consisted of salted flesh of sheep that had died of braxy (an intestinal condition). Scott wrote that pork had not been much consumed, "till within the last generation," but in 1730, Burt noted pickled pork was a standard winter provision in Aberdeen.

Rabbits, mountain hare, ptarmigan, capercailzie, black game, red-deer, grouse, partridges, and pigeons were common in the soup cauldrons from the days of the Auld Alliance

(1295), and Winterblossom of the Cleikum Club credited the quality of Scots soups with a French influence.[29]

Hunter's soup utilized any game available. "A Lady" wrote in *Murray's Modern Cookery*, "When sportsmen bivouac on the moors, the produce of the game bag must be put into the soup kettle with any odds and ends of other meat, and a bottle or two of any wine or beer that can be spared; then, filling it with water commence the brew which may be entrusted to any servant he being only required to begin early in the morning and let the game stew long enough to extract from it the entire of its juices."[30]

Rabbits were often used in friar's chicken soup instead of chicken. Friar's chicken was served "old style," with the chicken cut up into the broth. Meg Dods added a little mace, and some recipes used a little cinnamon. The consistency varied from soup to a thick ragout.

On the Isle of Skye, soup was made from sea-cormorant (a strong fishy-tasting bird), and throughout Scotland recipes were published for lobster soup and partan (crab) *bree* by the early 18th century. Numerous writers wrote of the vast quantities of oysters, mussels, crabs, salmon, cockles, limpits, whelks, and clams which no doubt made their way into the soup pot.

Hen and duck eggs were used to pay rent for working-class Scots, however, eggs of wild sea-birds were in much demand and therefore collected several basketsful at a time. Pennant wrote that eggs were usually to be had in the "public huts," and that he freely partook of them.

A receipt book kept by Martha, Lady Castlehill[31] (1668–1752) contained numerous recipes penned between 1712 and 1713. Her artichoke broth was made from chicken, veal, lettuce, spinach, eggs, vinegar and sugar or white wine and seasoned with mace. The artichoke leaves were scraped and the edible parts put into the soup. The chickens were served separately with herbs. Osgood MacKenzie wrote[32] in 1921 that Scots larders contained strings of dried artichoke bottoms used to make soup, indicating this was a fairly common soup.

The author of the published version of *Lady Castlehill's Receipt Book* compared the recipes to the food served to servants as documented in Lady Grisell Baillie's household books— broth, boiled beef and herring, eggs, haggis, half a loaf of oat or flour bread per meal, and an ample supply of beer.

Fare for Lady Castlehill's family usually included *skink* for the first meal of the day and broth for the midday meal despite the shortage of receipts in the manuscript.

Given the large number of Scots and Irish who emigrated to the United States and Canada, it is important to make mention of the foods those emigrants found on arriving in Canada. In 1841, Robert MacDougall wrote *The Emigrant's Guide to North America*, which discussed the abundant food available. Foods included Indian corn, barley, peas, wheat, potatoes, onions, oats, rye, apples, pork, beef, mutton, fowl, cheese, butter, cabbage, cucumbers, venison, eggs, herring, squirrels, rabbits, badgers, leek, and pigeon. There were likely more foodstuffs readily available, but since MacDougall wrote the book in Gaelic for a target readership of Gaelic-speaking Scots, he most likely included the foods he knew his readers would recognize. He instructed serving the meat and the broth of squirrels and badgers.

Native people of Alaska, Canada, and Greenland (Esquimaux) relied heavily on walrus for food, and some of it was made into soup. It is not known how emigrants felt about that particular soup.[33]

Terms associated with Scottish soup:

Bree— soup or broth. Bawd bree — Scots hare soup

Chacklowrie— barley broth with mashed cabbage

Friar's chicken—chicken broth thickened with eggs (according to Mrs. Dalgairn, chicken, veal, eggs, salt, pepper, parsley, water)

Hairst bree— harvest broth, hotchpotch (mutton and vegetable broth)

Hen broth— barley broth made with chicken

Lithe— to thicken the soup

Neep brose— turnip soup

Parritch— soup/porridge (soup parritch)

Partan—crab. Partan bree—crab soup. Also used commonly were winkles, whelks, mussels, oysters, and cockles.

Turkey beans— Meg Dods put these into barley soup.

Shilling broth— made from shilled (freed from husk) corn

Yule brose—fat brose (soup made from ox head, cow heel or shin of beef, oatmeal, salt and water) often served on Yule Day.

12. England and Wales

The Romans introduced many vegetables and herbs into England that have been consumed for so long they appear, on casual inspection, to be native.

Vegetables and herbs used in the 1806 *Culina Famulatrix Medicinae* included parsley, carrots, leeks, onions, turnips, celery, coss lettuce, white beet leaves, chervil, marjoram, thyme, mint, cucumbers, peas, and cayenne. Soup recipes also contained lemon juice, Madeira wine, Parmesan cheese, mace, allspice, peppercorns, cloves, and macaroni.

There are contrary reports on the prevalence of soup in the English diet. John Jefferson said, "So long as the English of every social grade were habitual consumers of pottage, their dames and soldiers were as clever at making palatable broths, 'out of nothing,' as the French are at the present time [1875]."

> The Englishman has a proverb—"I don't like slops"—by which he means, he does not like soups or broths; and he is right, if we refer to the manner the English generally make them. Broth or soup is in all parts of Europe, save the United Kingdom, a regular dish at dinner, and is very often the only breakfast. It is made of meat, game, fish, or vegetables; and each is excellent in its kind if well made, and both savoury and nourishing. Broth is also not only used as a dish, but also for dressing other dishes, instead of water, butter, and flour, called melted butter. In England, it is customary to buy coarse pieces for soup to stew them down, and give the meat to the dogs; or, if we boil a piece of meat, we throw the water away—that water (as we call it); with a few vegetables would make a comfortable meal for half, or perhaps, all of the family. On the Continent, the best parts of the beef are boiled for soup and bouilli, which latter is the name they give to the fresh beef boiled. The great secret of making soup is to let it simmer slowly for a considerable time, but never boil. The vegetables are thus saturated with the juices of the meat. An earthen pot that will stand the fire is better than an iron one. The meat must be put into cold water, and the water should be soft.[1]

Andrew Boorde shed a different light on the preparation of English pottages in 1542.

> Pottage is not so much used in all Christendom as it is vsed in Englande. Pottage is made of the juice in which flesshe is cooked in, with puttyng-to Chopped herbs, and otemel and salt.[2]

Boorde further commented that pottage and broth filled a man with wind, herbs used in pottage must be of good quality (free of worm-eaten parts), frumenty was indigestible yet nourishing, pease pottage was preferred to bean pottage (as it produced less gas), rice pottage made with almond milk restored comfort, and the use of herbs during times of pestilence was unadvised for fear of spreading the disease.

Grain-based pottages and sauces that evolved throughout Europe during the Middle Ages included **frumenty** (boiled or cracked wheat with some combination of milk, eggs, broth, almonds or almond milk, currants, sugar, saffron, etc.), **bukkenade** (a stew made from veal, kid, hen, or rabbit with fresh herbs and spices), **blancmange** (a bland stew made from milk or almond milk, shredded chicken or fish, sugar, and a mixture of rosewater and flour) and **blanc dessore** (similar but with the addition of red wine sauce), and **egerdouce** (sweet-sour pottage or a sour vinegar-like product).

The 14th-century *Forme of Cury*, compiled by Richard II's chefs, included several recipes for soups and pottages, which were poured over toasted bread or sops.

Cullis was a long-standing dish made by pounding cooked chicken and mixing it with broth. Its upscale cousin, mawmeny royal, was made from pounded pheasant, partridge or capon flesh mixed with pine nuts, spices, and almond milk. Civey (hare) and coney (rabbit) and wild birds were among the pleasures denied to the lower classes and reserved for landowners.

Richard Morris (1703–1779) stated that for a cullis the flesh of a seethed hen or chicken was chopped, pounded, and mixed with broth, oat groats or white bread. This was simmered and strained through a cloth and served.

The Guild of Poulterers was established in the 11th century to regulate the sale of birds, including swan, cygnet, crane, heron, bustard, pheasant, partridge, quail, blackbird, lark, sparrow, finches, stockdoves, thrushes, bittern, snipe (called brewe also), egret, gull, lapwing, mallard, plover, ruff, shoveller, and woodcock.

Rabbits, brought back to England by the Normans, represented the main, sometimes only, game for taking outside lands given to the royal deer and hare parks and hunting preserves. The penalty for taking game from one of those preserves was death.[3]

A few years after the death of Queen Elizabeth I in 1603 Fynes Morison, a Scot, wrote of the abundance of foods in England.

> The English have abundance of white meats of all kinds, of flesh, fowl and fish and of all things good for food ... the English eat fallow deer plentifully, as bucks in summer, and does in winter which they bake in pasties, and this venison pasty is a dainty rarely found in any other kingdom.... No kingdom in the world hath so many dove-houses.[4]

The last meal of King Charles II was a small quantity of soup. Charles was king when the bubonic plague ravaged Europe, and during the Great Fire of London in 1666, which actually brought an end to the plague by killing the rats through which it spread.[5]

Pottage for Charles II was documented by his chef, Giles Rose. Herb pottage was made of herbs, water, bread, and capers. Bran pottage was made of strained liquor from boiled bran, almonds, and sweet herbs. Snow pottage was made of milk, eggs, rice, and sugar.[6]

Elizabeth I is said to have taken only pottage in a time of mental anguish over circumstances resulting in the execution of the earl of Essex, a matter so grave that even Sir Walter Raleigh, who observed the execution, was moved to tears.[7]

Soup seems to have been the last meal of several monarchs including Scandinavian King Erik. Legend has it he was "irrevocably plighted" to seven women at the same time, one of whom was Queen Elizabeth, and the murderer of any number of men. After being imprisoned, he was offered his choice of dying by suffocation, opening a vein, or poison. He chose the latter, which he drank in a plate of soup.[8]

Marie Antoinette had nothing but soup in the last days before her execution. A girl was sent to her cell to offer her sustenance before her execution. She told the girl, "Oh, my good girl, all is over for me now." The girl admonished her, saying she needed support and insisted she should take some of the soup she had prepared. The queen relented but could swallow no more than two or three spoonfuls.[9]

Brawn (meat of a boar) was, according to Morison, standard fare for the lower-class English while venison graced the tables of landowners. The meat was cooked in cauldrons until tender, cooled and put into vessels. Then a mixture of small ale or beer, verjuice,[10] and salt was poured over it.

In order to understand the drastic culinary changes initiated during the Middle Ages it is necessary to understand the politics which set them into motion.

Up until the time of Henry VIII, the Church of Rome (Catholic) had imposed a series of dietary laws, the crux of which was that certain days were set aside as fasting days, certain days were fish days (meaning no meat could be eaten, but fish could be eaten), and some days when neither was acceptable.

In his zeal to produce a male heir to assume the throne, Henry decided he must separate himself from his first wife, Catherine of Aragon, who had produced only one child, a daughter. When the Church refused to grant an annulment for the marriage, Henry left the Church, thereby eliminating any need to follow doctrine, and thus was born the Church of England, and a new way of life.

With the Church of England came the abandonment of practices Henry wasn't especially fond of, and as he was very fond of food and feasting, dietary practices changed along with everything else. With his finances in ruins, he looked to the monasteries as a source of replenishing his coffers. Later, with the monasteries in ruins, it became apparent the land that had previously generously housed the masses in return for enlistment of soldiers to fill the ranks, was better utilized in producing profits. The era of the feudal system was slipping away.

Where cottages and villages had stood, grass was planted or cottages were taken to house and feed sheep which would produce those profits in the form of wool.

The poor became poorer as unemployment rose because, after all, not much labor is needed to maintain sheep, at least not enough to employ the men of a nation. Begging and soup kitchens kept some alive while many others fled, never to return.

The fishing industry failed because the absence of fish days lessened the demand for fish. This resulted eventually in a renewal of the ban of meat consumption on Fridays and during Lent. That change had far more to do with economics than actual religious doctrine.

Ironically, during this time of privation, Fynes Morison wrote of the abundance of bread and other good things on the tables of the wealthier English. It was for this class the cookery books such as *The Forme of Cury* were intended.

Henry's parting with the Catholic Church was an issue far from being put to rest, and under the reign of his daughter, Elizabeth I, came reform to ease the plight of those so harmed at the hand of Henry VIII and her half brother Edward VI. Her half sister, Mary I, a Catholic, saw Elizabeth, who had been raised a Protestant, as a threat. Because early leaders did not seem disposed to do anything in moderation, a chain of reactions resulted which eventually resulted in the puritanical movement exacerbated by the extremism of Oliver Cromwell.

During this period of extremism, food taboos blossomed overnight. Spices were felt to excite undue passion, and Christmas and its feasts became relics of the past. Anything other than plain fare, and that in modest quantity, was forbidden.

It was during Elizabeth I's reign that English colonization in North America was established. Virginia was named in her honor, she being known in some circles as "the Virgin Queen" because she never married. The puritanical beliefs of those early colonists survived an ocean voyage to become standard in the New World, thus it would be decades before the English restored any trace of enjoyment to their meals on either side of the ocean.

Elizabeth died in 1603. However, the puritanical movement survived until the death of Oliver Cromwell in 1658. Through the works of cookery writers, botanists, and others, English cuisine began an exultant rebirth as food taboos faded into oblivion.

Robert May gave extensive information on soup, pottages, and broths in his *Accomplished*

Cook (London, 1660). He was trained as a chef in Paris and served an apprenticeship in London. During his career he was employed in thirteen different households of minor English nobility. He did not fully break away from the prevalent food customs of the Middle Ages, but he did introduce new culinary concepts.

He included among his pottages French bisques and Italian *brodos*. He used ingredients such as lemon and lemon peel, nutmeg, mace, cloves, ginger, bay leaves, marjoram, rosemary, savory, parsley, garlic, horseradish, oysters, eggs, anchovies, wine and claret, vinegar, pepper and salt, chestnuts, "pistachas," fish, prawns, eels, asparagus, barberries, grapes, gooseberries, lettuce, cinnamon, rosewater, raisins, sugar, oats, barley, cream, saffron, capers, almond paste, oranges, beets, pomegranates, butter, mint, alexander, honey, ale, beer, peas, onion, rice, spinach, carrots, artichokes, potatoes, skirret, barley, almonds, herbs, and parsnips in his soups, bisques and pottages.

Like most authors of the time, his book included broth recipes for invalids, and he preserved the medieval custom of pouring the liquids over toasted bread. Recipes for pottages and soups make up almost 20 percent of the book, attesting to the importance of soup in the medieval English diet. An illustration showed a large pottage dish in the center of the table settings of the era.

Hares were made into soup, and were jugged by putting the pieces of meat into a crock with cider and putting the crock into a cauldron of boiling water to simmer for three to four hours. Raised game pies filled tables, and roasted joints tempted the strongest of men.

Lord Dudley stated a typical British dinner should consist of "a good soup, a small turbot, a neck of venison, duckling with green peas, or chicken with asparagus, and an apricot tart."[11]

> Of British soup, turtle always takes precedence in the list of honour, but as the turtle comes from Ascencion, or the West Indies, it can hardly claim to be a denizen of these islands. Hare soup and mock turtle soup, mulligatawny, mutton broth, and pea soup are distinctively British, though the curry powder in the mulligatawny..., of course comes from India. Oxtail soup has a good British sound, but I fancy that French housewives first discovered the virtue that there is in the tail of an ox.[12]

Green turtle was first brought to England between 1740 and 1750. By about 1800, a liberal portion per guest at dinner was six pounds live weight. During a dinner at the City of London Tavern in August 1808, 400 men consumed 2,500 pounds of meat. Samuel Birch, a confectioner, is credited with being the first to serve turtle soup in London, providing lemons, cayenne, and other condiments with toasted French bread on the tables.[13]

Giles Rose's method of making turtle soup was, "Take your tortoises and cut off their heads and feet and boyl them in fair water, and when they are almost boyl'd put to them some white wine, some sweet herbs, and a piece of bacon, and give them a brown in the frying-pan with good butter, then lay them upon your bread a-steeping in good strong broth, and well seasoned; garnish the dish with green sparrow-grass [asparagus] and lemon over it."

Throughout the Victorian and Edwardian eras, brown Windsor was a classic British soup made from lamb or beef, leeks, carrots, parsnips, bouquet garni, and Madeira. Later it sometimes contained onion and chopped parsley. It got its color from browned meat and flour.[14]

The famous singer Jenny Lind, who arrived in England in 1847, is supposed to have partaken of soup to soothe her throat before her performances.

> JENNY LIND'S SOUP. Make about three quarts of stock, which strain through a fine sieve into a middle-size stewpan; set it to boil; add to it three ounces of sago; boil gently twenty minutes; skim; just previous to serving break four fresh eggs, and place the yolk, entirely free from the white, into a basin, beat them well with a spoon; add to it a gill of cream; take the

pan from the fire, pour in the yolks, stir quickly for one minute, serve immediately; do not let it boil, or it will curdle, and would not be fit to be partaken of. The stock being previously seasoned, it only requires the addition of half a teaspoonful of sugar, a little more salt, pepper, nutmeg; also thyme, parsley, and bay-leaf will agreeably vary the flavor without interfering with the quality.[15]

The custom of foods for the sick dates as far back as Galen, a Greek physician in the 2nd century, and Hippocrates (born 460 B.C.) for whom the Hippocratic oath taken by graduating physicians is named.

Galen thought chicken soup capable of healing leprosy, migraine, constipation, chronic fevers, and "black humours." In 1190, the Jewish philosopher Moses Maimonides (1135–1204), studied Galen's use of soups in treating ailments and wrote that the soup of fat hens was effective in treating asthma. His patient was 40-year-old Prince al-Afdal.[16]

The 10th century Persian physician, Avicenna (980–1037), also praised the restorative powers of chicken soup. His treatise on health was well esteemed through the Renaissance period.

Samuel Pepys,[17] the famous English diarist, enjoyed food immensely. He wrote much in the 1660s on food and its preparation, and spoke of May's pease pottage, which was made thusly:

> Take green pease being shelled and cleansed, put them into a pipkin of fair boiling water; when they be boiled and tender, take and strain some of them, and thicken the rest; put to them a bunch of sweet herbs, or sweet herbs chopped, salt, and pepper, being through boild dish them, and serve them in a deep clean dish with salt and sippets around them.

Pepys usually dined much more sumptuously than on simple pease porridge, and stated in his diary that meat was so dear that, "hundreds of thousands of families scarcely knew the taste of it.... The majority of the nation lived almost entirely on rye, barley, and oats."

If he ever experienced the deprivation characteristic of the puritanical age, he made light of it in his writings as he described the affluent meals he ate, or perhaps his love of food was fueled by opportunity following such deprivation. There was no great appreciation of pottage in Pepys' writing; he believed pottage best left to peasants.

John Russell wrote in the 15th-century *Boke of Nurture* of a feast that began with pea soup with bacon, beef or mutton stew, and other dishes. He also instructed proper placement of trenchers on the table.[18]

In 1789, the Princess Royal gave a supper and ball at which 20 tureens of different soups constituted the hot part of the meal. The remainder of the meal was equally grand.[19] It was common practice in Europe to distribute any food left over after a banquet to the poor of the city, which explains to some extent the amount of food that was prepared.

For those of lesser importance, "rich soups and elegant dinner" could be had at Mr. Wooll's Room at the Denmark Arms, Surry side of Westminster.[20]

Elizabeth Moxon's *English Housewife Exemplified* (1764) contained 10 soup recipes and a recipe for hotchpotch which was given in a different section than the other soups. These were vermicelli, cucumber, hare, green pease, onion, common pease in winter, pease in Lent, craw-fish (sometimes a Lenten dish), soup without water, and Scotch *soop*. These represent the basic soups that remained popular from the medieval era.

Her hotchpotch was made of cubed beef, mutton, a fowl, broccoli, barley, chopped carrots and turnips, shelled peas, sweet herbs, onions, and salt to taste. Shredded spinach was added just at the last, before the soup was served, so as to preserve its color. When fresh peas weren't available, asparagus could be substituted, and if that failed also, savoy cabbage was used.

During the 19th century, English cooks were known as less than adequate in the preparation of soup. "Soup must be persuaded and reasoned with; it will not submit to the impetuous tyranny of a person in a hurry. The wine, spices, and anchovy are cast into the 'enchanted pot' too soon by us, and their subtle flavors volatilize and pass away into thin air."[21]

Auguste Kettner was a London restaurateur who opened his restaurant in 1867 with savings earned as chef for Napoleon III. An extant menu from the restaurant contains consommé borscht. His philosophy of soup seemed to echo the sentiment, "There has been a good deal of needless controversy about Soup, some people finding it a dinner in itself, and some refusing it as a weak wash, fit only for babies and invalids."[22]

The diet of the Welsh seems to have been basically that of the English if the following account is any indication.

> Almost all the people live upon the produce of their herds, with oats, milk, cheese, and butter; eating flesh in larger proportions than bread.
>
> In the evening, when no more guests are expected, the meal is prepared according to the number and dignity of the persons assembled, and according to the wealth of the family who entertains. The kitchen does not supply many dishes, nor high-seasoned incitements to eating. The house is not furnished with tables, cloths, or napkins. They study nature more than food, for which reason, the guests being seated in threes, instead of couples as elsewhere, they place the dishes before them all at once upon rushes and fresh grass, in large platters or trenchers. They also make use of a thin and broad cake of bread, baked every day ... and they sometimes add chopped meat, with broth.[23]

13. France

Thankfully, France escaped the extremism of Oliver Cromwell and French cuisine never experienced the stagnation that English dishes did; however, that is not to say every class feasted on rich food.

For the elite, the quality and originality of French food remained on a steady upward spiral. The peasant class was a study in contrast, however. They rarely ate meat, occasionally ate fish, and their general provision was soup with bread of wheat or rye.[1] Food shortages and riots fueled the French Revolution and led to the execution of Marie Antoinette and Louis XVI.

> The diet of a French peasant is fruital in the extreme. His two meals usually consist of cabbage-soup—in which on Sundays and other special occasions a morsel of bacon is boiled—accompanied with rye bread. We have known a very well-to-do couple make half a rabbit last them four days in the way of meat. Many kinds of fungi are common articles of diet with the French peasantry.[2]

In an age when the duty of master cooks was mainly to oversee less-skilled individuals in their charge, cookbooks were vague as to amounts and techniques. There was no point in giving specific amounts when most of the lesser cooks couldn't read and dishes were prepared "to taste" according to the wishes of the families employing them. Perhaps it was job security for the master cooks to be a little vague in their instructions.

An excellent insight into soups in medieval France comes from a book of instructions in domestic economy written by a Frenchman in 1392. Because he wrote the instructions for his 15-year-old unskilled wife so that she would be able to comfortably manage his household as he aged, he gave specific instructions for recipes that were usually painfully vague.

Spices such as cinnamon and ginger, today perhaps most common in desserts, were commonly found in soups made of flesh or fish.

The amazing reality of studying ancient cuisines is not their differences, but their similarities. The herb soup so well described in *Le Menagier de Paris* is little different from the one in a 17th-century Dutch manuscript translated by Peter Rose. The soup was so basic, utilizing common ingredients and the one-pot method of preparation, that it evolved simultaneously from one area to another.

The following were used and/or grown according to *Le Menagier de Paris*: sorrel, cabbage (four or more varieties), spinach, lettuce, beets, squash, lettuce, onions, chickpeas, shallots, garlic, carrots, mushrooms, chestnuts, turnips, peas, broad beans, leeks, parsnips, marjoram, sage, dittany, mint, clary, savory, parsley, fennel, borage, rosemary, basil, tansy, bayleaf, liquorice, celery, cress, and mustard.

Households throughout medieval Europe used various sorts of fruit, usually grapes, to make verjuice (an unfermented juice, similar to vinegar, made from unripened fruit) to flavor soups. Verjuice can be mail-ordered or replaced in recipes with diluted cider vinegar, citrus juice, (Seville oranges or lemons are best), or sour apple juice.

Fowl and farm animals were described along with game and wild fowl for well-flavored broths and stocks.

Soups made from green vegetables, leeks, cabbage, peas, cress, beet greens spinach, parsley, sprouts, chard, and fennel were called *porray*. White *porray* was made from the white part of the leek only, and if meat was used it was chine, chitterlings, and ham.

Pottages were generally heartier than other dishes, and were often made from grains and/or beans, peas, and other legumes. Vegetable pottages contained any vegetables the cook chose to throw into the pot.

Soup could include bacon or meat if the meal were served on a meat day (per Church decree meat and fish were not allowed on certain days, usually Wednesday, Friday, and Saturday). In fact, in *Le Menagier de Paris*, recipes often appear in three forms—vegetarian, with meat, and with fish—so the cook could choose the version to comply with the appropriate dietary law for the day the soup would be served.

City dwellers had almost an unlimited array of meats, vegetables, and spices, if their income was ample enough to pay for their choices, but what may have been readily available in the markets might have been beyond the reach of country folk. Major markets at the time included Paris, Florence, Milan, and Venice, with many smaller cities carrying a good amount of merchandise, though it did not compare to those cities.

Le menagier was written from the standpoint of a gardener and a cook, providing greater insight into the foods available in medieval France. Pottages mentioned included beans, peas, cabbage, thick pottage without meat, eel *brewet* (broth), *brewet* of pike and eel, fish *brewet* (mentioned specifically are salmon, tench, herring, carp, perch, pike, roach, and bream), *brewet* of capon, cinnamon *brewet*, almond *brewet*, *brewet* of verjuice and poultry, *brewet* of hare or veal, coney, white *brewet*, and yellow *brewet*. Recipes included several for *civey* (a thick stew or rag-out). Fish soups were made in the same manner as meat and poultry pottages and with the same spices; some contained sugar while others did not.

Le menagier lists numerous soups made of herbs and eggs mixed with spices, verjuice, vinegar, and saffron, one thickened with almond milk, and one made with onions and leeks cooked in milk and thickened with bread. Pottages made with milk were made without verjuice or wine.

"Poultry Flavored with Cummin" or *cominee de poulaille* instructed the reader to cook pieces of poultry in water and wine, then fry the pieces in fat, after which they were combined with bread moistened in broth, and brayed (pounded in a mortar) ginger, cumin, and verjuice. The soup was then colored yellow with saffron or egg yolks. If the latter were used, they were put through a strainer so that they slowly dropped into the pottage after it was taken away from the fire. The bread and eggs helped thicken the soup.

"Cominee for a Fish Day" instructed the cook to fry the fish, peel and bray almonds, and dilute with fish broth and/or cow's milk (preferred) or milk of almonds.

Cinnamon *brewet* (*brouet de canelle*) started with pieces of meat or chicken stewed in water with a little wine, then fried in fat. Raw dried almonds in the shell and cinnamon were brayed together and moistened with a little of the broth, then boiled with the broth, meat, and brayed ginger, cloves, and grain of paradise. It was thick in consistency.

White *brewet* (*brouet blanc*) was made with capons, pullets, or chicken, veal, and bacon prepared as above, with brayed almonds, white ginger (peeled or pared), red coriander and pomegranate seeds. To thicken it, flour of amidon or rice with a drop of verjuice was added with white sugar.

German *brewet* (*brouet d'Alemaigne*) was similar but contained minced cooked onions, nutmeg, and roasted livers which were brayed with ginger, cinnamon, grains of paradise, nutmegs, and saffron. A little verjuice and parsley leaves were added with bread to thicken it. When served, the meat was placed into a bowl and the broth was poured over it.

The cook was instructed to stir often so soups would not burn while cooking. However, if a thick pottage such as peas or beans should stick and burn, it was not to be stirred. Instead, the contents were poured into a fresh clean pot and anything that stuck to the burned pot was discarded. Putting a little yeast into the pot was thought to remove the scorched taste.

Spices were to be very well brayed but not strained before being put into pottages, it was felt best to add the spices near the end of the cooking time, rather than at the beginning.

The French were known as great epicures as early as the 1600s. In 1868, it was said, "A French epicurean writer of eminence asserts that ten solid volumes would not contain the recipes of all the soups which have been invented in these grand schools of good eating, the kitchens of Paris."

The following is extracted from an early poem:

> Now just such a mess of delicious hot pottage
> Was smoking away when they enter'd the cottage,
> And casting a truly delicious perfume
> Through the whole of an ugly ill-furnish'd room;
> "Hot, smoking hot,"
> On the fire was a pot
> Well replenish'd, but really I can't say with what;
> For, famed as the French always are for ragouts,
> No creature can tell what they put in their stews,
> Whether bull-frogs, old gloves, or old wigs, or old shoes
> Notwithstanding, when offer'd I rarely refuse,
> Any more than poor Blogg did, when seeing the reeky
> Repast placed before him, scarce able to speak, he
> In ectasy mutter'd, "By Jove, Cocky-leeky!"[3]

La Varenne instructed in the preparation of a wide array of soups, pottages and ragouts in his *The French Cook*. Samuel Sorbière wrote in 1663[4] of the plainness of English meals, saying that in homes without the talents of French cooks tables contained simply large dishes of meat. He described the English as strangers to "bisks and pottages."

Louis P. De Gouy stated the French were masters at using *dessertes de la table* (leftover food), or heads, tails, lights (lungs), livers, knuckles, and feet for soup, and pronounced soup "cuisine's kindest course." He went on to say soup was to the meal what the hostess's smile of welcome was to the party: "a prelude to the goodness to come."

Later, not everyone may have been privy to those delicious soups if the following passage is any indication.

> A man or woman may live in Paris for many years, and, unless peculiarly fortunate, or favoured by extreme circumstances, never get the entrée to the jealously guarded French home, which is not open to all comers like an American, but is an inner shrine, most carefully guarded against intrusion. Hence as the prophet in his haste said, "All men are liars," so the roving American readily decides there is no social home-life in France because he has never seen it, nor met those who have had the privilege denied to him. Finding his letters of introduction, which in England and America are always considered as "tickets for soup," giving admission to the family circle, do not answer the same purpose in France, and meeting the person for whom they are addressed only at the opera, the restaurant, and the public promenades, the conclusion is arrived at that the domestic hearth is ever cold, the table never spread at home

for the entertainment of friends, and that the modern Frenchman, like the old Greek, regards his home only as a shelter, a place to sleep in, his enjoyment being all taken out of doors.[5]

French soups varied greatly in consistency and ingredients. There were broths, soups, and stews, versions with and without meat, and versions made using fish, eels, or shellfish. Ragouts were relatively dry whereas broths and soups were more liquid in consistency. Stews might or might not have contained onions and spices.

Jean Baptiste Gilbert Payplat, called Julien, is a classic example of the French soup chef. He fled France during the Revolution, and opened an eatery in Boston which he named Restorator (a loose translation of the word *restaurant).* His creative and artfully prepared soups attracted the likes of the famous Jean Anthelme Brillat-Savarin.

Brillat-Savarin so valued soup that he once said a woman who couldn't make it ought not to be allowed to marry.

Prior to 1805, some credit Julien with inventing the very popular Victorian julienne soup, in which the vegetables are cut into long thin strips, or julienne.

> Frenchmen, they tell us, dine upon frogs and soup maigre, live in hotels; are educated chiefly at the theatre; have no "homes," are taught to dance before they learn to read; love revolutions, glory, and foie-gras, and believe in the remission of sins by the grace of holy water.[6]

As a general rule, the heavier the balance of the meal, the lighter the soup. A hearty stew or soup needed little accompaniment, whereas a heavy meal needed only consommé or a light cream soup to start the digestive juices flowing. Soup, tenderly prepared, excited the palate and left the diner with great expectations of that which was to follow.

> There is no French dinner without soup, which is regarded as indispensable overture; and believe it an excellent plan to begin the banquet with a basin of good soup, which, by moderating the appetite for solid animal food, is certainly a salutiferous custom.[7]

Bisque usually refers to fish or shellfish creamed soup, though it can in recent times refer to a vegetable soup such as tomato bisque. Early bisques instructed the cook to pound the shell of the crustacean, often crayfish, lobster, or crabs, with mortar and pestle and return the crushed shell to the soup. The word was first spelled *bisk* and early on also denoted a creamed soup made of poultry or game birds. Robert May spelled it thusly in 1685.

Simple cream soup may be made by adding any chopped meat, vegetable, or herbs to a base made from 2 tablespoons butter, 2 tablespoons flour, 1 cup milk or cream, 1 cup stock, 1/2 teaspoon salt, and 1/8 teaspoon pepper. Add the flour to the melted butter with salt and pepper, cook slightly but do not brown, and gradually stir in the milk or cream followed by the stock. Add chopped ingredients and any desired additional seasonings or herbs. It need only simmer 3 to 4 minutes before being served.

Blot stated French cookery was simple and rather coarse until the 16th century when Catherine de Medici, wife of Henry II and niece of Pope Leo X, brought Italian cookery to France. She sparked a competition to create the best dishes of France which provided incentive for Henry IV to develop *consommé à la reine,* and coin the phrase *poule au pot* (a chicken in the soup kettle to make broth).[8]

Legend has it that Louis XIV of France ordered his chef to create a soup so perfectly clear that he might see his royal countenance when looking at its surface. The chef accommodated his request by clarifying a broth with egg white. This broth became known as consommé, and remained a favorite of Louis XIV.[9]

By the 17th century French cookery had evolved in its own right, leaving the oil, oranges, and olives to the Italians.[10]

France's national dish of *pot au feu* is named for the pot in which the soup is cooked. During the reigns of Louis XV and Louis XVI, this invention of dishes continued with a fury. A dinner given for Lent included no less than 28 potages.[11]

> Who better to instruct the preparation of such a dish than a French cook? Get from the butcher a nice, smooth, pretty piece of beef, with as little skin, fat, strings, and bones, as possible: one pound does for me, but for a family we shall say three pounds. Put this into—not an iron pot, not a brass pot, not a tin pot—but an earthen pan with a close-fitting lid, and three quarts of filtered water, and some salt. This you must put, not on the fire, but on the top of the oven, which is heated from the fire, and which will do just the same as a hot hearth; let it boil up; skim and deprive it of all grease. When this is accomplished, take three large carrots, cut in three pieces—three, remember!—one large parsnip cut in two, two turnips, as many leeks as possible—you can't have too many; two cloves ground, and the least little idea of pepper, and onions if you like—I only put a burnt one to color. Now cover up, and let it stay, going tic-tic-tic! For seven hours; not to boil, pray. When I hear my bouillon bubble, the tears are in my eyes, for I know it is a *plat manqué*. When ready put the beef, what we country people call *bouilli* ... on a dish, and with tasteful elegance dispose around the carrots, parsnip, and turnip. Then on slices of bread at the bottom of a bowl pour your soup, and thank God for your good dinner.[12]

The writer decreed this was the "old version," and the new style allowed use of celery, parsley, "and a hundred other things."

The Bretons[13] had their equivalent of the French *pot au feu* called *soupe fraîche.* An elderly Breton man was asked in 1895 if he ate meat, to which he replied in the affirmative, explaining on Sundays and feast days his wife added "a little salt bacon" to the soup.[14]

The chef who is credited with some of those decadent dinners was Antonin Carême. He prepared meals for Talleyrand, Czar Alexander I, George IV, and baron de Rothschild. Of soup he stated, "Soup must be the agent provocateur of a good dinner." It was Carême who classified families of soups, sauces, and stocks so that cooks the world over understood recipes and techniques for making them. He also established roux as a basic thickener for soup, and established a practical cuisine for restaurants. He died in 1830, but his successes are still standard in the culinary world. In fact, *Harper's Weekly* once called him the "Raphael of the Kitchen."

Carême stated Napoleon ate little, and plainly, but other sources claimed that upon being named first consul in 1802, he began giving lavish dinners prepared by the best French cooks. His victories, marriage, and the birth of the king of Rome all occasioned great banquets. Some of the dinners given by Napoleon, the diplomat Talleyrand, and others along with the kings almost rivaled the excesses of the Romans.

Alexandre Balthazar Laurent Grimod de la Reynière, a 19th-century lawyer, felt soup was so important that "soup is to dinner what the portico or the peristyle is to an edifice. That is to say, not only is it the first part, but it should be conceived in such a way as to give an exact idea of the feast, very nearly as the overture to an opera should announce the quality of the whole work."

The name of the popular soup hotchpotch was derived from the French *hochepot*—*hocher* meaning "to shake" and *pot*. Although some cookery books changed the spelling to hodgepodge, Carrie Shuman advised that was not the general spelling. The dish refers to lots of ingredients shaken and gently boiled together in the same pot. It is more a ragout than a soup, and the French version contained oxtail, beef, ham, saveloy (sausage), and a long list of vegetables.

France and Spain each had their own versions of it, known respectively as *pot-pourri* and *olla podrida.*

Good Housekeeping contained a recipe for toast soup, served as an hors d'oeuvre in French kitchens, admitting it was rarely made in America. They instructed placing nicely browned pieces of bread in a tureen and adding just enough beef broth to wet the bread. After it had become saturated, the tureen was filled with more broth.

French onion soup is a prime example of soups descended from the medieval sops in that it is served with toasted bread and cheese, the bread soaking up the delicious onion flavored broth so that every last drop can be savored. It is also an example of soups made from ingredients that were sometimes thought medicinal and designed to alleviate a particular affliction in that onions were thought to relieve headache.

François Pierre La Varenne's 1651 potage of onion is one of the earlier recipes. Translation: "Cut your onions into very thin slices, fry them with butter, and after they are fried put them into a pot with water or with pease broth. After they are well sod, put in it a crust of bread and let it boile a very little; you may put some capers in it. Dry your bread then stove it; take up, and serve with one drop of vinegar."

In 1868 Charles Dickens wrote:

> French cooks in their versatile invention and restless desire to please and delight give strange and striking names to their new dishes. They have "The Soup of the Good Woman" and above all, "The Potage a la Jambe du Bois (The Soup of the Wooden Leg)."
>   But the wooden leg is an after ingredient. Like most receipts of the first class, this one is horribly expensive; but, like most other expensive recipes, it is just as good made more economically. Take a wooden leg — no, that is afterwards. Procure a shin of beef and put it in a pot, with three dozen carrots, a dozen onions, two dozen pieces of celery, twelve turnips, a fowl, and two partridges. It must simmer six hours. Then get two pounds of fillet of veal: stew it, and pour the soup over the meat. Add more celery; then mix bread and eventually serve up the soup with the shin bone (the real wooden leg) emerging like the bowsprit of a wreck from the sea of vegetables.[15]

There seems to have been some vying for the tourist dollar early on, as evidenced by numerous newspaper articles:

> French cookery, as you see at the table-d'hôte, admits of the most inferior parts of the meat being served as a stew or ragout; and as for French soups, they are chiefly "confectioned" from the dibrit of previous days dinners. The pot-au-feu is a well-known institution in French hotels. It is all the better that diners do not see the offal which is given to them in Franco, but which at home is given to the dogs.[16]

One of the major reformers of diet in the 19th century was Auguste Escoffier, who in 1898 began work on *Le Guide Culinaire*. Of soups, he said that in the old classical kitchen they were dishes unto themselves and contained a wide variety of meat, poultry, game and fish in a liquid and garnished attractively, but by the 19th century soup referred only to the liquid part of the dish. *Garnish* was at times used to describe the bits of solids added to the basic stocks.

The fact he considered any meal of importance to begin with soup is evidenced by the 438 soup recipes found in the book. Rightly, he credited Carême with many of the improvements to good-quality soup.

Escoffier was born in 1846 and served as an army chef in the Franco-Prussian war of 1870–71, during which he experienced difficulties in obtaining provisions much as his predecessors had in previous wars. In 1884, he was working in Monte Carlo and Lucerne, where he met Cesar Ritz. The two men went to London and combined their efforts to open the Savoy and Carlton Hotels. Their success led to the chain of hotels known as Ritz-Carlton.

Escoffier updated the kitchen to standards still maintained in those facilities and gave chefs and assistants a degree of professionalism not previously known while demanding an impressive level of cleanliness.

In 1910, Adelaide Keen's French soup recipes included petite marmite made in a clay pot, and consommé Colbert. The latter was made by clarifying 1 quart of beef stock, well flavored and made from fresh meat, adding 1 tablespoonful of sherry, and in each plate putting an egg, poached in water and vinegar, to keep it firm and white. Salt and pepper were added to taste.

Her Normandy frog soup was made by adding 1½ ounces of flour to 1½ quarts of white stock, an onion, parsley, celery, salt, and pepper. It was cooked 1 hour and strained. Then one dozen frogs' legs fried in butter were added, with a glass of sherry. The whole was then cooked ½ hour more and the yolks of 2 eggs added, blended with 1 cup of hot milk and a little butter.

Jean Anthelme Brillat-Savarin left a manuscript[17] called *The Physiology of Taste*, which remains one of the best-known tomes on food and its preparation, due in part to his observances from the point of view of someone enjoying fine food rather than someone responsible for preparing it.

Agreeing with everyone, he thought soup was wholesome and nutritious and a delight to the stomach. He naturally thought France produced the best potage anywhere in the world. Although *bouilli* was filling, he thought, it offered little nutrition, its essence having been released into the broth (bouillon). He called it "meat without its juice."

Early cooks used various methods of coloring soup to please the eye as well as the palate — brown burned sugar (caramel); pounded spinach leaves, chard, celery leaves, basil, parsley; tomato, cochineal (cactus beetles), red grape juice, saffron, alkanet, blackberry pulp, raisins, prunes, and darkly toasted bread. To make the caramel, ½ pound of sugar was mixed with ⅓ cup of cold water and slowly cooked until it turned dark brown. It was customary then to add another measure of water and boil the mixture until it reached the consistency of thick syrup. Caramel kept in a corked bottle was a kitchen staple.

Colored garnishes can add to the appeal of a bowl of soup while also conveying a subliminal message depending on the color used. Red tends to convey power and has been used for military uniforms for that reason. It excites the senses and is associated with passion and danger. Yellow evokes a sense of things to come, in the way that spring flowers herald summer. Green has been associated with the working class and farming, as has earthy brown. The effect of green is calming and peaceful. In centuries past, white evoked a feeling of innocence and immortality and was associated with mourning in China. It is this sense of immortality that fueled the concept of ghosts being white and the welcoming "light" many people believe leads the way to Heaven at the time of death.

In July 1841, the *Southern Literary Messenger* described the French diet as consisting of rye bread, soup made of millet, cakes made of Indian corn, "now and then" some salt provisions and vegetables, and rarely, if ever, butcher's meat. Elsewhere people dined on wheat bread, vegetable soup, potatoes and other vegetables, but seldom butcher's meat.

In 1869, it was reported in *Literature, Science, and Art* that French diners were not always served the freshly prepared fare one might expect. Cooks in aristocratic homes sold leftovers from meals to peddlers who cleaned, trimmed, and rearranged them. Then they were sold in stalls and passed on to those less fortunate — for a price.

Secondhand bakers likewise recycled scraps of bread brought to them. Some of it was rasped, dried in an oven, and sold for the making of a soup, very popular among the lower classes, called *croute au pot*. Larger pieces were cut into triangles and fried in butter after which they were sold to restaurants where they were served up with steaming bowls of pea soup — the diner none the wiser that these toasts were made from bread salvaged from the plates of others. As if that were not insult enough, diners ordering breaded cutlets consumed the worst of the leftover bread after it was pounded and sold to the restaurants.

Food had been served to travelers for centuries before the French coined the phrase *restaurant* for a place where guests could order from a varied menu. According to a 19th-century writer, A. Boulanger, a soup vendor who opened his business in Paris in 1765, is thought to have been the first to operate such a facility. The sign above his door advertised restoratives, or *restaurants*, referring to his soups and broths.[18]

From early days, the French were known for eating frogs' legs prepared in a number of ways, including in soup. During the American Revolution, a group of French officers stationed in Boston Harbor became friends with a local merchant. The soldiers and the merchant were invited to the home of Nathaniel Tracy who, along with most of the town, had heard rumors that the soldiers had been catching their "favorite food" in the Frog Pond on the Common.

When they sat down to dinner, a large soup tureen was placed on each end of the table and Tracy began to ladle out the soup. L'Etombe, consul of France and resident at Boston, put his spoon into the soup plate and fished up a large frog,

> just as green and perfect as if he had hopped from the pond into the tureen. Not knowing at first what it was, he seized it by one of its hind-legs, and, holding it up in view of the whole company, discovered that it was a full-grown frog. As soon as he had thoroughly inspected it, and made himself sure of the matter, he exclaimed, "*Ah! Mon Dieu! Une grenouille!*" Then turning to the gentleman next to him, gave him the frog. He received it and passed it round the table. Thus the poor *crapaud* made the tour from hand to hand until it reached the admiral. The company convulsed with laughter, examined the soup plates as the servants brought them, and in each was to be found a frog. The uproar was universal. Meantime Tracy kept his ladle going, wondering what his outlandish guests meant by such extravagant merriment. "What's the matter?" asked he; and raising his head discovered the frogs dangling by a leg in all directions. "Why don't they eat them?" he exclaimed. "If they knew the confounded trouble I had to catch them, in order to treat them to a dish of their own country, they would find, that with me, at least, it was no joking matter.'"

Had Tracy gone to the trouble to study French cuisine, he would have known only the hind legs were eaten.[19]

In 1854, Harriet Beecher Stowe described soup she ate in France.

> At Nantua, a sordid town, with a squalid inn, we dined at two, deliciously, on a red shrimp soup; no, not soup, it was a "potage"; no, a stew; no, a creamy, unctuous mess, muss, or whatever you please to call it. Sancho Panza never ate his *olla podrida* with more relish.

Contents aside, however, the French were rarely separated from their soups. It was said that "Frenchmen and soup are convertible terms. Whenever a Frenchman is ill, or exhausted, or hungry, or about to take a long journey, he orders soup. The first thing he orders when he gets up in the morning is soup. The last thing he takes at night before donning his night-cap ... is soup."

The French coined the phrase "pot luck." At the many French soup stands, "Each customer was given election — a bowl of soup or pot-luck. Armed with an iron fork whose handle was three feet long, he had the right to try his pot-luck; if he speared a bit of meat, it was added to his soup-bowl. These picturesque kitchens have been improved out of existence. Pot-luck has been lost."[20]

14. Germany and Poland

Though Germanic peoples have been documented in the area since soon after the life of Christ, Germany as we know it wasn't formed until 1871. Assessments of the quality of German food through the early 19th century varied with the appreciation of the writer, many Americans commenting on the common unhealthy practice of eating raw smoked ham and greasy soup. In 1853, *Harper's* thought all German soup was of poor quality, and in 1844 *Blackwood's* commented on the Germans' propensity for using odd mixtures of ingredients, as in a soup "full of round balls of a pasty substance." References to the greasy kitchens of the Germans were common.

Bothmer divided German food into three categories — salt, sour, and greasy — with soup falling in the third category. However, Germany's soup offerings were many, with their claim to fame being fruit soups, as evidenced in this mid–19th-century recipe found in the *Brooklyn Eagle, Godey's,* and other publications.

> A receipt for cherry soup is given by the Salut Public of Lyons. Take, it says, a quantity of fine ripe cherries, cook them in water with sugar and a little vanilla; fry some slices of bread in fresh butter, throw them into the decoction of cherries, mix well up, and serve hot. This soup seems a favorite dish in Germany.

In 19th-century America, fruit soups were served ice cold in hot weather. An acid flavor was preferred, and the soup was often served with croutons of bread sprinkled with sugar and toasted in the oven.

In the 1880s, Germans were eating milk soup with semolina, beef tea with balls of marrow, eggs and bread crumbs, and cauliflower cut up in small pieces, bullion with eggs floating on top, meat broth with barley, and *potage à l'Espagnol.*

They favored soup made with beer as the principal ingredient. It was made from half beer (less alcohol content by volume), grated stale bread, sugar, raisins, water, and spices. The French also made a soup from beer called *soupe à la bière.*[1]

> Cooked beer is a comparatively old drink among the Germans. They have many ways of preparing it, even going so far as to make it the principal ingredient of a soup. It is well known in Germany, especially in student towns like Stuttgart, where many a carousal has it for a principal dish.[2]
>
> Bread in Germany means rye bread.... The German "Suppe" is not soup, but means all dishes taken with a spoon.[3]

Ludwig von Beethoven, the great composer, was exceedingly fond of bread soup, and once threw a bowl of the soup at his cook when it did not meet his expectations.[4]

Henriette Davidis published a book in the U.S., originally published in Germany in 1897, which contained 106 recipes for soups reflecting German influence, including those made from fruit, beer, wine, and milk.[5]

Various religions have been associated with dietary food laws over the years. The Catholic practice of not eating meat on Fridays was lifted by Vatican II, especially in America. Many churches still practice dietary laws during Lent (the period from Ash Wednesday to Easter Sunday representing the 40 days Jesus spent in the wilderness and other significant events, each lasting 40 days).

Early cookery books often contained recipes for Lenten dishes. Dr. Kitchiner's 1829 *Cook's Oracle* contained a section titled, "A Complete System of Cookery for Catholic Families."

The German cookery book *Das buch von guter spise* (The Book of Good Food) was written in Wurzburg in about 1350, and *Kuchenmeysterey* (Kitchen Mastery) was printed in Nuremberg in about 1485. The first contained no soup recipes, probably not because soup wasn't eaten but because it was so commonly eaten and made in so many ways that it didn't need documenting.

Goose soup is classic. Make it as follows: Set a large pan under the goose while it is roasting. Let the fat drip into it. After that, simmer good milk with sugar and put toasted bread into it.[6] A similar recipe was found without the goose fat: Grated wheat bread, a couple of eggs and flour, boiled in water or milk. Put sugar thereon.[7]

Water soup was made by seething water with green parsley or parsley roots, sieving after simmering, and adding butter and hen eggs which were simmered to thicken the soup. It was dished up over slices of toasted bread. Chicken with broth was made by seething rice in the broth after boiling chickens.

Wine soup without eggs was made from wine, bread, honey, herbs, and raisins.

"A Good Broth From Salmon, Sturgeon, Pig's Game or Other" was made from apples, red onion, and sweet beer (without hop flavor). They were seethed together until the apples and onion softened, then toasted bread was grated in with the apples and onions and the whole sieved together with herbs. The type of herb was not specified.[8]

The Germans enjoyed crawfish soup and almond soup as well as the English, and made them in a similar manner.[9]

Alfred Sidgwick stated in 1908 that nearly all German soups were good, some of the best not known in England. *Nudelsuppe* was noodles in strong chicken stock, the *nudeln* (noodles) of the early soups rolled by hand as thin as paper. He claimed, "All over Germany dinner begins with soup."

In 1913, Henry Finck wrote that Munich was the main tourist destination for Americans, and there a host of soups awaited: bouillon with egg, bread soup, noodle soup (with or without a large portion of chicken), liver noodle soup, and brain soup.

Germany borders Poland and France, and shares culinary similarities with both, perhaps through the early colonization of Germany by the Romans about A.D. 96. At that time, the German diet was described as mostly meat, bread, and mead. By the 18th century, King Edward of Prussia had introduced items such as sugar, potatoes, and rice into the German diet.[10]

Medieval Poland's cuisine was shared through translations of two cookery books by Maria Dembinska, who found similarities in spices and ingredients between German and Polish food.[11] Polish beer soup was one example. It contained beer, egg yolks, and cheese. Soup made from cheese, eggs, and pepper was routinely served in German monasteries through the Middle Ages.

Meats were favored in the order of beef, pork, and then poultry in Poland with little mention of game. Fish, however, was very popular, possibly because of its importance on fast days and Lent. Catholics were forbidden to eat meat on Wednesday and Friday during that time unless granted special permission, which usually came with a price attached to it.

Spices from Asia were plentiful through the Middle Ages and less expensive in Poland than in most of Europe.[12]

Commonly used soup ingredients included field peas, cabbage, parsley, lentils, grains, greens, and wine.[13] Leeks, carrots, celery and other cultivated vegetables became popular in 1518 when Italian and French cooks were brought to Poland.

In medieval Poland, millet was used, sometimes combined with field peas, to make a thick pottage which could be sopped up with bread and there was millet flour soup (*zacierki*), oat flour soup (*kucza*), barley flour soup, and turnip gruel.

A modern recipe for zacierki instructs the cook to mix 1 cup flour, 3 tablespoons parmesan cheese, and egg to make a dry dough which is grated and added to simmering soup.

15. Remaining European and Mediterranean

Ancient Swiss culinary skills were perhaps less refined than those of other countries, if 1885 newspaper articles are any indication. That year, Zurich was holding an exhibition of the culinary arts, and U.S. newspapers claimed the Swiss were in need of instruction, their diet consisting of thin soup, pale meat, and watery unseasoned vegetables.[1]

Switzerland is a good example of using what was most plentiful to create a cultural cuisine. The country's rich heritage of dairy products has been the basis of its diet since the country was established. The French culinarian Brillat-Savarin said Swiss fondue was created before the 19th century in an effort to use hardened cheese. The Swiss also pioneered the production of soup powder in bags and cubes through companies like Maggi and Knorr.

Soup played an important role in history when Zurich tried to persuade Strasbourg that the two cities should form an alliance in 1576. To prove the connection between the two, legend has it, a pot of hot gruel was placed on a ship going down the Limmat and Rhine rivers bound for Strasbourg. When it arrived the gruel was supposedly still hot.

Viking warriors founded settlements in various parts of Europe and North America, and no doubt took Scandinavian food customs into the lands they settled. For example, *svartsoppa*, or black soup, which contains goose blood (or, less traditionally, pig blood) as the main ingredient, is traditionally served at dinners on the eve of St. Martin (November 11) in memory of Martin of Tours. Legend has it that Martin, an impressed Roman soldier who objected to military service, and later a bishop, once hid in a goose house, was given away by the cackling of the geese, and then cooked one of the geese for his dinner as a sign of revenge — thus the use of goose blood in the soup, and the custom of serving the goose following the soup.

Norway is bordered by Sweden, Finland, and Russia. Archaeologists have documented people living there for 12,000 years. The 8th to 12th centuries are known as the Viking years, and during that time kingdoms were established in Iceland, Greenland, Ireland, and parts of Britain. A historian wrote, "Northmen or Normans, who inhabited Denmark, Norway, and Sweden, first laid waste and then settled in part of France, and afterward conquered England."[2]

An American traveler in 1860 described Norwegian *rodgrod*, or red porridge, which was customarily served alongside a plate of pickled fish and potatoes. The porridge was made from thin, sweetened water-arrowroot flavored with red wine or cherry juice. Cinnamon, almonds, and raisins were added to the soup before it was served.[3]

Norwegian cuisine into the late 19th century was characterized as only sufficient to keep body and soul together. Food was basic, not unlike that of Ireland — principally porridge, milk, fish, potatoes, bread, oatmeal soup, salted herring with sour milk, rye meal soup, salt beef and bacon with pea soup, dried meats, cheese, butter, and polonies (sausage) made of blood and barley.[4]

Various cultures have consumed the blood of fowl and animal through the centuries, and this practice has been somewhat controversial. Ancient Spartans routinely made black soup which was made from boiled pigs' blood, pork, and vinegar. Legend has it that an Italian once said he understood why the Spartan soldiers were readily willing to die after he tasted the black soup.

Does it seem possible to separate Italian food from rich tomato-based sauces and soups? Perhaps not, but the tomato didn't enter prominently into the Italian diet until the 17th century. The Indians in the mountains of Ecuador and Peru discovered them thousands of years ago and took plants with them into Central America, but it is unknown at what point they began to consume them.

Spain was consuming tomatoes, roasted or boiled into sauce and soup, by the year 1590 according to Gerard's *Herball.* Consumption of tomatoes throughout northern Africa, Egypt, Italy, Spain and other countries, where they were either boiled with vinegar, salt and pepper, and splashed with oil, sometimes with lemon juice or eaten raw with oil, vinegar, and pepper, was documented in 1710 by William Salmon. Accounts of tomatoes in soups and raw in salads were published throughout the 18th century in English.

Tomatoes were first introduced to Italy as an ornamental plant. The exact date of their introduction is unknown, but they were being grown by about 1540. Some accounts say they were thought poisonous and not eaten until sometime afterward, perhaps about 1575, while others classify the poison theory as legend only.

The first known version of tomato sauce printed in recipe form dates from 1692 in Naples. In England, Hannah Glasse included a tomato recipe in her *The Art of Cookery* in 1758. The Italians are credited with having cultivated the original tomato fruit, about the size of a modern cherry tomato.

Tomatoes were introduced into the diet of various other European cultures during the 18th century. England was slow in accepting the tomato, for the most part due to John Gerard's insistence that they were poisonous in his printed work of 1597.

It seems that the tomato, first discovered in the Americas, made its rounds through Europe before being consumed by colonists in the New World. In the United States, herbalist William Salmon wrote about tomatoes in 1710. By the mid–18th century they were being cultivated on Carolina plantations and probably in other areas as well. He described having seen them growing in the southeast part of Florida. (Between 1565 and 1700, Florida was colonized by the Spanish. Forts and missions were established among native people and soon reached across north Florida as far north as the area now designated as South Carolina, therefore much of the area Salmon called Florida was actually part of the Carolinas.)

Thomas Jefferson grew tomatoes, and helped educate citizens regarding their culinary uses. Many believe them to have been used in Philadelphia by a French refugee from Santo Domingo in 1789 and in Salem, Massachusetts, in 1802, by an Italian painter. They were reportedly being eaten in New Orleans by 1812, probably due to the French and Spanish influence on cuisine.

In 1906, William T. Davis, then over 80 years old, described his youth in Plymouth, Massachusetts, saying that in 1831 his mother was given tomato seeds for her garden. They bore luscious fruit which was at first considered ornamental, but within a few short years rivaled the potato in culinary importance. He called the tomato "the most remarkable change in our gardens."

A conundrum appearing in an 1857 newspaper shows a rise in popularity in tomatoes. "Why is a man with corns and tight boots like a certain garden vegetable when boiling? Because it's a toe-martyr in a stew!"

Clifford Wright credits the cabbage as the foundation of the Italian diet with cabbage soup at the heart of medieval Mediterranean cuisine. Leeks and onions also found their way into the gardens and soup pots. Early cabbage was a loose-leaf green which later evolved into the headed varieties we know today.

For centuries, soup has been at the heart of Mediterranean cuisine, even for breakfast.

Popular Spanish soups included *sopa de gallina* (chicken soup), *sopa de verdure* (vegetable soup), *sopa de familia* (family soup), and *guisado con chile* (stew with green chili peppers), which was quite hot.[5]

Portuguese *sopa secca* was typical of the "dry" soups found in various cultures. It was made of wheat bread, beef, cabbage and mint, and is considered almost the national dish of Portugal.[6]

Cooking techniques in medieval Italy were essentially the same as those in other parts of Europe. Food was stewed in a cauldron hung from a hook or roasted on hooks suspended from tripods.

Aelfric's instruction of Latin through a series of dialogues about various occupations has the cook commenting, "If you expel me from your company you'll chew your cabbage green ... nor can you have fat broth without my art." This shows the importance of the use of soups and broths.

Because soup was inexpensive to make and could be made from anything on hand, Anglo-Saxon monasteries served two dishes of soup daily, with peppered broths being classified as dishes of delicacies.[7]

Soups usually contained cabbage along with herbs, game, chicken, salt pork, grain, or turnips.

Pumpkin or winter squash soup containing onion, verjuice, parmesan cheese, egg yolks, and spices, red chickpea soup, soup of fresh fava beans with herbs, meat ravioli in broth, and soup made from eggs, cheese and breadcrumbs with meat broth and saffron are typical of the recipes recorded by Maestro Martino. He also used Swiss chard, borage, parsley, and mint to make herb soup. (See Redon for translated recipes.)

Ravioli and other pasta dishes were being served by about 1284.

Since most of the recipes from the medieval era do not specify how much liquid to add, it is often difficult to tell whether a recipe was intended to be a wet soup or a drier soup which could, in theory, be described as a meat or vegetable dish. In these cases it is left to the cook's discretion which he or she prefers.

Only the wealthy and nobility consumed anything like the feasts popular with many living history organizations today.

Some soups and dishes such as ratatouille were not created in Italy until the tomato was firmly established as a culinary ingredient. The French *touiller* meaning "to stir" forms the basis of the word *ratatouille*, and *rata* was a French soldier's slang term for a rough chunky stew. Its main ingredient is tomatoes with various other vegetables added to taste.

In 1875, Bayard Taylor toured the Bible lands and wrote that the poor used pieces of broken bread to form spoons to eat mouthfuls of thick soup, always with the right hand, and when the bread became too saturated to be of service it was eaten and another piece obtained.

Pillau, or *pilaf*, as it is called today, which has been a Persian and Turkish favorite for centuries, might be categorized as soup given the nature of the ingredients being cooked together to stretch the meat. Recipes date from as early as 1634: "A dish of Pelo, which is rice boyled with Hens, Mutton, Butter, Almonds, and Turmerack."[8] It was initially made of rice and mutton fat, and sometimes mutton meat, chicken, peas, or saffron were added.

In 1873, pillau was defined as "a favorite dish of the South," by a Miss Beecher. She defined pilaf as a "Turkish stew." In America, chicken and rice has been a standard southern dish for perhaps 300 years, probably because rice was the prime cash crop in some southern states, primarily South Carolina, Louisiana, and Florida.

It is sometimes prepared thick enough to eat with a fork, and is sometimes a soup to be eaten with a spoon. Depending on the region in which it is served, it can be spelled or pronounced any number of ways. Many countries had a version of it, and here pronunciation is primarily a hold-over of language patterns of the nationalities that settled different regions of the United States. Floridians enjoy *pur-LOO* while South Carolinians most likely partake of *pur-LOW* and other Southerners are content with *PEE-Laf*.

In 1832, Mrs. N. M. K. Lee's *The Cook's Own Book* instructed making pillau by boiling 2 pounds rice with a little water, half a pound of butter, salt, pepper, cloves, and mace in a covered saucepan, then combining that with two boiled fowls cooked with a half pound of bacon. The dish was garnished with fried onions and boiled eggs.

Yet another spelling was penned by Taylor in 1874: "...basins of soup, pilao in huge bowls, big sheets of bread, and numberless dishes of food..." were served on his visit through central Asia.[9]

Turkish cuisine improved greatly during the height of the Ottoman influence (1453–1909). The Hittites, Seljuks, Persians, Greeks, and Romans have all ruled the area at one time or another, and Turkey has both Asian and European contact. Its geographic location was at the heart of the spice routes, giving cooks access to the freshest spices, grains, and produce, all of which were used extensively in traditional soups. Turkey is bordered by several countries, each of which influenced its food.

Traditional *tarhana* soup, made from spices, vegetables, and fermented dough, is said to have become popular during this era. Other traditional soups are *yayla chorbasi* (chicken broth with rice, yogurt, and mint), and wedding soup (lamb in egg broth).

The history of Syria dates to approximately 1800 B.C., when King Shamshi-Adad I established a capital near what is today Tell Leilan in northeast Syria. For many centuries conflict plagued the area until it melded with the Ottoman Empire in 1516, and its food then evolved similarly to that of the Turks through common vegetables and grains. Muslims are subject to Islamic dietary rules which forbid consumption of pork, but lamb is commonly eaten.

Saul of Tarsus' conversion on the road to Damascus is a significant part of history along with the creation of the Christian Church at Antioch. The area has a long history of warfare and involvement in the Crusades.

Its cuisine was influenced by many cultures, including Mediterranean, Greek, Middle Eastern, Turkish and French.

Lentils were produced in all parts of the area and were made into soup flavored with onion, the favorite of hardworking men. Lentils were unearthed near the Euphrates River and estimated to be approximately 10,000 years old. They were also found in third century B.C. tombs near Thebes. Spicy red lentil soup and bean stew are traditional Syrian soups.

When traveling through Greece and Russia, Taylor gave a recipe for *potage aux voyageurs* with which he was especially pleased. Two fowls were boiled for the broth, a sufficient quantity of vermicelli added and, when nearly cooked, four egg yolks beaten with a gill (4 ounces) of water were stirred in, followed by the juice of half a lemon.

He found *shchi* or *shchee*, Russian cabbage soup, worth mentioning, which isn't surprising given it has been made since man first began to combine ingredients into a stew pot. Food historians trace its ancestry back at least a thousand years, and it was so basic to Russian culture it knew no class boundaries, being consumed equally by rich and poor alike.[10]

Russia's native cuisine is credited to the Mongols or Tatars during the 13th century (the Mongol invasion lasted from 1223 to 1236). By the time of Catherine the Great, affluent households imported ingredients and cooks to prepare them, resulting in an improvement in the traditional dishes. Basic ingredients include fish, poultry, game, mushrooms, berries, and honey.

The Russian diet has always been one rich in soups, many of which were created in the medieval era and vastly improved during the 18th and 19th centuries. Traditional Russian soups include *botvinia*, iced soup of cucumbers and fish, sorrel, onions, spinach, horseradish, and lemon juice; *ukha* which came to be known as fish broth around the 17th century; *rassolink*, created during the 19th century, but named for the practice of making soup from pickle liquid during the 15th century (made from vegetables or from veal or beef kidneys or chicken giblets whitened with sour cream); and noodle soup made from chicken, mushroom, or milk adapted from the Tatars.

Debow's Review noted,

> The food of the [Russian] peasant is rye bread, his chief sustenance sour cabbage soup, salted cucumbers, eggs, salt-fish, bacon, lard, mushrooms, and onions. His favorite dish is a mixture of meat and rye flour seasoned with onions and garlic. Of meat he eats but little. His common drink is quas, a fermented liquor made by pouring boiling water on rye or barley.[11]

An 1885 article on Italian trattoria in New York spoke pleasingly of the décor of the café as well as the inexpensive but appreciated fare.

> *Antipasti* sounds grander than hors d'oeuvre ... *zuppa* is a strange yet pleasant rendering of soup; *pesco* of course means fish; *bollito* and *fritti*, boiled and fried dishes respectively, are comprehensive enough; but what a charming, strange, musical word is *intingoli*, which corresponds entrees? It sounds not unlike an Arabic word, and there seems to be a quaint metallic ring to the syllable. *Arrosto* means roast, of course, and *insalata* is evidently salad; but is there not something peculiarly pleasing in the name *verdusi* for vegetables? Does not *dulei* (sweets) suggest that it is almost time for the *dolco far niente*, when you have got so far in the bill of fare? And don't you almost hesitate to engage any of the delicious cheeses which look so formidable under the name of *formogge*? ... On my visit I had the following: *Morue à la hollandaise*, which is codfish with butter and boiled potatoes; then breast of veal stuffed, with spinach and tomato sauce; Parmesan cheese, bread, and a pint of very fair claret for the total of thirty-five cents.[12]

In 1877, Caleb Cushing wrote to Secretary of State William M. Evarts, describing the crops of Spain. He included apples, pears, peaches, grapes, maize, wheat and cereal grains, oranges, sweet pepper, lemons, figs, rice, carobs, sugar, potatoes, beans, garbanzos, and olives. Domesticated animals were basically the same as those in the United States, but the Spanish were as likely to drink milk from goats, sheep, or asses as cows. Cushing's letter described the food of all classes:

> The lower classes [in Spain] live on poor food, rarely eating meat; but laborers on the farms fare better. The common food of the latter is bread, soup, garlic, bacon, and garbanzos (Spanish beans), together with wine and oil. The middle and higher classes have chocolate for breakfast, and eat beef, mutton, and pork, accompanied by cabbage, garbanzos, onions and *chichoros* (large peas). A favorite dish is *olla* or *cocido*; and the sausages (chorizos) of Castile are esteemed great delicacies out of Spain.[13]

Cocido was "meat stewed to rags after removing the broth (*caldo*), with vegetables and rice" (perhaps a boiled pottage of chickpeas or beans with salt pork, meat, or sausage).[14]

Spain was invaded and settled by various cultures throughout the Middle Ages, thus its food was influenced by the Basques, Arab cultures, Greeks, Romans, German Visigoths, Jews, Celts, Moors, and so on. Potatoes, tomatoes, peppers, and beans were introduced through Spain to other parts of Europe. The Spanish diet differs from one region to another. Early ingredients included cabbage, mushrooms, ham, onions, artichokes, legumes, and garlic. Fish and seafood is abundant.

Olla podrido (stew of bacon, ham, meats, fowl, and vegetables), paella, fish and lamb stew, chickpea stew, and vegetable stews have been popular soups for many years.

The word *olla* refers to a kind of prepared food as well as the earthen vessel in which it was prepared. It was common in Andalusia under that name while in other parts of Spain it was called *puchero* and "made from dry beef, garbanzas, and sausage."[15]

Purists thought *olla podrida* must be made in an earthen vessel, or two, actually. Ford wrote, garbanzos were soaked overnight and put into a pot with a piece of beef, a chicken, and a large piece of bacon. That was brought quickly to boil, then simmered for four to five hours. In another pot, vegetables (lettuce, cabbage, a slice of gourd, carrots, beans, celery, endive, onions, garlic, and long pepper) were brought to boil in water with chorizo and a pork face (cheek). When served, the meat and vegetables were put into a serving dish and the broth poured over.

Romania claims the oldest human remains in Europe, some 42,000 years old, found in the "Cave with Bones." First called Dacia, the area was settled as early as the 2nd century B.C. Herodotus left one of the first written accounts of the area in 513 B.C. Romania was heavily settled by the Romans who sought to unearth its rich deposits of silver and gold. It has since been ruled by a host of cultures.

In the Middle Ages, Romanians lived in three provinces, Transylvania, Wallachia, and Moldavia. Its most well known ruler is Vlad the Impaler, who was the inspiration for Bram Stoker's vampire, Count Dracula. In the first chapter of Stoker's book, the character spoke of porridge of maize flour. *Ciorbă de burtă* is a Romanian soup made of tripe, and *borsh* is also common.

Pasta was a medieval Italian staple, and the pasta dishes such as ravioli and lasagna were often considered pottages even though they were served almost dry. Gnocchi dates to the medieval era, when they were made of flour, cheese, eggs, and salt. Potato wasn't used in making them until much later.

In 1850, Leigh Hunt wrote of macaroni in Italian markets, saying it was yellow in color, and even deeper in color when dyed with saffron, as was common with the Genoese. Hunt referred to *minestra* as soup made from macaroni, sometimes with meat, oil or butter added, and always cheese.

The Persian Empire, now better known as Persia or Iran, has at its heart a cuisine which relied heavily on spinach, citrus, saffron, and pomegranate. Its proximity to the trade routes brought spices and other foods easily within reach. The country converted to Islam after it was invaded by the Arabs in the 7th century at which time the use of wine passed out of favor in keeping with Islamic dietary rules.

Persian soups include *eshkeneh* (onion soup) and three basic types—an economical and commonly served soup made from lamb stock and beans, sometimes containing also grains and fruits or juices; a vegetable-based soup which usually contains some combination of rice, grain, spinach, peas, and lentils seasoned with lemon juice; and a thin soup most often served as a first course.

The area of Libya has been ruled by a succession of peoples including the Phoenecians, Carthagians, Greeks, Romans, Vandals, and Byzantines. It was inhabited as early as the 8th millennium B.C., and archaeologists have uncovered a great deal of evidence to show the residents were highly productive. It became part of the Ottoman Empire in 1551 and remained so until 1911 when it was seized by Italy. Its cuisine then gained an Italian influence combined with that of the greater Mediterranean and Northern Africa. Pork is not eaten.

A thick soup of lamb broth, vegetables, spices, and grain is a national dish and known simply as Libyan soup. *Sharba* is a Libyan spicy soup of lamb, onion, tomato, lemon, orzo, salt, red pepper, and cinnamon.

Because of Austria's location and complex political history, Austrian foods were heavily influenced in early years by many cultures, including Turkish, French, Alsatian, Swiss, Spanish, Dutch, Italian, German, Bohemian, Hungarian, Polish, Croatian, Slovenian, Slovakian, Serbian, and Jewish. Austrian *suppes* include *fiaker goulash* (similar to chili or Hungarian *gulyas*), and *Rindsuppe* (beef soup).

Albania is in southern Europe, bordered by Greece, Montenegro, Kosovo, Macedonia, and the Adriatic and Ionian Seas. It suffered violence at different times from the Greeks, Romans, Byzantines, Venetians, and Ottomans, each of whom influenced its food and culture.

Albania has been ruled by the Romans, Greeks, and Turks, each leaving an indelible fingerprint on the cuisine. *Supë borsh me patate e lakër* is Albanian potato and cabbage soup. *Tarator* is made from yoghurt, garlic, cucumbers, walnuts, dill, oil, and water. Lemon and bean soups are also traditional favorites.

Portugal sits on the westernmost part of mainland Europe, bordered by the Atlantic Ocean and Spain. Its location on the Iberian Peninsula left it vulnerable to attack, but inland it has been settled since prehistoric times and its culture is as rich as its cuisine.

The Romans referred to the whole of the peninsula, now Spain and Portugal, as Hispania, and the Greeks referred to it as Iberia. Its name derives from *span* (rabbit), meaning "the land of rabbits."

The earliest settlers were the Celts, and Portugal's history as an established country began in 1128. Economic prosperity came in 1498 with the discovery of a route to India. Portuguese traders brought spices such as pepper, ginger, curry, saffron and paprika to Europe along with tea and rice from the Orient, coffee from Africa, and peppers, tomatoes, and potatoes from the New World.

Fish, shellfish, meat, olive oil, tomato, and spices are the heart of Portuguese cuisine, and it is rich in hearty soups, chowders, and stews. *Caldo verde* (green broth) is made from a type of kale thickened with potato and flavored with chorizo sausage; *canja de galinha* is chicken broth, *caldeirada de lulas à madeirense* is squid or seafood stew flavored with curry and ginger, and *acorda* is a dry soup of vegetables, seafood, and bread.

16. Asia

Of the wide array of foodstuffs available in ancient China, the most plentiful were grains and game. *The Book of Songs*, an ancient book of poetry, mentions clearing away grass and trees so crops can be planted, "many sorts of grain," mulberry trees, hunting fields, peaches, jujube, pears, a reference to earlier times with four dishes per meal, millet, wine, rice, and baking and boiling. Various farm animals were mentioned.

Volume 3 of *The Chinese Recorder and Missionary Journal*, (published in 1871 in Foochow [Fuzhou]) elaborates on beef, mutton, pork, canine flesh, duck and fish. A translation of ancient writings, it is quite informative. It gives the original writing alongside the translated English and lists the following as used in the diet of the ancients: guinea corn, plums, peaches, apricots, jujube, pears, apples, oranges, wild berries, lemon, a citrus with finger-like projections (today called Buddha's hand), various kinds of rice, yellow beans, black beans, and soja beans with bean curd, said to be of primary importance in the Chinese diet.

In 1830, a visitor wrote of the extravagant number of dishes served at meals and stated stews were the most common. Along with dried fruit and poultry, rats were offered in the markets, as were eggs, fish, and snails. It was said that the lower classes ate mostly rice with a trifling addition of fish and vegetables.[1]

In the absence of actual recipes for the soups and stews, it is necessary to study the available foodstuffs to understand what went into them.

Shiu Wong Chan wrote that Chinese cooking was invented by the Emperor Pow Hay Se in the year 3000 B.C. She thought Confucius was responsible for the practice of cutting food into small pieces before cooking, a practice that endures today.

Asian cuisine wasn't particularly known to the Western world until the mid–1800's when Chinese emigrants settled in San Francisco while building railroads.

Through the 19th century some Americans looked upon Asian foods with suspicion and considered them unfit for consumption. Stories abounded of Chinese dishes containing rat, cat, and dog, and the concept was sensationalized in print as first one paper then another printed the accounts.

In 1848, prolific food writer Samuel Williams noted that the art of cooking had not reached any high degree of perfection among the Chinese. He claimed that Chinese food consisted mainly of stews of various sorts, "in which garlic and grease are more abundant than pepper and salt."

Foods he listed included king crab, cuttlefish, sharks, rays, gobies, tortoise, turtle, crabs, prawns, crawfish, shrimp, fresh and saltwater fish, oysters, clams, grasshoppers, water snakes, rice, millet, wheat, oats, buckwheat, beans, peas, cabbage, colworts, broccoli, kale, cauliflower, cress, lettuce, sow thistle, spinach, celery, dandelion, succor, sweet basil, ginger, mustard,

Food vendors, Canton, China. Stereo card ca. 1919. Soups and stews were the bulk of the Asian diet.
Library of Congress, Prints and Photographs Division, Reproduction Number LC-USZ62-49135.

radishes, artemissa, amaranthus, tacca, pigweed, purslane, shepherd's purse, clover, garlic, leeks, scallions, chives, carrots, gourds, squashes, cucumbers, watermelons, tomatoes, turnips, brinjal (eggplant), pumpkin, water chestnuts, taro, sweet potatoes, and a wide array of fruits, citrus, and nuts. He stated that, next to pork, poultry was the most common meat.

Williams asked a native man about the preparation of *lau-shu tang*, or rat soup, and was told he had never seen it. Williams concluded, "Rats and mice are no doubt eaten now and then, and so are many undesirable things by those whom want compels to take what they can get, but to put these and other strange eatables in the front of the list, gives a distorted idea of the everyday food of the people." He also stated, "There is a wider difference, perhaps, between the rich and poor of China than in any other country."

An officer on the U.S. ship *Vincennes* attended a banquet of some 23 courses at Canton, and according to newspapers, found the first dish of bird's nest soup so unacceptable he refused to taste any of the other dishes.[2]

> Frequently have we seen the coolies skinning a newly caught rat, trussing it on sticks like a squirrel, and hanging it up to dry, with a sprinkle of salt for the winter's store, while they prepare the skin to line and warm their jackets; and often have we observed a plump and comely cur borne in a wicker coop on the end of a pole, counterpoised at the other end by a couple of corpulent cats, whilst around the throat of the pedlar, coiled a sleek but harmless snake, all of which he was ready to sell or gamble away, as materials for a wholesome soup.[3]

In 1874, a banquet of Chinese specialty dishes was prepared for the eminent men of San Francisco to celebrate the opening of a theater. Only one man tasted every dish. The others squeamishly picked at some of the dishes and refused others.

Bird's nests were gathered by men dangling off the cliffs from ropes in China before the birds had a chance to soil them. They were boiled to make soup, and in San Francisco brought $40 to $60 per pound. *Bah kop* was made from chopped pigeon meat with green onions and peas in the pod. *Moo goo* was made from bamboo sprouts, ham, Chinese water nuts and mushrooms. *San suey* was a stew of Chinese soft-shell terrapin. *Yee chee* was stew made from pike, fungus, eggs, and ham. A stew made from boned chicken and chestnuts was called *Lut chee-kee*.[4]

> This viand is not merely an artificial name for a dish, like the French "*pommes de terre en chemise*," or the fish "*en matelot*," but a genuine soup made of the gelatinous substance with which certain water-fowl of the Javan and Chinese seas construct their nests on the Islands. As it is precious from its extreme rarity and the danger with which it is obtained by hardy adventurers among the rocks and cliffs, it is of course to be found only on the tables of the rich, to whom it is sold at from twenty to thirty dollars a pound, according to its purity.
>
> We were skeptical upon the subject of this food as the most incredulous of our readers, until we visited the shops where the nutritive matter is separated from the rubbish of the nest; and when cooked, we found it to be a luscious compound, which, eaten in faith, may be pronounced equal to the most delicate broth that was ever seasoned for the palate of a valetudinarian.[5]

Birds' nests were consumed in 19th-century Cambodia as well, and in Canton were said to bring twice their weight in silver.

> These birds often build in rocks; these are rocks hollow within and pierced with a great number of openings, some large enough for a man to enter with ease, others very difficult to access. To the walls of these caverns the birds affix their nests in rows very close to each other. They prepare these nests from the remains of their food, which consists of all sorts of insects, and they are two months in making them. To procure the nests is a difficult and hazardous business. The men, whose employment it is, make ladders of reeds and bamboos, by which they climb up to the holes and pull out the nests, which they sell at a very great price.... About two hundred and fifty thousand pounds weight are brought to Canton itself every year, and the best are sent to the Capital for the use of the Celestial Court.[6]

The nests were made by swallows and were found in Borneo and throughout the East Indies. The nest was cleaned and boiled with pigeon eggs, spice, and "other ingredients." The soup thickened when it cooled due to the gelatin-like properties of the nests.

Shark fins were much in demand in China for making soup, with 10,000 to 15,000 hundredweight exported annually from various parts of India. It was reported that 40,000 sharks were killed annually off Kurachee, near Bombay, for their back fins, which was the only part of the animal harvested. Today, the number of sharks killed annually to make shark fin soup has risen to some 73 million.

One has to wonder how difficult it was in previous centuries to obtain Asian vegetables in the United States for authentic dishes such as *fu kwa*, today known as bitter melon, which was used in pork soup, or *chit kwa*, which used another member of the squash family in soup.

> A bowl of fish soup isn't worth more than a few cents; Yet, made as in the days of the former capital, it brings smiles to the imperial face. So people come in droves to buy it at twice the price; In part, they are buying the imperial gesture, and in part they buy the soup.[7]

The passage above attests to the importance of soup in Chinese culture. Perhaps this is indicative of the difference between the fine soups of the fortunate, such as shark-fin and bird's nest, as compared to the watered-down versions found in the peasant household.

In 1867, soup offerings in Chinatown (New York) included sponge squash soup (*sue kwa kiang*), mushroom soup (*tso you kiang*), beach de mare soup (*hoy shum kiang*), balsam pear and pork soup (*too kwar kiang*), and dried oyster soup (*ho she kiang*). In second-class restaurants, a bowl of soup was furnished with dishes at no additional charge, variety not specified.[8]

In 1891, John Ross included in the foods of ancient Korea rice, beef, pork, mutton only rarely, fish, boar, venison, pheasant, ptarmigan, partridge, fowls, ducks, geese, pulse, French beans, turnips, cabbage, radish, spinach, garlic, onion, wheat, barley, buckwheat, and millet.

Sei Shonagon (born c. 966), an author and a great court lady, wrote on the eating habits of Japanese carpenters, saying, "The moment the food was brought, they fell on the soup bowls and gulped down the contents."[9]

We do not know the ingredients in the soup she noted, but if an article in the *Brooklyn Eagle* on June 19, 1868 is any indication, they might have been quite exotic: "The natives of Japan refuse beef and milk, but eat rats with avidity."

Japanese miso soup was a favorite of samurai warriors about 750 years ago. It remains popular and is often served at breakfast.

President U. S. Grant ate soup of carp, mushrooms, and aromatic shrub in Japan.[10] This may have been *chawan*, a thin watered fish soup with seaweed and mushrooms.[11]

In August 1869, *Harper's* published a bill of fare for a dinner given in Japan by Prince Satsuma, Kagosima in July 1866. The dinner lasted five hours and consisted of 40 courses. The soups included one of mushroom, green vegetable, and fish, one of seaweed and vegetables, one of lobster and mushrooms, one of loochoo pork fat and vegetables, another of wild-boar and bamboo shoots, one of fish and seaweed, one of white berries and sprats, one of acorns, another of fowl and fruit, one of fish and roe with ginger leaves, one of vermicelli with soy and red berries, and finally three thick soups with unspecified contents.

Spring chicken soup with mushrooms, seaweed soup, and Chinese white vegetable soup were included in *The Chinese-Japanese Cookbook*, published in 1914 in New York. This book was published to encourage the preparation of these foods in the American kitchen.

PART TWO : THE NEW WORLD

17. American Indian

European cuisine wasn't the only one undergoing a slow evolution. The Americans[1] combined indigenous ingredients into pottages for the reasons of economy and ease of preparation in the same way as other cultures.

South American soup was somewhat of an evolution from pre–Columbian and European influences. It was sometimes hot and heavily spiced, typically consisting of hot peppers, water, herbs, and game meat. This soup is referred to as pepper pot in Guiana. Types included Colombian *ajiaco* (traditional chicken soup) or *sancochos* (stew), Brazilian *cozido* (meat and vegetable stew), Venezuelan *hervidos*, Argentinian or Paraguayan *puchero* ("*Puchero* is to Mexican cooking what the *pot-au-feu* is to French"), Peruvian *chupe de camarones* (shrimp chowder), Chilean *chupe de porotos* (bean chowder), or the Suriname national dish, pea soup with sausages and potato.[2]

Brazilian *mingau* was a soup made from tapioca and bananas that was traditionally served as a first meal of the day.[3] A similar soup was described in 1805 in the West Indies: "a kind of claret-colored soup seasoned with bananas, Seville oranges, salt and pepper, enriched with many yards of pork and interspersed with chicken-bones from which the meat had probably dissolved in boiling."[4]

Tambos (inns) served soup made from beans, potatoes, and the like. Stores of *charqui* (jerky made from fresh or salted beef, horse, or in earlier days llama) which benefited from slow simmering to render it tender were used to make soups, stews, or ragout.[5]

In 1850, when a group of American travelers put meat, onions, and pepper into a pot to make soup only to discover after an appropriate cooking time that the meat remained raw, a miner explained that in mountainous altitudes water begins to boil long before it reaches 212 degrees Fahrenheit, and cannot get hotter than the temperature at which it reaches the boiling point, except as steam.[6]

The North American diet shared similarities with that of South America in the type of pots used and favored ingredients.

In order to understand what Indians cultivated and collected from the earth, and how they prepared it, one must study the multitude of lengthy books by early explorers and naturalists who wrote of the culture of the natives. A study of tribes in multiple regions of the country turns up specific instances of wild foods used in particular locations, however, the basic elements of diet varied little from tribe to tribe. For example, tribes who lived where sugar maples grew utilized the sap as a sweetener while others may have used honey locust[7] (not to be confused with honey, which didn't come into use until bees were introduced by the Europeans) or something similar.[8]

Cultivated crops were fairly standard, though the eras when they became common and

Florida Indians planting seeds of beans or maize which, combined with squash, made the "Three Sisters," standard Indian fare for the soup kettle. Timucuan men cultivate the field and women plant the seeds. Engraving, Theodor de Bry, 1591. Library of Congress, Prints and Photographs Division, Reproduction Number LC-USZ62-31869.

the extent to which tribes grew them varied. The techniques and types grown changed after the people were sent to the reservations.[9] One of the oldest combinations of cultivated vegetables was corn, beans, and squash, known as the Three Sisters. An 18th-century author wrote, "They likewise plant a Bean in the Same Hill with the Corn, upon whose stalk it sustains itself."[10]

One major difference in diet was that while some Indians (including Cheyenne, Sioux, and Arapaho) ate dog and other small animals such as skunks, others did not.[11]

In 1698, Edward Ward listed the major portion of the New England Indian diet as fish, fowl, wildcat, raccoon, deer, oysters, lobsters, lampreys, moose tongues, broth thickened with pulverized hardboiled eggs, Indian corn and kidney beans, "Earth-nuts," chestnuts, lily roots, pumpkins, melons, and berries. Along with porridge, which was much esteemed, these foods were adopted by white settlers very quickly.

William Bartram wrote in 1789 that the Cherokee and Creek did not eat horse, dog, cat, "or any such creatures as are rejected by white people," and in addition to wild game they did have domestic poultry, cows, goats, and pigs.[12]

In 1775, Bernard Romans wrote of the Creek, saying they ate the previously listed game and foodstuffs, as well as acorns. He also said that the women did the gardening while the men hunted or fished, and added a few specifics. "They dry the tongues of their venison; they make a salt out of a kind of moss found at the bottom of creeks and rivers." He mentioned may apple [maypop] and corned venison, saying, "They have naturally the greatest plenty imagineable."[13]

Bartram claimed the Creek (Alabama) did not eat Irish potatoes though they did eat sweet potatoes and smilax. He said they did not use plows to plant grains, had no knowledge of salads, and planted rice in hills which he claimed seemed to produce better than that cultivated in water in the Carolinas.[14]

Pickett quoted references to native foods dating from the 1500s which were echoed by writers throughout the 18th and 19th century.

> [In] 1540 — The productions of the country were abundant. Peas, beans, squashes, pumpkins and corn grew as if by magic. Persimons, formed into large cakes, were eaten in winter, together with walnut and bear's oil. A small pumpkin, when roasted in the embers, was delightful, and resembled, in taste, boiled chestnuts. Corn was pounded in mortars, but Narvaez [1528] saw stones for grinding it upon the Florida coast.[15]

Not much changed over the next 140 years. H.S. Caswell wrote, "In 1647 the Confederacy of the Six Nations of the Long House ... their food was the flesh of wild animals, [including buffalo, bear, deer and elk] the corn, and beans, and squashes raised by the women."[16]

There seems to have been little difference in the diet of the native Creek and Alibamon and the French marines who occupied Fort Toulouse (near modern Wetumpka, Alabama) within their midst. Narratives list an abundance of game and fish including bear, deer, rabbit, turkey, partridges, and pigeons, and "rich lands that produced without cultivation." There are references to the marines in the Louisiana territory seeking food from the Indians in times of shortage, and of living off fish and oysters from the sea.[17]

The Indians apparently had little appreciation of the indulgences of the French, however. An Indian once imagined himself poisoned after tasting prepared mustard he'd seen the marines putting on the roast turkey they were consuming.

Swanton listed 13 feasts observed by the Indians of the lower Mississippi Valley which represented their primary food sources: the first moon was deer, second strawberries, third little corn, fourth watermelons, fifth peaches, sixth (August) mulberries, seventh maize, eighth turkeys, ninth bison, tenth bears, eleventh cold meat (January), twelfth chestnuts, and last, nuts.[18]

Lafitau's 1724 account of the eating customs of the Huron was referenced by many later historians. In times of plenty, they ate meat as fresh as possible, and in times of scarcity, they were thankful for even tainted meat. He noted that in order not to waste even a small amount they never skimmed the soup cauldron as did virtually all whites.

> They cook frogs whole ... dry the intestines of deer without cleaning them ... they have not abandoned the acorn ... gather beech-nuts with care and crush them. They eat potatoes with pleasure, various insipid roots, and all sorts of wild and bitter fruits.[19]

Many wild tuberous roots such as the *pomme blanche*, also known as breadroot, were dried, pounded, and put into soup. The root vegetables Kalm observed Indians and some Swedes eating, which he compared to potatoes, included the following, which were documented in multiple sources. Some varieties may be listed as endangered today, and great caution should be exercised by inexperienced gatherers so as not to confuse them with poisonous species.

Gray referred to some members of the *Arum genus* as Indian turnip, and Kalm mentioned the Indians' reaction when they saw the Swedes' turnips (rutabagas) for the first time.

> Indian turnip (*Arisaema triphyllum, Cammasia Esculenta*) is also known by the names wake robin, jack-in-the-pulpit, prairie turnip, breadroot, teepsinna,[20] and dragonroot. It produces violent inflammation of the mouth and salivary glands if not

boiled or dried before consumption. The plant produces red berries on a single stem, and the root, the part consumed, is bulbous, resembling a turnip.[21]

A woman who went out in the morning could, by around 2 P.M., dig enough with her stick to produce half a bushel of "hulled" roots. This labor was exclusively that of women and children.[22]

The Indian turnip measured up to 20 inches in circumference. It was called *pomme blanche* and *pomme des prairies* by the French. Several sources indicate there was another variety of this plant which was poisonous, and it was often compared to the mushroom, of which there are edible and nonedible varieties.[23] Audubon claimed bears were fond of it, which might have complicated gathering it.[24] A book about Minnesota said,

> When this root [Indian turnip] is chopped up, dried, and beaten, the Sauteaux make a soup of it, which, when mixed with a little meat, becomes very nourishing; and thus, the food which would scarcely have sufficed a single day, is made to last several days. There is also a wild onion, of which they make much use. The ginger which grows in the woods, is employed as pepper in their repasts. In the spring, they find a kind of root, the shape of which resembles a ligne, vulgarly called a rat's tail. It is very abundant, of a good flavor, and very nutritive. Another root, named *ashkibwah*—that which is eaten raw—is very abundant, and contains much nutritive substance.[25]

Hopniss or Hapniss, which Dr. Linne called *Glycine apios*, is the *Apios Americana*, commonly called groundnut. It grows throughout the southeastern United States, mainly in light woodland areas. The roasted roots are similar to sweet potatoes and can be dried to add to soups. The seeds were prepared like beans, as Kalm reported seeing the Indians do.[26]

Sagittaria was called *katniss* by the Indians and Swedes, and still bears that common name. It is also called arrowhead and duck potato. An aquatic plant, it has been harvested in North America and Asia for its tubers since ancient times.[27] Kalm compared it to the variety Pehr Osbeck described in his *Voyage to China* (1771).[28]

Arum virginicum (Taw-ho/Taw-him/Tuckah/Tuckahoe) This is a pond or bog plant that requires thorough cooking and/or drying to be edible. Kalm wrote that the Indians were aware of this and never ate them raw. Doing so produced intense burning of the stomach, throat, and tongue, but cooking rendered them quite palatable. When dried, the tubers were used to make bread and soup. The seeds and berries were also consumed after cooking.[29]

Orontium aquaticum (Golden Club/taw-kee) Like other Arums, it contains calcium oxylate, which produces intense burning if eaten raw. It requires thorough cooking or drying to be edible. The roots can be dried, powdered, and used when making bread or thickening soups. It was found throughout eastern North America, from Massachusetts to Kentucky and south to Louisiana and Florida in sandy or peaty shores and shallow water. When properly prepared, the seeds are edible and were eaten by the Indians in Kalm's day.[30]

Kalm said the natives originally made spoons and trowels of laurel wood, and bowls of sassafras.[31]

Tripe de roche, or rock tripe, is a lichen which grows in rocky areas and was often used as food by Indians, soldiers, and explorers. George Washington's troops are said to have prepared this at Valley Forge.[32] A 19th-century writer observed, "With this, and a duck, a partridge, or a fish, one can make a succulent soup sufficient to nourish several men."[33]

Thomas Harriot was sent to describe the expedition of the first European settlers in present-day North Carolina by Sir Walter Raleigh. He wrote about the diet, customs, and lives of the Indians, leaving one of the first such records. He encountered the usual maize (hominy), venison and other wild game, and fish, and thought their diet a very healthy one. These ingredients often found their way into earthenware cauldrons in the form of soup and stew.

> Their woemen know how to make earthen vessels with special Cunninge and that so large and fine, that our potters with lhoye wheles can make noe better: and then Remove them from place to place as easelye as we can doe our brassen kettles. After they have set them on an heape of erthe to stay them..., they putt wood under which being kindled one of them taketh great care that the fyre burne equallye Rounde abowt. They or their woemen fill the vessel with water, and then putt they in fruite, flesh, and fish, and all boyle together like a galliemaufrye, which the Spaniarde call, *olla podrida*. Then they putte yt out into disches, and sett before the companye, and then they make good cheere together. Yet are they moderate in their habit wher by they avoide sicknes. I would to god wee would followe their exemple. For wee should bee free from many kynes of diseasyes which wee fall into by sumptuous and unseasonable bankett, continuallye deuisinge new sawces, and provocation of gluttonnye to satisfie our unsatiable appetite.[34]

For most native cultures maize was the mainstay of the diet, and the term *corn* soon came to mean specifically maize rather than any grain as it had in Europe. In addition, numerous wild and cultivated plants are mentioned in early accounts, though not every one was found in every region. The following were documented before the 18th century; those in italics were documented during De Soto's expedition: *Beans, corn*, gourds, orache, peas, dock, *squash, pumpkin*, sunflower, angelica, blackberries, black gum berries, cherries, *chestnuts, chinquapin*, crabapple, gooseberries, Jerusalem artichoke, purslane, pennyroyal, sumac, spicebush, elderberry, dewberry, *grapes (both native muscadines and scuppernongs)*, groundnut, *hickory nuts*, honey locust, huckleberries, moss, *mulberries*, mushrooms, *acorns, persimmons, plums*, yellow pond lilies, dandelion, fern, plantain, marsh marigold, prickly pear, raspberries (Swanton thought these were blackberries), wild rice, seagrape, serviceberry, smilax, *strawberries*, sugar maples, wild sweet potato, *walnut*, cattail, cress, lambs'-quarter (pigweed), coneflower, ramps, poke, hazelnuts, cucumbers, cabbage, turnips, peaches, melons, wild *onions*, pinon nuts, cactus and yucca fruits.[35]

To that list, MacCauley added cabbage (sabal) palm for the Seminole of Florida.[36] The center bud of these palms is the part eaten, but harvesting it kills the tree. Getting to the heart is intensive labor. He also listed oranges, bananas, limes, lemons, guavas, pineapples, and coconuts.

Various nuts, usually hickory or walnuts, were pounded in mortars, formed into balls, and dried for storage. When nuts were put into soup, it was strained to remove the shells.

Through a process known as thermogenesis, skunk cabbage can generate enough heat to force itself up through ice and snow, thus it was often one of the first green shoots seen in the spring. Though the reticulate leaves are very astringent, many Indian tribes were able to consume them by boiling them in several changes of water.[37]

The contents of the pots changed somewhat with the introduction of the white man's vegetables and grains, and some tribes accepted these new foods quicker than others. Most sources agree the Cherokee were among the first to adopt new foods, pots, and agricultural practices.

Of the Cherokee, Drake said, "Their soil is excellent for corn, cotton, tobacco, wheat, oats, indigo, sweet and Irish potatoes."[38] Wood wrote that records of Cherokee farming practices dating from the 1740s documented their growing sweet potatoes and that by then the sweet potato had begun to replace the wild potato in the Cherokee diet.[39] The Reverend Jedediah Morse echoed the cultivation of corn, sweet potatoes, pumpkins, beans, and a "considerable quantity" of beef produced by the Cherokee by 1822.[40] Bartram added the Cassine yapon from which the Cherokee, Creek, and other southern tribes made the celebrated black drink.

In 1828, a Cherokee paper, *The Phoenix*, took a farmer's census and reported the growth of *corn*, gourds, *melons*, cucumbers, squash, cymlings, *beans*, and red *pease* (probably kidney beans) during the colonial era. Those in bold were listed by Timberlake in 1761. By 1826 McLoughlin added wheat, rye, oats, sweet potatoes, and apples,[41] and by the mid–18th century, Hurt added *pumpkins*, sunflowers, *cabbage*, *potatoes*, peaches, leeks, and garlic to that list.[42]

Even among the Cherokee, however, it shouldn't be assumed that once they began growing other vegetables they lost interest in the native varieties.

> I ought to have stated that these people derive a portion of their subsistence regularly from the wild fruits their country abounds in. Walnuts, hazelnuts, pacons [pecans], grapes, plums, papaws, persimmons, hog potatoes, and several other nutritious roots all these they gather and preserve with care.[43]

Others, such as the Hidatsa, were slow in adopting new crops. Buffalo Bird Woman, born 1839, recounted her agricultural practices through 1917, saying her people didn't like potatoes and planted them only at the insistence of government agents. The potatoes and, to a lesser degree, watermelons, onions, turnips, and large squash, were often left unharvested because the people either didn't like them or didn't know how to preserve them.[44]

Lafitau said cultivation of fields was woman's work, and observed that the women worked together, going from one woman's field to the next until all were planted. He also stated that several tribes roasted grain before grinding it, similar to practices of the ancients. This intensified the flavor of grain pottages.

Grinnell stated that the Cheyenne and Sioux raised corn and beans annually, at least through 1876, and the Cheyenne also grew squashes and tobacco. The women claimed to use 35 to 40 types of wild plants for food, some of which were berries and roots.

There were two methods of making meal from acorns and other nuts. The oldest was to remove the nuts from the husks and roast them in hot ashes. A more recent method was to boil the nuts to loosen the husk, then cook the nuts until soft and mash them in a mortar. Acorn meal was then placed into running water until the tannin was removed and the meal no longer tasted bitter. It was then made into soup or bread.[45]

In the 1840s, the Mechoopda of California still routinely ate soup and bread made from acorns, and a missionary left details of how the acorns were processed.

> Shallow circular depressions, some two feet in diameter, were made in the sand for washing the acorn meal, to remove the bitter astringent properties. The acorns after being dried were pulverized in stone mortars of rude construction with stone pestles, and put into these shallow cavities. Water was then repeatedly poured on till the bitterness was gone. Then with the finger the dough was marked into squares, lifted by one hand, and the adhering sand removed with a dexterous application of water with the other. It was then transferred to the heated stones on which fresh grass or leaves were hastily laid to receive it. Then another handful of grass on top of the dough, and hot stones upon that, until it was baked.... The meal not made into bread was diluted with water and boiled into soup in large water-proof baskets of beautiful shape and ornamentation, made of grass roots, wild smilax, and certain shrubs. The stones were lifted from the fire with two long pointed sticks, dipped into a basket of water to remove the ashes, then dropped into the soup and on cooling returned to the fire. This was

repeated until the soup was thoroughly boiled, bubbling like a mud geyser. The very aged still adhere to some of the old customs.[46]

The California Academy of Sciences Department of Anthropology estimates acorns had been part of the California Indian diet since 3000–2000 B.C. Before being processed, the acorns were cracked open, and the kernels removed, and dried in the sun.

The Indians of the Rocky and Cascade mountains collected acorns which they put into bags weighing approximately 80 pounds. These were buried in the sand. After a sufficient time they retrieved the bags, separated the kernels, dried and pounded them into flour, which was used to make soup.[47]

Overland Monthly in February 1896 contained an obituary of sorts for an elderly Indian, but no location was given for where the incident happened. The woman who wrote it had lived in close proximity to the man and his sister and often ate "two finger" soup with them.

> They found me on one occasion, after hours of frightened searching, sitting in Lucy's lap eating "two finger soup" from the same dish with her and Yat. Two finger soup is a sort of mush of acorns (and other unknown but to me then secret ingredients) of such consistency that it could be conveyed to the mouth on two fingers. One finger soup was very very thick, while three, four, and five finger varied in thickness, or rather thinness to the last degree, when it was necessary to hollow the hand like a cup and use it as such.

Early writers were unfamiliar with the sunflower and usually described it as a sort of giant marigold. The Indians in Virginia made "bread and broth" from it.

In Arizona and California trees were plentiful which produced the piñon nut (pine nut) which, a writer noted, "is quite an article of diet among the Indians, and it is also relished by the whites." The *Pinus edulis* was a nut about the size of a hazelnut, rich and sweet.[48]

Piñon nuts ripened in early autumn. To extract the nuts or seeds from the pine cones, the cones were thrown into the fire, and when slightly burned the nuts could be easily extracted. They were stored in dry ravines and pits. The harvest was good only every other year.[49]

Arizona Indians ate the beans produced by the mesquite plant. Hodge thought them to have a pleasant sweet taste, and indicated they were eaten green and dried, and Olive Oatman said the mesquite beans, a "staple of their existence," were strung and dried for use when other foods ran out.[50]

California Indians' list of foodstuffs included salmon roe, "the highest luxury the Indian mind can conceive," berries, clover, and buckeyes.[51]

Manzanita berries were gathered in a basket and beaten with a stone pestle. The flour was then cooked with heated stones into a, "panada ... sweet and nutritious, or a thinner porridge which is eaten with the shaggy knob of a deer's tail."

Girls ages 12 to 14 who were to undergo the Puberty Dance abstained from animal food for three days, eating only acorn porridge after which they took a sacred broth called *chlup*. To prepare it, buckeyes were roasted (to remove poison) then boiled to a pulp in small sandpools with hot stones. They also performed the Pine Nut Dance when the piñon nuts were ready to gather.[52]

Depending on availability in a particular region, game consumed by the Indians included (those mentioned by De Soto's party are in italics) *rabbit*, *deer*, *bear*, beaver, *bison*, elk (wapiti), *opossum*, panther, skunk, raccoon, rat, squirrel, wolf, wildcat, otter, porpoise, whale, snake, manatee, lizard, alligator, wasps or yellow jackets in the nest (larvae was used to make soup), partridge, pigeon, *turkeys*, duck, geese, prairie dog, brant, crane, hawk, eagle, prairie chickens, crows, blackbirds, larks, water hens, plover, snipe, woodcock, and dove.

It was said that the Florida Indians shoved the sharpened end of a pole down the throat of the alligator, flipped it over to gain access to its soft underbelly and attacked it with arrows and clubs.[53]

In 1761 Timberlake stated that in the Cherokee lands there were "an incredible number of buffaloes, bears, deer, panthers, wolves, foxes, raccoons, and opossums.... There are a vast number of lesser sort of game such as rabbits, squirrels, of several sorts, and many other animals, besides turkey, geese, ducks of several kinds, partridges, pheasants, and an infinity of other birds.... The rattle-snake is extremely good; being once obliged to eat one through want of provisions, I have eat several since thro' choice."[54]

The Hidatsa ate chiefly buffalo until approximately 1870, and prepared it by roasting, broiling or boiling in earthenware pots. They sometimes boiled meat in skins while hunting, a method they learned from the Assiniboine. Bones were pounded into fragments and boiled to make soup. A contemporary account claimed, "The flesh of a fat buffalo-cow is perhaps the best beef that can be eaten; wholly free from the rank flavor which markes the fat of the male."[55]

Charles de Rochefort, Thomas Harriot, and Reuben Thwaites commented on the number of fish caught by the Indians. Harriot described their technique of setting up reeds or twigs in the water in such a manner that the enclosed area grew progressively narrower, allowing the Indians to either spear the fish or catch them by hand.[56] They caught fish with traps, nets, poison, spears, and bow and arrow.[57]

Depending on location, several early writers wrote that fish and shellfish used for food included cod, catfish (mud, blue, and spoonbill, also known as sturgeon and paddlefish), bream, brook trout, smelt, bass, flounder, alewives,[58] sturgeon, mullet, whiting, rockfish, porgy, shad, blackfish, salmon, gar, oysters, crabs, cockles, mussels, crawfish, scallops, periwinkles, whelk, lobster, snail, turtles, and tortoises. Wood said the alewives arrived in such multitudes, "as is almost incredible pressing up such shallow waters as will scarce permit them to swim."[59] Beverley also mentioned a green snake, beetles and locusts as part of the native diet in Virginia.[60]

The biggest differences in diet seem to have been between the Eastern bands and the Plains bands, and the main reason was because of differences in native plants, fish, and animals.

The Blackfeet ate a great deal of meat and meat stew, and used buffalo, serviceberries, wild cherries, buffalo berries, June berries, wild turnips, wild onions, wild potato, bitter root, smart weed, wild rhubarb, wild ducks and geese, and beaver tail, most of which went into a soup pot suspended from a tripod. They ridiculed the Cree habit of eating dog, skunk, badger, prairie dog, wolf, and coyote.[61]

John Lawson wrote in 1703 on the lives and customs of the Indians of the Carolinas. Foods they consumed included sturgeon, bass, herring, trout, crawfish, skate, oysters, cockles, bilberries, pigeons (he mentioned obtaining fat from the pigeons), red pease, turkeys, ducks, and corn for bread. He also said "They plant a great many sorts of pulse, part of which they eat green in summer."[62] He elaborated:

> As to the Indians' food, it is of several sorts, which are as follows: Venison, and the fawns in the bags, cut out of the doe's belly; fish of all sorts, the lamprey eel excepted, and the sturgeon, our salt water Indians will not touch; bear, and beaver, panther, polecat (The Indians love to eat their flesh which has no manner of ill smell when the bladder is out), wild cat, possum, raccoon, hares, and squirrels, roasted with their guts in; snakes, all Indians will not eat them, though some do; all wild fruits, that are palatable, some of which they dry and keep against winter, as all sorts of fruits, and peaches, which they dry and make quiddonies [a sort

Native Americans attack and kill alligators by ramming a pole down its throat, turning it over, beating it with clubs, and shooting it with arrows. They sometimes ate alligator. Engraving, Theodor de Bry, 1591. Library of Congress, Prints and Photographs Division, Reproduction Number LC-USZ62-373.

> of jelly] and cakes, that are very pleasant, and a little tartish; young wasps, when they are white in the combs, before they can fly, this is esteemed a dainty; all sorts of fish and terebins [terrapin], shell fish, and stingray, or scate, dried; gourds, melons, cucumbers, squashes, pulse of all sorts; rockahomine meal, which is their maiz, made into several sorts of bread; ears of corn roasted in the summer, or preserved against winter.[63]

The Cheyenne diet included sweeteners made from box elder or maple, wild rice from the Great Lakes area, acorns pounded and boiled into soup with buffalo fat, various small animals, and the eggs of wild fowl.

Wild rice was a grain resembling oats that grew in marshy areas. When it was ripe, women of some tribes tied several stalks together with bark and stored it away or they would paddle into the marshes in canoes and beat the grain off directly into the canoe.[64]

Like medieval European soup cauldrons, the Indian soup cauldron was ever-present, with fresh ingredients added to seethe as the cooked ones were removed. Any cultivated or wild plants, fish, fowl, flesh, shellfish, tuckahoe, berries or nuts were added to the stew, and it was thickened with maize.[65] A culinary observer wrote:

> The kettle is swung over the fire, and whatever is on hand, or whatever has been obtained by the day's labors for the day's food, is boiled and served out in the common wood dishes, to be eaten with knives or horn spoons.[66]

In speaking with Native American historian He Who Stands Firm, it became apparent that native soups were simply made, layer upon layer, adding to the base flavor, until the desired effect was obtained. Records of early writers bear this out. Most of the soups started with hominy and beans, the most flavorful of which were toasted before being used. If available, meat or fatback was added to make it richer. Bones, especially marrow bones, heightened the flavor. Wild leeks or onions added another dimension and were often browned before being added for even more flavor. If available, squash completed the addition of the Three Sisters, and shellfish or fish could be added in place of, or in addition to, any other meat. Harriot wrote,

> They breake them [nuts] with stones and pound them in mortars with water to make a milk which they use to put into some sorts of their spoonemeat; also among their sodden wheat, peaze, beanes, and pompions which maketh them have a farre more pleasant taste.

He Who Stands Firm stressed the prevalence of some basic ingredients. Based on items excavated from middens,[67] "Oysters were harvested to the extent that near the Hudson River it can be established that various tribes from many parts of the Southeast went to this area to harvest oysters. They were often strung and dried in the sun, or smoked so that they could be taken home."

With regard to native agriculture, he noted references to crops by Hudson in 1609 and Champlain in 1603. Hudson stated after visiting a native village that there was so much maize strung for drying it would have filled three ships, and Champlain stated he once saw fields planted on both sides of the river as far as he could see.

Lawson was offered a "loblolly made with Indian corn," San Miguel, a monk, wrote in 1595 on the Georgia coast of *atole*, "made of parched corn and very thick." Dumont wrote of corn porridge in 1753. Peter Hudson wrote of *tanlubo*, which was made by soaking corn in a kettle with water and fresh pork seasoned with salt. This was cooked into a thick and rich pottage.

The primary method of preservation was to fill clay vessels or baskets and bury them in pits. A scouting party from the *Mayflower* discovered such a cache on Cape Cod, which they dug up and looted.[68]

Porridge called *sappaan* was a favorite.[69]

Although many Indians also grilled food or roasted it coated in mud, soup seems to have been the primary cooking method for the Dakota, as evidenced by Riggs' description:

> The flesh is put into the kettle.... The fire is made on the ground, in the center and a hole is left on the ridge for the smoke to pass out. But, with the best arrangement and the greatest care, a Dakota summer or winter house is often a very smoky place.

Riggs said ingredients that found their way into the soup pots had at times included live turtles, otter, crane, and ducks, and the Digger Indians roasted grasshoppers during the summer, a good amount of which were pounded and put into the soup cauldrons.[70]

Writers said both fish and game were *barbakued*, or roasted over heat, often on a gridiron made from saplings.[71] Wrote John Lawson in 1703:

> They boil and roast their Meat extraordinary much, and eat abundance of Broth, except the Savages whom we call the naked Indians, who never eat any Soupe.
>
> After they have taken store of fishe, they gett them vnto a place fit to dress yt. Ther they sticke vpp in the grownde 4. Stakes in a square roome, and lay 4 potes vpon them, and others ouer thwart the same like vnto an hurdle, of sufficient heighte. And laying their fishe vpon this hurdle, they make a fyre vnderneath the to broile the same, not after the manner of the people of Florida, which doe but schorte, and harden their meate in the smoke onlye to Reserve the same during all the winter. For this people reseruinge nothinge for store, thei do broile, and spend away all att once and when they have further neede, they roste or seethe

fresh, as wee shall see heraffter. And when as the hurdle can not holde all the fishes, they hange the Rest by the fyrres on sticks sett upp in the grounde against the fyre, and than they finishe the rest of their cookerye. They take good heede that they bee not burned. When the first are broyled they lay others on, that weare newlye brought. When the first of their meate in this sorte, untill they thincke they have sufficient.

Heckewelder stated the pre–1770 Iroquois were described by other bands as being less clean with their foods. They reportedly dried the entrails of animals without benefit of cleaning them of their contents and used them to season their pottage. One traveler said at first he thought the specks floating on the broth were pepper.

Various records show that some Indians weren't opposed to eating skunk when it was properly prepared. A traveler wrote, "If suddenly killed and the scent bag removed intact, the flesh of the animal [skunk] is highly esteemed and the skins made into tobacco pouches."[72]

General James Brisbin ate, squeamishly at first, until he grew accustomed to the idea, soup the Indians had made from dog meat, wild artichokes and corn.

Indians were not the first in history to consume dog and puppy meat. That distinction belongs to the Romans, according to Pliny. "The meat of nursing puppies was considered such a pure foodstuff that it was used to appease enemy gods more than any other sacrificial offering. Genita Mana (the goddess of childbirth) was honoured with a dog sacrifice, and puppy meat is even today, served at meals in honour of the deity."

The Indians' earliest method of boiling and making soup was boiling in hides heated with hot stones, as has been described in the chapters on Scotland and Ireland.[73]

During his travels between 1831 and 1837, George Catlin observed Indians known as the Stone Boilers, a name obtained from their methods of cooking with hot stones. They dug a hole and lined it with the hide, pressing it in by hand to form a basin in the hole. The hide was filled with water and the meat put in, and stones which had been made red-hot in a nearby fire were dropped in. As the stones cooled they were removed and replaced with hot ones until the meat was sufficiently cooked. He stated this method of cookery was almost relegated to antiquity by the 1830s except for traditional feasts honoring the ancient customs.[74]

The Sioux were documented using wooden kettles heated by dropping in red-hot stones in 1744 (a practice Lafitau documented for earlier tribes some twenty years earlier). Even in 1744, this method of cookery was said to be fast disappearing due to the Sioux being able to readily trade with the whites for iron pots or pottery from other tribes. Other tribes which were documented during that time to use the hot stone method of cooking included the Blackfeet, Cree, Shoshone, and Eskimos.[75]

Lafitau commented that the Iroquois women were skillful at making earthen vessels of a "spherical form at the bottom and considerable width at the top" before Europeans arrived with metal kettles. They dried the vessels in the sun then tempered them in a slow fire before use.

Indians west of the Rockies plaited tightly woven baskets of roots in which they prepared boiled salmon, acorn porridge, and other dishes by dropping in hot stones. The baskets were called *watape*.[76]

Other instances of basketry used in cooking include those used as sieves, water vessels, and so on. As late as 1900, some tribes made coiled baskets waterproof by lining the interior with pitch or clay. Others preferred birch bark containers to traditional basketry. The type of vessels used depended, to some extent, on the materials available and the preference of the user.[77]

In 1863, naturalist H. W. Bates stated he was served turtle soup cooked in the turtle's shell while exploring the Amazon.[78] It is not a hard stretch of the imagination to envision this being done by American Indians as well.

Peter Kalm wrote that by the 1740s the natives had long since given up making clay pots

An Eskimo woman in her outdoor kitchen, 1916. Library of Congress, Prints and Photographs Division, Reproduction Number LC-DIG-ppmsc-02305.

for cooking, choosing instead the "pots, kettles, and other necessary vessels of the Europeans." He further stated that "this art is entirely lost among them. Such vessels of their own construction are therefore a great rarity, even among the Indians."[79]

Native vessels were made of clay or potstone. The clay had particles of white sand or quartz and was burned in a fire. Most of the kettles had no legs for sitting over coals. Many had two holes near the upper edge through which a stick or leather thongs were inserted to hold the kettle over the fire. They were not glazed inside or out. The pots of potstone averaged an inch thick. Caswell wrote:

> Here and there the Indian kettle in which their favorite soup is being prepared for the feast hangs over a fire.[80]

When not hung, clay pots were balanced on three or four stones next to the flames with a ring of coals around the pot rather than placing it directly over the flame. A close observation of the illustration from Harriot's account reveals the pot to be sitting behind the fire on a base of wood.

Bowls made from bark or knots in the trees held individual portions. These were sometimes elaborately carved, especially those used during feasts.

Bowls and spoons were made of shells as recently as the 18th century, and by some tribes into the 19th. Various writers documented the use of wooden ladles for eating. Many had some sort of effigy carved onto the handle. The ladles were described as "omnipresent," and the craft of making them survived into the 20th century.

A single earthenware pot, a knife, a few trenchers, and water-gourds were typical furnishings of the 19th-century Mexican kitchen, and *tolle* (gruel) made from flour with water or milk was standard fare.[81]

Elk-horn spoons. Photograph by Edward S. Curtis, ca. 1923. Spoons, or ladles, for eating soup were a common Native American utensil. They were also carved from wood with various effigies on the handles. Library of Congress, Prints and Photographs Division, Reproduction Number LC-USZ62-118597.

Fruit and nuts ended up in the soup pot along with anything available. One enjoyable soup was made of wild grapes thickened with cornmeal.

Zebulon Pike wrote of Indian corn soup thickened with dried pumpkin, and James Edwin left one of several descriptions of corn soup made from green (fresh) corn boiled in water with slices of bison meat, grease, and beans.[82]

Misickquatash (succotash), a favorite stew, was made from corn and beans (either dried or green beans) with sometimes the addition of walnuts and/or pumpkin.[83] A memoirist wrote,

> When the Indian told us the green corn feast consisted of succotash, a soup of corn and beans boiled together, our pride in this purely Yankee dish received a shock. It is centuries old and we received it from the Indian![84]

The *Gettysburg Compiler* published a recipe for what it claimed was a New England dish, with no mention of its Native American roots, as early as September 12, 1853. To make it, the kernels were cut away from a dozen ears of sweet corn. The cobs were boiled with a quart of lima or other beans and a pound of salt pork in 3 pints of water for ¾ of an hour after which the cobs were removed and discarded, and the corn kernels put in to boil with the beans another 15 minutes.

Another 18th-century Indian favorite was *poussole*, a soup made from wheat, maize, peas, and beans: "The indispensable item of an Indian feast was corn mush. A large kettle was suspended over a fire in the yard and the mush was made by putting in tallow and stirring in meal or flour. When cooked the kettle was taken indoors and placed on the floor,"[85] wrote a 19th-century pioneer. And a historian recorded:

> The women sometimes made cakes of their corn and baked them in the ashes, but, more commonly, they made a sort of porridge of it, or rather soup, for they usually put in a part of some

animal, which the husband had brought home from the chase, to enrich and flavor it. The pounded corn and the piece of meat were boiled in the same vessel until they were sufficiently cooked, and then the whole was eaten together.[86]

The maize soups were very little different from sailors' burgoo (mush made out of Indian corn, meal, and water, sometimes sweetened with molasses) which was known as hasty pudding by New Englanders.

Sagamite was a popular Indian soup made from wild oats (or corn), usually harvested from cane brakes, sometimes with beans, meat, fish, or squash added if available.[87] It is similar to any number of hominy pottages, or "a kind of Meale Pottage, unpartch'd,"[88] as a 19th-century linguist put it. Lafitau wrote,

> *Sagamite* of the Indians is only a sort of stew made of their Indian corn leached in ashes, ground by hand labour in wooden mortars, passed through grossly made sieves of little branches knotted together and winnowed in bark or pliant baskets made of rush. I do not know the origin of the word *sagamite*, used by the French Canadians for this stew which the Iroquois call *onnontara*.

Lafitau went on to say the *sagamite* was prepared and each person came to eat as their appetite directed rather than at a specific meal time. A portion was set aside as a repast for any visitors who might appear, one of many accounts of native hospitality.[89]

Eschionque was a soup of squash cooked in meat or fish broth, and thickened with corn meal.[90] Bartram ate soup made from blossoms and squash thickened with meal, but was not very impressed with it.[91]

In *The Voyages of Samuel de Champlain*, Indian soup was described as, "A kind of broth made of maize crushed between two stones, together with meat and fish which was cut into little pieces, the whole being boiled together without salt." Champlain also described *migan*, a thin soup made from pounded corn with the bran and fresh or dried fish or venison.[92]

Some accounts specify the lack of salt in various tribes' diets, while others apparently had enough to use for trade. Swanton devoted several pages to the methods of obtaining salt, trading it, tribes that used it, among others.[93]

The American Society of Naturalists observed, "The [Miami] Indians also eat otter oil cooked in soup, and consider it very nutritious."[94]

In about 1800 an Ohioan documented Wyandot Indians living off "corn pounded into coarse meal or small hominy — this they boiled in water, which appeared like well thickened soup, without salt or anything else."[95] When that ran out, an elder took two boys with him in a canoe to hunt deer. One of the boys held a light to mesmerize the deer while the old man took aim and killed three.

Whether made into soup or bread, dried corn first had to be separated from the dry hulls. The corn was added to boiling water with hardwood ashes. Lye from the ashes softened the hulls after 30 minutes to an hour. The corn was then removed, and placed in a basket, which was then placed in a stream so that the hulls were washed away. When the hulls could be removed by rolling the corn between the fingers it was ready to be washed. The cleaned corn was then pounded using a mortar and pestle or returned to the pot with clean water and boiled until tender.

Prepared foods that were described included a fat boiled goose, venison, raccoon, groundnuts, cattle, cranes, geese, barbecued turkeys and venison, Indian peas, beans, oil, chinkapin nuts, corn, and peaches (from which they made peach bread).[96]

He stated the Indians of the Carolinas made regular use of bear oil, blackberries, huckleberries, hickory nuts to thicken broths and soup, barbecued shad, wild hogs, raccoons, opossum, turtle, curlew, gulls, gannets, pelicans, duck, mallard, swans, teal, widgeon, and pigeon oil. He said they kept pigeon oil in great quantities and used it like butter. One village of 17 houses was in possession of 100 gallons of oil.[97]

In 1709, a common pottage was "a loblolly made with Indian corn and dried peaches" which was made in an earthenware porridge pot. Another was made from teal, possum, and scraps of venison which made a "curious ragoo."[98]

Ground chinkapin nuts and hickory nuts were the basis of "soop" made from plain water or meat broth. Venison broth thickened with acorn meal made a "palatable soop."[99]

The Cherokee make a soup from yellowjackets. However, it is uncertain how early this practice can be documented. One of the earliest accounts may be from *The American Naturalist* (1878), which discusses the preparation of wasp larvae.[100]

Various Indian tribes perfected forms of outdoor cooking such as the clambake, and they roasted corn and meat, the precursor of the barbecue.

La Salle described the Indians of Illinois as farming a little and hunting a great deal.

Brunswick stew has undergone several stages of evolution since first recorded in American cookery books, and any number of people and states claim to have discovered it. However, the basic ingredients seem clearly native in origin. The most logical origin seems to be the stew cooked in the earthenware vessels of the Indians or the huntsman stew of early hunting parties. While Brunswick stew is today made of chicken, it was originally made of squirrel, and sometimes rabbit, corn, potatoes, and beans. Later versions included onion, tomatoes, and pepper.

Corn and bean dumplings made from dried beans and corn flour sometimes accompanied Cherokee soups and stews.

Heckewelder wrote in his journal of having turkey for supper with "a very good soup made of dumplings." A favorite described by Heckewelder in 1762 was a pottage "of corn, dry pumpkins, beans, and chestnuts, shell-barks and hickory nut kernels, boiled." Pots were covered with large pumpkin, cabbage, or other leaves. The Indians used very little water in preparing pumpkin and squash dishes, and the pottage was sometimes sweetened with maple syrup.

> Another very good dish is prepared by boiling with their corn or maize, the washed kernels of the shell-bark or hickory nut. They pound the nuts in a block or mortar, pouring a little warm water on them, and gradually a little more as they become dry, until, at lst, there is a sufficient quantity of water, so that by stirring up the pounded nuts the broken shells separate from the liquor, which from the pounded kernels assumes the appearance of milk. This being put into the kettle and mixed with the pottage gives it a rich and agreeable flavor. If the broken shells do not all freely separate by swimming on the top or sinking to the bottom, the liquor is strained through a clean cloth, before it is put into the kettle.[101]

The flour from blue corn was mixed with a little water and cooked into a thick pottage. Blue corn has a delicious nutty flavor.

He documented the use of beans in making bread as well as other additions such as pumpkin, chestnuts, dried pounded venison, and whortleberries. Cherokee bean bread was a staple.

Beach wrote, not only about what the Indians ate, but how they ate it. He wrote of a banquet with the Chippewa in which a bear killed by a warrior was portioned out among those holding claim to it, then the head, backbone, ribs, feet, heart, liver, and fat were served up for a feast. The receipt of a red feather was recognized as an invitation to partake of the meal, which began with smoking, "for the Indians invariably commence their ceremonies by smoking."

The next step was to place upon a fire in their midst a large kettle containing the remnants of the bear, which were boiled to a kind of soup, without the least particle of seasoning. While this was cooking, one of the orators of the day delivered a speech, wherein he thanked the Great Spirit for telling his red children where to find the bear, and concluding with some remarks upon the characteristics of the animal. When the bear chowder was done, it was equally distributed among the assembled crowd, and each one requiring to eat the whole that was placed before him, and this too without a ladle or lifting his dish, but on his hands and knees in the common attitude of a bear.[102]

In 1819, another account of bear soup was recorded by Christian Fast, an Indian captive. He stated the body was roasted, cut into small slices, and served on new bark plates while the unskinned head and feet were boiled in a copper kettle, and a sort of soup made from them was passed around in wooden vessels.[103]

A Michigan trader described a meal he was given by an Indian family in their lodge: "Corn soup seasoned with fish; the only provisions they had. Without salt or anything else. But I had now got so accustomed to voyagers fare that I found it very good."

Dried pumpkin soup served in a huge earthen bowl and eaten with the fingers was included in *The American Naturalist*. The writer said the Pah-Utes (Paiutes) ground and cooked alfalfa seeds into mush or gruel; boiled the flowering ends of spring cattails in water for a soup delicacy; and the plants and seeds of western wild cabbage (*Caulanthus crassicaulis*).

In 1858, a captive of the Apache described meals he had shared of bean soup and "burned" dough. "Their meat was boiled with water in a 'Tusquin' [clay kettle], and this meat-mush or soup was the staple of food among them."[104]

The same author included a reference to Indians making bean soup, and described a feast which several Indians and their families attended with:

> each bearing upon their heads a *Coopoesech*, containing a cake, or a stone dish filled with soup, or boiled vegetables. These cakes were made of wheat, ground, and mixed with boiled pumpkins. This dough was rolled out sometimes to two feet in diameter; then placed in hot sand, a leaf and a layer of sand over the loaf, and a fire built over the whole, until it was baked through.[105]

One of the first attempts at recording actual recipes used by the Native Americans was made in the 1930s by the Indian Women's Club of Tulsa, Oklahoma. Soup recipes included hominy and hickory nut soup which was made from finely ground hickory nuts, hominy, chicken broth, sweet potatoes, and salt.

The Cherokee also made soup from dried (smoked) fish similar in flavor to the Scottish finnan haddock soup known as cullen skink.

A significant contribution to preserving native foodways was made approximately 10 years later by Mary Ulmer and Samuel Beck on behalf of the Cherokee Indian Museum of North Carolina.

Brigadier General James H. Carleton wrote at Santa Fe, New Mexico in 1864 the following regarding the Indians at Crow Creek.

> The whole animal [for the Indians], including what the butchers call the "head and pluck," must be issued.... The economy in the use of food in all things must be observed. The making of soups, which is by far the best way to cook what they have, must be inculcated as a religion. And let me observe that one pound of solid food made into nutritious soup — nutritious because well and thoroughly boiled for each man, woman, and child, per day, for a Frenchman — is more than he wants, and more than he gets as a rule.

A subsequent notation confirmed that Carleton had conferred with Colonel Kit Carson, Governor Connelly, and Major McFerran, and they agreed that adequate rations were one pound of flour or meal or meat per day to each man, woman, and child, if cooked into a porridge was sufficient nutrition to feed a race of people who had for some time been accustomed to the ways of the whites, but found themselves virtual prisoners with no guns with which to hunt to provide their own food.

By far, the most offensive documented soup was a product of the U.S. Army and recorded by the government printing office in 1867.[106]

> Somehow this instruction became so perverted that a huge cottonwood vat was constructed six to eight feet round and as deep into which went, beef, beef heads, entrails of the beeves, some beans, flour, and pork. I think there was put into the vat two barrels of flour each time, which was not oftener than once in twenty-four hours. This mass was then cooked by the steam from the [sawmill] boiler passing through the pipe into the vat. When that was done, all the Indians were ordered to come there with their pails and get it.... The Indians would pour off the thinner portion and eat that which settled at the bottom. As it was dipped out of the vat some of the Indians would get the thinner portions, and some would get some meat. I passed there frequently when it was cooking, and was often there when it was being issued, and it had a very offensive odor; it had the odor of the contents of the entrails of the beeves.[107]

A Sarsi woman cooking over a campfire, Alberta, Canada. Various ingredients are seen displayed in the foreground. Similar scenes were common throughout North America. Photograph Edward S. Curtis, ca. 1927. Library of Congress, Prints and Photographs Division, Reproduction Number LC-USZ62-101189.

Testimony proved that the cows in question had been worked at hauling freight until they were so emaciated they "reeled as they walked." Often the meat was piled into warehouses, sometimes packed in a little snow and sawdust, until it was rotten before being put into the vat.

At an inquiry several men testified that the mass cooked in the cottonwood vat reeked of the stench of unwashed beef entrails and that many of the starving Indians vomited as they tried to eat it, and that many of the children and elderly died from consuming the putrid soup.

18. Colonial America

Colonial America was a patchwork of cultures. Immigrants from many countries contributed their own customs to the proverbial melting pot. William Penn outlined the Dutch, French, Swiss, Germans, Danes, Finns, Scots, Irish, Spanish, and English as the major contenders in the colonies, and detailing the customs and holdings of each is too lengthy to go into detail here. Suffice to say the culinary history of these countries is repetitive in Colonial America so far as available ingredients allowed.

Kalm stated the French colonists ate clear soup, wheat bread, and various sorts of relishes for dinner with cooked meat, fish, or fowl, and peas. For the evening meal, there was usually meat and/or fish or fowl and salad.[1]

A good indication of what went into the earliest colonial soup cauldrons is the list of supplies those making the trip to the New World were advised to bring with them. As the Reverend Francis Higginson stated regarding the importance of packing well for the voyage, "When you are once parted with England, you shall meete neither markets nor fayres to buy what you want."

John Josselyn said ship rations consisted of "beefe, porke, salt Fish, Butter, Cheese, Pease, Pottage, Water gruel, Brisket, and six-shilling beere." Given the prevalence of pease soup recipes the peas no doubt ended up in one of the pottages.

He suggested that those making the voyage take with them "some Conserves, and good Claret wine ... Sallat-oyle ... Prunes ... Sugar ... White Biskets, and Eggs, and Bacon, Rice, Poultry ... Juyce of Lemons well put up."

Most early histories of colonial villages mention bean or pea porridge, "broth with a few beans thrown in," or a "thick, rich soup seasoned with fried pork, pepper-pods and salt," as the common food for any time of day.[2] In the Connecticut colony,

> The breakfast of the farmers often consisted mainly of a soup made of salt meat and beans, and seasoned with savory herbs. This dish was called "bean porridge."[3]

Citizens of Long Island, New York, made a "celebrated," porridge from samp (hominy), salted beef or pork, potatoes, and any other vegetables at hand, which was reheated and served daily until it was all eaten.[4]

The preparation of venison was unknown to some new settlers because in parts of Europe only the nobility claimed the right to hunt, but it quickly became a staple. In some countries fishing fell under the same scrutiny, but in the new world, streams abounded with fish, and oysters and other shellfish were plentiful for the taking.

In Europe, William the Conqueror established restrictions allowing only the monarch or aristocracy the right to hunt wooded land, heath, or anywhere that supported game. Laws of forest and restriction existed, at times, from the 11th century.

One of the first chores for colonial women was to put in a kitchen garden to supply the pot herbs and vegetables needed for the soup cauldron and salad bowl.[5]

Gulielma Penn (1644–1694), wife of William Penn, left receipts for soups, though none were actually called soup, and having grown up in England her recipes reflected an English influence.[6] One was rich bisque of beef, another was "cabidg poridg without flesh," a typical early soup recipe using available ingredients and bread to soak up the broth.

A basic version of cabbage soup: Roughly slice or chop the cabbage, put into a pot of salted water, and boil until tender. Add butter, season to taste with mace, pepper, and salt, and simmer together 10 to 15 minutes to blend the flavors. To serve, place browned, buttered toasts in a tureen or in individual serving bowls. Slightly beat 6 egg yolks with ½ cup of cream that has come to room temperature, and stir into the soup. Ladle the soup over the toasts, and serve hot.

Thomas Harriot left an excellent accounting of the foods eaten by natives and colonists in 16th-century Virginia. The following is a summary of those used for soup.[7]

Pagatowr. Corn, red, white, yellow, and blue. Called turkey wheat or guinea wheat initially by the English.

Okindgier. Beans, varied in color.

Wickonzowr. Peas.

Macocqwer. Pumpkins, melons, and gourds. (Beverly [1705] added the cushaw.)

Melden. Herb. Similar to wild spinach (orach). Seeds were used to make broth or soup. Natives used it as a seasoning in soup instead of salt.

> OPENAUK are a kind of root of round forme, some of the bignes of walnuts, some far greater, which are found in moist and marsh grounds growing many together one by another in ropes, or as thogh they were fastnened with a string. Being boiled or sodden they are very good meate.
>
> OKEEPENAUK [wild potato] are also of round shape, found in dry grounds: some are of the bignes of a mans head. They are to be eaten as they are taken out of the ground, for by reason of their drynesse they will neither roast nor seeth. Their tast is not so good as of the former rootes, notwithstanding for want of bread, & sometimes for varietie the inhabitants use to eate them with fish or flesh, and in my judgement they doe as well as the household bread made of rye here in England.
>
> Kaishucpenauk [probably duck potato] a white kind of root about the bignes of hen eggs & near of that forme: their taste was not so good to our seeming as of the other, and therefore their place and manner of growing not so much cared for by us: the inhabitants notwithstanding used to boile & eate many.
>
> Tsinaw [probably a smilax (lily family)] is a kind of roote much like unto the which in England is called the China root brought from the West Indies. And we know not any thing to the contrary but that it may be of the same kind. These roots grow many together in great clusters and do bring foorth a brier stalke, but the leafe in shape far unlike; which being supported by the trees it groweth nearest unto, wil reach or climbe to the top of the highest. From these roots while they be new or fresh being chopt into small pieces & stampt, is strained with water a juice that maketh bread, & also being boiled, a very good spoone meate[soup or pottage] in manner of gelly, and is much better in tast if it bee tempered with oyle. This Tsinaw is not of that sort which by some was caused to be brought into England for the China roote, for it was discovered since, and is in use as is afore saide: but that which was brought hither is not yet knowne neither by us nor by the inhabitants to serve for any use or purpose; although the rootes in shape are very like.
>
> Coscushaw, some of our company tooke to bee that kinde of roote which the Spaniards in the West Indies call Cassavy, whereupon also many called it by that name: it growth in very

muddie pooles and moist groundes. Being dressed according to the country maner, it maketh a good bread, and also a good sponemeate, and is used very much by the inhabitants: The juice of this root is poison, and therefore heede must be taken before any thing be made therewithal: Either the rootes must bee first sliced and dried in the Sunne, or by the fire, and then being pounded into floure wil make good bread: or els while they are greene they are to bee pared, cut into pieces and stampt; loves of the same to be laid neere or over the fire until it be soure, and then being well pounded againe, bread, or spone meate very good in taste, and holsome may be made thereof.

Habasoon [possibly cow parsnip] is a roote of hoat taste almost of the forme and bignesse of a Parseneepe, of it selfe it is no victual, but onely a helpe being boiled together with other meates.

There are also Leekes differing little from ours in England that grow in many places of the countrey, of which, when we came in places where, wee gathered and eate many, but the naturall inhabitants never.

CHESTNUTS, there are in divers places great store: some they use to eate rawe, some they stampe and boile to make spoonemeate, and with some being sodden they make such a manner of dowe bread as they use of their beanes before mentioned.

WALNUTS: There are two kindes of walnuts, and of them infinit store: In many places where very great woods for many miles together the third part of trees are walnut trees. The one kind is of the same taste and forme or little differing from ours of England, but that they are harder and thicker shelled: the other is greater and hath a verie ragged and harde shell: but the kernel great, verie oylie and sweete. Besides their eating them after our ordinarie maner, they break them with stones and pound them in mortars with water to make a milk which they use to put into some sorts of their spoon-meate; also among their sodden wheat, peaze, beanes, and pompions which maketh them have a farre more pleasant taste.

MEDLARS [probably persimmon] a kind of verie good fruit, so called by us chieflie for these respectes: first in that they are not good until they be rotten: then in that they open at the head as our medlars, and are about the same bignesse: otherwise in taste and colour they are farre different: for they are as red as cherries and very sweet: but whereas the cherie is sharpe sweet, they are lushious sweet.

METAQUESUNNAUK [prickly pear], a kinde of pleasaunt fruite almost of the shape & bignes of English peares, but that they are of a perfect red colour as well within as without. They grow on a plant whose leaves are verie thicke and full of prickles as sharp as needles....

GRAPES [probably fox grapes and scuppernongs or muscadines] there are of two sorts which I mentioned in the merchantable commodities.

STRABERIES there are as good & as great as those which we have in our English gardens.

MULBERIES [crabapple, huckleberries (blueberries), cranberry, whortleberry], Applecrabs, Hurts or Hurtleberies, such as wee have in England.

SACQUENUMMENER a kinde of berries almost like unto capres but somewhat greater which grow together in clusters upon a plant or herb that is found in shallow waters: being boiled eight or nine hours according to their kind are very good meate and holesome, otherwise if they be eaten they will make a man for the time franticke or extremely sicke.

There is a kind of berrie or acorne, of which there are five sorts that grow on severall kinds of trees; the one is called Sagatemener, the second Osamener, the third Pummuckoner. These kind of acorns they use to drie upon hurdles made of reeds with fire underneath almost after the manner as we dry malt in England. When they are to be used they first water them until they be soft & then being sod they make a good victual, either to eate so simply, or els being also pounded, to make loaves or lumpes of bread. These be also the three kinds of which, I said before, the inhabitants used to make sweet oyle.

An other sort is called Sapummener which being boiled or parched doth eate and taste like unto chestnuts. They sometimes also make bread of this sort.

The fifth sort is called Mangummenauk, and is the acorne of their kind of oake, the which being dried after the maner of the first sortes, and afterward watered they boile them & their servants or sometime the chiefe themselves, either for variety or for want of bread doe eate them with their fish or flesh.

Deare, in some places there are great store: neere unto the sea coast they are of the ordinarie bignes as ours in England & some lesse: but further up into the countrye where there is better seed they are greater: they differ from ours onely in this, their tailes are longer and the snags of their hornes looke backward.

Conies, Those that we have seen & al that we can heare of are of a grey colour like unto hares: in some places there are such plenty that all the people of some townes make them mantles of the furre or flue of the skinnes of those they usually take.

Saquenuckot & Maquowoc [perhaps otters or muskrats, and beavers]; two kindes of small beastes greater than conies which are very good meat. We never tooke any of them ourselves, but sometime eate of such as the inhabitants had taken & brought unto us.

Squirels which are of a grey colour, we have taken & eaten.

Beares which are all of black colour. The beares of this countrye are good meat; the inhabitants in time of winter do use to take & eate manie, so also sometime did wee....

I have the names of eight & twenty severall sortes of beastes which I have heard of to be here and there dispersed in the countrie, especially in the maine: of which there are only twelve kinds that we have yet discovered, & of those that be good meat we know only them before mentioned. The inhabitants sometime kil the Lyon & eat him: & we sometime as they came to our hands of their Wolves or wolvish dogges, which I have not set downe for good meat....

Turkie cockes and Turkie hennes: Stockdoves: Partridges: Cranes: Hernes: & in winter great store of Swannes & Geese. Of al sortes of foule I have the names in the countrie language of four escore and sixe of which number besides those that be named we have taken, eaten, & have the pictures as they were there drawne with the names of the inhabitants of severall strange sortes of water foule eight, and seventeene kinds more of land foul...

For foure monthes of the yeere, February, March, Aprill and May, there are plenty of Sturgeons: and also in the same monethes of Herrings, some of the ordinary bignesse as ours in England, but the most part farre greater, of eighteene, twentie inches, and some two foote in length and better; both these kindes of fishe in those monethes are most plentifull, and in best season, which wee founde to bee most delicate and pleasaunt meate.

There are also Troutes, Porpoises, Rayes, Oldwives [alewife], Mullets, Plaice, and very many other sortes of excellent good fish.... Sea crabbes, such as we have in England.

Oysteres, some very great, and some small; some rounde and some of a long shape: They are founde both in salt water and brackish, and those that we had out of salt water are far better than the other as in our owne countrye.

Also Muscles, Scalopes, Periwinkles, and Crevises.

Seekanauk, a kinde of crustie shell fishe which is good meate, about a foote in breadth, having a crustie tayle, many legges like a crab; and her eyes in her backe. They are founde in shallowes of salt waters; and sometime on shoare.

There are many Tortoyses both of lande and sea kinde ... they are very good meate, as also their egges...

The array of foods Harriot recorded, some of which may be difficult to read from the original, included wild onions or ramps, Jerusalem artichokes, sweet potatoes, blackberries, raspberries, huckleberries, grapes, buffalo, bear, venison, rabbit, opossum, squirrel, wild turkey, pigeon, quail, shellfish, turtles, and fish.

Bear lard was as important as the meat. It was used to season soups, to fry in the earthenware vessels, and as a substitute for butter. When the lard is rendered it makes excellent bread. It is rendered the same way as lard from hogs. The meat was often made into bacon, some of which still found its way into the soup cauldrons.

In 1709, Lawson added to the list of available vegetables and pot herbs, including carrots, leeks, parsnips, turnips, potatoes ("of several sorts"), ground artichokes, radishes, horserad-ish, beet, onion, shallot, garlic, chives, onion, cabbage, lettuce, spinach, fennel, samphire (from the marshes), dock, wild rhubarb, rocket, sorrel, cresses of different kinds, purslane (both wild and garden varieties), two kinds of parsley, asparagus, muskmelons, cucumbers, pumpkins, cushaws, squashes, and gourds.

Pot herbs included angelica, balm, borage, burnet, clary, marigold, marjoram, savory, columbines, tansy, wormwood, mallows, lambs'-quarter, thyme, hyssop, basil, rosemary, lavender, dill, caraway, cumin, anise, coriander, elecampane, comfrey, and nettle.

Early planters ate very similarly to the English, including the mainstay, bean porridge: "They ate and drank what she [nature] provided for them, and thanked God that it was so bountiful and so nourishing."[8]

A good example of classic 18th-century soups can be found in the receipts recorded by Edward Kidder. These include "Strong Broth, Gravey, Brown Pottage Royall, Pease Soop, Green Pease Soop, Crawfish Soop, and A Bisk of Pigeons."

Kidder's "Crawfish Soop" is very similar to recipes recorded a century later. He instructed boiling the crayfish in salt and spices, pulling off the feet and tails, and breaking the remain-der in a stone mortar. It was seasoned with savory spice, onion, hard [boiled] eggs, grated bread, and sweet herbs simmered in a strong broth. The soup was strained, and chopped parsley and mushrooms were added with lemon slices. The crayfish feet [claws] and tails were used as garnish. French rolls or bread were served with it.

His "Pease soop" was made by boiling the peas, diced turnips, and onion, straining them, adding milk, and flavoring with spearmint. His Green Pease Soop recipe also included pars-ley, sweet herbs, and nutmeg.

His "Brown Pottage Royall" contained duck meat and broth, spinach, parsley, lettuce, cockscombs, lambstones, and "vermachelly boiled" [vermicelli], all simmered in a strong broth.

Perhaps the most appreciated soup was turtle. The green sea turtle, so named because of its greenish fat, has been consumed for several hundred years and was once a major source of fresh food for exploring Europeans and pirates. Pliny wrote about cave-dwellers who ate turtle flesh though they worshipped the turtle.

Throughout the 1600s and beyond, seafarers caught the great turtles and kept them on board the ships until they were killed and cooked. Ancient Hawaiians and South Sea Islanders depended heavily on them for food. They had been over-harvested for so long that by 1700 numbers were dwindling. They are now on endangered species lists around the world. Some estimate there are less than 200,000 turtles remaining worldwide.

William Dampier wrote in the late 17th century that many English and Dutch pirate ves-sels had a native Miskito man among the crew whose chief duty it was to "strike fish, turtle, and manatee ... for this they are esteemed by all privateers, for one or two of them in a ship will maintain 100 men, so that when we careen our ships we choose commonly places where there is plenty of turtle or manatee for these Miskito men to strike; it is very rare to find pri-vateers without one or more of them."[9]

Turtle soup's virtue was that it did not "cloy," or produce ill effects, no matter the quan-tity eaten, even though it was often richly spiced. One person who had eaten it recalled, "When, after having eaten, one is obliged to rest with his mouth wide open, and cool the fevered palate with Madeira or Port."

Dampier wrote, in 1699, that the Spaniards and Portuguese showed a great antipathy for turtle, thought by some a reflection of the conflict between England and Spain at the time. Someone was certainly impressed with it, though, given that by 1808 Raffald's *The Experienced*

English Housekeeper contained a recipe for mock turtle soup. Isabella Beeton later pronounced turtle soup "the most expensive soup brought to the table," and advised that when live turtle was too dear, many cooks used tinned turtle meat.

Smooth terrapin, red-bellied terrapin, freshwater terrapin, loggerhead, diamondbacks, salt-marsh turtles, snapper, box turtle, and pond turtles have been consumed over the years. James Johnson wrote:

> Among the luxuries of the season much prized by American epicures, of which I partook at this party, the salt-water terrapin, *Emys palustris*, was new to me. It is a small species of tortoise, from 5 to 7 inches in length, and 1 to 2 ½ in breadth, which is found exclusively in salt or brackish streams near the sea-shore. It buries itself in the mud, and at this season is very fat, and is taken in great numbers. Along the mud banks, which are accessible at low water, it is met with from the Gulf of Mexico as far north as New York; but it is especially abundant in the Chesapeake and the Delaware. Other species found in fresh water, such as the wood terrapin, *E. insculpta*, the red-bellied terrapin, *E. rubric-ventris*, and the painted tortoise, *E. picta*, are also eaten along the coast, especially the two former; but the salt-water species is the only one that is valued by connoisseurs.[10]

By the 1890s, crews employed natives to watch for the turtles as they came onto land to lay their eggs. The *Gracie* left New York shortly after the first of the year in 1895, bound for Jamaica, where they caught the turtles and canned them onboard the ship. They sent approximately 500 cases of canned turtle meat home in the first month and returned to port with another 600 cases. Such an astonishing quantity of canned meat did not satisfy the crew, however, "but owing to the rough weather we were not able to bring back as much turtle as we might have done. We will make another trip."[11]

The canning equipment consisted of an eight horsepower boiler connected to a cast-iron processing kettle. There were three 25-gallon copper cauldrons and 150,000 empty cans. The canning was done by a chief and six canners. They boiled the turtle in the cauldrons, packed the meat into the cans, and soldered the lids, after which the cans were processed in the steam kettle.[12]

George Steller wrote in 1741–42 of soup made from "a couple of ptarmigans." A ptarmigan is a small bird of the grouse family. He also wrote of soup made from dried berries, bread, and mixed with roots; a soup made from a root which resembled a sweet potato; and *cowse* (a root resembling a sweet potato or ginseng). In his case, portable soup (a dried mixture) was purchased in 150 pounds or more, and sometimes he mentioned that it was boiled in melted snow to make the soup.

The journals went on to say the peeled Indian turnips were sliced, strung on cord, and dried by the fire or in the sun for storage, and coarse flour from the root of the cowse was used to thicken soup.

The following groundwork for good soup during this era was laid during the 17th century by Sir Kenelm Digby.[13]

> CONCERNING POTAGES. The ground or body of Potages must always be very good broth of Mutton, Veal and Volaille [chicken: the flesh of a chicken used for food]. Now to give good taste, you vary every month of the year, according to the herbs and roots that are in season. In Spring and Summer you use Cersevil [chervil], Oseille [sorrel, French], Borage, Bugloss, Pourpier [purslane], Lettice, Chicoree, and Cowcombers [cucumbers] quartered, etc. The manner of using them is to boil store of them about half an hour or a quarter, in a pot by it self, with some bouillon taken out of the great pot; half an hour before dinner, take light bread well dryed from all moisture before the fire; then cut in slices, laid in a dish over coals, pour upon it a ladleful of broath, no more then the bread can presently drink up; repeat this three

or four times, a good quarter of an hour in all, till all the bread is swelled like gelly (if it be too long, it will grow glewy and stick to the dish) and strong of broth; then fill it up near full with the same strong broth, which having stewed a while, put on the broth and herbs, and your Capon or other meat upon that, and so let it stew a quarter of an hour longer, then turn it up.

In winter, boil half an hour a pretty bundle of Parsley, and half as much of Sives [a small pot herb, alliaceous in nature, resembling an onion or garlic], and a very little Thyme, and Sweet-marjoram; when they have given their taste to the herbs, throw the bundle away, and do as above said with the bread. Deeper in the Winter, Parsley-roots, and White-chicoree, or Navets [turnips], or Cabbage, which last must be put in at first, as soon as the pot is skimmed; and to colour the bouillon it is good to put into it (sooner or later, according to the coursness or fineness of what you put in) Partridges or Wild-duck, or a fleshy piece of Beef half rosted. Green-pease may some of them be boiled a pretty while in the great pot; but others in a pot by themselves, with some Bouillon no longer then as if they were to eat buttered, and put upon the dish, containing the whole stock a quarter of an hour after the other hath stewed a quarter of an hour upon the bread. Sometimes Old-pease boiled in the broth from the first, to thicken it, but no Pease to be served in with it. Sometimes a piece of the bottom of a Venison Pasty, put in from the first. Also Venison bones.

William Davis' memories of the ca. 1800 kitchen of his youth are an excellent reference to the ingredients, utensils, and dishes of a late colonial era household.

...open fireplace wide enough to take a four foot stick for a forestick ... on the left side was a fire hole by which a wash boiler set in back in the sink room was heated. Over the fire was a long iron crane with its pot hooks and trammels from which a teakettle always hung, never permitting any usurpation of its place by pots and kettles of less royal station. By its side hung the boiling kettle from whose recesses came at times those wonders of the culinary art, the hard boiled puddings tied in a bag, of which the present generation knows nothing, and with which nothing has ever been seen since to furnish comparison. They were the hard boiled rice, plum rice, apple, Indian, Indian suet, batter, bread, and huckleberry...

On the right hand side of the fireplace was a brick oven with an opening into the ash pit in front of the door to receive the coals and ashes when the oven was sufficiently heated. This kind of oven is often called the "Dutch oven" but it lacks that distinctive feature of the Dutch oven, a door on the outside of the house opening into a small lean-to under which the baking was done. In front of the fireplace was the tin kitchen, in which all the roasting was done, having a long spit running through it to hold the meat or turkey, the basting being done in the oven when it happened to be heated, was done either in a creeper or in a tin yankee baker before the fire.[11]

Davis credited noodles put into soup as having come from the Dutch *noodlegees*.

Each fall for winter stores his parents put by 20 bushels of potatoes, a bushel each of turnips, carrots, and onions, five bushes of apples, a firkin of good butter, a jar of tamarinds, a jar of Malaga grapes, and 50 pounds of well-selected codfish — thick and not more than 18 inches in length including head and tail.

A rather strange account of preparing soup was written regarding the pioneers of Marion County, Iowa. Pioneer dwellings were universally crude in nature and Donnel stated snakes were often attracted to the heat and the smell of food. "They would creep into the walls and roofs, and sometimes fall inside. Not unfrequently, one of these sneaking hateful representatives of Satan, regardless of consequences, would drop himself down the sod chimney into the fireplace, and into the soup that was being cooked to make the most, if not the only, article of food for the meal."[15]

In addition to the Native American soups, there are types of soup that are purely American in ancestry, a fact that was recognized throughout the world in the 18th and 19th centuries.

A Colonial era couple saying grace at a small table set with two spoons, two pieces of dark bread, and a bowl of stew while the dog sits patiently nearby. The floor is covered with reed mats, and the cooking apparatus is visible in the fireplace. Library of Congress, Prints and Photographs Division, Reproduction Number: LC-USZ62-90595.

Some 19th-century books claimed chowder originated in New England and referenced it back to the Indians and the pilgrims at Plymouth, but there are also European references. The *Oxford English Dictionary* states it was served in southwestern England and in the northwestern region of France in the 16th and 17th centuries.

Though no recipe was given, the first account of chowder this author found was in the diary of Benjamin Lynde, chief justice of the Province of Massachusetts Bay, in 1732: "Dined on a fine chowdered cod which the captain caught." Practically daily he recorded where he dined and with whom, including the governor frequently, but the chowder was one of only a very few instances when he seemed impressed enough to note what he ate.

The word *chowdered* appeared elsewhere, as in *Putnam's* in January 1857. With regard to residents of Cape Cod, "His fare, too, is simple — at breakfast fish, fish — at dinner, fish — fish fried, broiled, boiled, baked, and chowdered!"

The Boston Evening Post published a chowder recipe on September 23, 1751, predating the first American cookery book chowder recipe by 49 years. It is given in poetic form, as were many early receipts, and though it gives no amounts, the phrase "no turning" is significant to show chowders were not stirred during cooking. Amelia Simmons' second edition, published in 1800, included a recipe, as did Mary Randolph's (1828), Lydia Maria Child's (1832), and Sarah Hale's (1841).

First lay some Onions to keep the Pork from burning,
Because in Chouder there can be no turning:

Then lay some Pork in Slices very thin,
Thus you in Chouder always must begin.
Then season well with Pepper, Salt, and Spice;
Parsley, Sweet-Marjoram, Savory, and Thyme,
Then Biscuit next which must be soak'd some Time.
Thus your Foundation laid, you will be able
To raise a Chouder, high as Tower of Babel:
For by repeating o're the Same again,
You may make Chouder for a Thousand Men,
Last Bottle of Claret, with Water eno' to smother 'em
You'l have a Mess which some call 'Omnium' gather 'em.

Lydia's recipe already offered variations—sliced lemon, tomato catsup, or a cup of beer. While some were appalled at the idea of tomato in fish or clam chowder it eventually evolved into Manhattan style chowder. Potatoes become a more popular ingredient after the publication of Daniel Webster's chowder method in 1842 in which he instructed using potatoes and just "a few of the largest Boston crackers."

The Boston cracker may have been Crown Pilot Crackers, which were first produced in 1828. They remained in production until recently, and the company's decision to cease producing them was met with much disappointment.

The practice of using ship biscuits (hardtack) in chowder is the product of the "waste not, want not" philosophy. As the biscuits soaked in the broth they softened and became edible. Eventually they were replaced by potatoes when the latter was readily available.

Chowder also seems not to have been unknown to our ancestors, for Grose speaks of it as a "sea-dish," but the very indifference with which he, a man of infinite taste, mentions it, proves that it cannot have been the famous dish produced by the inventive genius of the venerable and pious pilgrims of Plymouth.... It is well known that Mr. [Daniel] Webster excelled in his chowder, which he did not disdain to make himself, as he had caught the fish for it with his own hands. It is described as, "a many-sided dish, of pork and fish, potatoes and bread, onions and turnips, all mixed up with fresh chequits and seabass, blackfish and long clams, pumpkinseed [sunfish] and an accidental eel, well peppered and salted, piled in layers and stewed together." Cider and champaigne are not unfrequently added, and the "matelote," as the French would call it, is a most tempting dainty—to very hungry people.[16]

Another writer left a concise definition of chowder: "Chowder, a favourite dish in New England—a stew of fish, pork, onions, and biscuit, often prepared by pic-nic parties, who visit the sea-shore, from fish caught at the time—is not unknown at our tables [Dutch settlements in New York], though not usually prepared after the approved New England fashion."[17]

Amelia Murray[18] claimed to have been "introduced to chowder, a most praise-worthy preparation, enabling you to eat soup and fish at one time," in the early 1850s, and another account published in 1856 sheds some light on the manner in which it was cooked in the home:

The Cauldron was removed from the iron hook on which it hung, and its contents which proved to be that standing dainty of New England, a rich chowder, were poured into a large tureen of Delft ware.[19]

Amelia and other non–French travelers were unfamiliar with chowder until they journeyed through the United States. However, de Guoy credits the creation of chowder to Brittany fishing villages. He stated that when fishermen returned from the sea, local families each contributed something for the soup cauldron and shared the steamy contents when it had cooked. He connected the name *chowder* to the phrase *faire la chaudière*, or "prepare the cauldron." Some also speculate it came from the word *jowter*, a fishmonger.

He went on to say these French fisherfolk crossed the Atlantic with their cauldrons, settling in Newfoundland, and their custom of making this soup then spread into New England where the name was corrupted to *chowder*.[20]

Like barbecue, chowder was a popular choice in enticing large crowds to attend a function such as a political rally. One of the largest described was prepared in a kettle weighing 3,500 pounds and was made from 350 pounds of fish, 3 barrels Crackers, 3 barrels Potatoes, 200 pounds of butter, 2 ½ pecks of onion, 14 pounds pepper, 90 gallons of milk, and a half bushel of salt. These ingredients produced 800 gallons of chowder for a Fourth of July celebration in Pawtucket, Rhode Island in 1857.[21]

Farmhouse chowders such as corn chowder descend from Native American stews, but recipes for these weren't published until the 1880s. The first may have been that of Mary J. Lincoln in 1884.

Of note, is similar Spanish *caldeirada a pescadora* (fish soup made with onions, sorrel, parsley, garlic, olive oil, and white wine with thin bread slices). This soup is popular in Portugal, and de Guoy credited early Portuguese fishermen who settled in New England with having spread the tradition of chowder through their *caldeirada*.

Commercial fishermen often sold the fish they caught in the markets, and prepared the heads, either by frying or making chowder for their own tables. This begins to sound more logical when the size of the fish caught is taken into consideration, for there was sufficient meat on the heads alone to prepare a meal. Elijah King noted, "There's nothing equal to a cod's head for a chowder."[22]

Chowder was historically made from clams or fish, usually cod (fresh or salted), although crabs, mussels, oysters, lobster, flounder, haddock, halibut, crayfish, perch, eels, frogs' legs, chicken, rabbit, dried beef, pork, salmon, shrimp, scallops, snapper, sturgeon, turtle, and even a host of vegetables have all been the star of the show in their own right.

Even catfish or oily mackerel wasn't safe when thoughts turned to chowder, as evidenced by one that was served to future president Franklin Pierce. "No time was lost in getting under way, and we all began to catch fish for the chowder which was the pretext for our expedition. The mackerel were running in innumerable shoals, and we soon had a supply far in excess of our expected wants. An expert in a red flannel shirt then commenced, with fish, salt pork, potatoes, and biscuits, the preparation of the savory dish, which was soon steaming under our watering mouths. I had never tasted chowder before, and have never tasted it since — at least not the genuine, simon-pure article, served up to appease appetites sharpened by the sea air."[23]

Lewis and Newhall stated in 1865 that potatoes were "among the articles to be provided for the Massachusetts settlers and sent over by the Company," by 1628 and, given the prevalence of fish in the waters, it wasn't long before someone "boiled, and ate them with fish."[24]

> Chowder, a national dish peculiar to the Eastern States, was first produced by the inventive genius of our venerable and pious ancestors at Plymouth. Our reverence for them created a fondness for this dish, and we still cherish it for that and its intrinsic merit. The refinements introduced into its composition, while they have added to our enjoyment, have not entirely effaced its simplicity, or diminished our gratitude. The French "matelote" is an imitation, but is so much tinctured with monarchial ornament as to be far removed from the simplicity of the original.[25]

Kentucky burgoo is an American soup. The term first appeared in Edward Coxere's 1650 *Adventures by Sea,* and it initially referred to a mush-like dish made from oatmeal or possibly bulgur wheat, the corrupted pronunciation of which could account for the stew's name. The term may have originated on seafaring vessels in the 17th century. From that grain soup grew the slow-cooked substantial stew that is standard fare across Kentucky. Burgoo is very similar to *Brunswick stew*, also an American soup.

Specific soups began to emerge during the medieval era and became perennial favorites in many locales, often at about the same time. They found their way into colonial America through the knowledge of European cooks and the cookery books brought with the first settlers.

English cookery books were used in America, with editions reprinted in America for Americans either with no changes or with few changes. As America began to produce its own culinary prodigies, recorded recipes began to change, reflecting not only the difference in available ingredients, but also in evolving techniques of preparation.

Cookery books in German, Italian, French, and so on were reprinted in the United States for use by immigrants who could read those languages, and for those who couldn't, translated versions soon followed. Many contain the same sorts of common soup recipes.

The first tomato soup recipes were simply tomatoes added to basic vegetable soups. As the popularity of tomatoes spread from the South through the North, so did the number of recipes for using them. Between 1832, when N. M. K. Lee's first tomato soup recipe was published, and 1841, when Lettice Bryan's version was published, the multitude of other vegetables were left out and the purely tomato soup we know today emerged.

Andrew Smith's remarkable *The Tomato in America* contains recipes taken from cookery books and papers as early as 1790. He stated tomatoes were used in soup "at least as early as the mid-eighteenth century" in colonial America. The earliest soup recipes he included were Mrs. Read's tomato and ochre (1813), and Mary Randolph's tomato and okra and gazpacho (1824).

Harriott Pinckney Horry included in her receipts one for keeping tomatoes for winter use for soups or sauces, in 1770.

Lawson shed light on the types of soup made in colonial America in his summary of the Carolinas. Pea soup was one of the most common. He described the Indian *rounceval* which the colonists called the "Miraculous Pease," "so call'd from their long pods and great increase," other pulses which he felt too numerous to name but which they had gotten from the natives and which afforded them two crops a year, and several types of English pea (white, gray, field-pease, sickle-pease). He also stated the Indians had grown the kidney bean long before the arrival of the English.

Cookery vessels in colonial America were at first whatever was typical in the country from which the family had emigrated. When necessary they may have used pottery vessels, and pottery bowls, wooden trenchers, or noggins held individual portions. The following was penned in 1854 regarding cookware from the *Mayflower*.

> There is still in the possession of Treat Davidson, of Roxbury, an iron kettle, which was brought to this country some forty years later, in 1660, and has descended to the present owner from Nathan Botsford, one of his ancestors, who himself brought it from England. This, doubtless, is the oldest culinary utensil in the territory [Woodbury, CT].[26]

19. Bartram and Kalm

In the 1770s, naturalist William Bartram's party ate soup made from crane. Bartram stated it made excellent soup, but that he should prefer its seraphic music in the sky.[1]

Much of what he ate was taken from the land, for example, squab made into "pilloe with rice" (pilau), turtle, "fat and delicious," sunfish, "delicious food," trout stewed in orange juice, and so on. He enjoyed oranges, palms which produced juicy fruit, and others.

John and William Bartram, Peter Kalm, and others wrote about the colonies, natives, and settlers. In many cases soldiers in the forts were also part of the social fabric of the territories.

In 1750, the lands of New France extended from the Gulf Coast northward, extending into Canada above the Dakotas and Minnesota, into Hudson's Bay, and into eastern Canada (including Newfoundland and Acadia). The territory was divided into Upper Louisiana, encompassing Illinois and the surrounding area, and Lower Louisiana, encompassing all of present-day Louisiana and parts of present-day Texas, Mississippi, and Alabama. Military districts of New France were Mobile, Biloxi, Alabama, New Orleans, Yazoo, Natchez, Arkansas, Illinois, and Natchitoches in 1718.[2]

Florida was held by the Spanish, and eastern Georgia and the Carolinas northeast into Canada by the English. The divisions of territories directly influenced the diet of each group through their native foods, and of subsections within each group through the native plant and animal foods in each area.

For example, the saltwater fish and shellfish found near French New Orleans, Biloxi, and Mobile were nonexistent in Upper New France, and those families near Fort de Chartres, Fort Massac, St. Genevieve, and so on prepared an abundance of freshwater fish, turtles, and the like.

Wild plant foods differed with climate and growing patterns; however, the cultivated crops described by early explorers seem to have been remarkably similar.[3]

Pierre Delliette wrote in 1702 of the multitudes of bison hunted on the prairies of what would become Illinois, while in Alabama the plains bison was rare enough by 1750 for historians to question its habitat, many saying any remaining had retreated into Mississippi, Kentucky, or the Appalachians. An elderly Hillabee chief born about 1750 stated that as a child he had seen large herds in the vicinity of Talladega.[4] Bison remained a plentiful food source in Mississippi through the remainder of the century. A contemporary report said, "The buffalo is the chief food of the Natives, and of the *French* also for a long time past.... They hunt this animal in winter; for which purpose they leave *Lower Louisiana* and the river Missisipi." Du Pratz, Gallatin, and others discussed at length the presence of the bison at various points. Bison were common in large numbers as far south as Nashville, Tennessee and west of the Mississippi river.[5]

A Currier & Ives depiction of an Indian encampment on the St. Lawrence. The ever-present soup caul-dron hangs from a wooden tripod over a slow fire. Similar ingredients and techniques were used by white explorers and settlers. Library of Congress, Prints and Photographs Division, Reproduction Number LC-USZ62-2898.

The French Canadians, even in a bad year, had more food than a peasant remaining in France — wheat and rye bread, corn cakes, salt pork, eels, game, fish, peas, beans, cucumbers, melons, potatoes, and wild fruits and nuts (walnut, cherries, plum raspberries, strawberries, gooseberries, and several roots and herbs. *Soupe aux pois* (pea soup) nourished whole families to the extent that some called it the national dish.[6]

Frenchmen consumed hominy, a dish they learned of from natives.[7] A French priest who claimed he was unable to eat the smoked game or fish of the natives subsisted on gruel made from pounded corn and on tripes-de-roches, a fungus harvested in the North which produced a blackish pulp when cooked. Fish and smoked game formed the principal diet at Michili-mackinac (Michigan) with mention of pigeon broth, meat pasties, and capon.[8]

Kalm wrote of the settlement called New Sweden, and his travels covered parts of modern-day Pennsylvania, New York, New Jersey, and southern Canada. His journey began in 1748 and resulted in the publication of his travel notes in 1753. New Sweden was founded March 29, 1638 at Fort Christina, present-day Wilmington, Delaware, which was part of New Nether-land. Settlers were primarily Swedes, Finns, and Dutch.

Dutch foods are those from the Netherlands, often called Holland, in northwestern Europe, and are what the settlers brought with them to the New World. The country is bordered by the North Sea on the north and west, Belgium on the south, and Germany on the east.

Kalm was much appreciative of the maize he encountered in his travels, and of meals he partook with the inhabitants he wrote, "The meal begins with soup with a good deal of bread in it. Then follow fresh meats of various kinds, boiled and roasted, poultry, or game, fricas-ees, ragoos, &c., of several sorts together with different kinds of salads. They commonly drink red claret at dinner mixed with water; and spruce beer is likewise much in use. The ladies drink water and sometimes wine."

Two important Dutch soups were *ertensoep* (split pea) and *bruinbonensoep* (brown bean). The pot herbs described in the following recipe translated by Peter Rose were standard break-fast fare; the more substantial soups were eaten later in the day.

> Take clean well-water, add one or two stale round white breads, depending on how much you want to cook, hang it [the pan] over the fire. In the meantime cut the pot-herbs: chervil, beet, a few blades of Mace, Borage, or Bugloss, the first tiny leaves of the black Currants and of Calendulas, also Leek and Catnip, a little Spinach, but not Sorrel that would make it too gray-ish [in color], when it [all] is cut up fine and the water and bread have boiled for a while until it [the bread] has dissolved. Add [the pot herbs] to it and let it boil until done then Butter and Salt as you desire.[9]

Such soups as an early-day meal may have come about because most medieval cultures ate only two, sometimes only one, meal per day, partly due to the labor involved in prepar-ing food, partly due to religious influence, and sometimes due to scanty provisions. King Alfred of Wessex noted, "They [monks] lived naturally and temperately. They always ate but once a day, and that was in the evening."[10]

Foods Kalm documented which could and did find their way into the soup cauldrons echo some of the accounts by other writers.

"When the [guinea pepper] fruit is ripe it is almost red; it is added to a roasted or boiled piece of meat, a little of it being strewed upon it or mixed in the broth. Besides this cucum-bers are pickled with it."

Squirrel flesh is "eaten and reckoned a dainty." Game, including raccoon, beaver, deer, and bear flesh, "was prepared like pork.... Their flesh is eaten by both rich and poor since it is reckoned equal in goodness to pork." As was customary in Europe, popes often declared the beaver a fish so its flesh could be eaten by Catholics on Friday.

"I was told that some people eat the thighs and hind legs [of frogs, especially bullfrogs], and that they are very palatable."

Birds, including partridges, cranes, pigeon, and bobolink (rice bird), were much appre-ciated in soups, and oysters abounded and were taken to market throughout New Nether-land. Mussels were eaten by the Indians and some Europeans as well.

As for peas, "in all parts ... inhabited by the French, the people sow great quantities of them and have a large crop." Potatoes and Bermuda potatoes (sweet) were "planted by almost everyone." Cabbage was added to soup and salad. Squashes and pumpkins were "prepared for eating in different manners." Okra is "a plant which grows wild in the West Indies but is planted in the gardens here." Asparagus "we frequently saw growing near the fences." Onions were "very much in use here," as were pumpkins, melons, lettuce, wild chicory, endive, beans, Turkish beans, carrots, cucumbers, beets, horseradish, thyme, marjoram, turnips, and parsnips. These were "sometimes eaten, though not very commonly."

> Few people took notice of potatoes, and neither the common or the Bermuda ones were planted in Canada.... When the French here are asked why they do not plant potatoes, they answer that they do not like them and they laugh at the English who are so fond of them.[11]

Poke and sorrel were eaten, "partly as green kale and partly in the manner we eat spinach." Clams were prepared in many ways, including being "boiled and placed in meat-soups." Wild garlic and wild onions, called by some wild leeks, were frequently found in soups.

Those dishes were followed by sweetmeats of walnuts, almonds, raisins, hazelnuts, currants, cranberries, and preserves of strawberry, raspberry, blackberry, and moss berries with cheese and milk.

Thomas Holm added the availability of filberts, chestnut, mulberry, sassafras, plum, damson, pear, and peach. He wrote of bears, elk, deer, otter, wild boar, hares and various animals trapped for fur. There were swans, geese, turkeys, pheasant, cranes, sea-culvers, herons, eagles, hawks, pigeons, turtledoves, ducks, parrots, partridges, quails, various singing birds, and sturgeon, cod, salmon, trout, mackerel, rock pike, horn pike, perch, roach, herring, eel, lamprey, oysters, lobsters, sea and land turtles, cockles, and mussels.

> Friday and Saturday they eat no flesh according to the Roman Catholic rites; but they well know how to guard against hunger on those days they boil all sorts of kitchen-herbs and fruit, fishes, eggs and milk prepared in many ways. They cut cucumbers into slices and eat them with cream, which is a very good dish. Sometimes they put whole cucumbers on the table, and everybody that likes them takes one, peels it, slices it, and dips the slices in salt, eating them like radishes.... Loaves are oval and baked of wheat flour.[12]

By this time cook pots were made of clay, tin, copper, brass, or iron, wrought iron having preceded cast iron.

Peter G. Rose translated *The Sensible Cook* (1683), and although the book contains little about the preparation or consumption of soup by the Dutch, she says soup and stew were very prevalent in the Dutch diet both in the Netherlands and in colonial America. She believes the reason there are so few recipes for soup in the book is that soup is such a common dish that can be successfully prepared in so many ways that it was left to the discretion of the cook what to put in it, and the author saw little need to include actual recipes.

Heartier soup and stew were standard fare in colonial America at dinner. The latter was eaten daily, and was usually made from some combination of vegetables, and inexpensive cuts of meat such as knuckles or pig's feet.

Soup spices were reflective of those of Dutch seafarers, especially nutmeg and mace, and it is this combination that makes these soups distinctively Dutch in origin.

Even in colonial America butter was used quite liberally in Dutch soups, reflecting the abundance of dairy products in the Netherlands. Also, the Dutch had always eaten more vegetables than their European neighbors.

The Sensible Cook has recipes for chervil soup and currant soup along with several recipes for *hutspot* and *olipodrigo*, dishes similar to hotchpotch but often containing an impressive list of ingredients. Mrs. Rose described *hutspot* as a thick stew, not to be confused with soup or pottage.

She quoted Lambertus Burema's study of Dutch foodways regarding the prevalence of soup in the diet of theology students in Leiden, which both thought typical of the average 17th-century diet. Soups and *hutspots* included wheat bread soup, white bread soup, mutton broth, and barley porridge. Porridge soup was eaten by all social classes.

20. Portable Soup

Lewis and Clark carried a vast quantity of portable soup with them on their expedition; however, it does not appear to have been much appreciated by them or the men under their leadership. By their words, it doesn't appear to have improved in flavor or consistency during the previous years.

Their journals (1806) include numerous mentions of soup, including the root vegetables mentioned by Stellar. Foods they ate included soup from cakes of cured bread made from a root resembling a sweet potato. They also purchased six bushels of the root the Indians called cowse, "a white meley [mealy] root which is very fine in soup after being dried and pounded," white apples (breadroot, Indian turnip, or as the French called it, *pommes blanche*), heath hen (probably pheasant or grouse), dried and pounded salmon roe, dried sunflower seeds pounded between two stones, and portable soup, though they seemed to use the latter only when "we have nothing else to eat."[1]

Numerous sources claim portable soup can be traced to the Magyar warriors in the 14th century. They boiled salted beef until it fell into pieces, chopped it, dried it, and carried it as they rode across Europe on horseback. This powdered soup base was added to hot water to make a nourishing meal. An account of Hungarian soup used to feed troops was recorded in 1533.[2]

> The driver put a big iron pot full of water on the fire and when the priest and gypsy had rapidly skinned the sheep, he chopped it up with a practiced hand and dropped the pieces in. Onions followed and plenty of paprika.[3]

Hugh Plat made portable soup in 1607, Ann Blencowe recorded her method in 1694, and Hannah Glasse followed suit in 1747. Baron Justus von Liebig, a chemist, produced his version in 1848. By the 1860s it was used by explorers who appreciated its lightweight, and later it evolved into the bouillon cubes such as Oxo marketed to housewives as a base for soups and sauces.[4]

Count Rumford (Benjamin Thompson) popularized portable soup while serving the duke of Bavaria. He produced large quantities of portable soup made from bones, inexpensive meat, and other ingredients which he fed to the soldiers under the duke's command. He later used his research to feed the hungry when he established soup kitchens for the poor.

James Boswell and Samuel Johnson mentioned the use of portable soup on their trip through the Hebrides in 1773: "A page of my Journal is like a cake of portable soup. A little may be diffused into a considerable portion."

Nathaniel Portlock, on a voyage around the world, including Hawaii and America, in the 1780s wrote in his journal several entries on soup, particularly of portable soup. In one entry he spoke of portable soup with barley, celery seed, mustard, cress, and rapeseed boiled in it.[5]

Written documentation of portable soup can be found from 1743 in *The Lady's Companion*. However, it has probably existed in primitive form since cookery vessels came into use.

> To make a Veal Glue or Cake Soup to be carried in the Pocket, take a Leg of Veal, strip it of the skin and the Fat, then take all the muscular or fleshy Parts from the Bones; boil this flesh gently in such a quantity of water and so long a Time, till the Liquor will make a strong Jelly when it is cold: This you may try by taking out a small Spoonful now and then, and letting it cool.
>
> Here it is to be supposed, that though it will jelly presently in small Quantities, yet all the Juice of the Meat may not be extracted; however, when you find it very strong, strain the Liquor through a Sieve, and let it settle; then provide a large Stew-pan, with Water and some China Cups or glazed Earthenware; fill these cups with Jelly taken clear from the Settling, and set them in a Stew-pan of Water, and let the Water boil gently till the Jelly becomes as thick as Glue; after which, let them stand to cool, and then turn out the Glue upon a piece of new Flannel, which will draw out the Moisture; turn them once in six or eight Hours, and put them upon a fresh Flannel, and so continue to do till they are quite dry, and keep it in a dry warm Place: This will harden so much, that it will be stiff and hard as glue in a little Time, and may be carried in the Pocket without inconvenience.
>
> You are to use this by boiling about a Pint of Water, and pouring it upon a Piece of the Glue or Cake, about the Bigness of a small walnut, and stirring it with a Spoon till the cake dissolves, which will make a very strong good Broth. As for the seasoning part, every one may add Pepper and Salt as they like it, for there must be nothing of that kind put among the veal when you make the Glue, for any Thing of that sort would make it moldy.... So may a dish of good Soup be made without Trouble, only allowing the Proportion of Cake Gravy answering to the above laid Direction: Or if Gravy be wanted for Sauce, double the Quantity may be used that is prescribed for Broth or Soup.

William Byrd II (1674–1744), founder of Richmond, Virginia, and owner of an elaborate library of over 4,000 books, got into the act of using portable soup. He advised, in 1737, using stock made from different kinds of meat, bones, vegetables, and anchovies which was boiled down to a thickened mass and then dried in the sun: "Dissolve a piece of portable soup in water and a bason of good broth can be had in a few minutes."

Throughout the 1790s, English and Scottish newspapers advertised portable soup, espousing several uses for it. "Gentlemen going to the muirs or retiring to the country will find it highly convenient to have along with them a few canisters of portable soups by which they can in a few minutes be provided with a wholesome, pleasing, and ready beverage." They could be made into soup or used to make gravy for family use.

Robert Burns wrote of hunters in Scotland packing portable soup, and numerous sources recommended it for sea voyages. Samuel Fraunces was selling portable soup and other goods for travelers from a tavern as early as 1761.

Portable soups from Buenos Aires, refined in England, were recommended for use in hospitals for the consumption of patients.—*Times*, London, June 27, 1794.

In 1855 Alexis Soyer took up the cause of soldiers fighting in the Crimea, where scurvy and other conditions were widespread, and where men died because weakened undernourished bodies could not heal themselves. Soyer used dried vegetable cakes he called "coarse julienne," which produced food enough for 100 men. His cakes contained per hundredweight 20 pounds carrots, 20 pounds turnips, 10 pounds parsnips, 15 pounds onions, 20 pounds cabbage, 5 pounds celery, and 10 pounds leeks combined with 1 pound aromatic seasoning made up of 4 ounces each of thyme, winter savory, pepper with 1 ounce cloves and 2 ounces of bay leaf. The quality of the desiccated vegetables was said to be well above average, so soup made from them was apparently better quality than that consumed by Lewis and Clark.

21. Army and Military Soup

Broth and porridge were the daily food of Highland children, yet once grown, the Scots were known for their endurance and tenacity in battle. "Let those who have quailed under the charge of a Highland Regiment, tell the results," warned a writer.[1] Another seemed to concur: "A Highlander will scale mountains all day upon a diet of oatmeal."[2]

Sir John Froissart was one of the first to extol the virtues of oats in 1327. He stated that when the Scots invaded England they did so with no provisions other than "a little bag of oatmeal" tied behind the saddle. The English initially thought oats fit only for animals.[3]

Soup was the ever-present sustainer of life for soldiers of early wars, from the Roman legions on, so much so that Napoleon Bonaparte said, "An army travels on its stomach. Soup makes the soldier."[4]

In 1813 Napoleon's troops were in great need of food, warmth, and other necessities. Upon taking shelter, "some were occupied in cooking the soup; others kneaded the biscuit which will be baked under the ashes." The soup was made from the carcass of a horse that had died earlier, each man taking a piece and all contributing his share to the soup kettle.

> Soup is the most common nourishment. Now, see what that soup is. As it was impossible to procure water because the ice covered all the springs and every lake, they melted in a pot a sufficient quantity of snow to produce the amount of water which they needed; they afterward mixed with that water, which was black and dirty, a portion of the flour, more or less defiled, which had been provided, and thus they thickened the mixture to the consistence of soup, which they seasoned with salt, or in default of that they threw in two or three cartridges, which in giving it the taste of powder, took away its extreme insipidity, and colored it with a deep, dark tinge which made it resemble the black soup of the Spartans. While they prepared this porridge they covered the coals with bits of horse-flesh, which they also seasoned with powder. The meal finished, each one lay down to sleep, immediately overcome with fatigue and depressed by the weight of his misfortunes.[5]

At times, Napoleon's troops dined on portable soup, which "gave nourishment to the soldier and whilst this food was light and easy of digestion, it did not subject him to dysentery."[6] This may have been felt prudent after 3,000 soldiers suffered greatly from dysentery at Witespk due to tainted rye in their soup.[7]

In 1750 Kalm said the soldiers in French Canada received generous rations—a pound and a half of wheat bread daily, plenty of peas, bacon, and salted or dried meat. They sometimes received among them freshly slaughtered beef, usually had milk, and kept vegetable gardens.[8]

Early accounts indicate the French ate little differently than natives in Canada. The most common dish was pottage made of pounded corn and scraps of meat or fish. Brass and iron kettles replaced the natives' pottery and wooden utensils after the arrival of the French.

The same accounts state no attempt was made by the French in Louisiana to clear land to plant corn or peas, though the writer's knowledge was limited to what he saw. Champlain was said to have planted the first wheat in Canada in 1608.[9] Near New Orleans there were six inhabitants cultivating the land.

Legend has it that pepper-pot soup was born of necessity during the siege at Valley Forge when General Washington instructed his cook to prepare a tasty meal, regardless of the difficulty in doing so, to boost the morale of his troops during the Revolution. The men were in rags and supplies were always inadequate, and the chef, finding nothing but peppercorns, tripe, and a few odds and ends, combined them in soup.[10]

That hot nourishing meal filled hungry bellies, bolstered confidence, and encouraged the men to rally for independence, but it seems to have been a well-established dish prior to this incident.

In 1698, Edward Ward described pepper-pot in Jamaica: "Three spoonfuls so inflamed my mouth, that had I devoured a peck of horse-radish and drank after it a gallon of brandy and gunpowder ... I could not have been more importunate for a drop of water to cool my tongue." A 1790 account refers to pepper-pot as native to Jamaica, and numerous accounts indicate it was common to India.

An 1869 article in the *Galveston News* called pepper-pot a West Indian dish and indicated English ladies had made it for over a hundred years. "Tradition states that daily, monthly, yearly, for a whole century this beautiful pot was kept boiling and steaming away, never ceasing at breakfast and dinner to send forth its odorous welcome to hungry guests ... a very large, very thick, deep earthen pot is placed over the fire and into this are thrown pieces of beef, mutton, salt, pork, fowls, ham bones, crabs, lobsters, all kinds of vegetables ... with a very large quantity of a West Indian vegetable called calalue."

Philadelphia street vendors in Washington's day chanted, "All hot, all hot, pepper pot, pepper pot; makes backs strong, makes lives long; all hot, pepper pot" as they served up steaming bowls of the tripe-laden soup.[11]

During the early days of the American Revolution, the colonies fed their militia, a practice that became increasingly more difficult as the army grew. After Washington became commander-in-chief, the Continental Congress appointed Joseph Trumbull the first commissary general of stores and provisions. His service in feeding the Connecticut militia was felt to qualify him for the position.[12]

In November 1775, the first allowance of food in the form of army ration was established at 16 ounces beef (or ¾ pound pork or 1 pound salted fish), 1 pound flour or bread, 16 ounces milk, 1 quart spruce beer per week, with 3 pints of beans or peas, 1.4 ounces rice or 1 pint Indian meal. Soap and candles were issued weekly.

In 1780, Congress issued supplies and depended on each state to properly distribute them. The system soon failed and more changes were instituted to make sure soldiers received adequate food. A gill (4 ounces) of rum and vinegar was added to the ration in 1785.

Sutlers were established during that time and remained a part of army life until 1866. Their role was to make available for purchase by the soldiers any items not supplied in the ration, such as vegetables, coffee, chocolate, tobacco, and liquor.[13]

A Virginian kept a brief diary following the surrender at Charleston, the first entry dated May 12, 1780. The British were apparently amazed that "an army of not more than three thousand troops, composed of regular soldiers, militia, sailors, and marines," defended their post for 31 days against a force of 10,000 British soldiers. After surrendering he stated the Americans were in great need of provisions. They were nearing starvation. Two days later they had not received any provisions, but they had somewhat relieved their hunger through their own ingenuity.

> This afternoon we were in some measure relieved from hunger, by means of a poor sheep a Hessian was driving by our quarters, that ran round the house and went in our cellar, and was immediately concealed by some of our waiters. The Hessian hunted for some time for his poor sheep but could not find it, and we soon made some good hot soup.[14]

A British army manual written in 1798 sang the praises of soup for weary troops.

> Nothing is so agreeable and at the same time so wholesome to a soldier, after a fatiguing and perhaps wet march, as some warm soup. The use of broth or soup is particularly advantageous after great fatigue, because, on these occasions, the digestive organs are weakened and less liable to bear solid food than at other times.[15]

That manual went on to enumerate the items usually available for the army mess's soup kettle. Among these were cabbage, carrots, parsnips, onion, and potatoes. They could be supplemented with foraged items such as wildcress or watercress, scurvy grass, sorrel, and lettuce found in every field. Those items, with barley, decorticated oats, cut groats, dried peas, rice, and fresh meat, produced wholesome soup.

Salted meat that had not yet turned bad was supposed to be a faint red color and have no "putrid smell" when cut into. Soldiers were so advised because of the frequency with which they were issued tainted meat in their rations.

Officers were to be provided with quantities of portable soup for use after marches. *The Soldier's Friend* said:

> In all cases where butcher's meat constitutes a bulky or essential part of the food of the privates, whether in camp, or elsewhere, they should be obliged to boil and make soup, or barley broth of it: and for that purpose barley should make a part of the stores of every camp.

Boiling was thought healthy, and by boiling the meat and making soup the broth also became a valuable addition to the soldier's diet, making the quantity of meat go further. The men, however, were said almost always to prefer broiling the meat and fish if left to their own methods of preparation.[16]

The manual said that any time the army was in a fixed camp the soldiers should be encouraged to grow fresh vegetables, especially potatoes, a philosophy that would later be recommended for American troops by John C. Calhoun in 1818.[17]

Barbara Leucke, author of *Feeding the Frontier Army*, supplied the following list of seeds ordered for the soldiers' gardens at Fort Snelling in 1821: yellow onion, red onion, blood beets, turnip, yellow Swedish turnips, head lettuce, scarlet radish, salmon radish, carrot, parsnips, cucumbers, long cucumbers, early June peas, bush beans, early cabbage, Drum winter cabbage, Savoy cabbage, red cabbage, sage, red pepper, French turnip, watermelon, winter squash, summer squash, pepper grass, parsley, saffron, and burnet.

With the exception of watermelon, cucumbers, and radishes, the entire list would have gone into the soup cauldrons of the soldiers and their dependents in whatever combinations suited the cook. Nonmilitary persons employed by the army, such as washerwomen, received rations with the troops and prepared their own meals.

In 1836, the seed list included spinach, thyme, summer savoury, cauliflower, and carrots. The soldiers utilized the typical methods of preservation for keeping the vegetables—pickling, drying, and storing in a root cellar.

The following is an excellent description of the military method of preparing soups.

> A cross-piece set upon two forked stakes, so soon as the fire was started, supported the four or five long black three-gallon camp-kettles in which each meal was cooked. One contained coffee or tea, another salt meat, a third fresh meat, a fourth bean soup or soup made from the

Photograph from the main eastern theater of war, 1864–1865. An African-American cook at work in City Point, VA. He has metal tripods from which the kettles hang rather than the wooden poles used by other units. The log behind the fire is likely a wind break. Library of Congress, Prints and Photographs Division, Reproduction Number LC-DIG-cwpb-02010.

dessicated vegetables ... then the sergeant would cry, with a loud voice, "Company A, fall in for soup."[18]

Growing vegetables was still encouraged in 1864. On a hundred-acre farm attached to Hampton Hospital in Virginia, convalescent soldiers sowed the following seeds: Three and a half bushels of beans, four pounds beets, 2 pounds cabbage, 1½ pounds carrots, 2 ounces celery, 1½ pounds cucumbers, 3 bushels of sweet corn, ¾ of a pound of lettuce, 2 pounds muskmelon, 2 pounds watermelon, 2 pounds onions, 7 barrels of onion sets, ½ pound parsnips, 6 bushels of pease, ¼ pound pepper, 225 bushels of potatoes, 5,000 sprouts of sweet-potatoes, 1¼ pounds of radishes, ½ pound salsify, ¾ pound spinach, 2 pounds squash, ¾ pound tomatoes, and 3 pounds of turnip seed. There was also an acre of strawberry plants and 250 cuttings of currants. Six businessmen from in and around New York donated the seeds and cuttings.[19]

Revolutionary War rations proved inadequate during the 1790s for soldiers on the frontier, and rations were then set at 1¼ pounds of beef, 18 ounces flour or bread, 4 pounds of salt, 4 quarts of vinegar per 100 rations, and soap and candles.

When in established quarters, wives of enlisted men were sometimes able to move to the forts and continue housekeeping with their husbands. While this made for happier, generally better-fed soldiers, it also meant economizing to stretch rations, especially if there were children to provide for.

The soldier in the War of 1812 received rations of 20 ounces beef, 18 ounces flour, 1 gill of rum, 1 gill of vinegar, .64 ounces salt, and soap and candles. The soldier's diet remained deficient in vitamin C but high in protein.[20]

Andrew Jackson, like most commanders, suffered for want of supplies when fighting the Creek in 1813. With 2,500 troops under his command, he was furious when supplies promised him did not arrive. "Such a body will consume ten wagon-loads of provisions every day. For a week's subsistence they require a thousand bushels of grain, twenty tons of flesh, a thousand gallons of whiskey, and many hundred weight of miscellaneous provisions."

Days later, with still no sight of the expected supplies, Jackson wrote to friends and several public authorities saying, "Give me food, and I will end this savage war in a month." On the evening of October 24, he started for the Ten Islands of the Coosa, "fifty miles distant," with only two days' supply of bread and six of meat, swearing that he would "neither sound a retreat nor suffer a defeat." It was later realized that the parties who had contracted for the supplies "failed to meet their engagements," and the army began to live off foraged supplies. Colonel Dyer and a party of 200 soldiers raided the Indian village of Littefutchee and after taking a "good supply of corn" torched the village.[21]

A Canadian soldier thought the Canadians more skilled at woodcraft, but the English excelled gastronomically. Rather than frizzle away rations on the end of a bayonet, they sent out one man from each mess who gathered pot herbs in his haversack. Combined with a little flour, these made "a capital kettle of soup."[22]

An English officer during the Peninsular War (1813) compared the monotony of his diet, a wooden bowl of rice soup and a piece of tough beef daily, with that of the 80-year-old archbishop of Burgos, who prepared his own daily breakfast of soup.

> The simplest sort of pottage imaginable; — some heads of garlic are kept simmering on the ashes in an earthen vessel which holds about two quarts of water; a few minutes before it is required for use, his Excellency puts in with his own Episcopal hands, a certain quantity of red pepper, and a small cup of oil; and the process is completed by pouring the whole over some thin slices of Spanish bread.[23]

Another peninsular soldier described the diet he consumed in 1811. It may have been monotonous, but he seemed to like it:

> We had a camp kettle in which we cooked all our rations together; there was an abundance of the finest vegetables, very cheap, so that with some rice in addition, we turned out excellent soup and bouilli ... sometimes we got a bullock's head to add to the rations.[24]

He recalled invitations to "come to dinner to-morrow in camp fashion," which meant to send your rations, your servant, your chair, knife, fork, spoon, and plate: "Three or four rations of fresh beef made a better soup than three fourths pound with a bone in it then there might be a bit of liver and bacon and some roast tatties."

He stated that when issued raw wheat, instead of bread, it was thrown into the soup kettles. In Calcutta he had a large pot for broth and combined a buffalo's head with the ration of beef to make a "most excellent soup."

In the hope of improving the system whereby rations were distributed, Congress placed the responsibility on the commissary general and his assistants in April 1818. The president had the power to make adjustments as he thought needed, the most noticeable one being the amount of spirits issued.

Navy rations per man per week in 1818 included ½ pound suet, 6 ounces cheese, 3½ pounds beef, 3 pounds pork, 1 pound flour, 98 ounces bread, 2 ounces butter, 7 ounces sugar, 4 ounces tea, 1 pint peas, 1 pint rice, and ½ pint each of molasses and vinegar. Adult men also received 3½ pints of spirits.

In 1790, the rum ration had been reduced to a half gill of rum, brandy, or whiskey. The president had the authority to boost this by another half gill for any soldiers he thought in need of an extra quantity. The quantity of rum issued varied, until in 1832 it was discontinued altogether and replaced with coffee and sugar. In 1846, money was deferred for rum ration when felt prudent, but that was discontinued by 1865.

A navy officer was quoted in the *Janesville Gazette* in 1879 as saying bean soup was so universally served on the ships that the officers should never be asked if they'd have it on dry land.

Mexican War soldier rations were established in 1838 and consisted of 20 ounces beef, 18 ounces flour, 2.4 ounces dried beans, .16 gill vinegar, 1.92 ounces sugar, .64 ounces salt, candles, soap, and .96 ounces green coffee beans.

A veteran remembered rations during the Mexican War: "six ounces of bread, a slice of salt pork, and a basin of bean soup." He recalled collecting oysters while in Tampa Bay from a bed some six miles from his garrison. Those no doubt filled the soup cauldrons as well:

> We often had turtle soup at Tampa Bay as turtle could be bought at two or three cents per pound. A species of land tortoise called a gopher ... made a very delicious soup which some preferred to turtle.[25]

Having found a large cauldron used by Mexican butchers to render lard, the men decided to use it to prepare a "gipsy hodge-podge, or Salmagundi" for all. They made use of Uncle Sam's bacon and pooled the hardtack from their haversacks which was combined with foraged supplies of a turkey, two fowls, a piece of mutton, some potatoes, chili peppers (the indispensable condiment of the locals), tomatoes, and onions. The cauldron was propped on three stones in the center of the room, the ingredients chopped, and put in with salt and pepper and boiled.

In his diary, Sergeant W. McMillan listed Crimean War rations as a pound of biscuit, a pound of salt beef or pork, a quarter ounce of tea or green coffee beans and a quarter of rum given out after dinner.[26]

Quite a stir was caused by the scanty rations during the Crimean War, enough that by 1860 British rations were 1½ pounds fresh meat or 1¼ pounds salt meat when fresh was not available, vegetables or peas or beans 1 pound, bread or biscuit or flour 1¼ pounds, tea ¼ ounce, coffee or chocolate ½ ounce, sugar 2 ounces, with mustard, pepper, vinegar, tobacco, soap, and matches.[27]

The *Galveston Daily News* quoted the *Pall Mall Gazette* November 23, 1869 in regard to European military rations which most likely referred to the Crimean War (1853–1856).

> England passes abroad for being the only country in which such a thing as a fat soldier is to be seen. The French soldiers and the Spanish soldiers are lean. Prussian soldiers are gaunt. Russian soldiers are squalid.
>
> As regards food, the most beautifully fed soldier is the English, next comes the French, then the Austrian. French soldiers have two pounds of excellent white bread a day, two rations of soup of about a quart each, and one ration of boiled beef of about eight ounces. The cooking is very good, the soup being rich and always well stocked with vegetables. The Prussian soldier eats black bread, their soup is mostly made of beans, or yellow peas; their meat boiled beef or fat bacon, is tolerable enough.... The soup of the Russian soldier is putrid. Turkish soldiers are fed on rice with which they mix up anything they can get. A Spanish soldier has

dined well enough to his taste when he has eaten a few spoonfuls of thick pea soup and rubbed his bread with garlic.[28]

Nineteenth-century Russian soldiers received daily rations of a bowl of cabbage soup, 1½ pounds of bread and dried meat.

In about 1809, an Irish trader at Prairie du Chien served as sub–Indian agent and justice of the peace, appointed to the latter position by the governor of the Territory of Illinois. Of trail food he said:

> The mode of traveling in those days was in a canoe, manned with six or eight men to paddle, and taking with them some flour, tea, and sugar for the Burgeois; and some hulled corn and deer tallow, enough to season the soup, for the men, depending upon shooting game by the way or buying wild fowl or venison from the Indians.[29]

Civil War rations again changed: 20 ounces beef, 22 ounces flour, 7 ounces potatoes, .045 ounces yeast, 2.65 ounces dried beans, 1.6 ounces green coffee, 2.4 ounces sugar, .32 gill vinegar, .64 ounces salt, .04 ounce pepper, soap and candles. The army recommended making soup whenever possible.

> The importance of soup as a diet for troops is not sufficiently apprehended except by veteran soldiers, those of experience in the field. It cannot be too highly esteemed, and should be used to a much greater extent than it is. Bean soup, when properly made, is one of the best that can be used; when improperly made, one of the worst. The beans must be washed, steeped in water overnight, put on the fire at reveille, and boiled slowly for six hours; a piece of pork, say one ration for three men, put in three hours before dinner; this, eaten with a little pepper and vinegar, makes a wholesome and palatable dish. The cooking is everything; if not well done, it is positively injurious; if well done, it is wholesome. The great principle in making soup is that it must be boiled slowly and for a long time; it cannot be boiled too much. In making beef soup all the bones should be used, together with half rations of beef, rice, and desiccated and fresh vegetables, with salt and pepper; the desiccated vegetables should be steeped in water for two hours, and boiled with the soup for three hours; the rice should be added, after having been washed half an hour before the soup is served; the beef must be put in cold water, and the soup kept at a low boil for five hours. Beef should not in any case be used for cooking until cold. Hard bread will be more palatable and more easy of digestion if placed in the ashes until thoroughly heated; it can also be improved by breaking it in pieces an inch or two square and soaking it thoroughly in warm water, then placing it in a frying-pan with a few slices of pork and cooked for five minutes, stirring it, that all may be cooked alike. Such portions of beef as are not used in making soup should be cut in pieces about the size of a hen's egg, with half a ration of potatoes and a small-sized onion cut in slices to one man, and half a ration of desiccated vegetables previously soaked in cold water for an hour, with a few small pieces of pork, adding salt and pepper, with water sufficient to cover well the ingredients, and stewed slowly for three hours, will make an excellent dish. Beef that is not used thus should be cooked on coals or held before them on a stick or fork, and no salt or pepper put on until cooked; the salt put on before cooking only assists in abstracting the juices of the meat and in making it dry and hard when cooked. The secret in using the desiccated vegetables is in having them thoroughly cooked. The want of this has given rise to a prejudice against them which is unfounded; it is the fault of the cooking, and not of the vegetables. Pork should be boiled three hours, having been previously soaked in water, to abstract the salt, for three hours, the water being changed twice in that time; when cold and cut in slices, with a piece of bread and a slice of onion, it makes an excellent lunch; cut in slices and toasted over coals it is sweet and good. Coffee should be roasted over a slow fire, constantly stirring it until it becomes of a chestnut-brown color, and not burnt, as is so commonly done. It should be boiled for twenty minutes, set on one side, sweetened, well stirred, and a little cold water added to cause the grounds to settle. Cabbage is more wholesome when cut in shreds

Cook house in the camp of the 71st New York Volunteers. Soldiers are getting ready to serve soup from a large iron cauldron using a tin cup as a dipper. Officers constantly stressed the importance of making rations into nourishing soup to provide as much bulk and nutrition as possible. Collodion image, 1861. Library of Congress, Prints and Photographs Division, Reproduction Number LC-DIG-cwpb-01678.

and eaten with a little vinegar, pepper and salt, than when cooked. All fried meats are unwholesome; they should be boiled or broiled.[30]

Spanish-American War rations were altered: quantity of potatoes was increased, baking powder was issued instead of yeast, flour reduced to 18 ounces, and dried beans were discontinued.

French troops were paid very little, and must have put quite a burden on the populace. In 1872 an article stated soldiers and tax collectors received little pay, but paid themselves by living on the people. "The wretched conscript, torn from his family and friends, receives five dollars a year, in addition to poor clothing and little food."

> The soldier has two meals a day. The first is composed of soup, and a quarter of a pound of boiled beef; the second of a small portion of vegetables, generally of potatoes and beans, with a quarter of a pound of mutton or veal. The only drink given is water.[31]

A sad occurrence was recorded by a French lieutenant, who was promoted to captain after commanding at Eylau following the death of his captain. On February 7 and 8, 1807, Napoleon's forces opposed an army of mostly Germans at the Battle of Eylau. Captain Rollin, "an old man, and half frozen," temporarily passed command to a lieutenant when his daughter brought him a bowl of hot soup, "which he began to eat a hundred feet in the rear on a small elevation." While he ate his soup, both he and the daughter were shot and killed.[32]

The *Manual for Army Cooks* was published by the U.S. Subsistence Department in 1896. It contained numerous instructions and recipes for using every part of the cow when making soup stock — heads, tails, and bones. Soup bones were cracked before being put into the pot and used for three days before being discarded.

Recipes in the manual included bouillon, vegetable, tomato, barley, dried bean, macaroni, sago, rice, tomato and rice, mutton or lamb broth, dumpling broth, oxtail soup, consommé, bean, pea, oyster, mock oyster, onion, beef tea, kidney, and St. Patrick's. There were even multiple versions of several of the types of soups.

The legendary Kit Carson wrote of a Fourth of July meal that he had enjoyed:

> The kindness of our friends at St. Louis had provided us with a large supply of excellent preserves and rich fruit cake. When these were added to macaroni soup and variously prepared dishes of the nicest buffalo meat, crowned with a cup of coffee, and enjoyed with prairie appetites, we felt as we sat in barbaric luxury around our smoking supper on the grass, a greater sensation of enjoyment than the Roman epicure at his perfumed feast. But most of all it seemed to please our Indian friends who, in the unrestrained enjoyment of the moment, demanded to know if our medicine days came often.[33]

In 1853, Wesley Bond's excellent soldier's soup made from two wild geese, onions, potatoes, and condiments[34] was probably better appreciated than one Colonel John Frémont had made from boiling the head of a mule for several hours, producing what he called a passable soup for famished people.[35]

While on an exploration through Kansas, Nebraska, Oregon, and California, Frémont wrote of his acquaintance with *yampah*, saying the Indians were fond of it and that a considerable portion of Americans and Europeans used its seeds to flavor soup.[36]

On a later expedition, Frémont was described in 1856 as having a fire burning in the center of his lodge with cedar limbs strewn around to sit upon, partaking of a dinner with some of the men. "First came the camp kettle with buffalo soup, thickened with meat-biscuit, our respective tin plates were filled and replenished as often as required. Then came the roast or fry, and sometimes both; the roast was served on sticks, one end of which was stuck in the ground, from it we each in rotation cut off a piece. Then the fried venison."

Seamen through the 1850s received ample rations from which they created an interesting array of dishes.

> Every mess has a liberal supply of beef, pork, potatoes, onions, flour, coffee, sugar, tea, and all the little etceteras which are so essential to the complete success of all cooking operations. These are served out every second or third day by the Purser's steward, who keeps an exact account of the amount distributed among the different messes. As our Government is very liberal in regard to rations, each man receives more than he can dispose of, unless endowed with unusual gastronomic powers, and as a general thing the amount supplied to every twelve men is abundantly sufficient for a whole mess of fifteen.[37]

Seamen were adept at preparing soups and dishes peculiarly their own, lobscouse and dunderfunk being two prime examples. Webster (1856) defined lobscouse as the food of seamen — a hash of meat with vegetables, a kind of olio, which referred to a stew mixture or medley.

John Mullaly wrote:

> Lobscouse — a dish in great favor among sailors, is a kind of stew, and is usually composed of salt beef, potatoes, onions, a liberal sprinkling of pepper, and the due allowance of water.[38]

The name may have evolved from the English pottage known as *loblolly*. *Lob* came from the English "to boil" and *lolly* meaning "broth." Gervase Markham said a seaman could expect no more wholesome and pleasant dish than loblolly made with whole groats boiled in water and liberally buttered.

Colton called lobscouse the last dish of gastronomic desperation in 1850. He said, "The culinary art is forced into its highest degree of perfection, and achieves its last triumph at sea. The cook, who, in a Parisian restaurant, can make a palatable soup from the carcass of a crow that has perished of inanition, is entitled to but little praise in comparison with him who can raise a good soup at sea after the third week out."[39]

Dunderfunk was made of hard bread, beef, or pork, beans, a little molasses, a small quantity of vinegar, "and not withstanding its startling title is, after all, as simple and easily made as fish, or any other kind of chowder."[40]

Although more a salad than a soup, another dish of seafaring men worthy of mention is salmagundi. Webster defined it as an olio or medley, a mixture of chopped meat, pickled herring with oil, vinegar, pepper and onions. Salmagundi appeared in various cookery books through the 18th century placing it on tables "at home" as well. Writer Tobias Smollett described it as follows:

> ... and ordering the boy to bring a piece of salt beef from the brine, cut off a slice, and mixed it with an equal quantity of onions, which seasoning with a moderate proportion of pepper and salt he brought it into a consistence with oil and vinegar; then tasting the dish assured us it was the best that he ever made.[41]

Skilligalee, or skilly, was a gruel or stew thickened with bread or meal. It was universally eaten by soldiers, sailors, and prison inmates. Some described it as very crude, but Horace Kephart was favorably impressed enough to recommend it for hunting camps.

> The best thing in a fixed camp is the stock-pot. Into it go all the clean fag-ends of game — heads, tails, wings, feet, giblets, large bones, also the leftovers of fish, flesh, or any and all sorts of vegetables, everything edible except fat. This pot is always kept hot. Its flavors are forever changing.... It is always ready day or night.... No cook who values his peace of mind will fail to have skilly simmering at all hours.[42]

The Civil War soldier was, out of necessity, a keenly creative cook, preparing whatever he could from rations or foraged and begged supplies. Just when many soldiers thought their meals couldn't get any worse, they found themselves captured and imprisoned, where shortages approached starvation levels. The following was penned by John McElroy who was imprisoned at Andersonville.

> But what savory meals we used to concoct around the campfires, out of the rich materials collected during the day's ride! Such stews, such soups, such broils, such wonderful commixtures of things diverse in nature and antagonistic in properties such daring culinary experiments in combining materials never before attempted to be combined. The French say of untasteful arrangement of hues in dress "that the colors swear at each other." I have often thought the same thing of the heterogeneities that go to make up a soldier's pot-a feu....
>
> My first experience with this "flat" soup was very instructive, if not agreeable. I had come into prison, as did most other prisoners, absolutely destitute of dishes, or cooking utensils. The well-used, half-canteen frying-pan, the blackened quart cup, and the spoon, which formed the usual kitchen outfit of the cavalryman in the field, were in the haversack on my saddle, and were lost to me when I separated from my horse. Now, when we were told that we were to draw soup, I was in great danger of losing my ration from having no vessel in which to receive it. There were but few tin cups in the prison, and these were, of course, wanted by their owners. By great good fortune I found an empty fruit can, holding about a quart. I was

also lucky enough to find a piece from which to make a bail. I next manufactured a spoon and knife combined from a bit of hoop-iron....

But, to return to the alleged soup: As I started to drink my first ration it seemed to me that there was a superfluity of bugs upon its surface. Much as I wanted animal food, I did not care for fresh meat in that form. I skimmed them off carefully, so as to lose as little soup as possible. But the top layer seemed to be underlaid with another equally dense. This was also skimmed off as deftly as possible. But beneath this appeared another layer, which, when removed, showed still another; and so on, until I had scraped to the bottom of the can, and the last of the bugs went with the last of my soup. I have before spoken of the remarkable bug fecundity of the beans (or peas). This was a demonstration of it. Every scouped out pea (or bean) which found its way into the soup bore inside of its shell from ten to twenty of these hard-crusted little weevil. Afterward I drank my soup without skimming. It was not that I hated the weevil less, but that I loved the soup more. It was only another step toward a closer conformity to that grand rule which I have made the guiding maxim of my life:
"When I must, I had better."[43]

Food in a rebel prison in Salisbury, North Carolina, consisted of bread and soup. The bread was sometimes wheat bread but most often cornbread, and the soup, when specified, was bean or rice. Sometimes there was the addition of potatoes, turnips, or a little beef.[44]

A soldier at Castle Thunder stated the rations there were bread made from coarse meal with cob ground into it, and sometimes 1½ to 2 ounces pork with soup made from cow-peas (Southern field peas) or rice.[45]

A Union soldier, obviously not as impoverished, described in an official record the boat he was on being hit by enemy shells: "She struck the *Calhoun* eight times. One shot carried away our soup tureen and our roast of beef into the paddle wheel."

Soup was the primary food served to wounded soldiers. It was easy to digest, and it helped to stretch limited supplies to feed as many men as were confined in the facility. Even for Union troops, who were better supplied than the Confederates, shortages often arose due to the difficulty of transporting the supplies over bad roads and in all extremes of weather.

> No pen can depict, and no tongue narrate the sufferings, hardships, and privations of our brave men in southern and eastern Tennessee, during the months of November, December, and January, of 1863 and 1864. Hunger and cold, famine and nakedness were their inseparable companions. Horses and mules starved also, ten thousand animals starving at Chattanooga. The reproachful whinnying complaints of the famishing beasts wrung the hearts of the soldiers, even when they were slowly dying themselves from lack of food.[46]

That writer went on to say the great Quaker reliever of suffering, Mother Bickerdyke, set up a field hospital at the edge of a forest five miles from the city in weather described as "arctic" where, aided by contrabands and recovering soldiers, she prepared soup, coffee, tea, and toast for 2,000 wounded Union troops. Another account recalled Mother Bickerdyke and Mary Livermore distributing soup from two six-gallon pails.[47]

On the opposite end of the scale was a state dinner given in the White House during Lincoln's administration which, like similar affairs, cost $1,500 to prepare and consisted of an unbelievable 29 courses. Mrs. Lincoln was opposed to such dinners, and this opposition "increased her personal unpopularity to an intense degree."

The first course at state dinners was soup of French vegetables. This soup was said to have "never been equaled by any other soup, foreign or domestic. It is said to be a little smoother than peacock's brains, but not quite so exquisitely flavored as a dish of nightingales' tongues; and Professor Melah is the only man in the nation who holds in his hands the receipt for this aristocratic stew."[48]

Those state dinners weren't nearly as decadent as those given under the reign of Louis XV and Louis XVI, "when *petits soupers* carried French cookery to its zenith." Even the corrupt rulers tended to adhere to the ceremonial rules of the Roman church, and meatless meals during Lent was one of those rules. One such Lent feast may have been void of meat, but certainly did not lack in quantity or quality of food served. In addition to dozens of other dishes no less than 28 soups, or potages, were served. These included, "two of vermicelli; 2 bisques of crawfish; 2 turtle soups; 2 of muscles; 2 of soles; 2 of smelts; 2 juliennes; 2 purees of asparagus; 2 of lentils; 2 of truffles; 2 of mushrooms; 2 of fish eggs; 2 of artichokes, and 2 of white onions."

Where one man sees a glass half empty, another sees it half full. Such was the recollection of army fare of an Ohio veteran compared to those of McElroy. "Some of the most delightful meals I have ever eaten I had in the army; the recollection of them lives with me still."[49]

The writer stated that whenever they could, they built ovens and baked fresh bread. Rations for the Union soldier included hard bread, salt pork, potatoes, and sometimes onions, though rarely both at the same time. An onion was readily available from the sutler when he wished to make an Irish stew. However, the writer recalled, "[It] looms up in my memory as a cloud of fragrance that will never fade. I get the folks where I live now occasionally to make me a stew just that way."

He went on to say they were often in areas where oysters abounded, and that "colored people" would go through the company streets selling them at 10 cents per pint, the pint being measured in an army tin cup which held about a pint and a quarter or a pint and a half. The oysters were the main ingredient in an oyster stew, and once he enjoyed a possum stew.

A Brooklyn newspaper carried a letter "from the boys" with a recipe for soup for ailing soldiers:

> Commence with a mild bean soup. This is got up by boiling two beans in a gallon of water, carefully stirring for an hour, after which the soup should be carefully strained through a fine sieve and then taken in doses of two teaspoonful in a pint of water every four hours. By following the above prescription for one week a certain cure is guaranteed.[50]

A unit of Union soldiers often took young pigs, despite orders not to forage off the local citizens, which they made up into "possum" stew. Two officers, Colonel Randall and Captain Whiting, were strict disciplinarians and not well liked to begin with, a situation that worsened when the captain caught the men making their stew and discovered the true identity of the "'possums" that went into it. He confiscated the prepared stew, leaving the men with no supper, and later served it himself at a poker game.

The stew makers decided to seek retribution, which they did by great deception. They confiscated four puppies and killed three. They buried the bodies and left the severed heads behind the officer's tent. They tied a card around the neck of the surviving puppy that read, "You have eaten my three brothers now eat me. Jeff Davis," and set the puppy loose to be discovered by the captain. In reality, the stew the captain confiscated was made of pigs and chickens, but the prank was so successful the soldiers said for a great while afterward the imitation of a puppy's whining or barking elicited great displeasure in their officers.[51]

In 1861, several newspapers published a block of information for cooking the U.S. soldier's rations. These included ¾ pound fresh or salt beef, 18 ounces bread or 1¼ pounds corn meal, 8 quarts of peas or beans per 100 rations or 10 pounds rice, 6 pounds Coffee, 12 pounds sugar, 4 quarts vinegar, and 2 quarts of salt. The soup recipes are given below.

Soldiers' Soup for 25 men: Take 15 quarts of water to 25 pounds of meat, small tablespoonsful of salt, half a one of pepper, about 2 pounds of rice, put in while boiling, and what vegetables, fresh or preserved, that can be procured—say 3 pounds.

Pork Soup for 25 men: In 6 gallons of cold water put 12 pounds of pork, 3 quarts of beans, 2 pounds of rice, season to suit; let boil one hour and a half; soak the beans overnight.

Irish Stew for 25 men: Take 25 pounds mutton, veal, beef, or pork, cut into pieces six inches square, 4 pounds of onions, 8 pounds of potatoes, 4 tablespoonsful of salt, 1 of pepper, 8 quarts of water, cook it from 1 to 2 hours, slowly thicken the gravy with flour mixed into smooth paste with water or potatoes mashed fine.

Peas or Bean Soup for 25 men: Take 14 pounds of pork, 8 quarts peas, or beans, 20 quarts of water, 25 teaspoonfuls of sugar, 12 of pepper, and several large onions; boil gently till the vegetables are soft-from four to five hours.[52]

Two surgeons in the U.S. Army published a manual in 1861 which contained recipes for soup in larger quantities taken from the recipes of Alexis Soyer. Compare the amounts with those above.

Soup for 50 men. Put into the boiler, 7½ gallons of water; fifty pounds of beef or mutton; three pounds of rice; eight pounds of fresh vegetables; ten tablespoonfuls salt; one tablespoonful of pepper. Simmer for three hours, and serve. Skim off the fat, which, when cold, is an excellent substitute for butter.

The bean soup made by soldiers in the army, is the best I have ever eaten. They prepare it by soaking the beans all night. The ration of pork is boiled in it, and any fresh or desiccated vegetables they can procure. Potatoes and onions are great favorites with them. It is seasoned to the taste with salt and pepper.[53]

The Treatise on Military Surgery and Hygiene included soup recipes for 50 men. The quantities for the bean soup were 4 quarts of beans, 15 pounds of bacon or pork, 3 onions, ½ ounce pepper, and 8 gallons of water.[54]

The Savannah, Georgia, newspaper requested citizens to gather and send culinary and medicinal herbs for use by the soldiers. The culinary varieties requested were thyme, parsley, marjoram, and red peppers. Newspapers throughout the South carried similar pleas.

A Confederate soldier told of marching into Leesburg, Virginia, with bands playing, colors waving, and men and women weeping.

I began to think we were marching into Bedlam. Bread, cheese, butter, eggs, meats, fruits-every thing eatable was strewn on the sidewalks; while loaves of bread were flying through the air in all directions, which were quickly caught and stuck on the men's bayonets ... while cups of tea, coffee, soup, and the like were freely handed to thirsty fellows who hastily drank and joined the ranks again.[55]

Hungry Confederates often killed small game, fished in streams, or foraged from locals to feed their hungry bellies. Sometimes they were taunted by the "well-fed-rice-cracker-fresh-meat-sago-ham-bean-pork-molasses-sugar-eating, and tea-coffee-and whiskey-drinking Yankees, in fine warm clothes," inciting them to risk life and limb in the process.[56]

In an 1864 account, a soldier stated he had known soldiers from the Gulf states who, unknown to the officers, strayed behind enemy lines to bring back provisions. "From experience in Indian warfare, [they] would scatter in the timber, prowl about the enemy's encampments, and return unscratched with a heavy load of eatables."[57]

After observing a flock of sheep and remarking what fine soup they would make for hungry men, that night after roll call a tall, beleaguered Texan crept toward the area where the sheep had been observed earlier.

> After a while I heard several shots fired in the direction of the sheep, but of course, took lit-
> tle notice of it, for firing was continued from morning till night. As "tattoo" was sounding I
> was about to repair to my own post, when some unaccountable object seemed to be crossing
> the dam.... I found he [the Texan] carried a large sheep and a fat lamb on his back, the legs
> tied round his neck, a bundle swung around his middle, four rifles hung from his shoulders,
> and his own trusty Enfield grasped firmly in the right hand, cocked and loaded. "But where
> did you get the rifles?" I inquired. "O! well, the darned fools wouldn't let me get the mutton
> peaceable, so I had to shoot four of 'em!"[58]

Robert E. Lee's last meal may have been beef tea, which was one of those restorative soups so important in earlier times. His great-niece quoted a letter from Mrs. Lee to Francis H. Smith, superintendent of Virginia Military Institute, dated October 10, 1870, in which Mrs. Lee stated the doctors recommended the general have some beef tea at once. Since she had no time to get the beef from the market before night set in, she had asked if he could send some.[59]

During the next war Colonel Teddy Roosevelt paid $60 a bushel for potatoes and $30 for onions, and his cook obtained beef to make a genuine beef stew for his Rough Riders.[60] The veteran who submitted the information to the paper proclaimed the soup manna from Heaven, and just one example of why Roosevelt was so loved by the soldiers under his command.

Bean soup was a favorite at Civil War veteran reunions. The James H. Perry Post 89 G.A.R. (Grand Army of the Republic) held a reunion in 1881 which commenced with a band and dancing followed by a meal reminiscent of those years long before:

> At the easterly end of the park the camp fire was burning and bean soup, spiced with pork,
> was boiling in a vast caldron, while at another fire the coffee was being prepared in true army
> style.... The bugle sounded a charge on the commissary department, and the whole company
> obeyed the call with alacrity and appeared to enjoy the "hard tack" and bean soup quite as
> much as if they had been the rarest delicacies of the season, the novelty of the situation prov-
> ing an appetizer to most of those present ... and drank coffee out of tin cups and eat the soup
> from little tin dishes with a tin spoon, and did it with relish; all because, as the veterans said —
> "This was the style in the army." They all seemed to appreciate the viands the more when it
> was stated that they were prepared by an old army cook, Mr. Frank Thompson, who went out
> during the war with Company G, Forty-eighth Regiment from Brooklyn.[61]

The Boys in Blue of the Mansfield Post No. 35, G.A.R., of Brooklyn served it in August 1900:

> A large tent was raised in the west end of the park and underneath it was arranged the huge
> kettle in which delicious bean soup was made and served during the afternoon and evening
> by an old Army cook, Louis Hamburger, and such bean soup! To have one serving meant
> another, and when that was gone another dish was called for.[62]

The veterans were joined by friends and family after the meal when the Columbian Guard, composed of some 60 daughters and granddaughters of the veterans, were drilled with their rifles amid "deafening" applause. Activities were concluded with songs and stories around a huge camp fire and dancing, after which the guests retired to their homes and the veterans to their tents.

In September 1898, a newspaper contained an article entitled, "Revolt in the 47th over poor rations, Company K Refuses to Eat the Food or to Drill. Six sent to Guard House." The men of the 47th New York Volunteers stationed at Fort Adams, Newport, Rhode Island, remained in their tents when the call for drill was sounded after being offered rancid pork, sour beans, soup and unbaked bread for breakfast, an act that likely would have had them court-martialed in earlier decades. They had for days received the "scantiest of fare," though "the men know that the ration allowed by the government is sufficient, and, if properly handled, they can live well upon it." Apparently the army did not appreciate the story being printed in the papers because "Private William F. Gill of Company K and Corporal Taylor of Company E are under arrest for furnishing information to newspapers."[63]

The menu for Brooklyn, New York's Navy Yard, in 1899, was printed in the newspaper. Beef stew was Monday's breakfast, and the noon meal included bean soup. Tuesday's lunch included vegetable soup. Bean soup was served at noon on Wednesday, and vegetable soup was served at noon on Saturday. The only day beans weren't on the menu was Saturday.

In 1896 army cooks were preparing meals in cookware of tin and iron. They were instructed not to leave soup sitting in an iron pot, but to pour it up into an earthenware or tin vessel when it was finished cooking. They were to keep a stock pot in use daily. Bones were to be placed in bags and marked before putting them into the pot. After the third day they were discarded and fresh bones added.[64] Soup was prepared by adding other ingredients to the stock in one-gallon measures.

The recipe instructions were simple enough that anyone could prepare the soups successfully with minimal effort, and if followed correctly were meant to produce not only soup with good flavor but with a pleasant visual effect as well. For example, the cook was instructed that frying the onions before putting them into the soup improved the taste and made the soup look better than putting them in raw.

The cooks were instructed on making a refrigeration device by fitting a wooden box inside a slightly larger wooden box and filling between the two with charcoal or sawdust for insulation.

The following parody of *Old Dan Tucker* was written about General Winfield Scott, known as Old Fuss and Feathers to his troops.

Scott Soup for the million, Boiled on Long Island

We are going to make a pot of soup,
To satisfy a big Scott Troup
Of men who fight and never fly,
But stand their ground until they die.
Out o' the way Old Dan Tucker
Out o' the way Old Dan Tucker
Out o' the way Old Dan Tucker
We'll take Scott soup for our supper,
We'll fill our pot with goodly things,
To ward off Loco Foco stings;
And first of all we will not feign
To give the Battle of Lundy's Lane.

Chorus

The next ingredient for our pot,
As good as any we have got,
In old Fort George, of which we brag
Where Scott tore down the British flag.

Chorus

As we now come to take for use,
A corner piece of Vera Cruz,
And to put in we'll have a speech
Away from old Chepultopec.

Chorus

The next good chance that we have got,
To put a mixture in our pot,
Is just to take up Mexico
Give it wholesale as we go.

Chorus

There's other things that we have got
To make a bowl of soup for Scott,
For forty years the Hero's stood
And fought to do his country good.

Chorus

Whoever wants a bowl of soup,
Will not be treated like a dope,
If he will call on General Scott
President of the Public Pot.

Chorus.[65]

Rations were increased by World War I to include butter or margarine, lard, and flavoring. The sugar ration was increased. Rations sometimes included bacon, rice, onions, and canned tomatoes. In 1907 an emergency ration of chocolate and dried food was authorized, and numerous changes were in place by World War II.

Between 1946 and 1963, the army developed standard recipes for use by the armed forces. The recipes were first published in 1969 and have been reprinted regularly since. Until that time, lucky was the mess containing a soldier who'd been taught to cook at home or in the hunting or fishing camp, for otherwise some mean and miserable meals were endured.

22. Overland Trail

Settlements in America spread slowly westward, sometimes via little-known routes and at other times along historically significant routes such as the Overland Trail, Santa Fe Trail, and the Oregon Trail. The hardships endured on the trail depended on the distance covered and the knowledge of the guide.

According to the *Standard Dictionary* in 1812, Robert Stuart's courier party discovered the passage that came to be known as the Overland Trail. In 1834, the first emigrants to the Pacific coast completed the journey following the trail. Julius Morton further said that sections of the trail had been used by the Indians "since time immemorial," and it was simply developed into a continuous route by the whites. By 1843, it was a well-traveled route.

Except for immigrants who knew how to pack wisely, the trip west by wagon train was a perplexing situation with regard to what to take along. Of primary importance was enough clothing and food to last the journey. Newspapers often carried notices advising what supplies would be needed for the average family, and books provided additional guidance. One of the best-known of the books was written by an army officer in the 1850s.[1]

Dagmar Mariager, with a female traveling companion and her daughter, not only made the journey west, but made a living in the process in the 1860s. "Our moving restaurant [a 16 × 30 foot canvas structure] and store had gathered us in a good many greenbacks."[2] During their travels the women fished the streams and hunted the woods to supplement their stores while braving extremes of weather, Indian encounters, and strangers whose intentions were undetermined.

Soup was usually the dish of choice at mealtime using packed and indigenous ingredients. In Texas, their soup was "a conglomeration of onions, chile, and little black beans, frijoles, flavored by bits of mutton or rabbit," which was ladled onto tortillas.

Soup played a big role in the fare cooked along the trail because those making the journey were advised to take "as few cooking utensils as are indispensably needed."[3] One writer said the major part of the kitchen furniture consisted of a frying pan and perhaps a Dutch oven.[4]

Cooking utensils recommended for the trip west included for every six to eight people a large wrought-iron camp kettle for making soup, a coffeepot, tin plates and cups, frying and baking pans of wrought iron, a heavy tin for mixing up bread, eating utensils, a bucket, ax, hatchet, spade, and mallet.

Mrs. Luzena Stanley Wilson began her journey with multiple cooking pots. However, like many others, after only a few days on the trail she wrote that she had left most by the side of the trail except for a coffee pot and one camp kettle; the burden of carrying the others was too great.[5]

Another writer learned to make do with the basics after packing his cookware onto a mule that became spooked and ruined almost the entire lot.[6]

Two women hard at work preparing supper on the plains. They wear typical hairstyles and clothing, although the skirts are somewhat shorter than normal, probably due to the close and constant proximity to the fires on which they cook. Smoke rises as one woman makes coffee and the other holds a spoon ready to stir. Soup and stew were the easiest meals to prepare under such conditions due to the need for only one cooking pot, and reducing the number of utensils that must be washed afterward. wood engraving from sketches by James F. Gookins, Library of Congress, LC-USZ62-133215, 1866.

Basic supplies usually included flour, bacon, beans, coffee, sugar, tea, rice, dried fruit, saleratus (Sodium bicarbonate, or baking soda. For recipes calling for 1 teaspoon of saleratus it is possible to substitute 1¼ teaspoons of soda. It originated about 1840), onions, meal, cheese, and butter. Packing lightweight provisions and preserving the supplies so that they lasted the duration of the trip were of paramount importance.

The bacon kept best when put up in 100 pound bags which were then placed inside boxes of bran. Pork packed in that way eliminated the weight of the barrels it was normally put up in. Flour was put into double canvas bags weighing 100 pounds each. Butter kept better if it was previously boiled and all scum removed. Sugar was packed in waterproof bags made out of gutta-percha or India rubber. Desiccated vegetables were far lighter than canned or fresh ones and could be made at home or purchased. Those used by the U.S. Army were purchased from Chollet and Co. in Paris through an agent in New York.[7] Civilians may well have ordered from the same source.

Those supplies were naturally supplemented with game and fish when possible, as evidenced

Emigrants on the plains of the West. Cattle, sheep, dog, horse, and wagons are seen in the background while the group gathers around a campfire near the tent. One man is holding two game birds; another has slain a deer, and the women are preparing the evening meal, soup or stew, in a camp kettle suspended from a wooden pole. Engraving by William de la Montagne Cary, illustration in *A Popular History of the United States* by William Cullen Bryant and Sydney Howard Gay, 1881, New York. Library of Congress, Prints and Photographs Division, Reproduction Number LC-USZ62-101163.

by a diary notation from 1846: "A soup of the hare killed on our march today constituted our supper and only meal for two days." The diarist continued:

> The tame rabbit is rarely if ever eaten. The wild hare of the South — in vulgar parlance, "old hare," although the creature may be but a day old — exactly corresponds with the rabbit of the Northern fields, and when fat and tender may be made into a variety of excellent dishes. Hares are unfit for eating in the early spring. There is thus much significance in "Mad as a March hare." The real English hare is a much larger animal than that which is known in this country by this name. To speak correctly, all our "old field hares" are wild rabbits.[8]

The same diarist wrote later, "Of the soup prepared from rancid bacon skins remaining in our provision sack, a single spoonful to each seemed to satisfy the desires of the whole party for this kind of food, if it did not satisfy their appetite."

Hunting to stave off hunger is a recurrent theme in the tales of those who journeyed across country.

John Ball was among the pioneers who was able to purchase food from the Indians when supplies ran out. He bought dried bear, other meat, and elderberries. He said members of his party ate large quantities, but did not say whether they ate the food in its dried state or prepared it, as many did, into soup.[9]

George Bonniwell wrote in his diary that the boys had gone hunting for ducks for a chowder, cooked over a fire of buffalo chips. Duck was not a typical chowder ingredient, however, it was much more substantial than the soups of boiled water and flour that followed a few days later. He next mentioned soup made from rice and pork purchased from a trader and cooked in the only pot mentioned, a camp kettle. Upon reaching a post, they had soup made of leeks, bones, bread, and flour.[10]

Those who left without adequately preparing for the journey soon found themselves in dire straits. A Wisconsin newspaper carried a notice in 1859 saying that for a period of seven months annually, travelers would find neither employment, food, or shelter within 500 miles.[11]

Those who flocked to the gold fields of California in 1849 and 1850 found supplies came at a great price for those who came unprepared. "Everything was high, merchandise of all kinds being scarce and gold plentiful. Pork and flour sold for fifty dollars a barrel ... milk a dollar and a half a quart; butter, same price, per pound, eggs, six dollars a dozen."[12]

Few men were skilled in the culinary craft. One miner was pleased to discover that dried beans soaked overnight and boiled for a while, before adding pork, made a much more pleasing stew than when everything was started together, resulting in the beans remaining hard when the pork was reduced to shreds.[13] Another wondered at the culinary genius of a group of neighboring French miners who dined on soup, bread and claret while he ate a "conglomerate" of ingredients, "tortured, simmered, stewed, and concentrated ... regardless of the assimilation of flavors."[14]

Miners may have stumbled across rare remaining olives, fruit, vegetables, and cereals for their soup pots given that wheat and grains were grown in California as early as 1770,[15] and olives, vegetables, and fruit were planted soon after the establishment of a mission at Loreto in 1697. These missions soon spread throughout the state, but their orchards were mostly "decayed and neglected" by mining, although individuals managed to resurrect some of the orchards through "pruning, irrigation and cultivation."[16]

23. Slave Food to Soul Food

Slaves from Africa have been credited with the introduction of various foods and dishes to the New World, but given the desperate circumstances under which they were captured and transported aboard ships, how could they have brought goods with them, except perhaps in a rare circumstance?

In short, the answer is, they didn't, at least not with any regularity, yet they were the vehicle by which native African foods found their way to America. During their passage individuals bound for enslavement in the New World had to be fed, and whatever foods were carried on the journey were collected or purchased at the site of departure by the ship captains. Whatever quantities remained at journey's end were dispersed into the areas where the ships docked.

Those foods were cooked, or the seeds planted in order to create sustainable crops, by the only individuals with the knowledge to do so—the Africans.

The foods included yams, black-eyed peas, cassava, okra, peanuts (original to South America), millet, sorghum, and sesame or benne. Through an incredible talent for turning basic foods into amazingly delicious meals those cooks brought worldwide recognition to southern foodways.

Peas were initially thought of as food for farm animals, but by the 1730s they were being eaten by whites and blacks. Okra, a southern staple, was usually boiled whole, fried, or made into gumbo. Peanuts found their way into soup as did sesame seeds. Historians credit slaves with advancing the rice culture of the Carolinas and other coastal regions.

Calalu is a thick stew similar to gumbo, except that its main ingredient is greens instead of okra. It was initially prepared in Africa and the Caribbean, then in America. The name also refers to a variety of greens which are commonly used to make the soup.

Slave cooks worked in slave cabins, plantation kitchens, and presidential residences. North American cuisine was influenced by all three.

Before the federal government was established in Washington, D.C., the business of running the new country was conducted in New York and Philadelphia. Meals were prepared for George Washington and his family by a slave known as Hercules, and by the family as "Uncle Harkless," who arrived by stage with another slave in 1790. George Washington Parke Custis remembered Hercules as quite a dandy, fashionably attired, due in part to the $200 he earned annually by selling leftover food from the kitchen.[1]

James Hemmings accompanied Thomas Jefferson to France, where he was expected to learn the art of cookery, after which he took charge of meals in Jefferson's home. He was chef at both Philadelphia and Monticello. Before he was freed, it was agreed that he would pass his knowledge along to his successor. He chose his brother, Peter, who became head cook at

Monticello. Cookery skills, probably passed on from one family member to another, made it possible for James' great-nephew, Peter Fosset, to establish a very successful catering business in 1850.[2]

After the Civil War, skilled African-American cooks continued to work in the White House. The Benjamin Harrison family enjoyed meals prepared by Dolly Johnson in Indiana and at the White House. After Franklin D. Roosevelt's mother passed away he brought her cook, Mary Campbell, to the White House.[3]

Numerous diaries indicate that a slave woman who prepared meals for the white plantation owner and his family could be a venerated member of the plantation hierarchy. A cook who excelled at manipulating ingredients into savory morsels might have learned her skills in Africa, and they passed from generation to generation.

> The Kru cuisine is rather limited. Animal food is used sparingly ... and chiefly in soup, so hotly peppered as to defy the palate of an East Indian. Cassava and rice are the principal articles of consumption. The Kru housewives are famous for their skill in boiling rice.[4]

Kru food was liberally spiced with grains of paradise, harvested from native Guinea pepper. By the 14th and 15th century grains of paradise was used as an upscale substitute for black pepper throughout Europe, and it found its way into the United States by the colonial era, perhaps through slaves captured in that area of Africa.

The food prepared and consumed by slaves in 19th century America varied widely from plantation to plantation. As a general rule, food supplies were coarse in nature, primarily vegetarian, and the quantity varied. The methods of preparation were sometimes reminiscent of the way in which foods had been prepared before they were taken into slavery.

Carpenters, millers, and others whose work did not allow time for growing crops usually received larger rations, enough to sell surplus if they chose. An 1850 census found, "The children and non-workers are fed on corn-bread, hominy, molasses, rice, potatoes, soup, &c."[5]

Corn was often ground in a hand mill which was shared by all, probably similar to the Scottish quern. A Georgia gentleman said the mills often stayed in use late into the night as everyone took their turn at grinding the corn issued to them into meal.[6]

The *Southern Quarterly Review* reported in April 1849 that supplies often consisted of a peck of corn, 2 pounds of bacon or a quart of molasses, or, if preferred, potatoes and peas. Many slaves were allowed to keep a piece of land, either consuming the produce themselves or selling it if they preferred. There were exceptions, however.

> My earliest recollections are of pushing a chair in front of me and toddling from one to the other of my Master's family to get a mouthful to eat like a pet dog, and later on as I became older, making raids on the garden to satisfy my hunger, much to the damage of the young onions, watermelons, turnips, sweet potatoes, and other things I could find to eat. We had to use much caution during these raids on the garden, because we well knew what we would catch if someone caught us, but much practice made us experts in escaping undetected.[7]

The food produced by slaves for their own use or for sale usually consisted of turnips, potatoes, corn or rice, butter, ducks, fowls, bees for honey, fish, shellfish, and turtles. *The Southern Quarterly Review* supplied this description:

> In the rear of their houses, they should have a small vegetable garden, fruit or shade trees in the front, with a hen house near, as all are allowed to raise poultry. When they are sick, in addition to the sugar and coffee supplied them from the house, they can have their chicken soup, and their own vegetables, which add greatly to their comfort.
>
> Supplying them with an abundance of wholesome food, is a matter of great importance; and, in order to make the meat ration, usually given, hold out, large quantities of vegetables,

usually turnips and potatoes, are cultivated. The latter is an invaluable article, and is raised in such quantities as to last throughout the year. As negro families prefer doing their own cooking, their rations are weighed out to them once a week. Three and a half lbs. of bacon are allowed to each hand over ten years old, and a peck of meal, or more, if required; though, with a plenty of vegetables, a peck is quite sufficient. The children are fed from the kitchen; large quantities of vegetables are boiled; soup is made, and this, with milk, and a small quantity of bacon, supplies them bountifully with wholesome food.[8]

The article went on to say that rations were usually passed out by the overseer on plantations, and obviously, if he was unscrupulous, measures may have been shortened. The rations would have produced several types of soup given that most items were typical soup ingredients.

Edna Lewis (1916–2006) is the prime example of cooks who used this culinary heritage to promote history through delicious food. Ms. Lewis was the granddaughter of emancipated slaves who helped found Freetown, Virginia after the American Civil War. She grew up there and never forgot her family heritage and the part food played in it.

As an adult, she was a respected author and chef in New York City, but in her introduction to *The Taste of Country Cooking* the pride she felt in her family and their accomplishments rang out loud and clear. Her purpose in writing the book was to preserve that legacy for future generations.

She included country beef consommé, kidney bean, oyster, pea, and vegetable soups, and advised using cleaned, scalded, scaled, and de-spurred chicken feet in making stock for vegetable soup because they gave it body.

Ms. Lewis was a talented writer, graciously inviting the reader into the home of her youth.

> My mother often served us a supper of kidney bean soup or a pot of baked beans on a winter night with crackling bread, buttered salsify, and the famous cake of that time, jelly roll, filled with one of the tart, homemade jellies from summer canning. Stews and thick soups cooked leisurely in the side of the hearth and were enjoyed before a lively fire that sent up loud reports of snaps and crackles as if it knew we were enjoying our meal after a day of ploughing through the snow to feed the stock and gather in the evening wood.[9]

In June 1892, *Overland Monthly* described the pillau of Somali-land as rice, meat, or fowls boiled together with dates. The origin of the dish could help explain its widespread acceptance in the South where the ingredients were staples.

Cornmeal mush with bacon, "to give the soup a taste of meat," was typical of the soups that used inexpensive, commonly available ingredients that kept well.[10]

The slave narratives conducted by the Works Progress Administration in the 1930s reflect memories of those who lived through slavery. Regarding food, some were more fortunate than others. Commonly mentioned foods were beans, grits, rice, opossums, raccoons, cornbread, molasses, sometimes biscuits, and garden vegetables.

Betty Curlett remembered cooking a washpot full of peas and roasting potatoes around the pot in the ashes. They always cooked hams and greens of all kinds in the big iron pots for there were so many to eat and "in slavery times the cook, cooked for her family in with what she cooked for the Master."[11]

Lucinda Davis, slave of a Creek Indian and his white wife, said until after the Civil War she knew nothing but the Creek language and food which was, "sho good stuff." They baked green corn on the ear in the ashes, fried some of it, and ground the dry corn or pounded it to make ash cake. They boiled wild greens of all sorts with chopped-up pork, venison, or wild turkey meat, or maybe all three at the same time, resulting in soup of varying kinds. They also had fish, turtle meat, and *sofki*, which was made by pounding the corn "real fine," pouring in water and draining it off to get all the skins off the corn, then boiling the grits. Sometimes they added pounded hickory nut meat which made it "real good."[12]

Not everyone was so willing to embrace corn. Mobile, Alabama was the scene of a feminine uprising known as the Petticoat Rebellion in 1706 when French women brought to the city to marry French colonists realized that corn was to be the staple food in their kitchens. They demanded the wheat bread they were used to and threw quite a tantrum, threatening to leave the city in a united front, over the prospect of a lifetime commitment to cornbread. It became quickly apparent that the French women would not likely succeed in teaching domestic skills to the native women as hoped.[13]

George Ball, a slave, supplemented his diet by catching turtles and gathering their eggs.

> I had by this time, become well acquainted with the woods and swamps, for several miles round our plantation; and this being the season when the turtles came upon the land to deposit their eggs, I availed myself of it, and going out one Sunday morning, caught in the course of the day, by traveling cautiously around the edges of the swamps, ten snapping turtles, four of which were very large. As I caught these creatures, I tied each one with hickory bark, and hung it up to the bough of a tree, so that I could come and carry it home at my leisure. I afterwards carried my turtles home, and put them into a hole that I dug in the ground, four or five feet deep, and secured the sides, by driving small pieces of split timber into the ground, quite round the circumference of the hole, the upper ends of the timber standing out above the ground. Into this hole I poured water at pleasure, and kept my turtles until I needed them.[14]

His method of keeping the turtles was the same as that used on many Louisiana plantations for, "on feast days you are entitled to terrapin, no plantation yard being perfect without a terrapin pen in it."[15]

Ball was born in 1781, and his life story was published in New York in 1832. The narrative was later shortened, published by an Edinburgh newspaper, and serialized by the *Southern Quarterly Review* in January 1853. He commented on the habit of slaves maintaining gardens for their own use. "They are really allowed to have gardens, besides patches of corn, potatoes, and pumpkins."

Because the slaves could sell baskets, brooms, horse collars, and other items of their own manufacture, George began making and selling wooden bowls and ladles which were often purchased by the plantation owners. With the money he made, he frequently purchased clothing, sugar, molasses, coffee, and tobacco.

> About ten days after my arrival, we had a great feast at the quarter. I was sent with a boy into the swamp, to find a bullock. This was killed, and cut into quarters, the hind quarters being kept for the family, and the "rest" cut into small bits, and salted for the slaves. At night, each family took a bowl to the house, and received two gallons of soup made of the tripe and offal, with bacon, green [ripe] corn, onions, tomatoes, and squashes boiled in it. This, with our bread, and peas from "our" garden, gave us an ample meal.... We were, also, to spend the "whole of Sunday" in rest and banqueting, as the two quarters were to be dressed for dinner; and we were permitted to send to the orchard for some early peaches. At one o'clock we received two gallons of soup, about a pound of beef, a small piece of bacon, and nearly two pounds of corn-pudding mixed with lard. This, with some molasses, which we had at home, made a good second course to our meat and vegetables.

Doc Quinn, a former slave, stated they often made a sort of cornmeal soup using cotton seed. They dumped cottonseed into a huge pot to boil, and as the seeds rose to the top they were skimmed off and discarded. Cornmeal was poured into the thick liquid and cooked. He said, "I has never eaten anything what tasted any better, or what would stick to your ribs like cotton-seed and corn-meal cake."[16]

An elderly African American couple eating at a table by the fireplace in a rural Virginia cabin at the turn of the twentieth century. The soup kettle is visible in the fireplace. Their eyes are closed as they say grace. Library of Congress, Prints and Photographs Division, Reproduction Number LC-USZ62-61017.

Susan Jackson described meals taken to the fields for field hands. She stated they had "cakes," most likely hoe cakes, a tray of cooked cabbage, and a bucket filled with pot liquor (broth left after cooking cabbage or greens). In its most simplistic form, pot liquor is soup, or, more aptly, broth, and it was mentioned often in the slave narratives.[17]

Millie Evans contributed several recipes, one of which was "beef dumplins." "Take the brough [broth] from boiled beef, and season with salt, pepper, and add your dumplins jus as you would make chicken dumplins," she instructed.[18]

Hopping John has been credited to slave cooks who combined some form of field peas, rice, and bacon, salt pork, or ham with peppers, onions, and so forth to produce a thick vegetable stew. It took on an aristocratic flair and bridged the social gap when the 1847 *Carolina Housewife* included a printed recipe for this down-to-earth dish.

A northern newspaperman was quoted by *Debow's Review* in November 1849 regarding several aspects of slavery he had witnessed.

I observed, one morning, a negro engaged over a large kettle of boiling cotton seed and corn, cabbage stumps, and turnips, cutting up and putting into the kettle a litter of pigs that had been overlaid by the mother and killed the night before; on inquiring what he was making soup for, he very honestly told me it was to feed them "young blacks," that I had just been looking at ... whether or not cotton seed soup, thickened with dead pigs, is a wholesome diet, that would be relished by young negroes, I am unable to say.[19]

The use of baby pigs in this soup wouldn't have stirred much interest in an era when roast suckling pig was a common dish, and cooking oil made from cotton seed was ordinary until about the 1950s.

Some positive comes from every negative, and in the case of slavery, the positive is a legacy of delicious, well seasoned food, basic in ingredients but rich in love, the dishes today known as soul food. Soul food knows no racial boundaries and no social class boundaries. Presidents have enjoyed fried chicken and sweet potatoes as well as any rural family that subsisted primarily on what they produced on the farm.

Whether you call it soul food or country Southern food, it is real food, basic, honest, and nonpretentious, but unforgettable and oh so comforting. Most Southerners couldn't survive long without it, though few may realize the intricate combination of Native American, African-American, and European influences that combined to produce this truly American cuisine.

24. Tavern Food

In the early days, "all diversions centered around the tavern."[1] For example, in the 18th century the Black Horse Tavern in New York hosted concerts, dinners, receptions, and balls.[2] Taverns were also called ordinaries, and as defined by *Bailey's Dictionary* in 1740, an "ordinary" was a victualling-house where persons may eat so much at a meal.

Such houses have been in business since the reign of Henry II (1154–1189) and were described by William Hazlitt in *Old Cookery Books and Ancient Cuisine* as serving viands of every sort including venison, guinea fowl, and sturgeon. Ordinaries were soon established in the New World, and, as in Europe, the quality of the service and the meals varied widely.

In 1844 the cost of a tavern meal was a shilling or 12½ cents. Foods served were usually similar to what the proprietor knew at home, and what could be made from the most readily available ingredients.

Cato's Road House, built in 1712, was owned and operated by an ex-slave who had saved enough money to purchase his freedom. He left South Carolina and went to New York, where he opened the tavern and ran it for 48 years. His specialties included okra soup.[3]

The 18th-century turtle feasts were called turtle frolics, and were sometimes hosted at taverns, or ordinaries.[4]

Chowder was the dish of choice in New England. Herman Melville's *Moby Dick* said a Nantucket tavern was the "fishiest of all fishy places ... for the pots there were always boiling chowders. Chowder for breakfast, and chowder for dinner, and chowder for supper."

> ... but when that smoking chowder came in, the mystery was delightfully explained. Oh, sweet friends, hearken to me. It was made of small juicy clams, scarcely bigger than hazel nuts, mixed with pounded ship biscuits and salted pork cut up into little flakes! The whole enriched with butter and plentifully seasoned with pepper and salt.

Based on the bill of fare offered by the Restaurant Dorval at Coney Island, Burtch's Dining and Oyster Saloon of Brooklyn, the Montague Hall Restaurant, and others, the most commonly served soups in restaurants during the 1840s and 1850s were beef, mutton, and chicken, followed by vermicelli and vegetable. More upscale restaurants served turtle soup or, like the steamship *Clara* in 1852, offered mock turtle soup made from veal.

In 1855, Boston's Parker House, a favorite of Charles Dickens, achieved fame by making food available to customers at any time of the day rather than at specific hours. This paved the way for establishments like Ladd's Eating House and the Penny Restaurant in New York to compete for customers by supplying hot lunches at the lowest possible price, and soup was invariably on the menu.[5]

Harper's Weekly said in 1856 that the customers bolted their food like a boa constrictor in an effort to return to work in the time allotted for their meal.

"Public Ordinary." A tavern was often referred to as an *ordinary*. This illustration is a satire on militia camps, showing people eating, drinking, and dancing. A dog seizes the roast suckling pig while two roosters fight. Tents in the camp are seen in the background. Library of Congress, Prints and Photographs Division, Reproduction Number LC-USZ62-86558.

In 1858, the *Brooklyn Eagle* printed the following article:

> FREE LUNCH AT THE EAGLE HOTEL. The well-known proprietor of the Eagle Hotel, No. 235 Fulton Street, Mr. DOMINICK COLGAN, and who that knows anything about Brooklyn, does not know him, has preferred arrangements for a FREE LUNCH every day, from the hours of 11 to 12 o'clock. M. Colgan's experience in the Oyster line, (and it is well known that he prepares the best stews to be found anywhere) is proof sufficient that all things will be done satisfactory and well. He proposes to confine his lunches for the present to oyster soups and clam soup, got up in first rate style. He has a good block of first rate liquors and segars, for the accommodation of those of his patrons who desire a choice article or a fine smoke. The lunch will be introduced on Saturday, 14th inst. Go and try the soup.

The above newspaper article differs from similar articles advising the poor of the possibility of a free meal in that it is aimed at upper-class clientele, and the purpose of the free soup is to bring in customers who will then purchase liquor and cigars, both of which were sold at higher-than-usual prices to recoup the cost of the soup.

Newspapers carried articles about the free-lunch counters, saying that those who needed a meal and had no money to purchase drinks would deliberately go in during the busiest times of day, order their soup, eating all they could and, when the staff was too busy to notice that they hadn't purchased anything, walk out the door.

Besides the free lunches, an inexpensive meal could be had in New York at St. Andrews coffee stands where patrons could obtain coffee, bread, and soup for 1 to 3 cents. Next, at 5 cents per dinner, were the so-called Five Cent Restaurants where thin and sour or thick and greasy soup, scraps of meat and antiquated pie were offered. These restaurants were located in the "dingy business and tenement houses district of the city," and were intended for the lower classes. The day laborer and mechanic ate breakfast and dined at home or in his boarding house, and took his lunch to work.[6]

David McRae wrote of meals taken at the Opera Restaurant in Chicago and the short time it took American businessmen to consume their noon meal. Diners walked along a counter and ordered brown soup which was downed before choosing chicken or ham, and within minutes they were on their way back to work.

The 1890s saw the birth of another sort of lunch counter, provided in large dry goods stores. Its purpose was to provide a hot lunch of soup in order to keep housewives in the stores longer, increasing the likelihood they would make more purchases. Soup cost 12 cents and coffee 8 cents in 1894. Such lunch counters remained in operation until the 1970s.

25. Modern Jewish Soups

Jewish people have lived in various parts of the world and their diet closely mimicked their non–Jewish neighbors. For example, Jews in Russia, Europe, America, and other parts of the world tend to prepare foods native to these countries while making whatever changes are necessary in order to comply with Jewish food laws. When they moved to other parts of the world, they continued to prepare what they knew, and in areas where larger groups of these immigrants settled their culinary practices sometimes spread to non–Jewish households.

The first account of Jewish emigrants in the New World is of 23 individuals who settled in Brazil, and then in North America. The Portuguese Jews who had been forced to leave Spain in 1492 were granted permission, "to sail to and trade in New Netherlands" on April 26, 1655, partly because they had invested heavily in the Dutch West India Company. Waves of Jewish emigrants who followed were German, Hungarian and Austrian, and Russian. Kosher food in America began in 1654–1655 with their arrival.[1]

American Jews found it difficult to prepare foods they knew from the foodstuffs available in the United States until in 1846 the first Jewish cookbook in English was printed in London.[2] In 1871 Esther Levy published the first cookbook in the United States for American Jews.[3]

Today Orthodox households may prepare certain foods primarily on particular days of the year. Separate sets of dishes are used for meat and dairy, and two similar sets are used only at Passover. Reform Jews do not usually keep kosher, and some Conservatives may keep kosher while others may not.[4]

Food may not be prepared on the Sabbath by observant Jews. This may mean eating cold foods in summer, or in winter putting the food to cook the day before in such a way that it maintains most of its heat until consumed on the Sabbath.

Soups have been a popular part of Jewish cuisine for many years. One of the most popular has been *krupnik*, which is a soup made from groats or grits often with potatoes and fat, ingredients not unlike those found in Scottish soups. Barley is used in Polish *krupnik*.

Dumplings added to soup have long been a favorite in western parts of Europe. *Kneidlach* were made with flour, eggs, water, fat, salt, and pepper and formed into small balls, after which they were dropped into the simmering soup. These soups may be made without fat or meat, especially among the less affluent.

Matzo balls are made from matzo (flat breads), or from matzoh meal (basically ground-up matzo). In preparing the matzo meal, the flour has been especially "guarded" against moisture in keeping with the teachings in the Torah, which says there is to be no leaven found in the house for seven days to commemorate Passover. When the Hebrews left Egypt, they quickly baked unleavened bread to take with them and no leavening is used as a remembrance of that. In Franco-German chicken soup, matzo replaced dumplings made from regular flour. The 1846 cookbook by Judith Montefiero included 25 recipes for soup, including matzo balls and matzo soup:

> Boil down half a shin of beef, four pounds of gravy beef, and a calf's foot may be added, if approved, in three or four quarts of water; season with celery, carrots, turnips, pepper and salt, and a bunch of sweet herbs; let the whole stew gently for eight hours, then strain and let it stand to get cold, when the fat must be removed, then return it to the saucepan to warm up. Ten minutes before serving, throw in the balls, from which the soup takes its name, and which are made in the following manner:
> Take half a pound of matso flour, two ounces of chopped suet, season with a little pepper, salt, ginger, and nutmeg; mix with this, four beaten eggs, and make it into a paste, a small onion shred and browned in a desert spoonful of oil is sometimes added; the paste should be made into rather large balls, and care should be taken to make them very light.

In parts of France and Germany matzo was saved from the Seder and placed into a cage where it was to remain, unmolested, until the next year during the search for leaven the night before Seder service.[5]

Examples of Passover soups in different cultures include beef bouillon with flavored matzo balls in France, leek soup in Spain, fava bean soup in Morocco, and, in Italy, chicken soup with matzo and additional flavoring of cinnamon and eggs.

Dumplings in Lithuania are made of mashed potatoes and dropped into warm milk.

Borsht can be made with beets and beet juice, or it may refer to soup made from cabbage, meat, onions, raisins, salt, sugar, and maybe tomatoes. Borscht was originally named for a wild plant, *borshchevik*, prevalent in soup-making in ancient times. Russians called it "sweet grass" or hogweed. It wasn't until the 10th or 11th century when beets had been imported into the Ukraine from Europe that they were added to this soup. Red beets were referred to as Roman beets by Gerard.

Maria Dembinska stated, in her history of soups from medieval Poland, that *barszcz* (beet soup) was originally made from the cow parsnips that grew wild. She indicated it was a soup of the poorer class and not of the nobility.

Mrs. Levy included 19 recipes for soup in her *Jewish Cookery Book* in 1871. Many were made from grains, meats, and herbs available in biblical days. They include: spring soup, barley soup, mock turtle soup, frimbel, noodle soup, julienne soup, mutton soup, potato soup (2), mulligatawney soup, pea soup, vegetable soup, ox-tail soup, sago soup, nice butter soup, ochre (okra) soup, gumbo, matzo cleis soup, drop dumplings for soup, a pepper pot, and forcemeat for soup.

Spring soup was made from mutton, beef, cabbage, lettuce, tarragon, chervil, asparagus, peas, cucumbers, beans, cauliflower, cayenne, salt, ginger, mace, and nutmeg.

Barley soup was made of beef and barley seasoned with ginger, salt, pepper, nutmeg, and chopped vegetables.

26. Nineteenth Century America

"What is the lightest, most nourishing, most wholesome, most savory, of all cooked food? Soup, of course." This newspaper article went on to say:

> Blessings on the man who invented soup! For it rejoices the tired stomach, disposes it to placidly digest, encourages the noble organ, and comes as a promise of future good things. It is a gentle experiment to test if the stomach be in sound working order. It contains the greatest amount of nourishment that can be taken with the least exertion. Chemically it is a wonder (the cooks of the future will all be taught the elements of chemistry), for Broth, which is the humble father of soup, is literally an extract of all the soluble parts of meat. The ozmazome melts first; then the albumen. To make good soup, it is chemically necessary that the water boil slowly, so that the albumen may into coagulate in the centre of the meat before being extracted. And the ebullition must be slow, so that the different ingredients of the extract may unite with each other easily and thoroughly.[1]

Soup was once a delectable precursor to a meal or a delicious meal in itself, unlike the canned concoctions common today. The basis of good soup, regardless of the century in which it was prepared or whether made for a cottager or cabinet member, was a flavorful stock.

> The soup is to a dinner what the portico is to a mansion; it is not merely the first thing to which you come, but it also serves to give an idea of what the architect intends to do afterwards; much as the overture of an opera conveys foreshadowing, and glimpses of what is to follow. A simple dinner should have the prelude of a simple soup; which, however, requires to be perfect and demands a care, patience, and waiting watchfulness, which good housewives are more likely to bestow than a professed cook. It has been often noticed by epicureans that thoroughly good soups are rare in great men's houses. The reason is that the kitchen-maids keep taking the soup for their ragout and side-dishes, and filling it up with water, till the crude adulteration has infected the whole. In small houses the soup is a principal object, and receives the most religious care. The chief fault in England is, that soups are over-spiced and under-vegetabled. They are also too hurried. By quick, violent boiling, all the soluble and finest parts of the ingredients pass off in puffs of indignant steam while the coarser parts only are retained in the solution. This process of soup making is a slow chemical process and nature will not be hurried without having her revenge.[2]

By the 19th century the French were considered the leaders in preparing delicious soups, followed in turn by the Scots and the Welsh. The English were often found lacking in ability in preparing soups.[3]

A Scots writer once said, "We of Scotland probably owe our superiority in this department to our long and close alliance with that nation which has ever been the most pronounced and skilled in the mysteries of the soup-pot. That Scotland is indebted to France for even the slender proficiency she has attained in cookery is abundantly evident from the culinary phraseology of the nation."

In studying the 19th-century diet, it is important to consider not only the types of foods eaten but the quantities. Alexis Soyer left little to the imagination in the following account of "the food and clothing a man may consume in a lifetime. Soyer's *Modern Housewife* gives the following calculation as the probable amount of food that an epicure of seventy years might have consumed.

> Supposing his gastronomic performances to commence at ten years, he will make 65,700 breakfasts, dinners, and suppers, to say nothing of luncheons and extra feastings. To supply the epicure's table for sixty years, Soyer calculates he will require 30 oxen, 200 sheep, 100 calves, 200 lambs, 50 pigs; in poultry, 1,200 fowls, 300 turkeys, 150 geese, 400 ducklings, 263 pigeons; 1,400 partridges, pheasants, and grouse; 600 woodcocks and snipes; 600 wild ducks, widgeon, and teal; 450 plovers, ruffs, and reeves; 800 quails, ortolans,[4] and dotterels, and a few guillemots and other foreign birds; also 500 hares and rabbits, 40 deer, 120 Guinea-fowl, 10 peacocks, and 360 wild-fowls. In the way of fish, 120 turbot, 140 salmon, 120 cod, 260 trout, 400 mackerel, 300 whitings, 800 soles and slips, 400 flounders, 400 red mullet, 200 eels, 150 haddocks, 400 herrings, 5,000 smelts, and some hundred thousand of those delicious, silvery whitebait, besides a few hundred species of fresh-water fishes, In shell-fish, 20 turtle, 30,000 oysters, 1,500 lobsters or crabs, 300,000 prawns, shrimps, sardines, and anchovies. In the way of fruit, about 500 lbs. of grapes, 360 lbs. of pineapples, 600 peaches, 1,400 apricots, 240 melons, and some hundred thousand plums, green-gages, apples, pears, and some millions of cherries, strawberries, raspberries, currants, mulberries, and an abundance of other small fruit, viz., walnuts, chestnuts, dry figs, and plums. In vegetables of all kinds, 5,475 lbs. weight, and about 2,434-¾ lbs. of butter, 684 lbs. of cheese, 21,000 eggs, 800 tongues. Of bread, 4-½ tons, half a ton of salt and pepper, near 2-½ tons of sugar. His drink during the same period may be set down as follows: 49 hogsheads of wine, 13,683 gallons of beer, 584 gallons of spirits, 342 gallons of liqueur, 2,394-¾ gallons of coffee, cocoa, tea, etc., and 304 gallons of milk, 2,736 gallons of water. This mass of food in sixty years amounts to no less than 33-¾ tons of weight of meat, farinaceous food and vegetables, etc., out of which I have named in detail the probable delicacies that would be selected by an epicure through life. But observe that I did not count the first ten years of his life, at the beginning of which he lived upon pap, bread and milk, etc., also a little meat, the expense of which I add to the age from then to twenty, as no one can really be called an epicure before that age; it will thus make the expenses more equal as regards the calculation. The following is the list of what I consider his daily meals:
>
> BREAKFAST.— Three quarters of a pint of coffee, four ounces of bread, one ounce of butter, two eggs, or four ounces of meat, or four ounces of fish.
>
> LUNCH.— Two ounces of bread, two ounces of meat, or poultry, or game, two ounces of vegetables, and a half pint of beer, or a glass of wine.
>
> DINNER.— Half a pint of soup, a quarter of a pound of fish, half a pound of meat, a quarter of a pound of poultry, a quarter of a pound of savory dishes or game, two ounces of vegetables, two ounces of bread, two ounces of pastry or roasts, half an ounce of cheese, a quarter of a pound of fruit, one pint of wine, one glass of liqueur, one cup of coffee or tea; at night one glass of spirits and water.[5]

No doubt many of these items were prepared as savory and delectable soups served with pomp and circumstance, but simple, delicious soups, stews, and chowders were also prepared and served informally.

One 19th-century writer stated everybody wanted clam chowder, from the millionaire to the patron of the cheap restaurant and the free lunch fiend. Fishing and gathering clams were often popular family outings, the product of which produced a generous cauldron of creamy chowder by evening, often at the water's edge, the cooking being part of the outing.

Mid–19th-century cooks were instructed to keep soup stock on hand for the base ingredient of soup, or for use in cooking other foods. Soup stock which wasn't wanted for soup could be used to make gravy or sauces, or given to the poor so that they could use it to make nourishing soup.

A cookbook writer advised,

> Of Soups: No good housewife has any pretensions to rational economy who boils animal food without converting the broth into some sort of soup.[6]

A brown stock was made by first roasting beef and bones, then putting them into a soup pot and boiling them. White soup stock was generally made with white meats and the step of roasting the meat before boiling it was eliminated.

Typical beef stock was made by simmering approximately 3 pounds of beef (preferably hind shin or buttock) with about 2 quarts of water. The beef was added to the stew pot with cold water and the contents brought to a boil and allowed to simmer slowly. The cook skimmed the scum that collected on the surface approximately every 10 minutes for the first half hour of cooking time and discarded it.

Adding the bones to the stock pot produced gelatin, which helped to give body to the soup. Soup could also be thickened by stirring in a tablespoon or so of flour mixed to a paste with a little water, and a teaspoon of good butter or drippings.

> If the meat to be boiled solely to make stock, it must be cut up into the smallest possible pieces; but, generally speaking, if it is desired to have good stock and a piece of savory meat as well, it is necessary to put a rather large piece into the stock pot, say sufficient for two or three days, during which time the stock will keep well in all weathers. Choose the freshest meat, and have it cut as thick as possible; for if it is a thin, flat piece, it will not look well, and will be very soon spoiled by the boiling.
>
> Never wash meat, as it deprives its surface of all its juices; separate it from the bones, and toe it round with tape, so that its shape may be preserved, then put it into the stock pot, and for each pound of meat let there be one pint of water; press it down with the hand, to allow the air which it contains to escape, and which often raises it to the top of the water. By skimming off and discarding the scum that rose to the top the soup would be certain of being clear.[7]

"If one's stock is good, what remains of the work is easy."[8]

The following table was published in an American-French cookery book in 1803. The quantities made basic soup sufficient to serve five people.

> Beef and bones.......5 lbs.
> Veal.................½ hock (about 2 lbs.).
> Fowl.................The body of 1 hen.
> Vegetables...........2 carrots, ½ turnip, 1 onion, some celery.
> Water................From 3 to 4 quarts.
> *Time.* — About 5 hours.

Savory herbs (thyme, marjoram, and parsley), salt, and a few peppercorns boosted the flavor.

> General stock, or Grand Bouillon, is the principle of all the soups and sauces which follow; it is used instead of water, to which it is much to be preferred. General Stock is made with legs of beef, knuckles of veal, and any fresh meat trimmings and bones. Cut all the meat from the bones; break them; and put them, together with the meat, in a stock-pot, with about 2½ pints of cold water to each pound of bones and meat; and add a little salt, and put on the fire to boil; skim carefully; and put in some carrots, onions, and leeks; simmer for five hours; strain the Stock through a broth napkin, into a basin, and keep it in a cold place, till wanted.[9]
>
> Stock is the basis of all meat sauces, soups, and purees. It is really the juice of meat extracted by long and gentle simmering, and in making it, should be remembered that the object to be

aimed at is to draw the goodness out of the materials into the liquor. It may be prepared in various ways, richly and expensively, or economically, and recipes for all modes are given in this work. All general stock, or stock which is to be used for miscellaneous purposes, should be simply made, that is, all flavoring ingredients should be omitted entirely until its use is decided upon. The stock will then keep longer than it would do if vegetables, herbs, and spices were boiled in it, besides which the flavouring can be adapted to its special purpose. To ensure its keeping, stock should be boiled and skimmed every day in summer, and every other day in winter. The pan and the lid used in making it should be scrupulously clean. A tinned iron pan is the best for the purpose. Those who need to observe economy will do well to procure a digester, which is a kind of stock-pot made with the object of retaining the goodness of the materials, and preventing its escape in steam. When ready, stock should be poured into an earthenware pan, and left uncovered until it is cold. It should on no account be allowed to cool in a metal pan. Before being used, every particle of fat which has settled on the surface should be removed, and the liquor should be poured off free from sediment. A few years ago it was customary for cooks to make stock with fresh meat only, the rule being a pound of meat to a pint of stock. Altered prices have necessitated the adoption of more economical methods, and now excellent stock is constantly made with the bones and trimmings of meat and poultry, with the addition or not of a little fresh meat, or a portion of Liebig's Extract of Meat. In a house where meat is regularly used, a good cook will never be without a little stock. Broken remnants of all kinds will find their way to the stock-pot, and will not be thrown away until, by gentle stewing, they have been made to yield to the utmost whatever of fresh meat is used it is better for being freshly killed. The liquor is which fresh meat has been boiled should always be used as stock.[10]

Thickened soups required more seasoning than thin soups—a proportion of about twice the amount.

Kitchiner said the basis of soup was good stock, and from that any sort of soup could be made with the addition of a few ingredients. Little has changed since his *Cook's Oracle* was published in the early 19th century, except that with the aid of purchased stocks and a few simple ingredients a hot, steaming homemade soup takes little more time than opening a can.

> Carrots, turnips, onions, celery, and a few leaves of Chervil make what is called Spring Soup or Soup Sante; to this a pint of green pease, or asparagus pease, or French Beans cut into pieces or a cabbage lettuce are an improvement.
>
> With Rice or Scotch Barley, with Macaroni, or Vermicelli, or Celery, —cut into lengths; it will be the soup usually called by those names.

Pierre Blot wrote in 1869 that July was an excellent month for harvesting and preparing vegetables and suggested various dishes he thought well suited for serving in that month. The potages were carrot, cauliflower, lima beans, peas, lettuce, squash, crecy [cress], sorrel, tomatoes, turnips, and bisques of lobster and crab.

In 1860, *Southern Field and Fireside* recommended that the best variety of carrots for soup were early horn and long orange, and the *Mississippian* claimed okra split and dried in the shade made as good a soup as that made from flesh.

Some books instructed the cook on the option of removing the meat used to make soup stock and mincing it for making into croquettes. This "waste not, want not" tip was much appreciated by families on a budget.

> It [soup] can be made from the merest scraps and trimmings of meat, from the heads, tails, and feet of animals; from the bones and skin of fish, from cereals and vegetables alone. Pot liquor in which meat has been boiled should always be saved and used for soup the next day, when by removal of all fat, by careful skimming, and the addition of a few vegetables or some dumplings, rice, or macaroni, it will make palatable broth.[11]

Inexpensive cuts were perfect for soup since the slow simmering tenderized the meat while making excellent stock.

> From the leg and shin excellent stock for soup may be drawn; and if not reduced too much, the meat taken from the bones may be served as a stew with vegetables; or it may be seasoned pounded with butter and potted; or chopped very fine and seasoned with herbs, and bound together by egg and bread-crumbs; it may be fried in balls, or in the form of large eggs, and served with a gravy made with a few spoonfuls of the soup.
>
> Of half an ox-cheek excellent soup may be made; the meat, when taken from the bones, may be served as a stew.[12]

Mid–19th-century cooks were cautioned to take great care of their tinware so that flavor was not lost with steam escaping the pot due to an ill-fitting lid. If the pot was cast iron, the seasoning of the pot could go rancid between uses, imparting a disagreeable taste to the soup. A good cook washed the soup pot, lid, and ladle before making soup so that any residue wouldn't produce a disagreeable flavor.

By the mid–1800s soups, sauces, and other foods that the cook wanted to keep hot, but not to continue cooking, were placed in a bain-marie, or water bath. "The bain-marie is a deep iron or copper pan, partly filled with salted water, the temperature of which can be raised higher than that of fresh water, and placed upon the back of the fire, to contain saucepans whose contents require heating without boiling; by increasing the heat, cooking can be done in a bain-marie. Small saucepans or tin pails are set in the water-bath to keep their contents hot after they are ready for the table." A cook could, when necessary, make a bain-marie out of a dripping-pan and several tin cans.

In 1863, *Peterson's* noted that French cooks made better soup because they paid more attention to skimming. French soup pots were generally earthen ones, and English pots were made of copper or iron.

A French emigrant said in 1849 she had accidentally broken her precious earthen pot on her passage across the Atlantic. She had since made soup in a black [iron] saucepan and a stew pan; but "we must admit not quite so delicate and perfect as in the identical *pot de terre*."[13]

Godey's noted in 1855 that the French rarely served dinner without soup, and that the *pot-au-feu* (soup kettle) was a necessary utensil in the kitchens of both the poor and wealthy. A thin white soup was intended to commence a set dinner, whereas a substantial thick soup with vegetables might be a satisfactory dinner in itself for the working class. *Godey's* writer elaborated:

> A common camp-kettle will be found an excellent utensil for making soup, as the lid is heavy and will keep in the steam. An earthen pipkin or jar, if of a long and narrow make, widening a little in the centre, is, perhaps one of the best vessels for soups, and universally used by foreign cooks, who insist "that it renders the gravy more clear and limpid, and extracts more savor from the meat than when made in tin or copper.

Recommended flavorings for soup included zest, soy, nutmeg, mace, curry powder, savory, ragout powder, soup herb powder, browning, ketchup, wine, sweet herbs, and savory spice.

According to the August 12, 1854, edition of the *Watertown Weekly Register*, ragout seasoning contained 2 ounces dried parsley, winter savory, sweet marjoram, and lemon thyme; 1 ounce lemon peel cut very thin and dried; sweet basil, and 1 drachm each of celery seed and bay leaves.

Prepared seasoning for pea soup included dried mint, sage, celery seed, and pepper.

The most commonly found ingredients in soup included carrots, turnips, peas, beans, leeks, onion, celery, potato, cloves, parsley, macaroni, vermicelli, parsnips, beet root, garlic, milk or cream, shallot and sweet herbs.

Sweet herbs for soup were typically parsley, thyme, lemon thyme, orange thyme, marjoram, sage, mint, winter savory, and basil. Tying sprigs of herbs into a bouquet garni with cotton string before adding them to the soup pot makes it easy to remove the tough stems and any remaining green leaves before serving the soup. If the string is cut long enough to extend out of the pot during cooking it is possible to remove the herb bundle without disturbing the contents of the pot.

Bouquet garni was a term used in both English and French cooking, and it was sometimes known as a "fagot of herbs."[14] Bouquet garni can be placed inside a muslin bag as well.

Typical 19th-century bouquet garni ingredients included parsley, thyme, marjoram, rosemary (an ounce of each), a medium-sized onion with three whole cloves stuck into it, a long pepper or a few peppercorns, a dried capsicum, a small piece of mace, and a quarter of a lemon. Another version included lemon thyme, sweet basil, mint, dill, rosemary, bruised coriander seeds, caraway seeds, cloves, a few chives or eschalots, or a small clove of garlic, half a lemon, and some peppers.

A bouquet garni for stew was made from an ounce of lemon peel, an ounce of sweet basil, 2 ounces each of parsley, sweet marjoram, and thyme. It was dried, pounded, and mixed together and kept in a glass jar.

A kitchen bouquet was made from one onion, one carrot, one celery root, one sweet potato, one parsnip, one red pepper, one shallot and from one to four cloves of garlic, according to taste. Remove the seeds from the pepper, peel the carrot, parsnip, onion and potato and chop all very finely. Add three large bay leaves, quarter of a teaspoonful each of cloves, mace, cinnamon, and allspice. Mix all together and season with salt and pepper. Put a layer of the vegetables in the bottom of a saucepan, sprinkle with brown sugar, then add another layer of vegetables, then sugar, and continue in this way until all is in. Bake in a quick oven and when a rich brown add half a cup of cold water; place on top of stove, stir, and cook for fifteen minutes or until you have a rich brown syrup. Strain off the sauce and bottle, corking tightly. Keep in a cool place. A little added to a soup, stew, or sauce will give color and flavor.

Housewives were encouraged to grow enough herbs in their kitchen gardens for their own use with enough left over to sell to their less fortunate neighbors.

Red onion, lemon juice or zest, mace, forcemeat balls, mushroom ketchup, mushrooms, asparagus, okra, catfish, eels, endive, lettuce, spinach, eggs, winter savory, allspice, nutmeg, curry, ginger, chervil, and sage were mentioned slightly less often in 19th-century receipt books.

Throughout history when the word *egg* was used it did not necessarily mean those from a chicken. In some countries lizard eggs were eaten. Iguana eggs were a delicacy in the West Indies. In Antilles alligator eggs were eaten; duck eggs are excellent for baking; and turtle eggs have been "much esteemed wherever they are found." Turtle eggs were prized, especially for adding to turtle soup.

The meats most often found in soups seem to have been chicken, beef, veal, lamb, mutton, rabbit or hare, game birds, venison, lobster, fish, mussels, oyster, crawfish, crab, and eel.

The quantity of wine recommended per pot of soup was one wineglass full.

To a pound of meat a knowledgeable cook added one quart of cold water. A few sources advised using soft water and cautioned against using leftover meats because it did not make a clear broth. The pot was covered well, the scum removed as the pot began to heat, and the heat reduced to a simmer so as not to waste the broth by evaporation.

OYSTER SOUP

Oyster soup. Wood engraving. Two men are served bowls of oyster soup from an outdoor stand. A container of cigars sits on the end of the counter, no doubt available for purchase by the soup eaters. Illustration in *Harper's Weekly*, volume 31, number 1588, May 28, 1887. Library of Congress, Prints and Photographs Division, Reproduction Number LC-USZ62-128026.

By bringing the meat very slowly to a boil it is sure to be tender, and any impurities such as clotted blood rise in the scum where they can be skimmed from the surface and discarded. Do not add vegetables and seasonings until the scum has ceased to rise. The meat was sometimes pounded with mortar and pestle and added back to the soup to thicken it as it was during the medieval era.

Godey's in 1855 advised using two tablespoons of salt for soup with lots of vegetables, and with fewer vegetables reducing the salt to one and a half tablespoons.

Pierre Blot said of ingredients for prepared dishes, "Materials for a dinner are exactly like materials for a dress: they require time and skilful hands to put both in proper shape for use."

Good cooks always chose the freshest meats and vegetables available. Slow simmering turned even basic ingredients into a delicious meal.

Simmering time for good soup should be between three and six hours, the pot closely covered, and not allowed to boil hard.

If the broth is made the day before, the fat can be removed and discarded before making the soup. When pouring up the broth allow the finest of the settlings to remain in the pot and discard.

Newspapers carried a notice for a "defaticater," which was an instrument for skimming soup, apparently to remove the fat. However, research to date has turned up no further information on the instrument.

Clear soups should be perfectly transparent, and thickened soups should be similar in consistency to heavy cream. Soup was thickened with bread, bread crusts, potato, wheat or rice flour, barley, rice, oatmeal, truffles, morels, dried mushrooms, scotch barley, pearl barley, peas, beans or, on rare occasions, isinglass.

Mrs. Colman thought pearl barley more wholesome than rice. Its chief use was in soup and puddings and it required five or six hours simmering. Quicker-cooking varieties are available today.

Clear soups should not be strong of the meat flavor, and should be of a light brown, sherry, or straw color. All white or brown thick soups should be rather thin, with just sufficient consistency to adhere lightly to a spoon when hot, such as those containing fish, poultry, or game. Simple brown soups, either of meat or vegetables, were somewhat thicker.

Victorian cooks kept broth and stock from spoiling by reheating it daily in hot weather and storing it in a cool cellar or spring house. In cooler weather reheating every other day was sufficient.

> Never put by any soup, gravy, &c. in metal utensils; in which never keep anything longer than is absolutely necessary for the purposes of cookery; the acid, vegetables, fat, &c. employed in making soups, &c. are capable of dissolving such utensils: therefore stone or earthen vessels should be used for this purpose.

Potato soup was started with stock. When reduced to about two quarts of broth, the potatoes were added. "Steam two pounds and a half of mealy potatoes, and mash them to a smooth paste; boil up the broth which has been made and which should measure about two quarts, and when boiling mix in by degrees the potatoes. Strain the soup and place it again on the fire for ten minutes, adding pepper, salt and a little finely chopped parsley. Skim it thoroughly, and add two ounces of onions, lightly fried and chopped small."

Early in 1861 *Godey's* advised that while celery was generally available year round for flavoring soup stock, the same results could be obtained by adding dried celery seed. A drachm (1/16 ounce) was said to be equivalent in flavor to two heads of celery, and sufficient for a half gallon of soup. Some sources advised adding a teaspoon of sugar when using celery seed instead of fresh celery.

Fresh or dried mushrooms flavored the soup, and in their absence, a small quantity of mushroom catsup could be substituted.

Ingredients such as wine, catsup (generally walnut or mushroom), and spices were best added just before the soup was served. Tomatoes sometimes flavored the soup.

If the cook felt onions were too strong in flavor she was instructed to boil a turnip with them which would produce a milder flavor.

Soups might be poured through a napkin, previously wet in cold water, to remove excess fat. The fat hardened and remained on top of the napkin while the soup went through, but this method was said to reduce some of the flavor and wise cooks were directed to reseason as needed after straining.

Vermicelli added to soup in the amount of a quarter of a pound per eight servings was well received. This pasta product was so named because the little rolls or threads of pasta resembled small worms. It was made of flour, eggs, salt, and saffron. Cooking the vermicelli in broth prior to adding it to the soup strengthened the flavor. Pierre Blot wrote in 1869, "A potage vermicelli is always good if the broth has been made properly."

Macaroni was a paste made with eggs and flour and extruded through an apparatus which gave it the hollow tube shape. It wasn't cut into the familiar elbow shapes until later on. It was dried for storage. In the United States, vermicelli and macaroni were used principally in soup.

Semolina flour was known during this era, and the debate over the origins of the product stem from the type wheat used and the method of cooking — boiling versus baking.

Cooks were instructed to stir soup with a wooden spoon and a good cook knew a "tureen of soup" referred to three quarts. A quart of soup was sufficient for three to four servings.

"Soup herb powder" was easily prepared from dried parsley, winter savory, sweet marjoram, lemon-thyme, 1 ounce of each; lemon-peel, cut very thin and dried, and sweet basil, the latter two added at 1 ounce each; and a drachm each of bay leaves and celery seed.

Herbs were dried by a fire or in a warm oven, then pounded with a mortar. The powder was passed through a sieve. If the powder was kept in a clean, tightly corked bottle it remained fragrant and flavorful for several months, and could be used in the absence of fresh sweet herbs.

A good pot of soup had a delicate and harmonious blending of flavors, with no particular ingredient or spice dominant over the others.

> You must observe in all broths and soups that one thing does not taste more than another, but that the taste be equal, and it has a fine agreeable relish, according to what you design it for; and you must be sure that all greens and herbs you put in be cleaned, washed, and picked.[15]

Soup was sometimes colored by adding grated carrots, tomato juice, spinach, browned flour, or caramel.

Some sources advised cooking potatoes separately and adding to the soup since they contributed nothing towards the flavor, and frying onions in butter before adding them to the soup to increase the flavor.

Beef stew was made by cutting the beef into small pieces, dredging it in flour, and browning it. Stock or water was added, and it was stewed for several hours, after which onions, "mixed spices," and bay leaf were added and the whole simmered for several hours. Chopped vegetables could be fried and then added if desired.

A ragout was a highly seasoned dish of greens, fish, or meat stewed together with salt and pepper.

The 1877 *Buckeye Cookery* recommended serving poached eggs with some soups. They were added just before serving, allowing one per person. The eggs could be poached in water and added to the soup or added directly into the pot of soup. Two or three eggs stirred into the hot soup just before pouring up into the tureen thickened it nicely.

A product called Maizen A was sold in the 1860s in Brooklyn to thicken sauces and meat soups. It was sold in one-pound packages with instructions provided for its use.

In 1868 and 1869, Pierre Blot wrote a series of articles that were published in *The Galaxy*. He gave bills of fare which he cautioned housewives to take with a grain of salt and be wise of what was available in the markets at the time they planned their meals.

Soups for hot weather included carrot, cauliflower, lima bean, peas, lettuce, squash, sorrel, tomato, turnip, puréed cress, vermicelli, and bisques of lobster and crab.

Consommé was generally taken without anything in it, being rich enough by itself. Blot proclaimed the richest and most delicate soup to be *potage à la reine*, and cautioned serving but a little due to its richness.

Winter soups were hearty and savory. Summer soups were served in cups and made a pleasing first course for country teas, "constituting the bit of something hot which guests are sure to appreciate" after archery, tennis, or a long drive.

Mary Randolph included a recipe for gazpacho in her 1824 *Virginia Housewife*. She stated the soup was Spanish in origin. "Put some soft biscuit or toasted bread in the bottom of a bowl, put in a layer of sliced tomatas with the skin taken off, and one of sliced cucumbers, sprinkled with pepper, salt, and chopped onion; do this until the bowl is full, stew some tomatas quite soft, strain the juice, mix in some mustard and oil, and pour over it; make it two hours before it is eaten." Some books considered gazpacho a salad.

The *Oxford Companion to Food* agreed the soup was Spanish in origin and pointed out that the addition of tomatoes was a relatively modern addition. The Arabs who occupied parts of Spain from the 8th to the 13th centuries are the originators of the dish which was initially made from bread, garlic, olive oil, vinegar, salt, and water.

Eugenia de Montijo of Granada, the wife of Emperor Napoleon III, is credited with introducing Andalusian gazpacho to France where it spread to the rest of the world.

Vichyssoise probably shares a 19th-century origin. While many sources credit its creation to Chef Louis Diat around 1910, a very similar version appears in Gouffé's collection in 1869. The difference is Diat's version was served cold while Gouffé's was served hot. Both are puréed soup made from potatoes and leeks.

In 1863, George Sala said that for bouillabaisse "indispensable ingredients are red mullet, tomatoes, red pepper, red burgundy, oil, and garlic. Soles, gurnets, dories, and whitings are admissible into this dish." He stated that at Marseilles a rolling pin was coated in several layers of melted tallow then put into the soup pot and swirled around until the tallow melted and mixed into the soup. He was not fond of this idea.[16]

If Sala paled at that vision of bouillabaisse, William Thackeray was so much enamored with the soup he memorialized it in "The Ballad of Bouillabaisse."

> A street there is in Paris famous,
> For which no rhyme our language yields,
> Rue Neuve de petits Champs its name is—
> The New Street of the Little Fields;
> And there's an inn, not rich and splendid,
> But still in comfortable case;
> The which in youth I oft attended,
> To eat a bowl of Bouillabaisse.
> This Bouillabaisse a noble dish is—
> A sort of soup, or broth, or brew,
> Or hotchpotch of all sorts of fishes,
> That Greenwich never could outdo;
> Green herbs, red peppers, muscles, saffern,
> Soles, onions, garlic, roach, and dace;
> All these you eat at Terré's tavern,
> In that one dish of Bouillabaisse.
> Indeed, a rich and savory stew 'tis;
> And true philosophers, methinks,
> Who love all sorts of natural beauties,
> Should love good victuals and good drinks.
> And Cordelier or Benedictine
> Might gladly, sure, his lot embrace,
> Nor find a fast-day too afflicting,
> Which served him up a Bouillabaisse.
> I wonder if the house still there is?
> Yes, here the lamp is as before;
> The smiling, red-cheek'd écaillère is

Still opening oysters at the door.
Is Terré still alive and able?
I recollect his droll grimace;
He'd come and smile before your table,
And hoped you like your Bouillabaisse.
We enter; nothing's changed or older.
"How's Monsieur Terré, waiter, pray?"
The waiter stares and shrugs his shoulder —
"Monsieur is dead this many a day."
"It is the lot of saint and sinner.
So honest Terré's run his race!"
"What will Monsieur require for dinner?"
"Say, do you still cook Bouillabaisse?"
"Oh, oui, Monsieur," 's the waiter's answer;
"Quel vin Monsieur desire-t-il ?"
Tell me a good one." "That I can, sir;
The Chambertin with yellow seal."
"So Terré's gone," I say, and sink in
My old accustom'd corner-place;
"He's done with feasting and with drinking,
With Burgundy and Bouillabaisse."
My old accustom'd corner here is—
The table still is in the nook;
Ah! Vanished many a busy year is,
This well-known chair since last I took.
When first I saw ye, *cari luoghi*,
I'd scarce a beard upon my face,
And now a grizzled, grim old fogy,
I sit and wait for Bouillabaisse.
Where are you, old companions trusty
Of early days, here met to dine?
Come, waiter! Quick, a flagon crusty —
I'll pledge them in the good old wine.
The kind old voices and old faces
My memory can quick retrace;
Around the board they take their places,
And share the wine and Bouillabaisse.
There's Jack has made a wondrous marriage;
There's laughing Tom is laughing yet;
There's brave Augustus drives his carriage;
There's poor old Fred in the Gazette;
On James's head the grass is growing:
Good Lord! The world has wagged apace
Since here we sat the Claret flowing,
And drank, and ate the Bouillabaisse.
Ah me! How quick the days are flitting!
I mind me of a time that's gone,
When here I'd sit, as now I'm sitting,
In this same place — but not alone.
A fair young form was nestled near me,
A dear, dear face looked fondly up,
And sweetly spoke and smiled to cheer me.
— There's no one now to share my cup.

> I drink it as the Fates ordain it.
> Come, fill it, and have done with rhymes;
> Fill up the lonely glass, and drain it
> In memory of dear old times.
> Welcome the wine, whate'er the seal is;
> And sit you down and say your grace
> With thankful heart, whate'er the meal is.
> Here comes the smoking Bouillabaisse!

He pronounced turtle, terrapin, oyster, and bisque all exquisite and mentioned Italian *zuppa marinara* and Russian *batwinia*. The stock for *batwinia* was *kvas* (half-brewed barley beer and oil), into which went fish (*starlet* or *sassina*) with bay leaves, pepper, and ice. A boys' adventure book of 1874 described it thusly:

> Kvas is a beverage of fermented rye. From this they [Russians] make an iced soup, into which they put meat, chopped herring, and cucumbers.... They have cabbage soup and fish soup we should call chowder.[17]

One of the earliest uses of the word *bouillabaisse* to describe fish stew such as that found in the Mediterranean came from the French writer Marie-Henri Beyle (1783–1842), pen name Stendhal, in 1806.

Researching the origins of chili is an exercise in fantasy since so many theories abound as to its earliest origins. However, one theory seems constant — it is of American origin, though many believed it to have originated in Mexico.

By the 1880s, newspaper ads carried notices for "real Mexican" chili con carne suppers at various restaurants, social clubs, and so on. It is possible the "ragout of pork with Spanish pepper" served in Mexican marketplaces as early as 1850 and reported on in newspapers in the 1840s and 1850s was the forerunner of chili.[18]

In 1731, a group of immigrants from the Canary Islands settled in San Antonio where the women prepared a spicy stew some believe evolved into chili con carne. It is fact that chili stands were a permanent fixture in San Antonio for cowpokes and tourists alike.[19] In support of that date, a decade later the *San Antonio Light* reported on the closing of the chili stands which they claimed had been in operation for approximately 200 years.[20]

A widely held notion regarding the origins of chili is that in about 1850 Texas cowboys on trail drives ate a spicy stew made from dried beef, fat, wild chili peppers, salt, and herbs which was later refined into what we know as chili con carne. The original ingredients were formed into cakes, in essence a variation of portable soup cakes, and boiled in water to prepare them.[21]

Frank Bushick stated that the Chicago World's Fair offered San Antonio chili to hungry fair-goers, bringing it out of Texas and into the wider world.[22] By that time, prepared chili powder (mostly a blend of chili peppers, cumin, and oregano) made it possible for anyone to prepare it. In the 1920s Cincinnati put a new spin on chili when it was served over spaghetti.

Note that the following 19th-century recipe does not contain tomatoes, and therefore, supports the notion that chili may have originated as trail food.

> Chili Con Carne. Remove the seeds and veins from 10 red peppers, and scald them until soft in sufficient boiling water to cover them. Mash them thoroughly with a potato masher, or pound in a mortar, then press through a colander, adding a teaspoonful of salt. Cut two pounds of round steak into inch-pieces and fry quickly until brown in a little butter or fat. Add the prepared peppers, one small onion and two cloves of garlic, chopped fine. Stew slowly for three hours, adding more water from time to time as may be necessary. This is a favorite Mexican dish, and is worthy of a trial.[23]

The 19th century saw several changes in the type of cooking pots sold and used. In the 18th century firms advertised light cast iron kitchen furniture, double block tin, and copper, which was sold both separately and in sets. By 1850 those were slowly beginning to give way to cast iron pots with porcelain interiors, not to be confused with the enamelware that was advertised beginning in the 1890s. Women were offered the opportunity of trading in their copperware when purchasing newer varieties of pans.

Soup was often served with toasts, crackers, or sippets cut into various shapes, particularly into Maltese cross, triangles, diamonds, paper-kites, or cocks' combs, "nicely fried" and served as garnish. Christian Johnstone wrote, "Fried bread is a most useful thing for this purpose, as it never fails to be eaten with the dish it is employed to ornament."[24]

Stale crackers were improved by spreading them with butter and salt and heating them in the oven.

In 1860, Solon Robinson wrote on a variety of topics to instruct frugality and survival skills for immigrants and others purchasing land and carving homes out of the wilderness. His account of soup was, naturally, aimed at producing a meal at the lowest possible cost.

> I went to the butcher's the night before, and bought five cents' worth of little scrap pieces of lean beef, and I declare I think I got as much as a pound, and this I cut up into bits, and soaked overnight — an all-important process for soup or a stew — cooking it in the same water. Then I bought two cents' worth of potatoes and one cent's worth of meal — that made the eight cents; two had to go for fuel every day, and the paper I got my purchases in served for kindling. The meal I wet up into stiff dough, and worked out into little round balls, about as big as grapes, and the potatoes I cut up into slices, and all together made a stew, or chowder, seasoned with a small onion and part of a pepper-pod that I got with the potatoes.[25]

A repast served in a Scots-American home was described well in *The Dutch Dominie of the Catskills*. Plates which had been hollowed out of basswood had broth described as "sheep's-head kail" ladled into them from a tripod pot.

> Clarence had seen, when he was standing by the fire, the nose of some animal pushing itself up among the vegetables in the pot like a black hippopotamus among the reeds of the Nile; but he did not expect to make his dinner of the mess. However, now like a good soldier, he sat down with a ready appetite for whatever was coming, asking no questions. To his agreeable surprise, the soup was white as milk, though the head — it might be of a ram from its size — was there in a large platter on the centre, without the horns, and the wool singed all off. Garden stuffs of all kinds, known, and some only known to Janet, had been boiled for two full hours, with the head among them; so that it would have defied a French cook to tell the prevailing flavor of what McDonald called this dish of hotch potch. Barley bread, unleavened, baked on a griddle, thin and tough as leather, was eaten to this soup; when at the close Janet put down a square bottle and a basket of oatmeal cakes alongside of a skim-milk cheese; all of which were intended as a dessert.[26]

Soup with the sheep's head, its wool singed off prior to going into the pot, had been standard fare in Scotland since before the 17th century.

The poor still lived on grain-based pottages and porridges, which many continued to eat after coming to the United States. They were known as *crowdie* in Scotland, *llymru* (flummery) in Wales, and hasty pudding or Indian pudding in New England.

Recipes for sheep's head broth were published in the United States, such as the one in *Peterson's* in March 1863. The recipe used the liver and lights as well as the head, with onion, carrot, turnip, pearl barley, salt, pepper, cloves, marjoram, parsley and thyme. Sherry was added just before serving. The recipe does not specify whether the head was served whole or whether the meat was picked from the bone.

In 1830, Mrs. Dalgairns instructed that the head be singed with a red-hot iron to prepare it for cooking, and thought it best to take it to the blacksmith to have this done. The brain and eyes were removed and discarded. She used the trotters in making soup, and instructed in other recipes that the head, trotters, or ribs of mutton could be substituted for chicken or fowl.

At about the same time the English began to refine their soups, cutting the meat into small pieces, seasoning with saffron, herbs, and other spices, and thickening with flour to produce a rich gravy.

Perhaps 19th-century Americans' talent for preparing tasty meals was a credit to cookery book writers, instructors of domestic economy (the precursor of the home economics movement), and a series of lectures and demonstrations of the culinary arts given in larger cities.

One of those lecturers was Mrs. Sarah Tyson Rorer, whose presentations are described in contemporary newspapers. At times between 300 to 400 women attended her programs. In November 1899 the menu for what Mrs. Rorer called a simple dinner was cream of celery soup, steak with oysters, glazed sweet potatoes, stuffed baked tomatoes, and apple float.

Similar classes were given in South Kensington and written up in the English newspapers. The Training School for Cookery offered, among other things, instruction in French bourgeois cookery meant primarily for persons who intended to make a livelihood as teachers. Students learned the proper way to clean pots, pans, and grates, build and maintain cooking fires, and clarify fat and drippings, after which they proceeded to learn actual preparation of dishes including soups and stews.

By the 1880s, kangaroo tail was being imported to the United States, and it was used primarily for making soup. The giant kangaroo had been discovered by Captain Cook in 1789 and often weighed up to 140 pounds. Its flesh was considered excellent, and the animal was much hunted in Australia. By the 1850s, it had been taken to England and bred there. The black-striped kangaroo of New South Wales was also hunted for food and leather.

The buttocks, loins, and thighs were good cuts for various methods of cooking, but the tail was most often used for soup. The following was written by an American touring Australia.

> At Newcastle we had our first experience of a dish of kangaroo. And a very good dinner we made off it. The meat requires to be young, or not too old at any rate; and it should be cooked with a bit of pork, to supply the fatness which it lacks, but when well served it is a very welcome variety to the tough steaks and scraggy mutton chops that form the usual bill of fare in Australian hotels. The tail of the kangaroo is the part of the animal that is most highly esteemed, the soup made from it being said to be not at all inferior to that made from the tail of the domestic ox.[27]

The gold rush of 1849 brought so many men to California that food became scarce and expensive. One miner remembered surviving on acorns and pepper grass. When that ran out they were grateful for the generosity of nearby Indians who, seeing their plight, brought them acorn bread and buckeye soup.

Another miner reached a point where he couldn't eat the coarse fare served at most establishments and asked a lady for some soup.

> She had eaten soup in New York, and thought it very poor stuff, filling one up with water and vegetables, or rather cattle fodder, such as turnips and carrots and celery, a sort of makeshift for want of something better. It was not customary to have it in the mines; but desirous of pleasing if she could, she stepped briskly to the great iron pot from which she had just lifted several cabbages, filled the bucket with the thick, steaming liquid, and saying smilingly that

she hoped he would like it, and if he did she would make him some every day, handed it back to the envoy and he departed.

Her efforts were for naught, however, as the man soon returned with the bucket of broth, angrily calling it "water poisoned in an iron pot." The woman had no knowledge of making soup and asked her husband for insight, but he remained as ignorant of the process as she.[28]

Such soup, made from cabbage or kale, was documented in *Le Menagière*, Taillevant, and others for centuries.

The *Ladies' Repository* in 1858 carried an article stating that Indians often ate roast fish and muskrat chowder served in wooden bowls.

When the French first came among the Indians they easily adopted the use of some kinds of meat they had not previously known. Dan Marsac's family at the mouth of the Flat River in Michigan provided a "bounteous" dinner for weary river travelers, which, over 20 years later, they remembered with hearty laughter, recalling that their principal dish had been muskrat soup.

Chowder parties were favorite pastimes of citizens across the country. In areas where clams were plentiful they were the heart of the creamy white stew, and in other areas fish of varying types were the main ingredient. A chowder party was an outdoor affair often held in conjunction with a social occasion such as a birthday or anniversary, political debate, tableau (still-life play), or a dance.

An English woman touring the United States in the 1850s pronounced chowder "a very famous dish," and the *Southern Literary Messenger* expressed disappointment in a cookery book in 1850: "What will be thought of a work on cookery, edited by an American, in which neither chowder or gumbo is mentioned, and which completely ignores terrapins and canvas-back ducks?"

> Chowder — A favorite dish in New England — a stew of fish, pork, onions, and biscuit often prepared by pic-nic parties, who visit the sea-shore, from fish caught at the time."[29]
> "We organized sailing parties and rowing matches; we picnicked under the 'tea party tree' in the pine woods, a well-known trysting-place for generations; and in cooler weather, enjoyed the fish and clam chowder parties, held in some of the many large kitchens in town, where the good cheer could be supplemented by music and dancing."[30]

According to James Fennimore Cooper, some 10,000 people reportedly attended a political rally in support of General William Henry Harrison, an old Indian fighter who was promoted on the Whig ticket for president, at which a clambake and chowder were prepared on July 4, 1840 in Rhode Island.

William T. Davis stated that at the end of the 18th century in Plymouth haddock were thought inferior fish and were difficult to dispose of in the market at 1 cent a pound. "But some critical person found worms between the flakes of a codfish, and then another discovered that a haddock made a superior fry and still another that in a chowder the flesh of a haddock was firmer than that of a codfish, and finally both came to be held in equal distinction."

A lengthy report of San Francisco eateries was published in *Overland Monthly* in December 1892. One of the most inexpensive places in the city to eat was in the vicinity of one of the factories where rooms were maintained for the factory girls to take their lunches. They could bring food from home, or be served bread, butter, soup, beans, milk, tea, or a sandwich for a nominal amount.

Hotel bars and saloons provided a choice of soup, fish, entrée, roast, and dessert at considerably more expense. A "three-for-two" establishment was where a diner could order items costing ten cents, or three for a quarter. They could choose from soup, fish, meats, vegetables, and desserts in whatever amount or combination they chose.

Of the European-style *table d'hôte* restaurants, the least expensive was a French shop where a meal of soup, fish, meat, potatoes, bread, butter, and a half bottle of claret cost 15 cents.

There were French versions of the three-for-two establishments which served similar fare, but better quality than the others, or for 75 cents to one dollar, portions and quality increased considerably.

> The soup is still brought to you in a large yellow earthenware bowl, from which you ladle out a portion suited to your appetite. The half-bottle of claret is still open to the suspicion of being largely water colored with logwood, and the portions are exasperatingly small to a hungry man.... They serve soup, a salad, a choice of several kinds of fish, and any one of half a dozen entrees, either of two kinds of roast, fruit, cheese, and black coffee with kirsch or cognac.

German restaurants served prune soup, herring salad, and a variety of sausages.

A block away a Mexican restaurant served *sopa* (soup), "always much the same though the name varies, as *sopa de gallina* (chicken soup), *sopa de verdure* (vegetable soup), or *sopa de familia* (family soup)." The restaurant also offered baked fish, feet, tongue, *rellenos de chile*, and *picadillo con chile colorado* (mincemeat with red peppers), or *guyisado con chile* (stew with peppers), *tamales, enchiladas, albondigas, chorizos con huevos.* The reporter said, "The first four are too complex to be readily explained to the stranger." Also offered were roast, vegetables, and puddings.

There were Chinese restaurants with the standard bird's nest soup, Scandinavian, Japanese, and Russian restaurants, coffee houses, oyster houses, and ladies' cafés.

George A. Sala recorded many accountings of soup in the United States in 1863, one of which was pepper-pot.

> Pepper-pot, that wondrous West-Indian dish, that salmagundi of fowl, beef, and mutton peppered up to the maintruck sauced with the cassareep or inspissated juice of the manioc root; the whole kept simmering and seething in a large jar or pipkin. I consumed vast quantities of pepper-pot. Dear old mess! I felt to the manor born of it; it was my pot-au-feu.

Sala contemplated the proposition that convicts be fed on bread and water, and stated, "We have heard a great outcry within these latter days against the assumed luxurious manner in which criminals are fed in gaol [jail]. The rogues it appears live on savoury soup, thickened with meal and seasoned with vegetables, salt, and pepper." Sala stated the "forcats of Toulon" (Marseilles) were fed on soup, beans, and wine. Sala spoke of meals with enthusiasm, of clear turtle and bisque and potage à la Bedford.

Soup has always played an important part in feeding the hungry, but perhaps never more so than onboard ships. Accounts of families who bought steerage tickets on ships bound for America in the 18th and 19th centuries relate harsh living conditions that one passenger later described as survival of the fittest.

Steerage referred to an area between decks of the ship where passage was cheap. Not for the faint of heart, steerage was dark, cramped, often accessible only by ladder, and stifling in the closed quarters with no fresh air and the stench of vomit when passengers were seized by fits of sea-sickness. Hatches had to be closed in high seas to prevent waves from filling the steerage compartment with water.

Steerage passengers were usually responsible for bringing along enough food to last the duration of the voyage and cooking it themselves. Rations of wood and water were included in the price of the ticket.

Typical foods brought aboard for the journeys were ingredients that would have been difficult to prepare in any way other than porridge and soup — salted pork or mutton, butter, cheese, rye or barley flour, dried peas, dried beans, pearl barley, potatoes, salt, pepper, onions, vinegar, and kegs of salted herring. Most brought strong drink, coffee or tea, and bread — either soft bread, hardtack, or flat bread.

Cooking vessels were limited to what could be carried in a bag — usually a coffee pot, water pail, kettle, and eating utensils.

Ole Ellingsen Strand made the trip in 1851 when he was 11 years old. He described the cooking area as a bin four feet wide and a foot and a half tall, filled with sand, on which fires were built by the steerage passengers to prepare food. The size of the area was inadequate, it was usually filled with smoke, and the timid usually found themselves doing without.[31]

Women would wait in line on deck for an opportunity to use the cooking area, but on days when it was too stormy, the men would go up to "steep tea, cook coffee, or even make a kettle of soup."

Stephen de Vere sailed for America in 1847. He described food preparation by saying, "The food is generally ill-selected and seldom sufficiently cooked in consequences of the insufficiency and bad construction of the cooking places. The supply of water, hardly enough for cooking and drinking, does not allow for washing."[32]

An 1845 article regarding German emigrants said passage cost $20 per adult, and children half price. This included rations of beef, pork, beans, rice, potatoes, bread, butter, coffee, and sugar.[33]

Sailors' meals were sometimes very little different from those of steerage passengers. An 1891 article described a group sitting on the foredeck three times a day dipping sop into a big wooden bowl while a smaller boat followed with poultry, rabbits, and a lamb or goat for the better-class passengers' meals.[34]

Emigrants remained dependent on simple soups and porridge as their main meals after their passage due to a limited array of cooking utensils with which to prepare meals. One traveler wrote,

> Scores of emigrants are encamping along the stream. One having caught a turtle as large as a peck measure, invited us to partake of a savory soup, which we imbibed from tin cups, sitting on a log.[35]

The 19th century was a great time of exploration as people who could afford passage traveled extensively within the United States and abroad. Magazines were filled with their culinary exploits.

> A cup and saucer was placed before me immediately, and dipping my spoon into the fluid it contained, I found it nothing but chicken water, and so meager in its composition that it would have shocked the sensibilities of every good old Aunty in Carolina, who would never have dreamed it nice enough for a convalescing invalid, much less for "company." One spoonful was quite enough, I did not get rid of the taste of garlic it left in my mouth for a couple of days.[36]

Exemplifying the 19th-century sense of humor, one publication wrote, "An 'old bachelor' of thirty years standing advertises in one of our agricultural exchanges for a receipt to make bean soup. A fair correspondent thus answers his request: 'Get a wife that knows how to make it.' Sensible advice."[37]

27. Cajun and Creole

New Orleans is known for its unique cuisine, which evolved from slaves, Native Americans, and Creoles in the region. As well, the French, Spanish, and English influenced the foods in the area, and the Acadians who first migrated from Canada to Louisiana in the 1700s lent their influence in the contents of the soup pot. Soup was the first course, "served at all ordinary dinners."[1]

Brennan's restaurant is an excellent example of the French custom of having a daily soup. They offered onion, turtle, and oyster on their three-course breakfast menu. Many French families began their day with a cup of bouillon at breakfast, and even peasant families began the day with a cup of claret and a portion of soup. Soup in France was standard at dinner "from palace to hovel," and this tradition continued with Creole French.

The word *Creole* evolved from Spanish and Portuguese terms that referred to individuals born in the colonies as opposed to those who emigrated. It doesn't particularly distinguish between races. Culturally Creoles were African, French, Spanish, and later German and Italian, and each ethnicity contributed to modern New Orleans cuisine.

The earliest cookbooks published in New Orleans did not use the word *Creole* in the title because, according to Liz Williams of the Southern Food and Beverage Museum, they simply viewed the dishes as everyday food and not as a distinct cuisine. The first cookbook calling itself *Creole* was *La Cuisine Créole* by Lafcadio Hearn, published in New Orleans in 1885.

Hearn was born on the island of Santa Maura off the coast of Greece and as a child also lived in Ireland and Wales before moving to New Orleans in 1877 where he worked as a journalist. He realized the foods of New Orleans were distinct from those in other areas, and when he compiled recipes from housewives and chefs into book form his title reflected the late 19th century influence in describing the food of New Orleans as *Creole*.

Paul Prudhomme and Emeril Lagasse were the leading proponents of New Orleans cuisine in the 20th century.

La Cuisine Créole states Creole food is a blending of American, French, Spanish, Italian, West Indian, and Mexican. Tanty's *La Cuisine Française* followed in 1893, and Eustis's *Cooking in Creole Days* in 1904.

Creole is not the same as Cajun, which denotes someone of Acadian background. Creole food is similar to a more sophisticated continental cuisine, and Cajun food is more of the one-pot-wonder type. Cajun food compares to French provincial cooking while Creole dishes are more like Parisian cuisine and are more dependent on sauces. Both use indigenous ingredients, although Creole food used more seafood and Cajun food tended to use more game than seafood. Cajun settlements were typically farther from the coast, which before refrigeration meant more difficulty in obtaining and keeping seafood.

173

The New Orleans pot-au-feu was made by boiling a good soup bone with a "soup bunch" (cabbage, turnips, carrots, parsley, celery, onion, sometimes garlic, thyme, bay leaf, and allspice). Macaroni, vermicelli, or vegetables were added to taste.

Bouillon was second only to the pot-au-feu in preference, and might have been served warm or cold. Proportions of ingredients were approximately 6 pounds boneless beef without fat, 6 quarts of cold water, 4 cloves, allspice, a cup of tomatoes, 1 teaspoon salt, 1 spoon celery seed, 1 bay leaf, red pepper, and a clove of garlic. It simmered slowly from breakfast until dinner. It was never allowed to stop simmering, and additional water was never added.

The 1903 *Good Housekeeping Everyday Cook Book* echoed these sentiments, suggesting various ingredients be added to clear soups, but consommé was to be made from browned diced steak with no added ingredients. By adding to consommé a cup of heated rich cream to four beaten egg yolks mixed with four tablespoons of chilled cream with a little powdered mace, a "velvet" soup was created.

Gumbo cannot be ignored in any discussion of Creole food. A traveler to a Creole home in Louisiana in the 1850s pronounced it, "the crown of all savoury and remarkable soups in the world — a regular elixir of life of the substantial kind. He who has once eaten gumbo may look down disdainfully on the most genuine turtle soup."[2]

Gumbo was thickened with okra, filé, or roux, although in recent history more than one is often used. Roux is flour mixed with fat and slowly stirred over low heat until dark brown. Its purpose is to thicken and to flavor the gumbo.

In recent years premade roux has become available. However, most die-hard gumbo makers haven't been impressed. Some have speeded up the process of making homemade roux by browning the flour in an iron skillet in a 350° oven before combining it with the fat.

The darker the roux, the less thickening power it retains, therefore, the dark roux used in gumbo probably contribute more to the flavor than the consistency. Dark roux, cooked until it is the color of an old penny, is used in highly flavored soups, while *roux blond*, made with the same ingredients but cooked only until it reaches a light golden brown, is used for more delicate sauces and soups. The liquid should be added to the roux rather than adding the roux to the liquid.

Rice was an important part of Cajun and Creole cuisine. No good cook would think of serving foods like gumbo without it, and a cook's ability to prepare it so that every grain was separate determined her reputation within the culinary circles of the community.

The word *okra* is thought to be derived from certain African dialects, and the more African influence in the dish the more likely it is to contain okra. It is not always used in Cajun gumbo. Okra found its way into America from Africa in connection with slaves who left their mark on Creole cuisine.[3] Okra was dried and pounded into powder known as gumbo powder.[4]

In 1851, Schenck instructed cooks to add equal amounts of chopped okra and skinned tomatoes with a sliced onion, salt, and pepper to make a stew he called gumbo.

Powdered sassafras leaves were referred to as gumbo powder for soup in a report on the Paris Exposition of 1867.[5] The dried leaves were pounded in a mortar and pestle into a fine powder called filé. Filé and bay were staples of Native Americans, and Indian women often sold sassafras and filé at the French market.[6]

There is another dish from New Orleans which modern Creoles wouldn't necessarily think of as soup. However, given the definition of soup in earlier chapters, they do fall into the thicker stew category.

Jambalaya is a thick ragout of rice, onion, broth, seasonings, and shrimp, chicken, or sausage, which historian Karen Hess compared to Carolina pilau. The pilau-type dishes may have gone to Europe with the returning Crusaders.

An aged Cajun woman using a crude mortar and pestle in the process of hulling rice near Crowley, Louisiana. Filé is a classic ingredient in gumbo, and sassafras leaves were dried and pounded in these devices as well. Native Americans used them for pounding corn. October 1938. Library of Congress, Prints and Photographs Division, Reproduction Number LC-USF34-031664-D.

There does not appear to be surviving evidence of the earliest origins of the dish sufficient enough to credit any one culture with its creation. It may have origins in Spain, France, or possibly even Africa, but the Cajuns and Creoles coaxed jambalaya into a celebration of flavors.

In 1849, Solon Robinson submitted a recipe to *The American Agriculturist* titled "Hopping Johnny (jambalaya)"— it was almost as if the jambalaya was an afterthought. The recipe is clearly not for Hopping John or at least any recognized version of it.

> Take a dressed chicken, or full-grown fowl, if not old, and cut all the flesh into small pieces, with a sharp knife. Put this into an iron pot, with a large spoonful of butter and one onion chopped fine; steep and stir it till it is brown; then add water enough to cover it, and put in some parsley, spices, and red pepper pods, chopped fine, and let it boil till you think it is barely done, taking care to stir it often, so as not to burn it; then stir in as much rice, when cooked, as will absorb all the water; which will be one pint of rice to two of water; stir and boil it a minute or so, and then let it stand and simmer until the rice is cooked.[7]

In 1846, Robinson suffered a fever which left him incapacitated for a while. At that time he arrived in New Orleans. From there he planned to go to Alabama and Florida, then to Georgia and the Carolinas the following spring. It was while traveling through these southern states that he was exposed to the foods that led to the publishing of the preceding receipt.

Another non–Creole who published a receipt for this dish was Mrs. Fisher who was a slave in South Carolina before moving to Mobile, Alabama after her emancipation. At the time her book was published (1881) she was living in San Francisco. Whether there was an Alabama preference for jambalaya or whether both authors having spent time there is coincidence, is food for thought.

The Creole version is loosely based on the Spanish paella and may have contained seafood as a main ingredient; Cajun versions may be made from alligator, turkey, wild boar, or venison.

Etouffée is a Cajun ragout or stew, usually made from a blonde roux, onions, pepper, celery, cayenne, garlic, salt, and seafood, chicken, or sausage. Some add tomato, but others think this alters the character of the dish. It is served over rice, bread, or grits.

28. Economic Depressions

The depression of the 1930s was only one of many eras of depressed economy. Financial panics occurred in 1809, 1814, 1819, 1825, 1837, 1839, 1841, 1857, and 1873, among other years.[1]

In 1819, the American economy experienced great upheaval when a financial crisis put an end to the progress experienced since the colonial era. Following the War of 1812, Americans had enjoyed a tremendous growth in trade which had spurred the economy to new heights, but this growth was halted in 1819. With unemployment, foreclosure, and failing agricultural prices came a reduction in family budgets that was keenly felt at the dinner table.

The collapsing economy brought extreme poverty, and cities like Philadelphia and Boston imprisoned hundreds of paupers in debtor's prisons. Property values plummeted. Soup kitchens were sometimes all that stood between families and starvation.

John C. Calhoun stated the panic of 1819 had been keenly felt in every part of the Union, and had reduced "enormous numbers of persons" to utter financial ruin.

By 1823, Americans had overcome that collapse. The period was partly blamed on reduced cotton prices, although tension occasionally surfaced regarding an economy based on the growth of cotton and slave labor used to produce it.

A recession extended through most of the 1850s and culminated in a major financial disaster on August 24, 1857 when the New York branch of the Ohio Life Insurance and Trust Company failed. New York bankers immediately restricted transactions, further prompting depositors to demand withdrawals of money in their accounts. By the next morning fortunes were lost.

On September 12, the steamship *Central America*, sank off the coast of South Carolina while underway from San Francisco with a load of gold and silver to relieve the New York banks. This prompted a drastic increase in withdrawals. Specie payment was suspended on October 13 and banks closed until November, resulting in a full-scale financial panic. Unemployment rose, stocks and real estate prices fell, manufactured goods piled up in warehouses, the railroads defaulted on loans, and land speculation ground to a halt. Grain prices fell and, to add misery to insult, British investors pulled their money out of American banks.

> In 1857 ... crowds of unemployed flocked into the Park and threatened the authorities unless they were given food and work.... The charitable societies and people of the city established soup kitchens for the needy and starving thousands, so that danger of an uprising was averted.[2]

In 1850, journalist Samuel Bowles and others of Massachusetts sent a petition asking Congress to revise the tariff of 1846 to protect U.S. labor and capital from foreign competition. The request had little effect.

In 1854, *Hunt's Merchant's Magazine* declared that "confidence is shaken everywhere" as foreign goods piled up and Americans begged for jobs.

> We do not come as beggars, but we ask what we deem right. We ask not alms, but work. We don't want a little soup now and cast-off clothing tomorrow. But we do want work and the means of making an honest livelihood.[3]

The hardships of the 1860s have been blamed on the Civil War, however, Americans were in dire straits before that war began. After the war and Reconstruction, America seemed destined to recover from devastating financial difficulties. Or so it seemed. In 1893 Grover Cleveland was president and America again took a financial beating. Gold reserves fell and the national treasury was drained because of sales of gold securities to foreign investors, the effect of the McKinley tariff and high veterans' pensions. On June 27 the stock market crashed, banks failed, some 15,000 businesses went bankrupt, and a third of the railroads were in default. This panic lasted until 1897.

America needed a savior, and people like Bavarian-born Nathan Straus answered their pleas. Straus, born in 1848, came to the United States as a child, settled in Talbotton, Georgia, and became a partner in L. Straus & Sons, importers of pottery and glassware. He held that position until 1888 when he became a partner in R. H. Macy & Co. and remained with Macy's until 1914, when he retired.

In 1893, Straus distributed pasteurized milk to infants, coal in winter to the poor of New York, and maintained lodging houses for the homeless. He was offered the nomination for mayor but declined. During the World War I era, Straus turned his attention to Palestine, where he opened soup kitchens and became chairman of the American Jewish Congress Committee.[4]

In 1894, Italian families of five or six persons lived off an average of $2 a week in New York City. Mrs. Janello, a dealer in secondhand clothing, repaired and remade cast-off garments, which she sold to provide two meals a day for her family: bread and coffee for breakfast, and macaroni, soup, or cornmeal for supper, "meat tasted not oftener than twice a year," according to Shepp in 1894.

> The good-hearted woman next door found a spare potato or two for the children; the neighbor across the hall, when she had corned beef for dinner, brought the water it was boiled in for soup.[5]

In 1903, the far-reaching effects of the panic were recalled in a speech before Congress:

> What I do know is this, Mr. Chairman, that after Grover Cleveland was elected President of the United States there came a change over this country.... Everybody knows that soup houses were erected in every city and village of the land to feed the people turned out of doors by this policy.... And, Mr. Chairman, we all know that in 1892 we stood on the summit of prosperity, and we know that a year later we were floundering in the quagmires of despair.[6]

During the panics, those who suffered the least were rural farmers who subsisted on simple hearty meals prepared from staples grown on the farm. Their fare sometimes consisted simply of soup or cornbread and bacon.

A stock market crash in 1929 precipitated the depression of the 1930s. Proud people who had always been able to work to provide for their families found themselves out of work, hungry, and watching their children beg for food. Soup kitchens and bread lines were all that kept body and soul together, and yet 95 cases of death by starvation were reported in New York City alone in 1931. This number did not reflect the number of deaths from diseases complicated by undernourishment.

> In Depression homes soup was served warm and was often thick and nutritious. Big families could be fed with soups from leftover meats, beans, and home-grown vegetables. Homemakers

Mulligan stew being prepared by a group of out-of-work men during the Great Depression. Library of Congress, Prints and Photographs Division, Reproduction number LC-DIG-ggbain-18190.

made many varieties of soup from available foods. The results included split pea, chicken-rice, potato-onion, bean, hamburger, and all vegetable. Dumplings were a filling addition to complement the soup. For some families, soup was the evening meal every night.[7]

During the 1930s, Mulligan stew was the name given to the stew prepared by tramps or hobos from whatever ingredients they could gather to go into it. Over time the use of the term was broadened to mean any conglomeration of ingredients or parts. The term first appeared in print in 1904, and the dish in that case was a crude form of Irish stew made from whatever was available.

Wild plants and vegetables grown from seeds given out as relief measures often ended up made into a hearty soup.

Another butcher by-product to be dealt with cleverly was bundles of chicken feet. Boiling chicken feet with greens, which could be obtained even in the city, resulted in a good pot of soup.[8]

During World War II, victory gardens would fill backyards and vacant lots.

29. Soup Kitchens

Soup kitchens have provided hot nourishing meals of soup for the underprivileged throughout history. Hillyer's Soup Shop was serving hot soup to those in need by 1799 in London.[1]

There were two schools of thought regarding free soup, one being the charity of helping those less fortunate, the other being that a ready supply of free food encouraged less responsible people to expect handouts instead of applying themselves more productively.

After the great Chicago fire of 1871, soup was provided to those who lost their homes. A soup house was erected, stoves put in, and kettles put to boil. While most recipients were appreciative, a few were not pleased. A single complaint of a maggot in the soup fired off a storm of rumors resulting in a panel of ladies being chosen to investigate the matter. They found only one woman who claimed she'd found a maggot "eight inches long" (which is an impossibility) in soup she'd been given. The ladies pronounced the facilities and the soup to be scrupulously clean and, to prove their findings, ate soup in each of the facilities.[2]

In 1893, Chicago was accused of bringing an undesirable element to a community through free soup. The papers said several hundred tramps arrived daily, filling the soup kitchens and lodging houses to overflowing.

Some of Chicago's facilities expected recipients to work in the woodyards in return for food and lodging, but few did. Of 19 able-bodied men sent to do a day's work at the Provident woodyard on North Clark Street, only one man actually reported for work, though each of the 19 claimed to be unemployed and destitute. The problem worsened until Mayor Swift ordered all freight yards to take anyone caught stealing a free ride into the city back to their point of origin upon discovery.

The issue was not confined to America. In Scotland, Glasgow was an example of the rough element sometimes associated with soup kitchens.[3]

> Even the soup-kitchens, which in 1816 were set up through the country, to avert starvation, had their evils. The recipients of the benevolence were discontented with its limited amount. At Glasgow some imaginary insult offered by a doler of the soup to the more unfortunate of that large community, stung the people to madness: the soup-kitchen, with its coppers [pots] and ladles, was destroyed; the outrage swelled to riot; the military were called in; and for two days the populous city was exposed to a contest between the soldiers and the mob.[4]

Good and decent people met with misfortune and needed aid in righting themselves. When work vanished, even those with property were disadvantaged because there was no market to sell it. An account from England said:

> The pawnbrokers' houses were crammed from the rafters to the door-step, till they would not hold one article more; and ... the pawnbrokers had no money.... It was touching to see how

Hard times in New York: the soup house, no. 110 Centre Street, one of the number instituted by Commodore James Gordon Bennett and superintended by L. Delmonico. Delmonico stands in the right foreground as soup is dispensed to those in need. Wood engraving 1873. *Frank Leslie's Illustrated Newspaper*, volume 37, page 429. Library of Congress, Prints and Photographs Department, Reproduction Number LC-USZ62-61255.

long the pride of the decent dressmaker, and the skilled weaver and his wife, leaning faint against their idle loom, stood out against the charity soup and loaf—declaring, even till it became no longer true, that they could point out some neighbors who would be glad of tickets, but that, for themselves, they could not say they had ever wanted bread.[5]

Nathaniel Hawthorne compared a London civic banquet of turtle soup, salmon, woodcock, and oyster patties, with "all manner of dirt and rags" worn by people he saw waiting for soup tickets on his way home.[6]

Newspapers, books, and journals contained articles on foods and cooking techniques and chapters advised the less fortunate in how to get the most in bulk and nutrition from what they could afford at the markets. The *Brooklyn Eagle* said, "A knowledge of the chemistry of foods would decrease the expense of most ordinary families fully by one-third."[7]

Soups were standard fare in penitentiaries. The Kings County (New York) Penitentiary served soup three times a week and the New Hampshire Penitentiary served "a soup or porridge of potatoes, beans or peas" daily for supper.[8] The Pennsylvania Eastern Penitentiary served meat soup and potatoes for dinner daily. Numerous American and English prisons relied heavily on bread and soup to feed the prisoners.[9]

In times past, one could be jailed for inability to pay debts, which left children at a terrible disadvantage. In 1885, Barrett wrote:

New York was comparatively a small place to what it now is, and yet 131 prisoners would be frequently locked up in the old jail in the Park for debt. The Society furnished these unfortunate individuals with food and fuel. Fifteen thousand and odd quarts of soup in a few months! Then there were the families of the poor prisoners to look after, and give soup, fuel and rent too, for when a man is locked up in jail for debt, he cannot provide for the wife and the little folks.

Benjamin Thompson, Count Rumford, is credited with developing the system whereby hungry children were fed inexpensive, but nourishing, meals of bread and soup in Germany in 1790. American born, Thompson emerged from the Revolutionary War considered less than trustworthy due to his contacts with Royalists, and in 1784 he embarked on a trip through Europe.

While in Munich, he founded the Poor People's Institute where the poor made clothing for the army in exchange for clothing and food. Children were required to study in between laboring with the adults.

Rumford fed the families soup made from potatoes, barley and peas; meat was felt too expensive. His programs eventually spread to England, Scotland, France, and Switzerland.

His efforts were on no small scale, feeding an estimated 60,000 people daily in London alone.

> John O'Conner, late of Parsontown, Kings Co., Ireland, addresses to the London Times the following letter, under date of New York, March 5:
>
> "In the name of God and humanity, I entreat you to use your powerful and influential paper to stop the emigration of my miserable countrymen from dear old Ireland. They are suffering all kinds of privation here, — thousands supported on public charity, lodging in the station houses, and the thermometer 10° below zero; no work, and no chance of any. In the midst of this distress 1200 people landed to-day, and thousands are expected. Are the people mad that they thus rush on death and destruction? The Americans are a liberal people; they do all they can, but millions will not sustain the poor foreigners here. Soup houses in all the wards are daily crowded with poor. The emigrants land here at the rate of 10,000 a week; 600,000 arrived last year, and there will be more this year if not stopped by the interference of humane men in England. The scene here is heart-rending. The work in the warerooms, canals, and factories is suspended, which adds to the misery I describe.[10]

In Glasgow, Count Rumford's plan for supplying the poor with potato soup and barley broth was adopted and showed "great promise of success."[11]

Soup kitchens were scattered throughout Scotland and England during the 18th century, in particular in Paisley, Glasgow, Stirling, Weymouth, and London. The societies that ran the soup kitchens sometimes had impressive-sounding names, such as the Society for Bettering the Conditions and Increasing the Comforts of the Poor of London, and nobility and gentry often donated the items from which the soups were made.

To comprehend the extent to which families depended on these meals, an examination of Dr. Kitchener's winter soup is helpful. It called for 210 pounds of beef forequarters, 90 pounds of legs of beef, 3 bushels of split peas, 1 bushel of flour, 12 bundles of leeks, 6 bundles of celery, 12 pounds of salt, and 11 lbs. of black pepper. The recipe produced 1,000 quarts of soup which fed some 600 families daily during the "late inclement weather and the cessation of ordinary employment."

The duke of Marlborough exemplified the benevolence of nobility with his contribution of 40 pounds of beef, made into soup daily, which was distributed along with a quart of milk per family.[12]

Money came from obscure sources to fund the endeavors. James Hamilton was fined for not giving way and driving his horses and carts on the Calder Road contrary to an Act of Parliament, payment to go to the soup kitchen.[13]

The Roman Catholic House of Mercy in New York City supplied families with soup, and appealed to the citizenry for charitable donations so it might purchase more food and increase the number of hungry it could feed.

The *Edinburgh Advertiser* stated on January 21, 1800, that soup houses had been established for indigent Jews whose religious principles did not allow them to "share in the general distribution of that species of charity."

In 1901, the Citizen's Committee of Tampa notified members of the Resistencia that the soup houses established by the union had to close because they encouraged cigar makers to remain idle. On discovering seven remained open, citizens poured the soup on the ground and put out the fires.

30. Life on the Home Front

Wartime has frequently been a time of shortages and substitutions, each generation turning to those older and wiser individuals who had been through it previously for guidance.

Soups provided the most bulk from a given amount of supplies for families just as it did for the soldiers. War meant using less meat, especially prime cuts, and more fish, game, grains, vegetables, and wild foods.

With few exceptions cookery books were not available to change the cooking habits of women during the Civil War, and logic and ingredients on hand determined the type of soups eaten. By World War I, books were being published to educate women in home economy during wartime shortages and rationing.

Many modern Americans have never known shortages, hunger, or stretching a dollar to put food on the table. Despite the tragedies of 9–11, domestic natural disasters and war in the Middle East, America has been a land of plenty since World War II, so much so that many Americans have no cooking skills, thus have a strong reliance on precooked foods.

During World War I and II, many women knew how to cook, how to garden, and how to preserve food to sustain them through winter. Many kept their own families fed and also contributed toward the welfare of friends and neighbors.

During World War I women were instructed to ask the butcher for chicken trimmings—head, feet, fat, and giblets—to add body to soup. Making fish and meat chowders, reusing liquid in which vegetables were cooked, and extending meat in "made-over" dishes with potatoes, rice, hominy, and beans meant more soup on the wartime table.[1]

America entered World War II in 1941, and although food habits didn't change overnight, they did change as virtually all resources were used to sustain the troops. Books such as Anne Pierce's *Home Canning for Victory* encouraged women to plant victory gardens and use that produce to sustain them through the winter. Even small amounts put away meant huge stores of food when multiplied by 45 million American women, "and will release just that much more to feed starving nations and our own men bearing arms in the far corners of the world."

Waste was not tolerable, and recipes underwent changes minimizing meat and bulking up the vegetables and grains. Success in the garden and kitchen was often carried over to the poultry yard since chickens could be raised for cooking and in canned broth and vegetable soup.

Anne Pierce gave a recipe for canning beans: "These will be like 'old fashioned' bean-hole beans and save much time when needed. Commercial canned beans may be hard to get." This refers to pioneer days when most homes and cabins had a "bean hole" built into the fireplace where a cast iron kettle nestled down in the hot coals to slowly simmer dried beans. They required practically no attention from the cook.

Some victory gardeners showing their fine vegetables. Library of Congress, Prints and Photographs Division, Reproduction Number LC-USZ62-69927.

A World War II recipe for canning chicken gumbo soup contained potatoes, corn, and lima beans and was more like Brunswick stew than traditional gumbo.

During that time, dried soup and bouillon were mass-marketed to save the housewife labor in the kitchen. The portable soups of earlier centuries sported new names and updated methods of preparation to impress women with their time-saving claims.

> A new branch in the food industry has sprung up rapidly since the start of the year and is beginning to contribute some funds to advertising. It is the soup mix business and at the rate companies are entering the field there will be at least a dozen contenders by the end of the year. The Thomas J. Lipton Company appeared to have started the parade earlier this year with numerous test campaigns on Continental Noodle Soup mix in newspapers. Since that time General Mills, with its Betty Crocker Noodle Soup Mix, Skinner and Eddy Corporation with its Minute Man vegetable, noodle, and chicken flavor rice soup mixes and Dainty Food Manufacturers, Inc., a Kraft Cheese affiliate, with its Dainty noodle soup mix have all entered the lists. These three companies are all using newspapers and radio to test campaigns in various cities.[2]

Canned soups were also mass-marketed for homes and restaurants, one of their biggest attractions being that two or more varieties could be combined to produce an interesting new flavor. Even better restaurants did this during the 1940s, sometimes adding a dollop of sour cream or a splash of sherry to enhance the flavor.

Gimbel's Department Store sold four varieties of instant soup at less than a dime per package in 1943. Three of them were Lipton brand mixes.[3]

In 1943, the Grocery Manufacturers of America elected L. J. Gumpert, director of sales at B. T. Baggitt, Inc., to head promotion of the sale of instant soups, which saw an increased revenue from $300,000 in 1939 to $40,000,000 in 1943.[4]

31. Outdoor Soup

Soup has been the meal of choice for outdoor enthusiasts since the first prepared dish because of its simplicity in preparation. When there weren't enough supplies for a dinner of separate meat and vegetables, the odd bits, when combined, produced enough hot soup to feed any required number.

Hunter's soup appears in numerous early journals. One, described by Bill Hugh in 1790–1791, included "the choisest bits" of buffalo, deer, elk, bear, and turkey.

Hunting and fishing supplied the bulk of the sports enthusiast's diet. Numerous lists were posted throughout the 19th century advising the basics needed to turn the game and fish into tasty dinners.[1]

For venison soup, the meat was cooked, then a sliced onion, potatoes, and salt and pepper were added and the soup simmered until the potatoes were tender. Black and white peppercorns, preferably freshly ground, and dried cayenne were used, and cloves, mace, and lemon or lime juice flavored the soup when they were available.

Soup was made in a similar manner from squirrels, hares, rabbits, grouse, and quail, and it was simmered half a day before serving it.

Any fowl was said to be palatable when simmered slowly for two hours and then simmered for another hour with a handful of rice, some mace, peppercorns, and salt. Adding port or madeira wine, butter, onion, and/or herbs heightened the flavor and produced a dish to suit even the most discriminating palate.

Turtle was easy to prepare outdoors. Though some dispensed with killing the turtle before dropping it into boiling water, it was felt best to remove the head and allow the turtle to bleed before cooking it. After its head was removed, the turtle, still in the shell, was dropped for a few seconds into a pot of boiling water. It was then removed and the shell cut through on the underside, lengthwise then across. The entrails and claws were removed and discarded, then the turtle boiled in the shell until the meat separated from the shell. The meat was cut up, salt, pepper, and onion was added, and it was boiled for three more hours. The turtle thusly prepared could be made into soup with the addition of diced salt pork or bacon and vegetables during the last simmering.

One account of capturing turtles amounted to roping them while they were locked in copulation and hauling them in for food. Occasionally both the male and female were caught, but since the male was the most accessible to his captors the female generally swam away.

> The turtle mounts ... it is done on the surface in such a way that they can be easily discovered: two or three people quickly jump in a canoe, race towards them, and easily coming alongside, pass a slip knot over the neck and flipper.[2]

A deer hunt near Deadwood in the winter of 1887-88. Two miners, McMillan and Hubbard, got their game. The man on the left prepares soup or stew; the other has returned from hunting, bringing another deer with him. John C. H. Grabill, photographer, 1888. Library of Congress, Prints and Photographs Division, Reproduction Number LC-DIG-ppmsc-02640.

Curry powder was used to season stews, and a ragout was simply a more highly seasoned stew containing sweet herbs along with the curry powder. Ragout was defined as a dish of fish, flesh, greens and the like simmered with salt, pepper, and cloves.

George Washington Sears was the preeminent outdoorsman of the 19th century. Under the name Nesmuk he wrote a series of articles about his adventures which in later years were combined into book form. Of soup he said:

> Soup is, or should be a leading food element in every woodland camp. I am sorry to say that nothing is, as a rule, more badly botched, while nothing is more easily or simply cooked as it should be. Soup requires time, and a solid basis of the right material. Venison is the basis, and the best material is the bloody part of the deer, where the bullet went through. We used to throw this away; we have learned better.[3]

He went on to say squirrels of any sort made almost as good a soup as venison. He instructed turning any soup into a stew by adding a three tablespoons of flour and two spoonfuls of melted butter, thinning to the consistency of cream with liquor [broth] from the kettle, and dripping this slowly into the stew while stirring briskly.

According to a historical marker in Brunswick County, Virginia, Brunswick stew was created when an African American cook, Jimmy Matthews, prepared it for members of a hunting party in 1828.

A dish bearing the name Brunswick stew was mentioned in May 1863 in a piece that discussed the virtues of several culinary offerings, including the stew. A lengthy search has not turned up any recipe titled "Brunswick stew" nearly as old as its claimed origins of

Two men and a boy pose with a giant sea turtle, July 1927. The boy appears to be wearing an apron, perhaps in preparation for dressing the turtle in order to harvest the meat.

1828, and it could be credited to Native Americans, slaves, or the camp dish called hunter's stew.

Brunswick County, Georgia, and Brunswick County, North Carolina, also claim to be the site of origin of this southern staple. All agree that the early recipes at least were cooked in a large pot outdoors and made primarily from corn and squirrels. By the 1870s, recipes appear in cookbooks, some using squirrels, some using chicken, and some specifying the use of both:

> The large gray squirrel is seldom eaten at the North, but in great request in Virginia and other Southern States. It is generally barbecued, precisely as are rabbits; broiled, fricasseed, or — most popular of all — made into a Brunswick stew. This is named from Brunswick County, Virginia, and is a famous dish — or was — at the political and social picnics known as barbecues.[4]

> Being tired of fried chicken and other every day Virginian dishes, the decree went forth for a Brunswick stew. That very evening, the squirrels were fetched from the tops of the tall oaks in the forest hard by, the garden furnished the vegetables, and the next day it was served copiously, superbly, royally, under a grand old walnut tree, whose mighty arms shaded half the yard. There was no other dish but the Brunswick stew, and that was enough; for it contained all the meats and juices of the forest and garden magnificently conglomerated and sublimed by the potent essence of fiery Cayenne, pod upon pod, lavishly thrown in. A dish capacious as the Mediterranean held it, and it towered aloft like Vesuvius, smoking gloriously.[5]

In 1852, outdoorsmen in Florida tried an experiment to determine what animals were actually edible providing one could give up any preconceived notions of what was acceptable for human consumption. While the English refused to eat frogs, the French were fond of them. Where some didn't hesitate to eat eel, they thought the snake beyond their acceptance. The man in question reported on his findings, saying, "Rattlesnake soup he found excellent, owl soup to be only tolerable, and turkey-buzzard soup he gave up as 'not good.'"[6]

Perhaps soup ingredients for the outdoorsman were like beauty, "in the eye of the beholder." Dr. Stimpson was quoted as saying soup made from sea cucumbers was very palatable but not very regularly used as food.[7]

32. Soup as a Weapon

December 11th Geneva celebrates "La Escalade," or "Scaling Day," and a great deal of fun (and food) is had by all. The day is the anniversary of the successful repulsion of the forces of the French Duke Charles-Emmanuel of Savoy in 1602 by the citizens of the city. The Duke had intended that two thousand of his men would scale the city walls by means of ladders, in the secret dead of night. The plot was foiled when Mère Catherine Royaume who lived with her family above one of the city gates, heard a noise, looked out, and promptly threw a hot pot of soup (and perhaps the pot itself) over the wall, killing one soldier — but not before he had made even more noise, thus alerting the whole city.

The townspeople generally have a good time on this day parading, dressing up symbolically smashing soup "marmites" while singing patriotic songs and enjoying the fact that they did not become French citizens. Naturally, food figures in the fun. It is winter, so mulled wine and hot chestnuts are popular, and of course soup is cooked and eaten, but, — this is Switzerland, after all — there is also much consumption of chocolates made in the form of soup pots filled with marzipan vegetables.

We can probably safely assume that the Mère Royaume's hot pot was a large one, as the good mother had fourteen children. Presumably she was up at that hour with one of the little ones, and thought she would cook the next day's dinner while she was about it. No official recipe appears to exist, but legend suggests it was a vegetable soup.[1]

Period newspapers are filled with articles pertaining to arsenic, rat poison, green vitriol, opium, binoxalate of potash, sliced root of aconite (wolfbane) or other toxins being added to soup in an attempt to poison someone, and occasionally of an accidental poisoning from soup made from poison mushrooms.

In November 1858, 23 people in a boarding house were poisoned after eating soup and salt, the latter from containers on the table, tainted with arsenic. The proprietor claimed ignorance of how the substance was put there, casting suspicion on a boarder who had left in anger a few days before.[2]

Additional stories included a man who claimed his wife put needles into his soup, a 15-year-old New York girl who was severely burned when soup she was preparing tipped over after a house cat upset the three-legged stool she was standing on, and a "colored lady who was irresistibly moved to kill somebody" and put rat poison into the soup served at a boarding house in New Orleans. She confessed her crime when suspected and was told to drink some of the soup herself. The cook, who said she bore no ill will against any of the individuals, was arrested.

Perhaps the most widely circulated story of poisoning from soup is that of the duke of Tuscany and his second wife, Bianca. When Johanna of Austria died, the duke married his mistress, who was apparently unable to give him a child. She concocted a plan to fake a pregnancy, at the end of which time a newborn was to be smuggled in which she intended to pass off as her own. The duke's brother, who stood to assume the throne in his brother's absence, accidentally discovered her secret. Later Bianca and the duke died on the same day, an event which gave rise to the legend in which Bianca had poisoned a tureen of soup she attempted to coerce her brother-in-law into eating. He did not partake, but the duke did, and when she realized she would be blamed with his death she, too, partook of the soup and thus both died.—*The Terrific Register*, 1825.

One of the most bizarre stories was of a man who put poison in his wife's soup at table, then withdrew in order not to witness her death throes. The wife returned, and discovered a spider had dropped into her portion. Being exceptionally squeamish of spiders, she dipped it out and swapped bowls with her husband who returned and consumed what he thought was his untainted portion. Before he died he confessed, otherwise the wife would have gone to jail innocent of the whole affair.[3]

Appendix I: Period Soup Vegetables and Herbs

Essences could be made or purchased for flavoring soup. The following is from *The Gazette of Health*, by Richard Reese, M.D., 1820.

> A case of the concentrated essences of celery, onions, garlic, shallots, mint, parsley, thyme, cayenne, &c. &c. for flavoring all kinds of soups: peculiarly adapted for the use of Captains of Ships, and of indispensable necessity in all Foreign Countries where these valuable ingredients are unattainable.
>
> These essences give a most exquisite flavour to Soups of every description, and are used by Cooks of the first celebrity. When the soup is ready to be served up, a small quantity of the Essence most agreeable to the palate should be added "the last thing," and the cover of the tureen be immediately put on to prevent the volatile parts from evaporating.

"Cultivated vegetables afford the principal part of our subsistence," wrote Phillips. This attests to the fact that crops are essential to feed humans and livestock. We may never know the full extent of their commonality, as English books on geography, astronomy and possibly herbals were ordered destroyed in 1552 in an effort to assuage witchcraft. Phillips recorded,

> In those early days the labours of the agriculturists were so duly appreciated, that the persons of husbandmen and the shepherds were held sacred even by the enemies of their country.
>
> Herodotus informs us, that one of the greatest princes of the East, Xerxes, when he led his army into Greece, gave strict orders to his soldiers not to annoy the husbandmen. Among the Indians, it was held unlawful to take these men in war, or to devastate their plantations.

The 1744 *Adam's Luxury and Eve's Cookery* listed artichokes, Jerusalem artichokes, asparagus, beans, beets, borage, borecole, broccoli, cabbage, carrot, celery, chervil, chives, cauliflower, cress, cucumber, currants, dill, endive, fennel, garlic, leeks, lettuce, marjoram, marigold, mint, mushrooms, mustard, nasturtium, onions, parsley, parsnips, peas, pennyroyal, potatoes, pumpkin, purslane, sage, savory, shallot, scorzonera, skirret, sorrel, spinach, tansy, tarragon, thyme, and turnip, from which excellent salads and soups were made.

Artichoke*: Greeks and Romans brought it from the African coast, and it was introduced to England about 1548. Stored by burying in sand or drying the bottoms. Made into soup and ragout; also fricasseed, fried, or pickled. Listed by Andrew Boorde in 1584, Reid in 1683 and Evelyn in 1699.

Asparagus*: Asparagus was cut when the young shoots pushed up out of the ground. It was used

Starred entries appear in Nicholas Culpepper's The Complete Herbal, *1653.*

to make soup, cooked as a vegetable, and put in salads. Once an asparagus bed was established it continued to produce for roughly 25 to 30 years. Gerard (1597) indicated it was English in origin. Phillips' references to early use include "two hundred years before Christ" during the time of Cato the Elder, who was particularly fond of it, Suetonius, Erasmus, and Pliny. Mentioned in the U.S. by Higginson in 1629 and Josselyn in 1660.

Barley: Phillips dated its use in Syria back 3,132 years in 1822, and Pliny pronounced it "the most ancient food in old times." Mentioned by Boorde in 1584.

Basil: Used in highly seasoned soups and meats, sometimes in salads. Can be dried for storage, but best method of storage is freezing.

Beans: Listed by Reid, Evelyn, Boorde, Higginson, and Josselyn. Grown by Native Americans.

Beet*: Used in borscht and salads. Tops were cooked for greens and soup. Beets were used in England from 1548, and the white variety from Portugal in 1570. Listed by Boorde in 1584, Higginson, and Josselyn.

Borage: Used in soups, native to Asia Minor.

Cabbage*: "Many there are, who have never heard of Indian corn, or salsify, egg-plants, okra, artichokes, sweet potatoes, or even of asparagus; but never yet was there one who had not heard of cabbage, or had never eaten it in some shape or other."[4] Cabbage has been used in soups for centuries. Phillips said it was important in spring soups. Varieties were quite extensive (green, red, and Savoy) and with varied plantings and root cellar storage, cabbage was easily available year round. Written of by Theophrastus, Columella, Pliny, Hippocrates, and others and listed by Reid, Evelyn, Higginson, Josselyn, and others.

Callaloo: West Indian green used in soups. Documented being grown in Mississippi in 1810 by Thwaites. Often referred to as Indian kale or cale. It appears in African soups.

Caraway: The leaves and seeds were sometimes used in soups. Seeds can be dried.

Carrot*: Phillips credited carrots as being introduced to England by the Flemings during the reign of Elizabeth I. He stated the French thought the purple carrot the sweetest. Used extensively in soup, stew, and French dishes. There were many varieties, each with its own distinctive characteristics. Shapes varied from turnip-rooted to long and narrow. Color varied from white to red. Storage: root cellar. Carrots were mentioned in literature in China by the 13th century, throughout Europe by 1536, in Virginia by 1609, in Japan by 1712, and in India by 1826. Listed by Boorde, Higginson, and Josselyn.

Cauliflower: Broccoli and cauliflower were initially considered one species, but by 1724 broccoli was listed separately in Philip Miller's *Gardener's Dictionary*.[5] He did think of it as a newcomer to England, though some food scholars claim to identify it in the writings of Apicius.

Celery: Used extensively in soup and stew, and by the 19th century eaten in its raw state alone or in salads. It was said to be the most commonly used salad ingredient. Celery seed was used to flavor soup. It grew best in the northern and middle states and was stored in root cellars or buried under mounds of earth. Before refrigeration it was wrapped in a cool cloth to keep it crisp. The fresh leaves were used in soups, salads, and as garnish.

Chard: Apicius included it in "soup for the stomach," and it is recorded by Charlemagne and *Le Menagier de Paris.*

Chervil*: Phillips said chervil was much cultivated by the French and Dutch and, "hardly a soup or salad but the leaves of chervil make part of the composition." Listed by Higginson in 1629 and Josselyn in 1660 in the United States.

Chickpea*: Original to the south of Europe, north of Africa, and parts of Asia. Used extensively in soups, especially *purée aux croutons* (bread-and-pea soup) in 19th-century Paris. Varieties were yellow, red, and white. Chickpeas were especially common in soups in France. In the *Iliad* Homer compared arrows bouncing off a breastplate to chickpeas being thrown from a winnower, and Charlemagne decreed chickpeas be one of the crops grown in the 9th century.

Collards: "In the garden [the Kentuckians] cultivate their collards."[6] Collards sometimes replaced the other porray greens in frontier America.

Coriander: Introduced from Europe, cultivated in England. Leaves were sometimes used in soup, the seeds primarily by confectioners. Planting at intervals of three or four weeks meant a steady supply of leaves. Listed by Higginson and Josselyn.

Corn: A Native American plant, it was used by the Indians for centuries before the arrival of Europeans. In its fresh, often referred to as green, state it is excellent in soups and stews, and when dried was used most often in the form of meal, hominy, or grits to make bread, soup, or porridge. Nineteenth-century varieties were white, red, blue, and yellow. They varied in the number of rows of kernels on the cob. There were both sweet and field varieties, and popcorn which could be ground into meal. Prior to this time *corn* was used to describe any type of grain and did not necessarily refer to maize.

Costmary*: Sometimes used as a pot herb in soups. Leaves were used in salads and for flavoring ale and beer.

Cress* (crecy): Native to Persia. Young tender leaves were used to make porray, cress soup, or made into salads. Watercress grew in ponds, ditches, and small running streams in the New World. The leaves and shoots were cut so that the roots would continue to put out new shoots. It was sometimes sold at market. It grew rapidly and was usually harvested weekly.

Cucumbers: Used in chilled soups which became popular in the 19th century, salads, pickles, and cooked.

Dill*: The leaves were used in pickling and occasionally in soups; seeds were used more often in pickling. Seeds were dried for storage. Fernleaf dill is grown for dill weed.

Fennel*: Leaves were used in flavoring soup and sauces, occasionally in salads. In 1822 the English considered it a native plant, but the French credited its origins to Syria. Pliny said the Romans cultivated it extensively as a garden herb. Listed by Boorde, Higginson, and Josselyn.

Garlic*: Used often in soup, stew, and other dishes. *Allium* in Latin. Listed by Boorde in 1584.

Leek: Commonly used in soup since antiquity and blanched like asparagus. Gerard said the use of leeks by the Welsh extended back as far as recorded history. Pliny thought the best examples from Egypt. Found in Charlemagne and Apicius and listed by Boorde and Josselyn.

Legume/Bean*/Pea: Beans were used in soups both fresh and dried. There were far more common varieties in the 19th century than are routinely cultivated today, but many of these can be obtained through heirloom food markets. They were classed as garden beans, pole or running beans, Limas, peas, and lentils. In Fearing Burr's 1863 treatise on field and garden vegetables, the section on beans is 68 pages long.[7] The variety of beans is amazing — consider cranberry beans, scarlet runners, white, kidney, green peas, field peas, china, green and mottled varieties of limas, and so on. The Cherokee and ancient Romans used beans to make bread and soup. The Roman agriculturist Columella said, "And herbs they mix with beans for vulgar fare." Phillips said kidney beans were introduced to England in 1509 from the Netherlands. Listed by Boorde, Higginson, and Josselyn.

Lettuce*: Lettuce was commonly blanched or added to soups through the 19th century. It was considered of English origin with some varieties indigenous to France and Germany, but few to America. Although some mid–19th-century varieties are described as heading, none produced a head as large or defined as today's iceberg. Col-

umella stated it was served at Persian tables for royalty from 550 B.C. Listed by Boorde, Higginson, and Josselyn.

Marigold* (calendula): Edible varieties of these flowers were native to Europe and used to flavor soup and stew. Gerard said the yellow petals were dried and kept in Holland for broths, and that markets kept them by the barrelsful. Flowers were rarely used in the United States through the 1860s. Dairymaids often put marigold petals in when churning to color the butter. Flowers are both single and double varieties. "Fair is the Marygold for pottage meet," according to Gay's *Pastorals*, quoted by Phillips. Listed by Higginson and Josselyn.

Marjoram*: Young shoots were used to flavor soups and meats, and dried for storage. It is found in Italy, Spain, and Portugal, and was introduced to England in 1573. Phillips credited its origins to Cyprus and Candia. He said pot marjoram came from Sicily and was cultivated in Britain in 1759.

Millet: Cultivated in Europe before 2000 B.C. The Greeks and Romans used it in porridge and European peasants put it into soups and porridge. Pliny stated inhabitants of Campania used it to make white pottage.

Mint*: Used in pea soup and salads. Written of extensively by the ancients.

Mushrooms: Cultivated in beds of horse manure throughout the 19th century or found in the wild. Morels and others were especially valued for making catsup, which was in turn often used to flavor soups, ragouts, and sauces. They were also dried and powdered for storage to be used in soups. Pliny the Elder, in the first century, called them one of the wonders of nature, and the French chef La Varenne used them extensively during the 17th century. Pliny stated Annaeus Serenus, the captain of Nero's guard, and several other officers died after eating poisonous mushrooms.

Nettle*: Popularly used as a pot herb for soup in Scotland, Ireland, Poland, and Germany. Listed by Boorde in 1584.

Oats: Known to the Greeks and Romans. Because there is no mention of oats in the Bible, scholars believe it did not grow in Egypt or Syria. Phillips quoted, "Oats for their feast the Scottish shepherds grind," and in his *Cotter's Saturday Night* Burns pronounced it "The halesome parritch, chief o' Scotia's food." Listed by Boorde in 1584.

Okra: Early recorders thought it native to Central America or the West Indies. Today it is known to have been grown by the ancient Egyptians and is thought native to Africa. It came to the American colonies in the 17th century on slave ships. The

---

*Starred entries appear in Nicholas Culpepper's The Complete Herbal, *1653.*

Africans knew its culture and culinary uses and it quickly became a southern staple. Young tender pods were sliced and dried for winter storage. When sliced into rings and dried, the rings could be threaded onto a cord for storage. It was chiefly used in soup, especially the gumbo of the South. In 1835 Edward Ruffin said gumbo was made by the Creole French and Spanish of Louisiana and Florida, the reference predating the first cookbook to use the term *Creole* by 50 years.

Onion*: Considered indispensable in soup making, and documented for at least 5,000 years. Pliny the Elder and others before him, including Theophrastus 200 years before Christ, wrote of onions. Onions varied in size, shape (round and flattened) and color (red, white, and yellow). "They used to form the favorite *bon bons* of the Highlander, who with oat cake would travel for days without other food. The Egyptians adored the onion almost as much as the ox; and the Spaniards have the same fondness for this pungent root.... Soupe a Poignon (onion soup) is thought highly restorative by the French. It is considered peculiarly grateful, and gently stimulating to the stomach after hard drinking or night-watching and holds among soups the place that champagne, soda water, or ginger-beer does among liquors."[8] Storage: root cellar. Listed by Boorde in 1584.

Orach: Native to central Asia. Not used by Apicius, but known to Charlemagne. Available from heirloom garden centers, and easily harvested through the summer.

Parsley*: Per Phillips it was native to Sardinia and not cultivated in England until 1548. Used extensively in soups and stews. It was grown in both flat and curled-leaf varieties. The seeds were sometimes used as a flavoring agent. It was dried for storage, but all flavor is lost with drying. Listed by Higginson and Josselyn.

Parsnip: Phillips stated the wild parsnip from which parsnips were cultivated was native to Britain. The Emperor Tiberius brought parsnips annually from Germany. A common soup ingredient, considered healthy with a pleasant delicate flavor. Storage: winters well in the ground. Listed by Boorde, Higginson, and Josselyn.

Pea: Burr stated the origin of the pea was unknown, though Valmont Bomare thought it native to France. Phillips thought them first cultivated in England during the reign of Henry VIII. Before the days of refrigeration green peas did not travel well, and they quickly passed their prime, resulting in a stale flavor. Varieties included green (commonly called English) peas, black-eyed peas, blue (seeds were a pale blue color), white (there were several varieties which produced white seeds varying from large and wrinkled to small wrinkled like the Carter pea), cream-colored (several varieties varying in size), and there were peas in which both pod and seeds were edible, like the sugar snap pea. One variety of the latter was described in 1859 as a cabbage pea (broad pod) that made good soup. However, no other sources or descriptions for this type of pea were located.[9] Listed by Boorde in 1584, Higginson in 1629, and Josselyn in 1660.

Pepper: Native to the New World, sweet and hot varieties including cherry, bell, and cayenne. Cayenne could be grown from a few seeds, unlike imported peppercorns. They were used green and after ripening to red. Sweet varieties were pickled while hot varieties were most often dried for winter storage, though they were added to pickled vegetables in quantities to taste. Black pepper and ginger formed the nucleus of the spice trade from Asia approximately 4,000 years ago. Peppercorns were commonly used in ancient Rome, and pepper was reportedly demanded as ransom for the city of Rome. Marco Polo was among those who wrote of pepper. White pepper comes from the same source as black. The berries are allowed to ripen on the plant and the outer hull removed before grinding.

Potato: Used extensively in soup, stew and other ways. Gerard said it was called *papus* by the Indians. Phillips says the potato, though some called it a "curious exotic" in the early 17th century, was a great (and expensive) delicacy in the time of James I, and was provided to the queen's household. He says it was grown in Scotland by 1683, and it was listed by Reid in 1683 in his gardening books. The potato was promoted in the United States by the 1600s and grown extensively by the early 1700s, but it wasn't until about 1800 that it underwent drastic improvements in size and flavor, making it by 1860 the "most important of all esculent roots." Flesh varied in color — white, yellow, and blue. Shapes included round, oblong, and kidney shaped. Storage: root cellar, or buried under a mound of earth.

The potato was the heart of the Irish diet, and when the crop failed in the 1840s starvation followed. Peter Lawson, who founded the Edinburgh nursery in 1770, described 175 varieties of potato. Sir Walter Raleigh is credited by many as having brought potatoes to England. Sir Robert Southwell, president of the Royal Society in December 1693, said his grandfather obtained potatoes from Raleigh which he brought to Ireland, probably about 1566. Raleigh is said to have had potatoes from America planted in his own Irish garden.[10]

The potato is a prime example of New World foods that Europeans were slow to accept, mainly because they did not know how to prepare them.

John Evelyn mentioned some people in New England eating roasted potatoes with sugar, although he included them in his book on sallets in 1699.

Pumpkins: Pumpkins were used extensively in soups, baked, and made into puddings and pies. Higginson listed *pompions* in the United States in 1629, and Josselyn included them in his list. Pumpkins and winter squash have often been used interchangeably. Burr listed a dozen varieties in 1863.

Rhubarb: One type of rhubarb was cultivated in England from 1573. Gerard said, "Patience [the French name for the herb] is an excellent holsome pot-herbe; for being put into the pottage in some reasonable quantitie." It had passed out of favor in pottage by 1822.[11]

Rice: "Ethiopian" grain known to the Greeks and cultivated by the Egyptians, Babylonians, Persians, and "all the eastern nations with whom they either warred or traded." It was used in Greece before the birth of Theophrastus about 300 B.C., and from there spread to the Romans. Pliny wrote, "As for us Italians we set the greatest store on rice." It has been grown in Africa since approximately 1500 B.C. England originally brought it from Spain and the Fortunate Islands and then from Carolina and the East Indies. Phillips wrote, "It thickens soups and broths without giving a taste." Rice was being grown in Carolina by the mid–1680s and soon after in Georgia. Carolina gold rice was "absolutely the best Rice which grows upon the whole Earth."[12] By the mid–19th century Louisiana and Texas cultivated it, and Arkansas followed after 1900. Modern accounts indicate rice culture appeared in various locations almost simultaneously. The oldest on record is carbon-dated to some 12,000 years ago, though most sources place its earliest documentation at about 6,500 years.

Rosemary*: Grew extensively on its own in Spain, Italy, Provence, and Languedoc. Phillips said it was first planted in England in 1548, though Gerard claimed that only one variety was native. Used often in soups and stews, especially in bouquet garni, it flavored eau de Cologne and was the principal ingredient in "Hungary water." It was dried for storage. It was placed in the hands of corpses before burial in France, giving rise to its popular use in funerals through the 1820s. Listed by Boorde in 1584.

Sage*: Both fresh and dried leaves were used in soups, stews, stuffing, and meat, especially sausage. There were green, variegated, and purplish or red-tinged varieties. Phillips said the French first called it sage because they thought it strengthened the memory and made people sage, or wise. The French pickled the leaves, and it was used early on to flavor cheese. "Marbled with sage, the hard'ning cheese she press'd" (from Gay, *Pastorals*, quoted in Henry Phillips *History of Cultivated Vegetables*, London, 1822). First cultivated in England in 1573, having come from Syria. Known to the Greeks. Listed by Boorde, Higginson, and Josselyn.

Sago: Naturally grew in Japan, Malabar, the Friendly Islands, and New Hebrides, according to Phillips. Introduced to England about 1758 by Richard Warner of Essex. Used to thicken soup, beverages, puddings, and an excellent invalid food.

Savory: Pot herb used in soup, known to the Greeks and Romans, said to have grown abundantly around Troy. There is a summer savory and a winter savory. Both are native to southern Europe, and were noted by Virgil. Cultivated in England about 1562 and praised by Gerard in 1597. Higginson listed "both kinds" in 1629.

Sorrel: Used in antiquity as documented by Pliny extensively in soups and sauces, especially in French cookery. It was as common as spinach in the markets of Paris. It was losing favor in England by 1822. It usually survived frost and quickly provided greens for the kitchen when others failed. The best was French sorrel from Provence. "In France there are few soups or sauces made without a portion of sorrel.... It is a common saying among the French that a good housewife is known by her pots of sorrel."[13] Listed by Boorde, Higginson, and Josselyn.

Spinach: Used as a pot herb in soup, sometimes mixed with sorrel, and as a salad green and cooked green. Eaten in salads during the reign of Elizabeth I and of Charles I. Wild spinach was native to Turkestan and Afghanistan. It was brought to Persia and to Great Britain, and naturalized to a lesser degree in the United States. Not listed in Apicius or Charlemagne, but was in *Le Menagier de Paris.*

Squash: Native to North America, eaten some 2,000 years before the arrival of Europeans. It is impossible to know exactly what varieties existed. Higginson and John Josselyn described varieties of *squontersquashes*, some green, some yellow, some longish like a gourd, some round like an apple, but all of them pleasant food for the Indians and the English.

Summer squash were consumed when fresh, and popular varieties included yellow crookneck and round scalloped varieties. In 1863 Burr listed several varieties of winter (hard skin) squash. Autumnal vegetable marrow was large and shaped like Hubbard squash. John M. Ives claimed to have perfected it from Native American seeds from New

---

*Starred entries appear in Nicholas Culpepper's The Complete Herbal, 1653.

York in 1831. Crookneck squash was described by Ray in 1686. It is similar in appearance to butternut, but with a crooked neck. Canada crookneck is a large round squash with a long, usually curved neck. It was said to be dry, sweet, and fine flavored, of a cream-yellow color. Cashaw grew well in the south. J. J. H. Gregory of Marblehead, Massachusetts popularized Hubbard and dated his efforts to about 1803, though it could have been grown in other areas earlier. Turk's turban has orange-yellow fine-grained flesh and is sugary and well flavored. Vegetable marrow is a term for squash more commonly used in England. When mature it is a pale yellow or straw color with white flesh. It was used both young and mature. Linda Newstrom reported in *Economic Botany* that the chayote (mirliton) is native to Latin America.[14] Numerous sources state it was eaten by the Maya and Aztec, however, it is not clear how early it was found in Louisiana and similar locales.

Winter squash keep well in a root cellar.

Tarragon: Used in soups, stews, salads, pickles and in flavoring vinegar.

Thyme: Commonly used in soups, stews, and ragouts, especially in bouquet garni. Dried for storage. Lemon thyme was popular in the mid–19th century. Listed by Boorde, Higginson, and Josselyn.

Tomato: It was native to America and in its wild state was approximately the size of a cherry tomato, and probably initially yellow in color. It sported various names throughout history, such as wolf peach and love apple. It was introduced into England as early as 1596, but not very commonly eaten until the 18th century, first in Italy, then other European countries before Americans followed suit. Thomas Jefferson helped popularize it for culinary purposes. In 1842 tomatoes were said to have been "brought into culinary dietetics during the French Revolution."[15] Burr stated in 1863 that its cultivation in the United States had increased fourfold in the previous 20 years.[16] They could be dried or bottled for winter storage.[17]

Andrew Smith documented tomato culture in South Carolina as early as 1764, and C. Margaret Scarry reported in 1991 that tomatoes had been found in excavations at Fort Matanzas, near Saint Augustine, Florida, indicating they'd been eaten there when the fort was constructed between 1740 and 1742. Lawson did not list tomatoes in his 1709 summary of the Carolinas, nor were they listed by Reid, Evelyn, or Phillips.

In 1856 the large red variety, "cultivated all over the Union," was said to reach six inches in diameter, and the cherry tomato was so named because of its size. "It is scarcely twenty years since its culture was commenced in this country [1836]. 'In 1828–9' says Buist, 'it was almost detested; in ten years more, every variety of pill and panacea was 'extract of tomato.'... It enters into soups and sauces and is prepared in catsups, marmalades, and omelets. The French, and the Italians, near Rome and Naples, raised them by the acre, long before used by other nations, and it is said prepared them in almost infinite variety of ways."[18]

One of the first mentions is Harriott Hory Pinckney's 1770 cookery book, in which she indicates they could be preserved for soup.

> Tomatoos— To Keep for Winter Use, H. Harriott: Take ripe tomatas, peel them, and cut them in four and put them into a stew pan, strew over them a great quantity of pepper and salt; cover it up close and let it stand an hour, then put it on the fire and let it stew quick till the liquor is entirely boild away; then take them up and put into pint Potts, and when cold pour melted butter over them about an inch thick. They commonly take a whole day to stew. Each pot will make two Soups.

This is commonly believed to be one of the earliest, if not the earliest, recipe for tomatoes in the United States.

Turnip: Used extensively in soup and broth. The purple-top white variety was most common. The yellow or Swede variety (rutabaga) was slower to be accepted, especially in Ireland. Eaten extensively in Wales. Baked, roasted in ashes during the time of Henry VIII, and young shoots (greens) were used as a spring salad, and boiled. Phillips proclaimed the greens an excellent vegetable. "Taprooted" turnips found in the Paris markets were considered excellent for pottage. Storage: root cellar. Listed by Boorde, Higginson, and Josselyn.

Watercress: "A good cook, who has a chemical knowledge of the virtues of culinary vegetables, will not fail to serve the table of his employer with spring soups and broths, in which this herb forms a principal ingredient."[19] Known by the ancients.

Swanton indicated the following were grown by early southeastern Indians:

Corn —flour or bread/dent, hominy or flint, and popcorn in colors of white, yellow, red, and blue.

Beans, kidney beans, wild peas, etc. Bartram stated the Creek and Cherokee cultivated all the species in use by the whites.

Pumpkin, squash, cushaw, and macock (possibly cymling)

Sunflower

Rice —Creeks and Cherokees grew enough rice for their own use as reported by Bartram.

Sweet potato and okra were introduced.

Appendix II: Period Recipes

The dates given with these recipes are but one source of documentation, and the soup may have been eaten for centuries. Through the 19th century "borrowing" recipes from books written by others was common practice and because of this the same recipes turn up time and time again. Except for the author's notes in brackets, the recipes are taken directly from the historical sources.

ALMOND POTTAGE, 1685, Robert May. Take a pound of almond-paste, and strain it with some new milk; then have a pottle of cream boiling in a pipkin or skillet, put in the milk; and almonds with some mace, salt, and sugar; serve it in a clean dish on sippets of French bread, and scrape on sugar.

ALMOND SOUP, *Peterson's Magazine*, 1859. Take a neck of veal, and the scrag end of a leg of mutton, chop them in small pieces, put them in a large pan; cut in a turnip with a blade or two of mace, and five quarts of water; set it over the fire, and let it boil gently till it is reduced to two quarts, then strain it through a hair sieve into a clear pot, and put in six ounces of almonds, blanched and beat fine; half a pint of thick cream, and as much pepper as you please. Have ready three small rolls, the size of a tea-cup (if larger, they will not look well, and will drink up too much of the soup). Blanch a few almonds, cut them lengthwise, stick them all over the rolls, and put the roll in your soup tureen; then pour the soup upon the roll.

APPLE SOUP, 1852. Clear the fat from five pints of good mutton-broth, *bouillon*, or shine of beef stock, and strain it through a fine sieve; add to it, when it boils, a pound and a half of good pudding apples, and stew them down in it very softly, to a smooth pulp; press the whole through a strainer, add a small teaspoonful of powdered ginger, and plenty of pepper, simmering the soup for a couple of minutes, skim, and serve it very hot, accompanied by a dish of rice, boiled as for curries.

APPLE SOUP, 1891. This is a German recipe. Take half a dozen good-sized apples, peel them and remove the core, and boil them in a quart of water with two tablespoonfuls of bread-crumbs; add the juice of a lemon, and flavor it with rather less than a quarter of an ounce of powdered cinnamon; sweeten the soup with lump sugar, previously having rubbed six lumps on the outside of the lemon.

ARTICHOKE SOUP, 1891. Take a dozen large Jerusalem artichokes about as big as the fist, or more to make up a similar quantity. Peel them, and, like potatoes, throw them into cold water in order to prevent them turning colour. Boil them in as little water as possible, as they contain a good deal of water themselves, till they are tender and become a pulp, taking care that they do not burn, and therefore it is best to rub the saucepan at the bottom with a piece of butter. Now rub them through a wire sieve and add them to a pint of milk in which a couple of bay-leaves have been boiled. Add also two lumps of sugar and a little white pepper and salt. Serve the soup with fried or toasted bread. This soup can be made much richer by the addition of either a quarter of a pint of cream or a couple of yolks of eggs. If yolks of eggs are added, beat up the yolks separately and add the soup gradually, very hot, but not quite boiling, otherwise the yolks will curdle.

ASPARAGUS SOUP, 1840. Asparagus soup may be made in a similar manner to that of green peas. You must have four or five bunches of asparagus.

Cut off the green tops, and put half of them into the soup, after the meat has been boiled to pieces and strained out. The asparagus must be boiled till quite dissolved, and till it has given a green colour to the soup. Then take the remainder of the asparagus tops (which must all this time have been lying in cold water) and put them into the soup, and let them boil about twenty minutes. Serve it up with small squares of toast in the tureen. You may heighten the green of this soup by adding the juice of a handful of spinach, pounded in a mortar and strained. The spinach juice should be put in fifteen or ten minutes before you take up the soup, as a short boiling in it will take off the peculiar taste.

ASPARAGUS SOUP, 1886. Cut the tops from about thirty heads of asparagus, about half an inch long, and boil the rest; cut off all the tender portions and put through a sieve, adding a little salt; warm three pints soup stock, add a small lump of butter and a tea-spoon of flour previously cooked by heating the butter and slowly stirring in the flour; then add the asparagus pulp. Boil slowly a quarter of an hour, stirring in two or three tablespoons cream; color the soup with a teaspoon of prepared spinach, made by pounding the spinach well, adding a few drops of water, squeezing the juice through a cloth and putting it over a good fire. As soon as it looks curdy, take it off, and strain the liquor through a sieve. What remains on the sieve is to be used for coloring the soup. Just before serving soup, add the asparagus tops which have been separately boiled.

AUTUMN SOUP. Begin this soup as early in the day as possible. Take six pounds of the lean of fine fresh beef; cut it into small pieces; sprinkle it with a tea-spoonful of salt, (not more); put it into a soup-pot, and pour on six quarts of water. The hock of a cold ham will greatly improve it. Set it over a moderate fire, and let it boil slowly. After it comes to a boil skim it well. Have ready a quarter of a peck of ochras cut into very thin round slices, and a quarter of a peck of tomatoes cut into pieces; also a quart of shelled Lima beans. Season them with pepper. Put them in; and after the whole has boiled three hours *at least*, take six ears of young Indian corn, and having grated off all the grain, add them to the soup and boil it an hour longer. Before you serve up the soup remove from it all the bits of meat, which, if the soup is sufficiently cooked, will be reduced to shreds.

BARLEY BROTH, Robert May, 1685. Take a Chine or Knuckle, and joynt it, put it in a Pipkin with some strong broth, and when it boils, scum it, and put in some French Barley, being first boiled in two or three waters, with some large Mace, and a fag-

got of sweet herbs bound up, and close hard tied, some Raisins, Damask Prunes, and Currans, or no Prunes, and Marigold-flowers; boil it to an indifferent thickness, and serve it on sippets.

BARLEY BROTH, 1832. Chop a leg of beef in pieces, boil it in three gallons of water, with a carrot and a crust of bread, till reduced to half; then strain it off and put it into the pot again with half a pound of barley, four or five heads of celery cut small, a bunch of sweet herbs, an onion, a little chopped parsley, and a few marigolds. Let it boil an hour. Take an old cock or large fowl and put it into the pot, boil till the broth is quite good. Season with salt, take out the onion and herbs, and serve it. The fowl may be omitted.

BARLEY BROTH, *Godey's*, 1862. Take half a pint of pearl-barley, boil it in a gallon of water gently for half an hour, then take three pounds of lamb or mutton chops, with the fat cut off, or lean beef; put them into a separate stewpan with a small quantity of water, add any kind of vegetables-carrots, turnips, small onions, celery, and green peas, if in season-salt and pepper; when tender add them to the water and barley; let the whole boil gently for two hours or longer, and serve it up all together.

BARLEY SOUP, *Godey's*, 1855. Two pounds of shin of beef, quarter of a pound of pearl barley, a large bunch of parsley, four onions, six potatoes, salt and pepper, four quarts of water. Put in all the ingredients and simmer gently for three hours.

BEAN SOUP, 1840. Put two quarts of dried white beans into soak the night before you make the soup, which should be put on as early in the day as possible. Take five pounds of the lean of fresh beef — the coarse pieces will do. Cut them up and put them into your soup pot with the bones belonging to them (which should be broken to pieces,) and a pound of bacon cut very small. If you have the remains of a piece of beef that has been roasted the day before, and so much underdone that the juices remain in it, you may put it into the pot, and its bones along with it. Season the meat with pepper and salt and pour on it six quarts of water. As soon as it boils, take off the scum and put in the beans (having first drained them) and a head of celery cut small; or a table-spoonful of celery seed. Boil it slowly till the meat is done to shreds and the beans all dissolved. Then strain it through a cullender into the tureen, and put into it small squares of toasted bread with the crust cut off.

BEAN SOUP, 1886. Boil a small soup-bone in about two quarts water until the meat can be separated from the bone, remove bone, add a coffee-cup white beans soaked for two hours, boil for an hour and a half, add three potatoes, half a turnip and a parsnip, all sliced fine, boil half an hour longer and just before serving sprinkle in a few dry breadcrumbs; season with salt and pepper, and serve with raw onions sliced very fine for those who like them.

BEAN SOUP, 1877. Soak a quart of navy beans overnight, then put them on the fire, with three quarts of water, three onions, fried, or *sautéed* in a little butter; one little carrot, two potatoes, partly boiled in other water; a small cut of pork; a little red pepper and salt. Let it all boil slowly for five or six hours. Pass it then through a colander or sieve, return the pulp to the fire; season properly with salt and Cayenne pepper. Put into the tureen *croutons*, or bread cut in half-inch squares and fried brown on all sides in a little butter or in boiling fat. Professor Blot adds broth, bacon, onions, celery, one or two cloves, and carrot to his bean soup. A French cook I once had added a little mustard to her bean soup which made a pleasant change. Another cook adds cream at the last moment. Or, a very good bean soup can be made from baked beans; the brown baked beans giving it a good color. Merely add water and a bit of onion; boil it to a pulp and pass it through the colander. If a little stock or some bones or pieces of fresh meat are at hand they add also to the flavor of bean soup.

MEATLESS BEAN SOUP, 1886. Parboil one pint beans, drain off the water, add fresh, let boil until perfectly tender, season with pepper and salt, add a piece of butter the size of a walnut, or more if preferred; when done skim out half the beans, leaving the broth with the remaining half in the kettle, now add a tea-cup sweet cream or good milk, a dozen or more crackers broken up; let it boil up, and serve.

TO STEW BEEF. It should be put in a pot with just sufficient cold water to cover it, and closely covered. After boiling three or four hours, according to the size of the piece, cut in small pieces, not larger than dice, two or three carrots and heads of celery, with a little sweet herbs and put them into the pot along with pepper-corns, mace, and a couple of large onions stuck full of cloves and let it then simmer by the side of the fire for two or three hours, taking care to skim off any fat that may appear on the top.

By this time the meat will probably be tender enough; when take out the whole onions, mince them, and fry them in butter, to be mixed in the gravy made by the meat, which season with salt and Cayenne, or Chili vinegar, to which add some

mushroom or walnut ketchup. Thicken the gravy with a little flour, and brown it, if necessary with a spoonful of sugar slightly burnt, which, besides imparting its color, adds an agreeable flavor. Such is the most simple mode; but the sauce may be much improved by a glass or two of port wine and a spoonful of curry powder; if the odor of garlic be not objected to, a clove boiled in the stew will be found to give it a fine flavor. Garnish with vegetables. [For mushroom catsup you may substitute liquid from purchased or home-canned pickled mushrooms.]

TO STEW BEEF, *A Mother's Book*, 1852. Take a good piece of fresh beef, not too fat, rub with salt and boil in water just enough to cover it. An hour before you take it up, add pared potatoes and parsnips, if you have them, split. Let them cook till tender, and turn the meat several times. Serve them up together with the gravy. The water should be cooked out, which will leave the vegetables a light brown. Sweet potatoes are good cooked in this way.

A FAMILY STEW OF BEEF. Take any piece of beef good for stewing, cut it into small pieces, slice two or three large onions, and put them into the stew-pan with two ounces of butter or good beef-dripping. When melted dredge in some flour, add the meat also dredged with flour, and enough water to keep it from burning. When the gravy has drawn, fill up with boiling water, let it come to a boil gently, skim the pot well, then add a spoonful of mixed spices and a bay-leaf or two; set the pan by the side of the fire to stew slowly for a couple of hours. Eleven pounds of meat will take four hours. This dish may be thickened like Irish stew, with potatoes, or it may be served with the addition of chopped vegetables of all kinds, previously fried.

SHIN OF BEEF SOUP, *Godey's*, 1861. Put on the shin at 7 o'clock in the morning to boil, at 9 o'clock add the vegetables; take a large head of cabbage cut fine, twelve carrots cut small, five or six turnips, two or three potatoes, two onions roasted in hot ashes, and, if tomatoes are in season, add two or three. Put in thyme, parsley, black pepper, salt, all-spice, and a little mace.

BEETROOT SOUP, 1891. This soup is better adapted to the German palate than the English, as it contains both vinegar and sugar, which are very characteristic of German cookery. Take two large beetroots and two good-sized onions, and after peeling the beetroots boil them and mince them finely, adding them, of course, to the water in which they were boiled, or still better, they can be boiled in some sort of stock. Add a very small quantity of corn-flour, to give a slight consistency to the soup, as well as a little pinch of thyme. Next add two tablespoonfuls of vinegar — more or less according to taste — a spoonful of brown sugar, and a little pepper and salt.

CRISP **BISCUITS**, *The Brooklyn Daily Eagle*, 1877. One pound of flour, the yolk of one egg, milk. Mix the flour and the yolk of the egg with sufficient milk to make the whole into a very stiff paste; beat it well, and knead it until it is perfectly smooth. Roll the paste out very thin; with a round cutter shape it into small biscuits, and bake them a nice brown in a slow oven from twelve to eighteen minutes. [Crackers. Based on the writings of Beeton.]

SIMPLE HARD **BISCUITS**, *Brooklyn Eagle*. To every pound of flour allow two ounces of butter, about half a pint of skimmed milk. Warm the butter in the milk until the former is dissolved, and then mix it with the flour into a very stiff paste; beat it with a rolling pin until the dough looks perfectly smooth. Roll it out thin; cut it with the top of a glass into round biscuits; prick them well, and bake them from six to ten minutes. The above is the proportion of milk which we think would convert the flour into a stiff paste; but should it be found too much, an extra spoonful or two of flour must be put in. [Crackers.]

BORSCHT, Penny (based on Russian recipe), 1939.

> 2 cups grated raw beet
> ¼ cup chopped onion
> ⅓ cup chopped cabbage
> 1 potato, chopped
> 1 turnip, chopped
> 2 tablespoons fat
> 2 quarts of beef stock
> pepper and salt
> 1 tablespoon sour cream, lemon juice, or
>   vinegar
> 1 carrot, chopped

Brown the onion in the fat, add other vegetables to the beef stock and simmer until tender. Season to taste with salt and pepper and serve topped with sour cream or add the vinegar, or lemon juice, just before serving.

BOUILLABAISSE, Gouffe, 1868. Put in stewpan 4 sliced onions, 4 cloves, 1 sliced carrot, 1 oz. parsley, 2 bay leaves, 1 sprig of thyme, 2 unpicked cloves of garlic, 4 shalots; Cut in 5 pieces about 5 lbs. of different fish, such as soles, flounders, small gurnet, red mullet, and whiting; Put the pieces of fish in the stewpan, with the vegetables and 1 gill [¼ pint] of olive oil, 1 oz. of salt, 2 small pinches of pepper, ½ oz. of capsicums, 2 quarts of water. Boil for

twenty-five minutes, keeping the stewpan closely covered. If whiting are used, they should not be added till the soup has boiled for fifteen minutes; Drain the fish carefully; remove any pieces of vegetable, or spice, which might be adhering to it, and pile it up on a large dish; Add a teaspoonful of powdered saffron to the liquor; strain it through the pointed gravy strainer, into the soup tureen; and serve.

BOUILLABAISSE, Blot, 1869. Put a gill of sweet-oil in a tin saucepan and set it on a sharp fire; when hot, add two onions and two cloves of garlic sliced; stir so as to partly fry them, and then take from the fire. Put also in the pan three pounds of fish, such as haddock, halibut, turbot, white-fish — of all if possible, but at least of two kinds; also a dozen muscles, just blanched and taken from the shell (some put them whole, properly cleaned). The fish is cut in pieces about two inches long. Then add one gill of Catawba or Sauterne wine, a bay-leaf, two cloves, two slices of lemon, the juice of a tomato, salt, pepper, a pinch of saffron, cover with cold water, and set the pan back on a brisk fire. After about thirty minutes add a teaspoonful of chopped parsley; boil ten minutes longer, and it is done.

COURT **BOUILLON**, *The French Cook*, 1828. Take three carrots, four onions, six shallots, and two roots of parsley, which pick and wash. Mince them. Put a small lump of butter into a stew-pan, with the above roots, and fry them till they begin to get brown. Moisten next with two bottles of red wine, a bottle of water, a handful of salt, some whole pepper-corns, and a bunch of parsley and green onions, seasoned with thyme, bay leaves, sweet basil, cloves, &c. Let the whole stew for an hour, and then strain it through a sieve, to use as occasion may require. If you should have no wine, put in some vinegar. The court-bouillon is better after having served several times than on the first day. It is a famous thing for stewing fish.

LIGHT **BREAD SOUP**, *Field and Fireside*, 1863. Boil in a saucepan a pint of water, to which add an egg well beaten, two slices of bread, toasted brown, a teacup of sweet milk, and a little butter. Heat, and salt and pepper to taste.

BRILLA SOUP, Godey's 1861. Take a shin of beef, cut off all the meat in square pieces, then boil the bone three hours; strain it and take off the fat, then put the broth to boil with the pieces of meat, a few carrots and turnips, cut small, and a good sprig of thyme, some onions, chopped, and a stick of celery cut in pieces; stir them all till the meat is tender. If not cooking brown, you must color it.

BRUNSWICK STEW, *Housekeeping in Old Virginia*, 1879. Take one chicken or two squirrels, cut them up and put one-half gallon water to them. Let it stew until the bones can be removed. Add one-half dozen large tomatoes, one-half pint butter-beans, and corn cut from half a dozen ears, salt, pepper, and butter as seasoning. [A similar recipe from the book states, "Cook until it is well done and thick enough to eat with a fork."]

BRUNSWICK STEW, Rufus Estes, 1911. Cut up one chicken, preferably a good fat hen, cover with cold water, season with salt and pepper, and cook slowly until about half done. Add six ears of green [fresh] corn, splitting through the kernels, one pint of butter beans, and six large tomatoes chopped fine. A little onion may be added if desired. Cook until the vegetables are thoroughly done, but very slowly, so as to avoid burning. Add strips of pastry for dumplings and cook five minutes. Fresh pork can be used in place of the chicken and canned vegetables instead of the fresh.

CABBAGE SOUP, Blot, 1868. Put in a kettle with two quarts and a half of water a pound of salted pork, same of breast of mutton; also, if handy, the remains of a roasted piece; set on a slow fire; skim before it boils, and then boil for about an hour and a half; strain, to remove the small bones, if any; put back in the kettle broth and meat, also one middling-sized cabbage, which you must have previously thrown in boiling water and boiled ten minutes; add then two carrots, one turnip, two leeks, half a head of celery, one onion with a clove stuck in it, a little salt and pepper, and about half a pound of sausage (not smoked); then boil gently about two hours, strain the broth, pour it on *croutons* in the soup-dish, and serve.

CAPON OR CHICKEN IN WHITE-BROTH, *The Gentlewoman's Companion: or, A Guide to the Female Sex*, 1675. First boil the Capon in water and salt, then take three pints of strong Broth, and a quart of White wine, and stew it in a Pipkin, with a quarter of a pound of Dates, half a pound of fine Sugar, four or five blades of large Mace, the Marrow of three Marrow-bones, an handful of white Endive; stew them very leisurely; having so done, strain the yolks of ten Eggs with some of the Broth. Before you dish up the Capon or Chickens, put the Eggs into the Broth, and keep it stirring that it may not curdle, and let it be but a little while on the fire; the Fowls being dished up, put on the Broth, and garnish the Dish with Dates, large Mace, Endive, preserved barberries. You may make a Lere of Almond-paste, and Grape- verjuice [juice of unripened fruit to replace vinegar in a recipe].

CARAMEL, Campbell, 1893. Half a pound of brown sugar; one tablespoonful of water. Put into a frying-pan, and stir steadily over the fire till it becomes a deep dark brown in color. Then add one cup of boiling water and one teaspoonful of salt. Boil a minute longer, bottle, and keep corked. One tablespoonful will color a clear soup, and it can be used for many jellies, gravies, and sauces. [Soups were for many decades colored with caramel to make them visually more appealing.]

CARROT SOUP. Take six or eight full-grown carrots, of the red sort, scrape them clean, and rasp only the outer rind, or soft red part, and if you have a single ripe tomato, add it, sliced, to the raspings, but use no other vegetable except onions. While this is doing, the broth of any kind of fresh meat which has been got ready should be heated and seasoned with a couple of onions fried in butter, but without pepper, or any other kind of seasoning, except a small quantity of mace and a little salt. When all is ready, put the raspings into two quarts of the skimmed broth, cover the stewpan close, and let it simmer by the side of the fire for two or three hours, by which time the raspings will have become soft enough to be pumped through a fine sieve; after which the soup should be boiled until it is as smooth as jelly, for any curdy appearance will spoil it.

Thus all the roots and most of such vegetables as can be easily made in to *purees* and combined with any sort of broth, will, in this manner, make excellent soup of different denominations, though all founded upon the same meat-stock. The gravy of beef is always preferred for savory soups, and that of veal or fowls for the more delicate white soups; to which from half a pint to one pint of cream, or, if that cannot be had, the same quantity of milk and the yolks of two raw eggs, should be added for every two quarts of soup; remembering, however, that the latter will not impart the richness of cream.

CARROT SOUP, *Godey's*, 1855. Four quarts of liquor to which a leg of mutton or beef has been boiled, [stock] a few beef-bones, six large carrots, two large onions, one turnip; seasoning of salt and pepper to taste; Cayenne. Put the liquor, bones, onions, turnip, pepper, and salt into a stewpan, and simmer for three hours. Scrape and cut the carrots thin, strain the soup on them, and stew them till soft enough to pulp through a hair sieve or coarse cloth; then boil the pulp with the soup, which should be of the consistency of pea soup. Add Cayenne. Pulp only the red part of the carrot, and make this soup the day before it is used. [An 1867 receipt book stated turnip soup could be made by following the same process by substituting turnips for the carrots.]

CATFISH SOUP, Miss Leslie, 1837 and 1840. Catfish that have been caught near the middle of the river are much nicer than those that are taken near the shore where they have access to impure food. The small white ones are the best. Having cut off their heads, skin the fish, and clean them, and cut them in three. To twelve small catfish allow a pound and a half of ham. Cut the ham into small pieces, or mouthfuls, and scald it two or three times in boiling water, lest it be too salt. Chop together a bunch of parsley and some sweet marjoram stripped from the stalks. Put these ingredients into a soup kettle and season them with pepper; the ham will make it salt enough. Add a head of celery cut small, or a large table-spoonful of celery seed tied up in a bit of clear muslin to prevent its dispersing. Put in two quarts of water, cover the kettle, and let it boil slowly till everything is sufficiently done, and the fish and ham quite tender. Skim it frequently. Boil in another vessel a quart of rich milk, in which you have melted a quarter of a pound of butter divided into small bits and rolled in flour. Pour it hot to the soup, and stir in at the last the beaten yolks of four eggs. Give it another boil, just to take off the rawness of the eggs, and then put it into a tureen, taking out the bag of celery seed before you send the soup to table, and adding some toasted bread cut into small squares. Before you send it to table, remove the back-bones of the cat-fish. Eel soup may be made in the same manner.

CATFISH SOUP, *Kentucky Housewife*, 1839. Take a catfish, weighing six or eight pounds; skin and clean it nicely, removing the head; cut it up in five or six pieces; season them well with salt and pepper, and boil them tender, leaving about two quarts of liquor when done. Cut up some of the nicest of it into tolerably small pieces, and reserve them to serve in the soup; take another small portion, pick out every particle of bone, and pound the meat to a paste, mixing with it an equal portion of Indian bread crumbs, boiled white potatoes, and boiled onions, moistening it with the yolks of eggs and seasoning it with cayenne pepper, nutmeg, and chopped parsley. When it is quite smooth, make it into a dozen little balls, half as large as a hen's egg, dust them lightly with flour, and let them dry a little. Strain the liquor into a soup-pan; add a pint of rich sweet milk, four ounces of butter, rolled in flour, and if not sufficiently seasoned, put in a little salt, pepper and mace. When it boils up, skim it, and put in your pieces of fish, having sprinkled them lightly with flour, and then drop in the balls.

Having beat very light the yolks of four eggs, mix them well with half a pint of cream, and stir it gradually into the soup. Stir it constantly till it raises the simmer, and pour it hastily into a tureen. Lay on the top some light sprigs of parsley, and send to table with it a plate of crackers, light bread, or bread and butter. You may for a change have more of the liquor, omit the cream and milk, and slightly acidulate it with lemon juice or good vinegar. Eel soup may be made in the same manner.

CATFISH SOUP, *Virginia Housewife*, 1860. Take two large or four small white catfish that have been caught in deep water, cut off the heads, and skin and clean the bodies; cut each in three parts, put them in a pot, with a pound of lean bacon, a large onion cut up, a handful of parsley chopped small, some pepper and salt, pour in sufficient quantity of water, and stew them till the fish are quite tender but not broken; beat the yelks of four fresh eggs, add to them a large spoonful of butter, two of flour, and half a pint of rich milk; make all these warm and thicken the soup, take out the bacon, and put some of the fish in your tureen, pour in the soup, and serve it up.

[In 1896 the *Chicago Record Cookbook* said few people were aware from what a "variety of tempting dishes this much abused fish can be made" belying the notion that catfish soup was a purely Southern dish. Their recipe was practically the same as those above except that it contained no onion.]

CAULIFLOWER SOUP, 1867. Clean and cut in small pieces three middling-sized cauliflowers. Put in a stewpan two ounces of butter, and set it on a moderate fire; when hot put the cauliflowers in; stir now and then till it turns brown, then add a sprig of thyme, same of parsley, a bay-leaf, one onion with a clove stuck in it, salt and white pepper; simmer gently till the whole is well cooked, throw away the onion, clove, thyme, and bay-leaf; mash well the cauliflowers, strain and put back on the fire with the broth; give one boil, pour on *croutons* and serve. [Modern cauliflowers are larger than earlier period varieties. Adjust amount of cauliflower according to the amount of soup required.]

CELERY SOUP. Celery soup may be made with *white stock*. Cut down the white of half a dozen heads of celery into little pieces and boil it in four pints of white stock, with a quarter of a pound of lean ham and two ounces of butter. Simmer gently for a full hour, then strain through a sieve, return the liquor to the pan, and stir in a few spoonfuls of cream with great care. Serve with toasted bre...d and, if liked, thicken with a little flour. Season it to taste.

CELERY SOUP, Miss Corson's, 1877. Pick over a cupful of rice, wash it in cold water, drain it, and put it over the fire in three pints of boiling water [or broth]; wash and cut in half-inch bits two cupfuls of the white stalks of celery, add it to the rice, with a teaspoonful of salt, and boil them together gently for an hour, taking care that there is always enough water to prevent burning. Then rub the rice and celery through a sieve with a potato-masher, return them to the saucepan in which they were boiled, set it over the fire, add to them two quarts of hot milk, or enough to make the soup about the consistency of thick cream; use a palatable seasoning of salt and white pepper, and a very little nutmeg, and stir the soup until it boils; then serve it at once.

CHEAP SOUP. A pound or a pound and a half of lean beef, cut up into small pieces, six quarts of water, stew in three large onions, with double the quantity of turnips; put in thyme, parsley, pepper, and salt, half a pound of rice, a pound of potatoes, peeled and cut in quarters, and a handful of oatmeal. Stew from three to four hours, not less.

CHEAP SOUP, *Godey's*, 1862. Put four ounces of scotch barley, well washed, into five quarts of water, with four ounces of sliced onions; boil gently one hour, and pour it into a pan. Then put into a saucepan from one to two ounces of fresh beef or mutton dripping, or melted suet, or fat bacon cut fine. When melted in the saucepan, stir into it four ounces of oatmeal, and rub them together till they become a soft paste. Then add, a little at a time of the barley broth, stirring it well together till it boils. For seasoning, put in a basin a little celery or cress seed, a little black pepper and allspice ground, and a very little Cayenne pepper; mix them smooth with a little of the soup, and stir it into the rest. Simmer greatly for a quarter of an hour, season with salt and it is ready. The flavor may be varied by any variety of herbs, or a larger portion of onions, or carrots and turnips, or green celery; add rice, or wheat flour, instead of oatmeal and barley.

CHEAP SOUP WITH MEAT, *Godey's*, 1862. Get two pounds of leg, shin, or neck of beef, cut it into pieces, and boil gently in six quarts of water, for about an hour and a half. Then add a pint of split peas, a pound of mealy potatoes sliced, and a head of celery cut small. Slice a few onions and fry them in a little fat, dredging them slightly with flour, till they are nicely brown; then stir them into the soup, with salt and pepper to taste. Let the whole boil till the vegetables are thoroughly tender, and the peas well broken in.

CHEESE SOUP, Blot, 1868. Put four ounces of butter in a soup-kettle, with an onion chopped fine; set on a brisk fire, stir now and then till it has a yellow color, then sprinkle on it half a tablespoonful of flour, keep stirring till it turns brown; then add two quarts of water, salt, and pepper; boil about five minutes. Have prepared in the soup-dish the following: a thin layer of grated cheese, Gruyere or pine-apple cheese; on it a layer of thin slices of bread, then another of cheese, again another of bread, etc., three or four of each; strain, and pour the liquor in the kettle on the whole; keep in a warm place five minutes, and serve.

CHERRY SOUP, 1868. Take ... a quantity of fine ripe cherries, cook them in water with sugar and a little vanilla; fry some slices of bread in fresh butter, throw them into the decoction of cherries, mix well up, and serve hot. This soup seems a favorite dish in Germany.

CHESTNUT (SPANISH) SOUP, Isabella Beeton, 1861. ¾ lb. of Spanish chestnuts, ¼ pint of cream; seasoning to taste of salt, cayenne, and mace; 1 quart of stock

Take the outer rind from the chestnuts, and put them into a large pan of warm water. As soon as this becomes too hot for the fingers to remain in it, take out the chestnuts, peel them quickly, and immerse them in cold water, and wipe and weigh them. Now cover them with good stock, and stew them gently for rather more than ¾ of an hour, or until they break when touched with a fork; then drain, pound, and rub them through a fine sieve reversed; add sufficient stock, mace, cayenne, and salt, and stir it often until it boils, and put in the cream. The stock in which the chestnuts are boiled can be used for the soup, when its sweetness is not objected to, or it may, in part, be added to it; and the rule is, that ¾ lb. of chestnuts should be given to each quart of soup.

CHESTNUT SOUP, Rufus Estes, 1911. Peel and blanch the chestnuts, boil them in salted water until quite soft, pass through a sieve, add more water if too thick, and a spoonful of butter or several of sweet cream, season to taste, and serve with small squares of bread fried crisp in butter or olive oil.

CHESTNUT SOUP, *The Times Cookbook.* One pound Spanish chestnuts, one pound good white stock, one-half pint cream, one-half pint milk, dash of grated nutmeg and mace, cayenne, and salt, one-half teaspoon sugar. Slit the husks and boil for ten minutes, remove the husks, and skin. Put the chestnuts in a stewpan with the stock and boil until they are soft, then rub through a fine strainer. Warm up with the milk, cream, sugar, and seasoning. [This version includes the step of removing the skins from the chestnuts, which would make the soup much more appealing.]

CHICKEN BROTH. Joint a chicken, wash the pieces, put them into a stewpan, with three pints of water, and add two ounces of rice, two or three blades of mace, some white pepper, whole, and a pinch of salt; let it come to a boil, skim frequently, and simmer for three hours; boil for five minutes, in the soup, some vermicelli, and serve with it in the soup.

CHICKEN MULLIGATAWNY. Cut up a young chicken, as for a curry; fry two sliced onions with butter until of a light brown color, when add a tablespoonful of curry, and half as much flour; mix these with the onions, and add one quart or three pints of rich gravy, previously made, either from veal, beef, mutton, or poultry. Boil it, skim off the butter, add a pinch of salt, and put into it the chicken cut as above. Simmer the whole until the fowl be tender, when the soup will be ready to serve in a tureen with a dish of boiled rice. A young rabbit may be substituted for the chicken.

CHICKEN SOUP. Cut up a large fowl, and boil it well in milk and water, thicken with cream, butter, and flour. Add vegetables of different kinds cut in small pieces, such as potatoes, turnips, the heart of cabbage, one or two onions, celery, etc., with thyme, parsley, Cayenne, or black pepper, and mace. Boil all together, and just before you dish it add wine, or a little lemon-juice, and salt to your taste.

GERMAN CHICKEN STEW, *Jewish Cookery Book*, 1871. Cut up a good sized chicken in small pieces, and put them in a saucepan, with a quart of water. Let it stew till tender; season with pepper, ginger, salt, chopped parsley, sweet herbs, and a little garlic; thicken with a tablespoonful of flour. Dish up, and garnish with lemon, parsley, and boiled carrots.

CLAM SOUP, *With Clams*, Blot, 1868. Wash and clean the clams well. Then put them in a saucepan with half a pint of water (say one quart of clams), set on the fire, and at the first boil, take off and drain. Put the pan back on the fire with two ounces of butter in it; when melted, fry a chopped onion in the butter, add then the liquor drained, a pint of water, salt, pepper, parsley chopped fine, and the clams; boil two minutes, add also a little butter,

and when melted and mixed, turn over some *croutons* in the soup-dish, and serve warm. [The book stated this could be made with mussels.]

CLAM SOUP, 1878. Open the clams by putting them in a pot with a little water, and steaming them until the shells begin to part, when they can be taken out with ease. Boil them well, and when they have been chopped fine add enough of the liquor to make them taste well, a lump of butter rolled in flour, two crackers rolled fine, a teaspoonful of mace, and half that quantity of cayenne pepper. When ready to be served, add a tea-cup of sweet cream.

BISQUE OF CLAMS, *Good Things to Eat*, Rufus Estes, 1911. Place a knuckle of veal, weighing about a pound and one-half into a soup kettle, with a quart of water, one small onion, a sprig of parsley, a bay leaf, and the liquor drained from the clams, and simmer gradually for an hour and a half, skimming from time to time; strain the soup and again place it in the kettle; rub a couple of tablespoonfuls of butter with an equal amount of flour together and add it to the soup when it is boiling, stirring until again boiling; chop up twenty-five clams very fine, then place them in the soup, season and boil for about five minutes, then add a pint of milk or cream, and remove from the fire immediately, and serve.

COCKY-LEEKY. Take a scrag of mutton, or shank of veal, three quarts of water (or liquor in which meat has been boiled), and a good sized fowl, with two or three leeks cut in pieces about an inch long, pepper and salt; boil slowly about an hour: then put in as many more leeks, and give it three-quarters of an hour longer: this is very good, made of good beef stock, and leeks put in at twice. [Cock-a-leekie soup is of Scottish origin, and recipes changed little through several decades except for the addition or deletion of prunes.]

COCOANUT SOUP, Dr. Allinson, 1915. 1 cocoanut grated, 2 blades of mace, 1 saltspoonful of cinnamon, 3 pints of water, the juice of a lemon, 2 eggs, 1 oz. Allinson fine wheat meal, pepper and salt to taste. Boil the cocoanut in the water, adding the mace, cinnamon, and seasoning. Let it cook gently for an hour; strain the mixture through a sieve and then return the soup to the saucepan. Make a paste of the eggs, wheat meal, and lemon juice, add it to the soup and let it boil up before serving; let it simmer for 5 minutes, and serve with a little plain boiled rice. [Similar soups date much earlier. Isabella Beeton, 1861, used rice flour to thicken her version of this soup.]

CORN AND TOMATO SOUP, 1881. Take a fresh beef bone, put on to boil with one gallon of water, and when boiling skim the grease off. Cut corn from cob and scald tomatoes with boiling water. Skin them and put both vegetables into soup, the corn ten minutes before dinner. Cut tomatoes in small pieces and let them boil in soup at least one hour.

CORN SOUP. Cut the corn from the cob, and boil the cobs in water for at least an hour, then add the grains, and boil until they are thoroughly done; put one dozen cars of corn to a gallon of water, which will be reduced to three quarts by the time the soup is done; then pour on a pint of new milk, two well-beaten eggs, salt and pepper to your taste; continue the boiling a while longer, and stir in, to season and thicken it a little, a tablespoonful of good butter rubbed up with two tablespoonfuls of flour. Corn soup may also be made nicely with water in which a pair of grown fowls have been boiled or parboiled, instead of having plain water for the foundation.

CRAB STEW, *Housekeeping in Old Virginia*, 1879. One peck live crabs, steam twenty minutes, bone and pick the claws and bodies. Stew with one pint milk or cream, the flesh and eggs of the crabs, fifteen minutes. Flavor with salt and cayenne pepper.

CRANBERRY SOUP, *Brooklyn Daily Eagle*, March 4, 1892. Put one pint of cranberries and one quart of water over the fire to cook for ten minutes; strain, return to kettle, add three-quarters of a cup of sugar; moisten two tablespoonfuls of corn starch in a little cold water; add to hot soup; stir a moment, boil and serve with strips of toast; this is a delightful soup for lunch in early spring. Currants, raspberries or strawberries may be substituted for cranberries.

POTAGE OF **CRAWFISH**, *The French Cook*, François Pierre La Varenne, 1653. Cleanse your Crawfish, and seeth them with wine and vinegar, salt and pepper. After they are sod, pick the feet and taile, and fry them with very fresh butter and a little parsley. Then take the bodies of your Crawfishes, and stamp them in a mortar with an onion, hard eggs, and crums of a loaf. Set them in stoving with some good herb broth or some other; if you will use pease porridge it must be very clear. After it is boiled, strain all together; after it is strained set it before the fire. Then take some butter with a little minced parsley and fry it; then put into your broth well seasoned, and stove it with your dry crusts, covered with a dish or a plate. Put also on your bread a little of a hash of Carp, and juice of Mushrums; fill up your dish, and garnish it with your feet and tails lf Crawfish, with Pomegranate and juice of Lemon, and serve."

CRAW-FISH SOUP, 1805. Cleanse them and boil them in water, salt, and spice; pull off their feet and tails, and fry them; break the rest of them in a stone mortar, season them with savory spice, and an onion, a hard egg, grated bread, and sweet herbs boiled in good table beer; strain it and put to it scalded chopped parsley, and French rolls; then put in the fried craw-fish, with a few mushrooms. Garnish the dish with sliced lemon and the feet and tail of a craw-fish. [This is an early 19th century recipe for Lent that appeared in several period cookery books.]

CROUTONS, 1867. Cut pieces of soft part of stale bread in different shapes, and fry them on both sides in butter or fat. [Some recipes specified cutting the bread into cubes]

CUCUMBER SOUP, Mrs. N. M. K. Lee, 1832. Make some broth with a neck of mutton, a thick slice of lean bacon, an onion stuck with three cloves, a carrot, two turnips, some salt, and a bunch of sweet herbs; strain it; brown with an ounce of butter the crumb of a French roll, to which put four large cucumbers, and two heads of lettuce cut small; let them stew a quarter of an hour, and add to them a quart of the broth; when it boils put in a pint of green pease, and as it stews, add two quarts more of the broth.

CULLEN SKINK

1 large smoked or finnan haddock,	2 tbsp butter
salt and pepper, mace, chopped parsley	1chopped onion
3 cups milk	2 to 3 tbsp
cream	
mashed potatoes as needed	

Skin the haddock and put into a shallow pan or casserole dish, and add just enough cold water to cover. Bring slowly to the boil. Simmer until the consistency of the haddock becomes creamy. Remove from the pan and part the flesh from the bones. Break the fish into flakes. Return the bones to the water in the pan and add the onion. Cover and simmer gently for 20 minutes. Strain this stock. Return stock to a clean pan and bring to the boil. In another pan bring the milk to the boil and add to the stock with the flaked fish. Simmer for three or four minutes but do not allow to stick to pan. Stir in hot mashed potatoes to make a creamy consistency. Add butter gradually and salt, pepper and mace to taste. Stir in the cream and, before serving, scatter the chopped parsley over the hot soup. Best served with finely sliced, dry toast. [This is a very wholesome and traditional Scottish soup.

The name derives from the Port of Cullen on the Moray Firth in Northeastern Scotland. *Skink* is Gaelic for "essence." Smoked haddock can be difficult to find in the United States. Fresh or frozen haddock may be substituted. To attempt to duplicate the smokiness of the smoked haddock, render enough drippings from smoked bacon to cook the onion, and omit the butter.]

CURRY SOUP, *Godey's*, 1861. Season two quarts of strong veal broth with two onions, a bunch of parsley, salt, and pepper, strain it, and have ready a chicken, cut in joints and skinned; put it in the broth with a tablespoonful of curry powder; boil the chickens till quite tender. A little before serving add the juice of a lemon and a teacupful of boiling cream. Serve boiled rice to eat with this soup. Always boil cream before putting it in soup or gravy. [Receipts for Curry and mulligatawny soup appear in cookery books from 1832, and are practically identical to the ones given here.]

INDIAN OR **CURRY SOUP**, 1867. Put in a saucepan one ounce of butter and set it on the fire; when melted, fry in it two large onions, one carrot, and half a turnip, all sliced; also one leek, a stalk of celery, and four of parsley, all cut fine. When the whole is fried, cover with about one quart of broth, season with two cloves, a bay-leaf, half a teaspoonful of cayenne pepper, same of pimento, two stalks of thyme; boil gently about one hour and a quarter, and drain. Put the liquor back in the saucepan and add four ounces of boiled rice, a little saffron to color, simmer about fifteen minutes longer and serve.

DUCK SOUP, 1847. Half roast a pair of fine large tame ducks; keeping them half an hour at the fire, and saving the gravy, the fat of which must be carefully skimmed off. Then cut them up; season them with black pepper; and put them into a soup-pot with four or five small onions sliced thin, a small bunch of sage, a thin slice of cold ham cut into pieces, a grated nutmeg, and the yellow rind of a lemon pared thin, and cut into bits. Add the gravy of the ducks. Pour on, slowly, three quarts of boiling water from a kettle. Cover the soup-pot, and set it over a moderate fire. Simmer it slowly (skimming it well) for about four hours, or till the flesh of the ducks is dissolved into small shreds. When done, strain it through a sieve into a tureen over a quart of young green peas, that have been boiled by themselves. If peas are not in season, substitute half a dozen hard boiled eggs cut into round slices, white and yolk together.

If wild ducks are used for soup, three or four will be required for the above quantity. Before you put them on the spit to roast, place a large carrot in the body of each duck, to remove the sedgy or fishy taste. This taste will be all absorbed by the carrot, which, of course, must be thrown away.

DUMPLINGS, *Miss Parloa's New Cookbook*, 1880. One pint of flour, measured before sifting; half a teaspoonful of soda, a teaspoonful of cream of tartar, one of sugar, half a teaspoonful of salt. Mix all thoroughly and run through the sieve. Wet with a small cupful of milk. Sprinkle a little flour on the board. Turn the dough (which should have been stirred into a smooth ball with a spoon) on it, roll to the thickness of half an inch, cut into small cakes, and cook ten minutes. By remembering that the soup should be boiling rapidly when the dumplings are put in; that they should not sink too deep in it; that they should fit tightly; so that the steam shall not escape; and that the pot boils all the time; so that the steam is kept up; and by following the other directions, success is insured.

CHICKEN **DUMPLINGS**, *Holland Cookbook*, 1923. Take 3 pints of flour, add 1 teaspoon level full of salt, 1 teaspoonful of soda, and stir thoroughly into the flour. Take shortening the size of a hickory nut, and mix with the flour until it is well rubbed together. Add half a pint of good sour cream, and buttermilk enough to make a dough stiff enough to roll; roll out thin, and cut in strips 4 inches long; have plenty of water [broth] around the chicken, and when boiling, drop them in, each piece in a separate place. Cook half an hour.

CORN **DUMPLINGS**, *Domestic Cookery*, Elizabeth Lee, 1869. When you boil corned beef, new bacon, or pork, you can make dumplings, by taking some grease out of the pot, with some of the water, and pouring it hot on a quart of Indian meal, mix and work it well, (it will not require salt), make it into little round cakes; (they should be stiff or they will boil to pieces); take out the meat when it is done and boil the dumplings in the same water for half an hour. [This recipe was also found in *Holland*, 1923.]

EEL, 1832. To make a tureenful, take a couple of middling-sized onions, cut them in half, and cross your knife over them two or three times; put two ounces of butter into a stewpan, when it is melted put in the onions, stir them about till they are lightly browned; cut into pieces three pounds of eels, put them into your stewpan, and shake them over the fire for five minutes; then add three quarts of boiling water, and when they come to a boil, take the scum off very clean; then put in a quarter of an ounce of the green leaves (not dried) of winter savory, the same of lemon thyme, and twice the quantity of parsley, two drachms of allspice, the same of black pepper; cover it close, and let it boil gently for two hours; then strain it off, and skim it very clean. To thicken it, put three ounces of butter into a clean stewpan; when it is melted, stir in as much flour as will make it of a stiff paste, then add the liquor by degrees; let it simmer for ten minutes, and pass it through a sieve; then put your soup on in a clean stewpan, and have ready some little square pieces of fish fried of a nice light brown, either eels, soles, plaice, or skate will do; the fried fish should be added about ten minutes before the soup is served up. Forcemeat balls are sometimes added.

TO MAKE AN EEL SOUP, 1803. Take eels according to the quantity of soup you would make; a pound of eels will make a pint of good soup; so to every pound of eels put a quart of water, a crust of bread, two or three blades of mace, a little whole pepper, an onion, and a bunch of sweet herbs; cover them close, and let them boil till half the liquor is wasted; then strain it and toast some bread, cut it small, lay the bread in the dish and pour in your soup. If you have a stew hole, set the dish over it for a minute, and send it to table. If you find your soup not rich enough, you must let it boil till it is as strong as you would have it. You may make this soup as rich and good as if it was meat; you may add a piece of carrot to brown it.

EGG BALLS FOR SOUP. Take the yolks of eight eggs, boiled hard, and mash them smooth with a little flour, salt, and the yolks of two raw eggs. Mix well together, roll into balls, and drop into boiling water.

EGG DUMPLING SOUP, *The Chicago Record Cookbook*, 1896. Into a quart or three pints of good stock drop from a spoon dumplings made according to this rule: Beat well two eggs, a very small teacup of flour and a larger cup of milk; melt in a spider half a cup of butter; when hot stir in the batter and cook, stirring constantly, until it leaves the side of the spider; set aside to cool; when cold beat in, separately, two eggs.

EGG DUMPLINGS FOR SOUP. To half a pint of milk put two well-beaten eggs, and as much wheat flour as will make a smooth, rather *thick* batter free from lumps; drop this batter, a tablespoonful at a time, into boiling soup.

EGG SOUP, Isabella Beeton, 1861. A tablespoonful of flour, 4 eggs, 2 small blades of finely-pounded mace, 2 quarts of stock. Beat up the flour smoothly in a teaspoonful of cold stock, and put in the eggs; throw them into boiling stock, stirring all the time.

Simmer for 1/4 of an hour. Season and serve with a French roll in the tureen, or fried sippets of bread.

EGG SOUP, 1867. Add to a pint of water the yolk of an egg well beaten, an ounce of butter, and the same quantity of sugar. Set it over the fire and stir it till it begins to simmer, then pour it several times from the pan to a basin, and back again till it is smoothed and frothed. This is a pleasant and good restorative.

FAMILY SOUP, *Godey's*, 1861. Take a shin or leg of beef that has been newly killed; the fore-leg is best, as there is the most meat on it. Have it cut in three pieces and wash it well. To each pound allow somewhat less than a quart of water, to ten pounds of the leg two gallons of water. Put it into a large stewpot and add half a tablespoon of salt. Hang it over a good fire a full eight hours before you dine. When it has come to a hard boil and the scum has risen (which it will do as soon as it has boiled); skim it well and set it on hot coals in the corner and keep it simmering, so as to continue a regular heat. About three hours afterwards put in a couple of heads of celery, four carrots cut small, and as many onions sliced and fried, with either a small head of cabbage cut into little pieces, or a large one whole if to be eaten with the meat; or if you have any objection to cabbage substitute a large proportion of other vegetables, or else tomatoes instead. Put in a bunch of herbs tied up in a thin muslin bag. It will require at least eight hours cooking; the vegetables should be put in three hours after the meat and the turnips only half an hour before it is done. If you wish to send any portion of the meat to table, take the best part of it out of the soup about two hours before dinner; let the remainder be left in the pot till you send up the soup, which must be strained.

Next day, take what is left of the soup, put it into a pot and simmer it for half an hour; a longer time will weaken the flavor. If it has been well made, and kept in a cool place, it will be found better the second day than the first.

FISH CHOWDER, 1808. Boil a pound of the best macaroni in a quart of good stock till quite tender; then take out half, and put it into another stewpot. To the remainder add some more stock, and boil it till you can pulp all the macaroni through a fine sieve. Then add together that, the two liquors, a pint or more of cream boiling-hot, the macaroni that first taken out, and half a pound of grated Parmesan cheese; make it hot, but do not let it boil. Serve it with the crust of a French roll cut into the size of a shilling.

FISH BROTH, 1864. Thick-skinned fish, and those

which have glutinous, jelly-like substances, are the best. The liquor which eels have been boiled in is good enough of itself, as they require but little water. The liquor in which turbot or cod has been boiled, boil again, with the addition of the bones. If purposely made, small eels, or grigs, or flat fish, as flounders, soles, plaice or dabs, or the finny parts of cod, will do for the purpose. A pound of fish to three pints of water; add peppercorns, a large handful of parsley, and an onion; and boil till reduced to half. A spoonful of catsup, or vinegar, is an improvement. This broth is very nourishing and easy of digestion; but for a sick person, leave out the catsup or vinegar.

FISH STOCK, Isabella Beeton, 1861. 2 lbs. of beef or veal (these can be omitted), any kind of white fish trimmings, of fish which are to be dressed for table, 2 onions, the rind of 1/2 a lemon, a bunch of sweet herbs, 2 carrots, 2 quarts of water. Cut up the fish, and put it, with the other ingredients, into the water. Simmer for 2 hours; skim the liquor carefully, and strain it. When a richer stock is wanted, fry the vegetables and fish before adding the water.

FORCEMEAT BALLS FOR FISH SOUP, *Brooklyn Daily Eagle*, 1877. 1 middling sized lobster, 1/2 an anchovy, 1 head of boiled celery, the yolk of a hard boiled egg; salt, cayenne and mace to taste; 4 tablespoonfuls of bread crumbs, 2 ounces of butter, 2 eggs. Pick the meat from the shell of the lobster and pound it, with the soft parts, in a mortar; add the celery, the yolk of the hard boiled egg, seasoning and bread crumbs. Continue pounding till the whole is nicely amalgamated. Warm the butter till it is in a liquid state; well whisk the eggs, and work these up with the pounded lobster meat. Make into balls of about an inch in diameter, and fry of a nice pale brown. [Based on the writings of Mrs. Beeton].

FORCEMEAT BALLS TO SERVE WITH SOUP. Chop meat boiled for soup finely, season with salt, pepper, parsley, and onion. Bind together with a raw egg mixed with a little flour. Make into balls and fry or boil before adding to soup. [*Murray's Modern Cookery Book* stated that forcemeat balls were regularly added to any soup the cook chose, whether it was fish, meat, or vegetable, and that they were often called "Passover Balls" because they were so often made by Jews.]

FRENCH GUMBO, 1867. Cut up one large fowl; season it with salt and pepper; dredge it well with flour; have ready a soup-kettle; put in a tablespoonful of butter, one of lard, a hand-ful of chopped onion. Fry the fowl then to a good brown; add to this four quarts of boiling water; cover close; let it simmer two or three hours; then put in fifty oysters with their liquor, a little thyme and parsley; just before serving, stir in a tablespoonful of the file powder; season high with Cayenne pepper. Turkey and beef-steak can make also very good gumbo. The filee or felee is what gives a mucilaginous character and excellence to the soup. The powder consists of nothing more than the leaves of the sassafras cured in the shade, and then pounded and sifted; therefore, any family in the country can always have it in their house.

FRENCH SOUP WITHOUT MEAT. Take a large lump of butter and a tablespoonful of flour; brown them in the saucepan in which the soup is to be made; then chop up finely some carrots, onions, celery, sorrel, and potatoes and mix them together; put them into the saucepan with pepper and salt, pour boiling water over them, and let them stew over the fire for three or four hours; they can hardly simmer too long. A little thyme, parsley, cress, and mint are a great improvement added to the other ingredients.

FROG-LEG SOUP, 1867. Skin and put the hind-legs of two dozen of frogs in cold water for an hour; drain and put them in a saucepan, and set it on a slow fire; stir now and then till they are turning yellow, then take them off and chop the flesh rather fine; put back in the pan with a carrot sliced, a stalk of celery, and one leek, both chopped, a little salt, and cover the whole with water. Simmer for about two hours; mash the whole through a colander, add butter which you stir and mix in, and it is ready for use.

GAME SOUPS, Burroughs. Cut in pieces a partridge, pheasant, or rabbit; add slices of veal, ham, onions, carrots, etc. Add a little water, heat a little on slow fire, as gravy is done; then add some good broth, boil the meat gently till it is done. Strain, and stew in the liquor what herbs you please.

GAME SOUP, 1855. In the game season, it is easy for a cook to give her master a very good soup at a very little expense, by taking all the meat off the breasts of any cold birds which have been left the preceding day, and pounding it in a mortar, and beating to pieces the legs and bones, and boiling them in some broth for an hour. Boil six turnips; mash them, and strain them through a tamis-cloth with the meat that has been pounded in a mortar; strain your broth, and put a little of it at a time into the tamis to help you to strain all of it through. Put your soup-kettle near the fire, but do not let it boil; when ready to dish your dinner, have six yelks of eggs mixed with half a pint of cream; strain through a sieve; put your soup on the fire, and as it is coming to boil, put in the eggs and stir well with a wooden spoon; do not let it boil or it will curdle.

GAME SOUP, 1865. In the season for game, it is easy to have good game soup at very little expense, and very nice. Take the meat from off the bones of any cold game left, pound it in a mortar and break up the bones, and pour on them a quart of any good broth and boil for an hour and a half; boil and mash six turnips, and mix with the pounded meat; then pass them through a sieve; strain the broth and stir in the mixture of meat and turnips, which has been strained through the sieve. Keep the soup pot near the fire, but do not let it boil. When ready to dish the soup for table, heat the yolks of five eggs very lightly and mix with them half a pint of good cream; set the soup on to boil, and as it boils, stir in the beaten eggs and cream, but be careful that it does not boil after they are stirred in, as the egg will curdle. Serve hot.

GAME SOUP, 1888. Two grouse or partridges, or if you have neither, use a pair of rabbits; half a pound of lean ham; two medium-sized onions; one pound of lean beef; fried bread; butter for frying; pepper, salt, and two stalks of white celery cut into inch lengths; three quarts of water. Joint your game neatly; cut the ham and onions into small pieces and fry all in butter to a light brown. Put into a soup-pot with the beef, cut into strips, and a little pepper. Pour on the water; heat slowly, and stew gently two hours. Take out the pieces of bird, and cover in a bowl; cook the soup an hour longer; strain; cool; drop in the celery, and simmer ten minutes. Pour upon fried bread in the tureen.

GERMAN SOUP. Boil a knuckle of veal, or any veal bones, and some good stock, then add one or two turnips (according to size), one carrot, and some onions, a little lemon, thyme, a very small stick of celery, and three or four cloves. Let all boil well, strain it off for use, thicken it, and add the yolks of six eggs to three quarts of soup, and one gill of thick cream; pepper and salt to taste. A little vermicelli, a little lean ham, and one blade of mace, will improve the stock.

GERMAN SOUP, 1867. Soak four ounces of pearl-barley in tepid water for eight or ten hours, and drain. Put it in a saucepan with one quart of broth, a piece of leek, one of celery, and boil gently about one hour and a half. While it is boiling, mix well together in a bowl one tablespoonful of flour and half a gill of broth, which turn into the saucepan, also grated nutmeg and sugar to taste; boil en minutes longer and serve.

GOOSE OR DUCK GIBLET SOUP, 1855. Scald and pick very clean a couple sets of goose, or four of duck giblets (the fresher the better); wash them well in warm water, in two or three waters; cut off the noses and split the heads; divide the gizzards and necks into mouthfuls. If the gizzards are not cut into pieces before they are done enough, the rest of the meat &c. will be done too much and knives and forks have no business in a coup-plate. Crack the bones of the legs, and put them into the stew-pan and cover them with cold water; when they boil, take off the scum as it rises; then put in a bundle of herbs, such as lemon-thyme, winter savoury, or marjoram, about three sprigs of each, and double the quantity of parsley, an onion, twenty berries of allspice, the same of black pepper, tie them all up in a muslin bag, and set them to stew very gently till the gizzards are tender; this will take from an hour and a half to two hours, according to the size and age of the giblets; take them up with a skimmer, or a spoon full of holes, put them into the tureen, and cover down close to keep warm till the soup is ready.

To thicken the soup. Melt an ounce and a half of butter in a clean stew-pan; stir in as much flour as will make it into a paste; then pour to it by degrees a ladleful of the giblet liquor; add the remainder by degrees; let it boil about half an hour, stirring it all the while for fear it should not burn; skim it, and strain it through a fine sieve into a basin; wash out the stew-pan; then return the soup into it, and season it with a glass of wine, a table-spoonful of mushroom catsup, and a little salt; let it have one boil up; and then put the giblets in to get hot, and the soup is ready.

Thus managed, one set of goose, or two of duck giblets (which latter may sometimes be had for 3d.), will make a quart of healthful, nourishing soup; if you think the giblets alone will not make the gravy savoury enough, add a pound of beef or mutton, or bones of a knuckle of veal, and heighten its *piquance* by adding a few leaves of sweet basil, the juice of half a Seville orange or lemon, and half a glass of wine.

GRAVY SOUP, 1845. Wash a leg of beef, break the bone, and set it over the fire with five quarts of water, a large bunch of sweet herbs, two onions, sliced and fried, but not burnt, a blade or two of mace, three cloves, twenty Jamaica peppers, and forty black. Simmer till the soup be as rich as you choose, then take up the meat, and put the soup away in an earthen vessel. The next day take off the cake of fat. Put into the soup such vegetables as you may wish, and a head of celery. Twenty minutes before serving, put in some vermicelli, and season. Add two spoons of mushroom catsup, and a small roll; serve in a tureen.

GROUNDNUT SOUP, *The Carolina Housewife*, 1847. To a half a pint shelled ground-nuts, well beaten up, add two spoonsful of flour, and mix well. Put to them a pint of oysters, and a pint and a half of water. When boiling, throw on a seed pepper or two, if small.

[Various accounts throughout history claim this soup was one of George Washington's favorites. *Groundnut* is an old term for peanut. The soup can be made by pounding a cup of peanuts into a paste in a mortar and pestle, or by pulsing them in a food processor, or use a cup of peanut butter. Mix the peanut paste and flour. Heat the mixture and stir in 3 cups chicken broth, the oysters, and the oyster liquor. Season with the dried pepper, and salt to taste. Simmer gently 10 minutes, stirring all the while to prevent scorching.

In *Resources of Southern Fields and Forests* (1863), Dr. Porcher stated both groundnuts and bemne (sesame seed) were valuable in making nutritious soup, and as a substitute for meat, and recommended them during war times to stretch inadequate food supplies. He stated they were already extensively used, and heartily recommended the seeds of *Glyceria fluitans*, or water fescue, for making nourishing soup and gruel. George Washington Carver included five peanut soup recipes in his 1940 bulletin.]

GUMBO SOUP. Cut up a chicken or any fowl as if to fry, and break the bones; lay it in a pot with just enough butter to brown it a little; when browned, pour as much water to it as will make soup for four or five persons; add a thin slice of lean bacon, an onion cut fine, and some parsley. Stew it gently five or six hours; about twenty minutes before it is to be served, make a thickening by mixing a heaping tablespoonful of sassafras leaves, pounded fine, in some of the soup, and adding it to the rest of the soup; a little rice is an improvement. If the chickens are small, two will be required, but one large pullet is sufficient.

TO PREPARE FILÉ FOR **GUMBO**. Gather sassafras leaves as late as possible in the season, before they turn red. Put them in the shade and open air to dry. When perfectly dry pound them, sift the powder, bottle it, and keep tightly corked.

CRAB **GUMBO**, 1878. Take one dozen large crabs, one cup of butter, and two or three onions. Wash the crabs, taking care to get them free from sand; take off the feelers and gills and divide the crabs into quarters; brown the onions in the butter with two tablespoonfuls of flour. Put in the crabs with about a hand-ful of chopped ham. Fill up the pot with three quarts of cold water. Just before serving

sift in about two tablespoonfuls of file.' Do not let it boil after the file' is put in. Serve with rice.

GIBLET SOUP, *Godey's*, 1862. The giblets must be well cleaned and singed; put them into some strong veal or gravy broth with shallots chopped very fine. Great care must be taken to keep the stock well skimmed; when properly stewed, put in a wine-glass of Madeira, salt, pepper, cloves, and mace, sifted fine and a little lemon pickle. When the rawness of the wine and lemon is gone so that no flavor predominates, pour it into a tureen and serve hot to table.

HARE SOUP, 1845. Take one that is good for nothing else, cut it up in pieces, and put it with a pound and a half of lean beef, two or three shank bones of mutton, well cleaned, a slice of lean bacon or ham, an onion, and a bunch of sweet herbs; pour on it two quarts of boiling water; cover the jar in which you put these, with bladder and paper, and set it in a kettle of water; boil till the hare is stewed to pieces, strain off the liquor, and give it one boil, with an anchovy cut in pieces, and add a spoonful of soy, a little Cayenne and salt. A few fine forcemeat balls, fried of a good brown, should be served in the tureen.

HARE OR RABBIT SOUP, 1874. Dissect the rabbit, crack the bones, and prepare precisely as you would the venison soup, only putting in three small onions instead of one, and a bunch of sweet herbs. Hares which are too touch to be cooked in any other way, make excellent game soup. Also, the large gray squirrel of the Middle and Southern States.

HARICOT SOUP. Cut some mutton cutlets from the neck; trim and fry them of a light brown; stew in brown gravy soup till tender. Have ready some carrots, turnips, celery, and onions; fry them in butter for some time, and clear the soup from the fat; then add the vegetables, color it, and thicken it with butter and flour; season, and add to it a little port wine and catsup. If the gravy be ready, the soup will require no more time to prepare than may be necessary to render the chops and vegetables tender, and is an excellent family dish. If wished to be made more highly flavored, put in a little curry powder.

FRENCH **HERB POTTAGE** FOR FASTING DAYS, Robert May, 1685. Take half a handful of lettice, as much of spinage, half as much of Bugloss and Borrage, two handfuls of sorrel, a little parsley, sage, a good handful of purslain, half a pound of butter, some pepper and salt, and sometimes, some cucumbers.

HERB SOUP, 1832. Wash and cut small twelve cabbage lettuces, a handful of chervil, one of purslane, one of parsley, eight large green onions, and three handfuls of sorrel; when pease are in season omit half the quantity of sorrel, and put a quart of young green pease; put them all into a saucepan, with half a pound of butter and three carrots cut small, some salt and pepper; let them stew closely covered for half an hour, shaking them occasionally to prevent their adhering to the pan; fry in butter six cucumbers cut longways in four pieces; add them with four quarts of hot water, half a French roll, and a crust of bread toasted upon both sides; and let the whole boil till reduced to three quarts, then strain it through a sieve; beat up the yolks of four eggs with half a pint of cream, and stir it gently into the soup just before serving.

A TUREEN OF **HODGE-PODGE**, OF DIFFERENT SORTS, 1845. Take either a brisket of beef, mutton, steaks, whole pigeons, rabbits cut in quarters, veal, or poultry; boil a long time over a slow fire, in a short liquid, with some onions, carrots, parsnips, turnips, celery, a fagot of parsley, green shallots, one clove of garlic, three of spices, a laurel leaf, thyme, a little sweet basil, large, thick sausages, and thin broth, or water. When done, drain the meat, and place it upon a dish, intermixed with the roots, sift and skim the sauce, reduce some of it to a glaze, if desired, cover the meat with it, then add some gravy on the same stew-pan, and broth sufficient to make sauce enough with pepper and salt. Sift it in a sieve, and serve it upon the meat. If brisket of beef is used, let it be half done before putting in the roots, which, if scalded first, will be more palatable. [A very similar recipe was found in a 1720 book.]

AN **IRISH STEW**. Cut six rather thick chops from the loin; when the square ends of the bones are cut off, these will probably weigh two pounds; lay them in an iron pot, and put four pounds of sliced potatoes, placed in layers, with the chops, and half a dozen small onions, with about a quart of water; cover the pan closely, and let them stew on a moderate fire for two hours, or until the potatoes have become nearly a mash, and absorbed all the water and gravy of the meat; the chops will then be found very tender, and the potatoes rich with the fat. The stew should be eaten hot, but without any kind of sauce.

JARDINIÈRE SOUP, Anna Collins, 1857. Wash a leg of lamb or veal of moderate size, and put it into four quarts of cold water. Boil it gently and when the scum rises, take it off carefully. Take of potatoes, cabbage, carrots, and onions, tomatoes, and turnips,

a tea-cupful of each, chopped fine. Add salt and pepper to your taste. Carrots should be put in first as they require most time for boiling and onions last. This soup must be boiled three hours.

JULIENNE SOUP, Anna M. Collins, 1857. This is a French dish and takes its name from the months of June and July; and to make it in reality as originally made; a small quantity of every description of vegetables should be used; including lettuce, sorrel, tarragon; however, some few sorts of vegetables mixed together make a most estimable soup. Weigh half a pound of vegetables, in fair proportions to each other; that is carrots, turnips, onions, celery, and leeks; which cut into small fillets an inch in length and the thickness of a running needle; when done wash, dry, and pan them in butter and sugar as before — preceding the same with the soup; adding just before it is done a little sorrel, cabbage, lettuce, and pease, if handy, but would be excellent without either.

KALE BROSE, Isabella Beeton, 1861. Half an ox-head or cow-heel, a teacupful of toasted oatmeal, salt to taste, 2 handfuls of greens, 3 quarts of water. Make a broth of the ox-head or cow-heel, and boil it till oil floats on the top of the liquor, then boil the greens, shred, in it. Put the oatmeal, with a little salt, into a basin, and mix with it quickly a teacupful of the fat broth: it should not run into one doughy mass, but form knots. Stir it into the whole, give one boil, and serve very hot.

KITCHINER'S CHEAP SOUP, initially published in 1829 as Dr. KITCHINER'S Receipt to Make a Gallon of Barley Broth for a Groat, 1864. Wash in cold water four ounces of Scotch barley, and put into five quarts of water, with four ounces of sliced onions; boil gently one hour, and pour it into a pan; then put into a saucepan from one to two ounces of fresh beef or mutton dripping. Dripping for this purpose should be taken out of the pan as fast as it drips from the meat; if suffered to remain in the pan it is apt to become rancid. If no dripping is at hand, melted suet will do, or two or three ounces of fat bacon minced fine. When melted in the saucepan, stir into it four ounces of oatmeal, and rub them together until they become a soft paste. Then add, by degrees, a spoonful at a time, the barley broth, stirring it well together till it boils. For seasoning, put in a tea-cup or basin a drachm of celery or cress seed, or half a drachm of each, and a quarter of a drachm of cayenne, finely powdered, or a drachm and a half of black pepper finely powdered, or half allspice; mix them smooth with a little of the soup; then stir it into the rest; simmer it gently another quarter of an hour, season with salt, and it is ready. The taste may be varied by any variety of herbs, or thickening with garlic or eschalot instead of celery; a larger portion of onions, or carrots and turnips, or rice, or paste, instead of oatmeal or barley.

PUREE OF **LENTILS**, Blot, 1869. The proportions vary according to taste; the more peas or lentils that are used with a certain quantity of broth, the thicker the potage will be and vice versa. Soak one pint of lentils (or split peas) in cold water over night and drain. Put them in a saucepan with a few slices of carrot, same of turnip, same of onion and salt. Cover with cold water, set on the fire and boil till done. Drain, and then mash through a colander. Put back on the fire with warm broth to taste–that is, to make the potage thin or thick, season with salt or pepper; boil gently for five minutes, turn into the soup-dish over croutons and serve warm.

GERMAN **LENTIL SOUP**, *Reform Cookbook*, Mrs. Mill, 1909. Scald 1/2 lb. German lentils for a minute in boiling water, drain and put on with quantity of boiling water required. Fry some onions, celery, and tomatoes— if to be had — in a little butter till brown, and simmer about 2 hours, and rub through a sieve. Add a little ground rice, corn flour, &c., to keep the pulp from settling to the bottom. A little milk or cream or ketchup may be added if liked.

LOBSTER SOUP. First prepare a veal stock with the following ingredients. A knuckle of veal, weighing from four to five pounds and one pound of lean ham, cut into pieces and freed from all the skin and fat upon it. Put these into an extremely clean saucepan and to every pound of meat add one pint and a half of water. Let these boil, and remove all the scum which rises to the surface, and continue to do so until the soup is quite clear; then add some salt, two onions, a head of celery, three carrots, white pepper, and a blade of mace. Let all simmer very gently together until the meat leaves the bones, which it should do in about five hours, when take the soup off the fire, strain it, and put it into a cool place until it jellies. Procure two fine hen lobsters, boil them, and when cold, pick the meat out of them, and break it into small, square pieces. Take out the spawn, pound it so as to separate it, pass it through a coarse strainer, and pound it again with a quarter of a pound of butter, which must be first melted before the fire. Break up the shells of the lobsters and stew them with a quart of the veal stock to which must be added a little ground allspice, beaten mace, and a small portion of scraped horseradish. Simmer these until the

strength of the ingredients has been extracted, then strain off the liquor. Pour it into a clean saucepan with another quart of veal broth, the meat of the lobster, the spawn, a dessertspoonful of anchovy sauce, and a half-pint of cream; let it simmer, but not boil, or else the color will be lost. Serve hot to table. Forcemeat balls are sometimes made with bread-crumbs, the meat out of the head of the lobster, and Cayenne pepper, mixed with two yolks of eggs; these are made up into small balls, fried, and added to the soup when it is going to table. N.B. Should the soup not be of the desired consistency add a little flour and butter.

TO MAKE A **LOBSTER SOUP**, An Original Scottish Receipt, 1736. Take 2 of the best Lobsters you can get, and boil them till they be of a red Colour, let them cool, then break open their Bodies, and pick out the white strings that is about the small Toes, take the Meat that is in the Body, but keep out all the red; take half of the Meat of the Lobsters, mince it very small, mix it with grated Bread, Mace, Nutmeg, Jamaica Pepper, a few Oysters and Muscles, then take the Yolks of 2 or 3 Eggs, work them up altogether in the shape of the body of the lobster, and fry it in clarified butter; take the other half of the Lobsters with a Mutchkin of claret wine, a Mutchkin of Oyster Liquer, a Pint of Water, a Piece of fresh Butter, boil all together an Hour, strain the Liquor thro a hair Search, put the fryed Lobster in the Middle of the Dish, put the Liquor about it, fry the Meat of the Toes in Butter, and garnish the Dish with them, keep it as whole as possible. [Mutchkin is a Scottish measure equal to 0.9 U.S. pints, or 0.42 liters]

LOBSTER SOUP, Burroughs, 1889. One large lobster or two small ones; pick all the meat from the shell and chop fine; scald one quart of milk and one pint of water, then add the lobster, one pound of butter, a teaspoonful of flour, and salt and red pepper to taste. Boil ten minutes and serve hot. [Simplified recipe.]

MACARONI SOUP. Take a quart of heavy gravy, break two ounces of Naples macaroni into pieces of little more than an inch long, putting them, by degrees, into a small portion of the boiling soup, to prevent them from sticking together, and let them boil until quite tender, but not soft or pulpy; from fifteen to twenty minutes if quite fresh, but nearly half an hour if at all stale. Vermicelli is used in the same manner. They will improve the consistence of the soup if the quantity above stated be added; but it is useless, and does not look well, to see, as at some tables, only a few strings of it floating in the tureen.

MACARONI SOUP, 1807. Boil a pound of the best macaroni in a quart of good stock till quite tender; then take out half, and put it into another stew-pot. To the remainder add some more stock, and boil it till you can pulp all the macaroni through a fine sieve. Then add together that, the two liquors, a pint or more of cream boiling-hot, the macaroni that first taken out, and half a pound of grated Parmesan cheese; make it hot, but do not let it boil. Serve it with the crust of a French roll cut into the size of a shilling. [Macaroni was a long hollow tube of pasta which was broken into desired size pieces when it was cooked. See Noodles below.]

MADEMOISELLE JENNY LIND'S SOUP, Eliza Acton, 1845. Wash a quarter of a pound of the best pearl sago until the water poured from it is clear. Then stew it quite tender and very thick in water or thick broth (it will require nearly or quite a quart of liquid, which should be poured to it cold, and heated slowly): then mix gradually with it a pint of good boiling cream, and the yolks of four fresh eggs, and mingle the whole carefully with two quarts of strong veal or beef stock, which should always be kept ready boiling. [Miss Bremer, a Swedish author, claimed the famous singer enjoyed the soup and thought it restorative to the voice.]

MATSO SOUP, *Practical Information in Jewish and Modern Cookery*, 1846. Boil down half a shin of beef, four pounds of gravy beef, and a calf's foot may be added, if approved, in three or four quarts of water; season with celery, carrots, turnips, pepper and salt, and a bunch of sweet herbs; let the whole stew gently for eight hours, then strain and let it stand to get cold, when the fat must be removed, then return it to the saucepan to warm up. Ten minutes before serving, throw in the balls, from which the soup takes its name, and which are made in the following manner: Take half a pound of matso flour, two ounces of chopped suet, season with a little pepper, salt, ginger, and nutmeg; mix with this, four beaten eggs, and make it into a paste, a small onion shred and browned in a desert spoonful of oil is sometimes added; the paste should be made into rather large balls, and care should be taken to make them very light.

MEG MERRILIES' SOUP, Miss Leslie, 1837. Take four pounds of venison, or if you cannot procure venison you may substitute the lean of fresh beef or mutton. Season it with pepper and salt, put it into a large pot, (break the bones and lay them on the meat,) pour in four quarts of water, and boil it three hours, skimming it well. Then strain it, and put it into another pot.

Cut up a hare or a rabbit, a pair of partridges, and a pair of grouse; or one of each, with a pheasant, a woodcock, or any other game that you can most easily obtain. Season them and put them into the soup. Add a dozen small onions, a couple of heads of celery cut small, and half a dozen sliced potatoes. Let the soup simmer till the game is sufficiently done, and all the vegetables tender. This is the soup with which the gipsy, Meg Merrilies, regaled Dominie Sampson. When game is used for soup, it must be newly killed, and quite fresh. [Meg Merrilies is from a poem by John Keats (1795–1821). Dominie Sampson was a school master in Sir Walter Scott's *Guy Mannering*, published in 1815.]

Meg Merrilies

Old Meg she was a Gipsy,
  And liv'd upon the Moors:
Her bed it was the brown heath turf,
  And her house was out of doors.

Her apples were swart blackberries,
  Her currants pods o' broom;
Her wine was dew of the wild white rose,
  Her book a churchyard tomb.

Her Brothers were the craggy hills,
  Her Sisters larchen trees—
Alone with her great family
  She liv'd as she did please.

No breakfast had she many a morn,
  No dinner many a noon,
And 'stead of supper she would stare
  Full hard against the Moon.

But every morn of woodbine fresh
  She made her garlanding,
And every night the dark glen Yew
  She wove, and she would sing.

And with her fingers old and brown
  She plaited Mats o' Rushes,
And gave them to the Cottagers
  She met among the Bushes.

Old Meg was brave as Margaret Queen
  And tall as Amazon:
An old red blanket cloak she wore;
  A chip hat had she on.
God rest her aged bones somewhere —
  She died full long agone!

MILK SOUP, Miss Leslie, 1837. Boil two quarts of milk with a quarter of a pound of sweet almonds, and two ounces of bitter ones, blanched and broken to pieces, and a large stick of cinnamon broken up. Stir in sugar enough to make it very sweet. When it has boiled strain it. Cut some thin slices of bread, and (having pared off the crust) toast them.

Lay them in the bottom of a tureen, pour a little of the hot milk over them, and cover them close, that they may soak. Beat the yolks of five eggs very light Set the milk on hot coals, and add the eggs to it by degrees; stirring it all the time till it thickens. Then take it off instantly, lest it curdle, and pour it into the tureen, boiling hot, over the bread.

MOCK BISQUE SOUP, *Good Housekeeping*, 1903. One quart of tomatoes cooked tender in one quart of water. Strain this and put the liquor back upon the stove; add one teaspoon of soda, a little butter, salt and pepper to taste, and, just before it is served, one quart of boiling milk. A little thickening and onion improves it for some tastes.

MOOR-FOWL SOUP, 1832. It may be made with or without brown gravy soup; when with the former, six birds are sufficient, when with moor-fowl only, boil five in four quarts of water, pound the breasts in a mortar and rub it through a sieve, put it with the legs, backs, and three more moor-fowl, cut down in joints, into the liquor, season with a pint of Port wine, pepper, and salt, and let it boil an hour. When only six birds are used, pound the breasts of three or four. [Chicken may be substituted.]

MULLAGATAWNY SOUP, 1851. Take a quarter of an ounce of China turmeric, the third of an ounce of cassia, three drachms of black pepper, two drachms of cayenne pepper, and an ounce of coriander seeds. These must all be pounded fine in a mortar, and well mixed and sifted. They will make sufficient curry powder for the following quantity of soup:

Take two large fowls, or three pounds of the lean of veal. Cut the flesh entirely from the bones in small pieces, and put it into a stew-pan with two quarts of water. Let it boil slowly for half an hour, skimming it well. Prepare four large onions, minced, and fried in two ounces of butter. Add to them the curry powder, and moisten the whole with broth from the stew-pan, mixed with a little rice flour. When thoroughly mixed, stir the seasoning into the soup, and simmer it till it is as smooth and thick as cream, and till the chicken or veal is perfectly tender. Then stir into it the juice of a lemon; and five minutes after take up the soup, with the meat in it, and serve it in the tureen. Send to table separately, boiled rice on a hot water dish to keep it warm. The rice is to be put in the plates of soup by those who eat it.

MULLIGATAWNY, 1893. This soup can be made from veal, chicken, or rabbit. Use one, or a mixture of two or more of these varieties of meat. It should always be highly seasoned with onions, curry powder, and apples, lemons, or some strong acid fruit. The best portions of the meat are usually removed as soon as tender and served with the strained soup. Rice should also be served with the soup. The following proportion is good: 3 pounds of chicken or young fowl, one pound veal bones, two onions, one tablespoonful beef drippings, four cloves, four peppercorns, two sour apples or the juice of one lemon, four quarts cold water, one tablespoonful curry powder, one teaspoonful each of salt and sugar.

MUTTON BROTH, *Godey's*, 1862. The best part for making broth is the chump end of the loin, but it may be made very good from the scrag end of the neck only, which should be stewed gently until it becomes tender, fully three hours, or longer if it be large, but not boiled to rags. A few grains of pepper, with a couple of fried onions, and some turnips, should be put along with the meat an hour or two before sending up the broth, which should be strained from the vegetables, and chopped parsley and thyme be mixed in it. The turnips should be mashed, and served in a separate dish, to be eaten, with the mutton, with parsley and butter, or caper-sauce.

If meant for persons in health, it ought to be strong, or it will be insipid. Cooks usually skim it frequently; but if given as a remedy for a severe cold, it is much better not to remove the fat, as it is very healing to the chest.

MUTTON SOUP. Cut a neck of mutton into four pieces and put it aside; then take a slice of the gammon of bacon and put it in a saucepan with a quart of peas and enough water to boil them; let the peas boil to a pulp, then strain them through a cloth and put them aside; add enough water to that in which the bacon to boil the mutton, slice three turnips, as many carrots, and boil for an hour slowly, adding sweet herbs, onions, cabbage, and lettuces chopped small; then stew a quarter of an hour longer, sufficient to cook the mutton, then take it out, and take some fresh green peas, add them, with some chopped parsley, and the peas first boiled, to the soup, put in a lump of butter rolled in flour, and stew till the green peas are done.

NOODLE SOUP, 1886. Add noodles to beef or any other soup after straining; they will cook in fifteen or twenty minutes, and are prepared in the following manner: To one egg add as much sifted flour as it will absorb, with a little salt; roll out as thin as a wafer, dredge very lightly with flour, roll over and over into a large roll, slice from the ends, shake out the strips loosely and drop into the soup.

NOODLE SOUP, Shuman, 1893. To make a good stock for noodle soup, take a small shank of beef, one of mutton, and another of veal; have the bones cracked and boil them together for twenty-four hours. Put with them two good sized potatoes, a carrot, a turnip, an onion, and some celery. Salt and pepper to taste. If liked, a bit of bay leaf may be added. When thoroughly well-done, strain through a colander and set aside until required for use. For the noodles, use one egg for an ordinary family, and more in proportion to quantity required. Break the eggs into the flour, add a little salt, and mix into a rather stiff dough. Roll very thin and cut into fine bits. Let them dry for two hours, then drop them into the boiling stock about ten minutes before serving.

NOODLES FOR SOUP, *White House Cookbook.* Beat up one egg light, add a pinch of salt, and flour enough to make a very stiff dough; roll out very thin, like thin pie crust, dredge with flour to keep from sticking. Let it remain on the bread board to dry for an hour or more; then roll it up into a tight scroll, like a sheet of music. Begin at the end and slice it into slips as thin as straws. After all are cut, mix them lightly together, and to prevent them sticking, keep them floured a little until you are ready to drop them into your soup which should be done shortly before dinner, for if boiled too long they will go to pieces.

NUT SOUP, *Holland Cookbook*, 1923. Two cupfuls shelled and blanched peanuts, 1 slice onion, 1 stalk celery, 1 pint white stock, 1 pint milk, 1/4 cupful butter, 1/4 cupful flour, seasoning to taste. Cook the nuts, with the onion and celery, in water to cover until tender. Press through a colander, add the stock, then the blended butter, flour and milk, and the seasoning. Reheat for a few minutes. Enough to serve six.

OCHRA GUMBO. Heat a large tablespoonful of hogs' lard or butter; stir into it, while hot, half a tablespoonful of flour; add a small bunch of parsley, a large onion, with plenty of ochra, all chopped up very fine. Let it fry till it is quite brown; then add a common-sized fowl cut up in small pieces, and let it all fry together until quite cooked. Then pour in about three quarts of hot water, and boil till reduced to one-half.

DRIED OKRA SOUP, Miss Corson, 1877. Pick over a quart of dried okra, wash it in cold water, and soak it over night in two quarts of cold water: be sure that the okra is tender, for if it is tough and full of woody fibre it will be exceedingly unpalatable. The next morning, pluck and singe a tender fowl weighing about three pounds, draw it [remove intestines] without breaking the intestines, wipe it with a wet towel, cut it in small joints as for a fricassee, and roll the pieces in flour seasoned with pepper and salt. Put a saucepan over the fire with a half cupful of lard and when the fat is hot put in the chicken, and fry it light brown; when the chicken is brown add it to the okra and water in which it has been soaking, with enough more water to together make four quarts of soup; season the soup palatably with salt and pepper and cook it gently until the chicken is tender. Meantime remove all bits of shell from a solid quart of large oysters, and strain their liquor, rub to a fine powder a tablespoon of dried sassafras leaves, sift the powder through a very fine sieve, and put it into the soup [filé], when the chicken is tender put in the oysters together with their liquor: let the soup again heat, and boil for two minutes, and then serve it very hot.

OCHRA SOUP. Boil a leg of veal with about four dozen ochras, an hour; then add six tomatoes, six small onions, one green pepper, a bunch of thyme and parsley, and let it boil till dinner-time. Season it with salt and red pepper to your taste, and if agreeable, add a piece of salt pork which has been previously boiled. The soup should boil seven or eight hours.

OLLA PODRIDA, Blot, 1869. Put four ounces of lean and fat salt pork into a saucepan and set it on a good fire; when partly fried, add half a pound of beef, same of mutton, same of veal (occasionally a chicken or partridge is added also), and four ounces of ham. Just cover the whole with cold water, and skim carefully as soon as the scum comes on the surface. When skimmed, add a gill of dry peas, previously soaked in water for an hour, half a small head of cabbage, pimento to taste, one carrot, one turnip, two leeks, three or four stalks of celery, same of parsley, two of thyme, two cloves, two onions, two cloves of garlic, ten pepper-corns, and some mace; fill up with water so that the whole is just covered, and simmer for about five hours. In case the water should simmer away too much, add a little more. When done, dish the pork, beef, mutton, veal, ham and chicken. Put the peas, cabbage, carrots, turnips, leeks, celery, and onions on another dish. Strain the liquor, pour it on croutons in the soup-dish, and serve the three dishes at the same time. [Blot stated that poorer families sometimes omitted the beef and veal, and that families of a higher social class served the soup first followed by the meat and vegetables as the next course.]

TO MAKE ONION SOUP, 1803. First, put a tea-kettle of water on to boil, then slice six Spanish onions, or some of the largest onions you have got; flour them pretty well, then put them into a stew-pan that will hold about three quarts, fry them in butter till they are of a fine brown, but not burnt; pour in boiling water sufficient to fill the soup dish you intend; let it boil, and take half a pound of butter rolled in flour, break it in, and keep it stirring till your butter is melted; as it boils, scum it very well, and put in a little pepper and salt; cut a French roll into slices, and set it before the fire to crisp; poach seven or eight eggs very nicely; cut off all the ragged part of the whites, drain the water from them, and lay them upon every slice of roll; pour your soup into the dish, and put the bread and eggs carefully into the dish with a skimmer. If you have any spinach boiled, lay a leaf between every piece of roll and send it to table.

ROBERT MAY'S **ONION POTTAGE**, 1685. Fry a good store of slic't onions, then have a pipkin of boiling liquor [broth] over the fire, when the liquor boils put in the fried onions, butter and all, with pepper and salt: being well stewed together, serve in on sops of French bread.

PLAIN **ONION SOUP**. Simmer turnips and carrots for two hours in weak mutton broth; strain it, and add six onions, sliced and fried; simmer three hours, skim, and serve.

RICH **ONION SOUP**. Put into a stewpan twelve onions, one turnip and a head of celery, sliced, a quarter of a pound of butter, and a quart of white gravy; stew till tender; add another quart of gravy, pulp the vegetables, and boil with the soup, strained, for half an hour, stirring it constantly; and, just before serving, stir in half a pint of boiling cream, and about eighteen button onions, nicely peeled, and boiled soft in milk and water. Season with salt. Spanish onions only are sometimes used; and the soup may be thickened, if requisite, with rice flour worked with butter.

OYSTER SOUP, 1807, Eliza Rundell. Make a rich mutton broth, with two large onions, three blades of mace, and black pepper. When strained, pour it on a hundred and fifty oysters, without the beards, and a bit of butter rolled in flour. Simmer gently a quarter of an hour, and serve.

OYSTER SOUP. Slice some onions, fry them a light brown in a quarter of a pound of butter, then put them on a fire to stew in some stock, as much as required for your soup. About half an hour is sufficient before you serve, add two or three dozen oysters, with their liquor strained. Thicken with the yolks of six eggs, and season it with white pepper, mace and salt; it must not boil after the eggs are put in, but thicken like custard. Any kind of good broth or stock makes the foundation. Some add to this, before the eggs are put in, a glass of white wine.

OYSTER SOUP, *Godey's*, 1866. To one hundred oysters, take one quart of milk, a half pint of water, four tablespoonfuls of flour, one teaspoonful of salt, a half cup of butter, and a little Cayenne pepper. Put the liquor of the oysters on to boil. Mix butter and flour and steam it in a bowl over the tea-kettle till soft enough to beat to a froth, then stir it into the liquor, after which add the other ingredients.

OX-CHEEK SOUP. An ox-cheek soup is made the same as an ox-tail soup. The broth is made with ox-cheek instead of with other parts of the beef, and the potage or soup made with the broth. A little wine — Madeira, Port, or Sherry — is sometimes added, as for mock-turtle. [This conversion appeared verbatim in several sources spanning a number of years.]

OX-TAIL SOUP, 1857. Take two tails, divide them at the joints, soak them in warm water. Put them into cold water in a gallon pot or stew-pan. Skim off the froth carefully. When the meat is boiled to shreds, take out the bones, and add a chopped onion or carrot. Use spices and sweet herbs or not, as you prefer. Boil it three or four hours.

PALESTINE SOUP. Take the liquor that a knuckle of veal has been boiled in, add one onion stuck with three cloves, a stick of celery, a sprig of parsley, a blade of mace, and a few white peppercorns; stew them altogether until reduced to the quantity required. In the meantime boil a sufficient number of Jerusalem artichokes to thicken the soup, in a small quantity of the liquor, until they are reduced to a pulp. Rub them through a fine sieve and add them to the rest of the liquor until it becomes the thickness of cream. Before sending it to the table add a little salt and cayenne pepper. Serve with fried bread.

PARTRIDGE SOUP, Eliza Rundell, 1807. Take two old partridges; skin them; and cut them into pieces, with three or four slices of ham, a stick of celery, and three large onions cut into slices. Fry them all in butter till brown, but take care not to burn them. Then put them into a stew-pan, with five pints of boiling water, a few pepper-corns, a shank or two of mutton, and a little salt. Stew it gently two hours; then strain it through a sieve, and put it again into a stew-pan, with some stewed celery and fried bread; when it is near boiling, skim it, pour it into a tureen, and serve it up hot.

OLD **PEAS SOUP**, *Godey's*, 1861. Put one and a half pound of split peas on in four quarts of water, with roast beef or mutton bones, and a ham bone, two heads of celery, and four onions; let them boil till the peas are sufficiently soft to pulp through a sieve, strain it, put it into the pot with pepper and salt, and boil it nearly one hour. Two or three handfuls of spinach, well washed, and cut a little, added when the soup is strained, is a great improvement; and in the summer young green peas in the place of spinach; a teaspoonful of celery seed or essence of celery, if celery is not to be had.

TO MAKE **PEA SOUP**. To four quarts of water, put in one quart of split peas, three slices of lean bacon (or a ham bone if at hand), and some roast beef bones, one head of celery, one turnip, and two carrots, cut into small pieces, a little salt and pepper; let all these simmer gently until the quantity is reduced to two quarts. Run it through a collender, with a wooden spoon, mix a little flour in water and boil it well with the soup, and slice in another head of celery, adding cayenne pepper, and a little more salt. Fry slices of bread in some butter until they assume a light brown color, cut them into small squares, and hand them with the soup, as well as a small dishful of powdered sage. [An 1867 receipt book stated asparagus soup could be made in basically the same way as pea soup by substituting asparagus for the peas. That book instructed that soup could be made from lima beans by following instructions for pea soup and substituting limas for the peas and that lentils could replace the peas in any pea soup receipt.]

For pea soup without meat: To make this soup without meat, put the peas, with some butter, two onions, seasoning, and a pint of water, into a stew-pan. Stew till the peas can be passed through a sieve, which being done, add to the liquor and pulp more after, half a pint of young peas, a few fine lettuce-leaves, and some mint, shred finely; stew all together till soft. Thicken with butter and flour, if requisite.

SPLIT **PEA SOUP**, *Godey's*, 1862. To three quarts of boiling water put a quart of whole or split peas; boil gently until the peas are dissolved, then pulp them through a sieve, and add three anchovies or a red herring, carrots, turnips, leeks, thyme, and sweet marjoram, and stew them together. Before serving add some catsup and slat, thicken the soup with butter, and send it up with fried bread. Frying the bread will make the soup richer. The addition of mushroom catsup will partly give it the flavor of meat.

PEPPER-POT. Stew gently in four quarts of water till reduced to three, three pounds of beef, half a pound of lean ham, a bunch of dried thyme, two onions, two large potatoes, pared and sliced; then strain it through a colander, and add a large fowl, cut into joints and skinned, half a pound of pickled pork, sliced, the meat of one lobster, minced, and some small suet dumplings the size of a walnut. When the fowl is well boiled, add half a peck of spinach that has been boiled and rubbed through a colander; season with salt and Cayenne. It is very good without the lean ham and fowl.

PHILADELPHIA **PEPPER POT**, *White House Cookbook*. Put two pounds of tripe and four calves' feet into the soup-pot and cover them with cold water; add a red pepper, and boil closely until the calves' feet are boiled very tender; take out the meat, skim the liquid, stir it, cut the tripe into small pieces, and put it back into the liquid; if there is not enough liquid, add boiling water; add half a teaspoonful of sweet marjoram, sweet basil, and thyme, two sliced onions, sliced potatoes, salt. When the vegetables have boiled until almost tender, add a piece of butter rolled in flour, drop in some egg balls, and boil fifteen minutes more. Take up and serve hot.

EDWARD KIDDER'S **PIGEON BISK**, 18TH CENTURY. Yor pigeons being clean washd & perboyld put ym into strong broth and stew ym yn make for ym a ragoo with gravy artichoke bottoms, potatoes & onions savory spice lemon juice & dicd lemon and bacon cut as for larding wth mushrooms truffles & pour ye broth into ye dish having dryd carved sippets yn place your pigeons & pour on ye ragooe wth 1/2 a pt of hott cream garnish it with scalded parsley beetroot & lemon.

JOHN EVELYN'S **BISK OF PIGEONS**. Take a legge of Beefe a knuckle of Veale boyle the[m] 6 or 7 houres be carefull to scume it when it boyles first up take the scum of[f] it as it rises for two hours after season it with whole peper cloves mace stick an Onyon with Cloves or a piece of Bacon tye a bunch of sweet herbs with a sprigged of Rosemary and a bay leafe or two and put it into the broth whilst it is boylying, get 2 or 3 Dozen of wild pidgeons ready boyle them in the broth about one houre before you mean to dish them take a Dozen of sweet breads not throats (pancreas, not thymus) parboyle them and cut them into dice as bigge as pease then take a frying pan put in a piece of sweet butter browne it with a slice of bacon and an Onyon strew in a little flower then put ye sweetbreads in frye them browne straine two ladles full of broth or gravy put it in a stew pan or pipkin with the sweetbreads sett them over a soft fire to stew, Blanche and slice two pallets (pullets) frye and stew them also Coxcombs when these are all in a readinesse get some [illegible word] crusts of French manchets dried also some farcemeant balls lett ye gravy be made with collops of beefe fryed browne in a frying pan straine broth to them sett them to stew with a Bunch of sweet hearbs and lemon all these being ready sett ye dish on a stove with ye dryed bread straine a ladle full of broth to it when you see the bread swell put in another ladle full of brot so by degrees fill the bottome then power on the sweetbreads then lay in order the pigeons round the Edge of the dish lay the pallats and Coxcombs the farced meat or balls and lemons Round the dish brim soe serve it in. [This soup is much more complicated and shows the range of variation in early recipes.]

A **POOR MAN'S SOUP**, *Field and Fireside*, 1863. Mince a handful of parsley leaves fine and steam over a little salt. Shred six green onions and put them with the parsley in a saucepan. Add three tablespoonfuls of oil and vinegar, with some pepper and salt. Pour over it a nice beef broth, and it is ready to serve. Note: Similar soups made from greens appeared in most cultures from antiquity.

PORTABLE SOUP. Put on, in four gallons of water, ten pounds of a shin of beef, free from fat and skin, six pounds of a knuckle of veal, and two fowls; break the bones, and cut the meat into small pieces; season with one ounce of whole black pepper, quarter of an ounce of Jamaica pepper, and the same of mace; cover the pot very closely and let it simmer for twelve or fourteen hours, and then strain it. The following day take off the fat, and clear the jelly from any sediment adhering to it; boil it gently upon a stove without covering the saucepan, and stir it frequently till it thickens to a strong glue. Pour it into broad tin pans, and put it in a cool oven. When it will take the impression of a knife, score it in equal squares and hang it in a south window, or near a stove. When dry, break it at the scores. Wrap it in paper, and put it closely up on boxes. There should always be a large supply of this soup as with it and catsup no one will ever be at a loss for dressed dishes and soup. [Portable soup receipts appeared multiple times from 1807 through the end of the century, many identical.]

PORTABLE SOUP, *The Frugal Housewife*, Susannah Carter, 1803. Take a large leg of beef, bone it, and take off the skin, and what fat you can; put it into a stoving pot, with a tight cover; put to it about four gallons of soft water, with six anchovies, half an ounce of mace, a few cloves, a half an ounce of whole white pepper, three onions cut in two, a bunch of thyme, sweet-marjoram and parsley, with the bottom crust of a two-penny loaf that is well baked; cover it close to let it have a constant fire to do leisurely for seven or eight hours; then stir it very well together, to make the meat separate; cover it close again, and in an hour try your broth in a cup, to see if it will glutinate; if it does, take it off, and strain it through a canvass jelly bag into a clean pan; then have China or well glazed earthen cups, and fill them with the clear jelly; put them into a broad gravy pan, or stew pan, with boiling water; set in the cups, and let them boil in that till they are perfectly glue. When they are almost cold, run a knife round them, and turn them upon a piece of new flannel, to draw out all the moisture; in six or seven hours turn them, and do so till they are perfectly hard and dry; put them into stone jars, and keep them in a dry place.

This is very good for soups, sauces, and gravies. When you intend to make it into soup, shred and wash very clean what herbs you have to enrich it, as celery, endive, chervil, leeks, lettuce, or indeed what herbs you can get; boil them in water till they are tender, strain them off, and with that water dissolve what quantity of portable soup you please, according to the strength you would have it. If you are where you can get it, fry a French roll, and put it in the middle of your dish, moistened first with some of your soup, and when your cakes are thoroughly melted, put your herbs to it, and set it over the fire till it is just at boiling; then dish it up and send it to table.

PORTUGAL BROTH (As made for the Queen), Knight. Make very good broth with some lean of Veal, Beef and Mutton, and with a brawny Hen or young Cock. After it is scummed, put in an Onion quartered (and if you like it, a clove of Garlick). Add a little Parsley, a sprig of Thyme, and as much Mint, a little Balm; some coriander seeds well bruised and a very little Saffron; a little salt, pepper, and a Clove. When all the substance is boiled out of the meat, and the broth very thick and good, you may drink it so. Or, pour a little of it upon toasted bread thin sliced, and stew it until the bread have drunk up all the broth, and then add a little more and stew. So you may add a little by little, that the bread may imbibe it and swell; whereof, if you drown it at once, the bread will not swell and make so good a jelly.

POT AU FEU, 1886. Take a good-sized beef-bone with plenty of meat on it, extract the marrow and place in a pot on the back of the range, covering the beef with three or more quarts of cold water; cover tightly, and allow to simmer slowly all day long. The next day, before heating, remove the cake of grease from the top, and add a large onion (previously stuck full of whole cloves, and then roasted in the oven till of a rich brown color), adding tomatoes or any other vegetables which one may fancy. A leek or a section of garlic adds much to the flavor. Rice may be added, or vermicelli for a change. Just before serving, burn a little brown sugar and stir through it. This gives a peculiar flavor and rich color to the soup.

PLAIN SAVOURY ENGLISH **POTAGE**, Sir Kenelm Digby Knight (1603–1665). Make it of Beef, Mutton and Veal; at last adding a Capon, or Pigeons. Put in at first a quartered Onion or two, some Oat-meal, or French barley, some bottom of a Venison-pasty-crust, twenty whole grains of Pepper: four or five Cloves at last, and a little bundle of sweet-herbs, store of Marigold-flowers. You may put in Parsley or other herbs.

Or make it with Beef, Mutton and Veal, putting in some Oat-meal, and good pot-herbs, as Parsley, Sorrel, Violet-leaves, etc. And a very little Thyme and Sweet-marjoram, scarce to be tasted: and some Marigold leaves, at last. You may begin to boil it overnight, and let it stand warm all night; then make an end of boiling it next morning. It is well to put into the pot, at first, twenty or thirty corns of whole Pepper. [Make sure the herbs are free of pesticides and other chemicals.]

AN ENGLISH **POTAGE**, Knight, 17th century. Make a good strong broth of Veal and Mutton; then take out the meat, and put in a good Capon or Pullet: but first, if it be very fat, parboil it a little to take away the Oyleness of it, and then put it into the broth; and when it hath boiled a little therein, put in some grated bread, a bundle of sweet herbs, two or three blades of Mace, and a peeled Onion. When it is ready to be dished up take the yolks of six Eggs, beat them very well with two or three spoonfuls of White-wine. Then take the Capon out of the broth, and thicken it up with the Eggs, and so dish it up with the Capon, and tostes of White-bread or slices, which you please; and have ready boiled the Marrow of two or three bones with some tender boiled white Endive, and strew it over the Capon.

POTAGE MEGRE OR A FASTING DAYES POTAGE, John Evelyn (1620–1706). Take a quart of Water 2 or 3 Onyons 2 slices of lemon salt whole peper mace and cloves tyed in a piece of tiffany lett these boyle halfe an houre then have spinache sorell white beets leaves cleane piked and washed and cut small so put them in, then put in a pint of blew peas boyled soft and strained a bunch of sweet herbs some pieces of bread lett these boyle together too houres then dish it with a French roule in the middle sliced round.

[To one quart of water, or better yet, broth, add 2 or 3 onions, 2 slices of lemon, salt, whole peppercorns, mace, and cloves tied in a piece of cloth. Let these boil half an hour and add spinach, sorrel, and/or white beet leaves which have been cleaned, washed, and coarsely chopped. Add a pint of peas. Evelyn may have been referring to a field pea which generally had a purple bloom, or to an *English* pea, which bloomed in a color other than the usual white. Either could be used in this recipe. Add sweet herbs to taste with half a cup of bread crumbs to thicken the soup. Simmer gently until all flavors have married and the vegetables are tender. Serve with slices of toasted French bread or croutons on top of the tureen.]

POTAGE À LA COLBERT, Blot, 1869. Scrape carrots and turnips and cut them in small dice or with a vegetable spoon; add green peas and string-beans, if handy, the beans cut in pieces; set them on the fire in a pan with cold water and salt; boil gently till done, and drain. Put them back on the fire, covered with warm broth, salt to taste, boil gently about two or three minutes, and turn into the soup-dish in which you have put as many poached eggs as there are or will be persons at table. A poached egg with soup is served to every person. Proportions of broth and vegetables vary according to taste.

CHICKEN AND RICE SOUP, OR **POTAGE À LA REINE**, *Miss Corson's Practical American Cookery*, 1877. To Three quarts of clear chicken broth add half a cupful of rice and boil it until the rice can be rubbed through a sieve with a potato masher; then return the broth and rice to the sauce pan; add enough hot milk to make them the consistency of cream, season them palatably with salt, pepper, and nutmeg, and as soon as the soup is hot serve it, as it grows too thick by standing.

Potage à la Reine was sometimes called **QUEEN SOUP**, *The Picayune Creole Cookbook*. 1 chicken, 1/4 pound of rice, 1/2 pint of cream, 1/2 blade of Mace, 1 sprig of thyme, 4 sprigs of parsley. 2 quarts of white veal [or chicken] broth, salt and pepper. Take a fine large chicken, clean it nicely and put it whole into a pot containing about 5 quarts of water. Add chopped onion, thyme, bay leaf, one carrot, a small bunch of celery, and one cup of rice. Let the chicken simmer well for about four hours, and when well cooked, take out the chicken from the broth. Cut off the white meat and cut it into pieces about the size of dice. Then strain the broth, mashing the rice well. Make a puree by taking another saucepan, putting in one tablespoonful of butter and one of flour, letting it melt together without browning. Moisten this well with the soup and a glass of milk, and season with salt and pepper and one-quarter of a grated nutmeg, and add to the broth. Then add the chicken, which has been cut up. Put in the tureen little dice of croutons of bread fried in butter. Pour the soup over and serve hot. The remainder of the chicken is used for croquettes, salad, etc.

[Of this soup Pierre Blot said, "*Potage à la reine* is the richest and most delicate potage that can be made and served at a well-ordered table. But little of it must be served on account of its richness." The version Blot wrote of most likely contained no rice as in the recipe above, but was, rather, a clear rich consommé. "Then came Henry IV (about 1589), who applied himself to making broth, and devised the *Consommé à la Reine* (chickens simmered, till cooked, in beef broth). It was after a grand dinner one day to some country nobles, and in answering a toast, that he pronounced that famous sentence which made him so popular with the peasantry, 'I hope that the day is not far off when all my subjects will have the *poule au pot*' (a chicken in the soup kettle with beef to make the broth)."]

POTATO SOUP MAIGRE, *Godey's*, 1861. Take some large, mealy potatoes, peel, and cut them into small slices, with an onion; boil them in three pints of water till tender, and then pulp them through a colander; add a small piece of butter, a little Cayenne pepper, and salt, and, just before the soup is served, two spoonfuls of good cream. The soup must not be allowed to boil after the cream has been put into it.

IRISH LEEK AND **POTATO SOUP**, 1884.

2 lb. potatoes	2 oz. butter
6 cups half stock and	
half milk, mixed	chopped chives or parsley
2 medium onions	
(or the same quantity of	
leeks if you prefer)	
6 rashers streaky bacon,	
fried crisp	salt and pepper to taste
1 cup light cream	

Melt butter in pan, add the sliced and peeled onions and cook lightly, but do not brown. Add the peeled and sliced potatoes, season to taste, and pour the milk over stock mixture over them. Cover and cook gently for about 1 hour. Either puree the soup, or use the back of a spoon to mash the potatoes against the side of the pot. Sprinkle the herbs on top with the crumbled bacon.

PUMPKIN SOUP. Take a quarter of a pumpkin, cut it in pieces, after removing the rind and seeds; add three pints of water, some turnips, celery, potatoes, parsnips cut in slices as for *julienne*; add two ounces of butter, salt and pepper; let it stew slowly till the vegetables are done and the pumpkin reduced to a marmalade. This is very good, but we prefer it made as follows: Boil in water about a quarter of a pumpkin till tender enough to pulp through a tammy: to this *puree* add milk enough to make it the proper consistency, a blade of mace, or a little nutmeg; about two ounces of butter must first be stirred into the pulp. Season it to taste with either a little Cayenne or white pepper, and salt. Before serving, add a few drops of orange-flower water, or you may in place add about an ounce of sweet almonds, pounded fine. It is a delicate and delicious soup maigre.

PUMPKIN SOUP, 1867. Peel, take away the seed and cut the pumpkin in small pieces; put them in a stewpan with water just enough to cover them, a little salt and white pepper, set on the fire and take off when cooked; throw away the water, mash and strain the pumpkin, put it back in the stewpan, cover with milk, add a little sugar, set it again on the fire, and take off at the first boiling; pour a little of it on *croutons* in the soup-dish, and keep covered in a warm place for ten minutes; then pour also the remainder in and serve.

QUEEN SOUP, Mrs. N.M.K. Lee, 1832. Pound in a marble mortar the white meat of three cold roasted fowls, and half a pound of sweet almonds blanched; add a little cream whilst pounding. Boil this with four quarts of well seasoned beef stock, then strain it, and just before serving it stir in a pint of cream.

RABBIT SOUP. An old rabbit is the best for this soup, but it should be a fine one. Skin it and put it into a saucepan with two quarts of new milk, and one quart of water, a quarter of a pint of rice, and eight moderate-sized onions, pepper, and mace and let all simmer together for two hours. Take the rabbit out of the saucepan, strain the liquor into a clean bowl, and then rub the rice and onions through a hair sieve to thicken the soup. Cut the rabbit into pieces, and put only the best and whitest parts in. Warm all up together, and serve hot in a tureen.

BROWN **RABBIT SOUP**, 1852. Cut down into joints, flour, and fry lightly, two full grown, or three young rabbits; add to them three onions of moderate size, also fried to a clear brown; on these pour gradually seven pints of boiling water, throw in a large teaspoonful of salt, clear off all the scum with care as it rises, and then put to the soup a faggot of parsley, four not very large carrots, and a small teaspoonful of peppercorns; boil the whole very softly from five hours to five and a half; add more salt if needed, strain off the soup, let it cool sufficiently for the fat to be skimmed clean from it, heat it afresh, and send it to table with sippets of fried bread. Spice with a thickening of rice-flour, or of wheaten flour browned in the oven, and mixed with a spoonful or two of very good mushroom catsup, or of Harvey's sauce, can be added at pleasure to the above, with a few drops of eschalot-wine, or vinegar; but the simple receipt will be found extremely good without them.

RICE SOUP, *New England Cookery*, 1808. To two quarts of water, put three quarters of a pound of rice, clean picked and washed, with a stick of cinnamon; let it be covered very close, and simmer till your rice is tender; take out the cinnamon, and grate half a nutmeg; beat up the yolks of four eggs, and strain them to half a pint of white wine, and as much pounded sugar as will make it palatable, put this to your soup, and stir it very well together: set it over the fire, stirring it till it boils, and is of a good thickness; then send it to table.

RICE SOUP, *The Brooklyn Daily Eagle*, 1877. Six ounces of rice, the yolks of four eggs, half a pint of cream, rather more than two quarts of stock. Boil the rice in the stock, and rub half of it through a tammy; put the stock in the stewpan, add all the rice and simmer gently for five minutes. Beat the yolks of the eggs, mix them with the cream (previously boiled), and strain through a hair sieve; take the soup off the fire, add the eggs and cream, stirring frequently. Beat it gradually, stirring all the time, but do not let it boil, or the eggs will curdle.

RICE SOUP, 1803. To two quarts of water, put three quarters of a pound of rice, clean picked and washed, with a stick of cinnamon; let it be covered very close, and simmer till your rice is tender; take out the cinnamon, and grate half a nutmeg; beat up the yolks of four eggs, and strain them to half a pint of white wine, and as much pounded sugar as will make it palatable, put this to your soup, and stir it very well together; set it over the fire, stirring it till it boils, and is of a good thickness; then send it to table. [Many period recipes call for what would to a modern palate be a large proportion of spice, so add the spice slowly, to taste, rather than the full amount called for.]

SAGO SOUP, *Godey's*, 1862. Take gravy soup, quite clear and brown; add to it a sufficient quantity of sago to thicken it to the consistence of pea-soup, and season it with soy and catsup; to which may be added a small glass of red wine. It may also be made *as a white soup* of beef, by leaving out the soy and catsup, and using white wine, adding a little cream and mace.

SAGO SOUP, Rufus Estes, 1911. Wash one-half cup sago in warm water, add desired amount of boiling broth (meat or chicken), a little mace, and cook until the sago is soft and tender.

SALMON BISQUE, *Good Housekeeping Cookbook*, 1903. Drain the oil from one-third can of salmon, remove the bones and skin and rub through a sieve. Add gradually one quart of scalded milk, one and a half teaspoons of salt, a dust of pepper, four tablespoons of flour and two tablespoons of butter rubbed into a paste to bind the soup.... Crab meat or lobster can be made into a bisque in the same way.

SALMON SOUP, Rufus Estes, 1911. Take the skin and bones from canned salmon and drain off the oil. Chop fine enough of the fish to measure two-thirds of a cup. Cook a thick slice of onion in a quart of milk twenty minutes in a double boiler. Thicken with one-quarter cup of flour rubbed smooth with one rounding tablespoonful of butter. Cook ten minutes, take out the onion, add a salt-spoon of pepper, one level teaspoon of salt and the salmon. Rub all through a fine strainer and serve hot. The amount of salmon may be varied to taste.

SALSIFY SOUP, *Blue Grass Cookbook*, 1904. One quart of salsify cooked in water until tender, 1 quart of new milk. Mash the salsify through a sieve. Add to boiling milk l tablespoon of flour and l large tablespoon of butter. Pour all together and season with salt and pepper. [Salsify is not as common as it used to be but it is available through heirloom seed companies. Many referred to salsify as oyster plant.]

SCOTCH BROSE OR CROWDY, 1864. Take half a pint of oatmeal; put it before the fire, and frequently turn it till it is perfectly dry and of a light brown. Take a ladle-full of boiling water, in which fat meat has been boiled, and stir it briskly to the oatmeal, still adding more liquor till it is brought to the thickness desired, which is about that of a stiff batter; a little salt and pepper may be added, if the liquor with which it was made was not salt. Kale brose is the same thing, but with the addition of greens, cut small, and boiled in the liquor.

SCOTCH BROTH, 1878. On four pounds of good beef pour one gallon of cold water. When this boils add one half pint of coarse barley. Then prepare and add one fourth of a small cabbage, four carrots, two parsnips, four turnips, one and a half pints of Irish potatoes; these should all be chopped fine before adding. Three quarters of an hour before serving, add one good-sized onion, cut fine, a sprig of parsley, and pepper and salt to taste. This should cook at least four hours. A pint of green peas is a good improvement, to be added with the onion, parsley, etc.

SCOTCH MUTTON BROTH, Eliza Rundell, 1807. Soak a neck of mutton in water for an hour; cut off the scrag, and put it into a stew-pot with two quarts of water. As soon as it boils, skim it well, and then simmer it an hour and a half; then take the best end of the mutton, cut it into pieces (two bones in each), take some of the fat off, and put as many as you think proper: skim the moment the fresh meat boils up, and every quarter of an hour afterwards. Have ready four or five carrots, the same number of turnips, and three onions, all cut, but not small; and put them in soon enough to get quite tender: add four large spoonfuls of Scotch barley, first wetted with cold water. The meat should stew three hours. Salt to taste, and serve all together. Twenty minutes before serving, put in some chopped parsley. It is an excellent winter-dish.

SCOTCH LEEK SOUP, Eliza Rundell, 1807. Boil a pound of the best macaroni in a quart of good stock till quite tender; then take out half, and put it into another stew-pot. To the remainder add some more stock, and boil it till you can pulp all the macaroni through a fine sieve. Then add together that, the two liquors, a pint or more of cream boiling-hot, the macaroni that first taken out, and half a pound of grated Parmesan cheese; make it hot, but do not let it boil. Serve it with the crust of a French roll cut into the size of a shilling.

To make **SCOTCH SOOP**, *Practical Housewifry*, 1764. Take a houghil of beef, cut it in pieces, with part of a neck of mutton, and a pound of French barley; put them all into your pot, with six quarts of water; let it boil 'till the barley be soft, then put in a fowl; as soon as 'tis enough put in a handful of red beet leaves or broccoli, a handful of the blades of onions, a handful of spinage, washed and shred very small; only let them have a little boil, else it will spoil the greenness. Serve it up with the fowl in a dish, garnish'd with raspings of bread.

SCOTTISH SOUP, 1736. Make strong broth of a thigh of beef, and a knuckle of veal cut in pieces, put it in the pot full of water, and some hail spice with a blade of mace, three great whole onions stuck with cloves, and a bunch of sweet herbs, boil all together on a slow fire, till the meat be all in pieces; then strain the broth thro' a callendar, and take some collops of beef, dust them with flower, and fry them very brown, take the Fat off the strong

broth, then put in the collops among the Broth, and let them soke over a slow fire; and have ready some pieces of tosted bread for your Soup Dish, put in a marrow bone in the middle, and pour in the broth on the bread, but keep out the collops, and serve it up. [Collops are small slices of meat.]

[In 1859 Mrs. Cornelius instructed that the richest soups were those made from multiple kinds of meat combined together such as mutton, veal, and beef. Her basic directions for making rich soup were to use a shank bone with little meat, boiling it one day for several hours, and the next adding vegetables and spices as desired. She advised having the butcher break the bone into pieces so that it would readily fit into the stock pot and offered suggestions for using the meat used to make the stock if it was not wanted in the soup.]

SEMOLINA SOUP. 5 oz. of semolina, 2 quarts of boiling stock. Drop the semolina into the boiling stock, and keep stirring, to prevent its burning. Simmer gently for half an hour, and serve. [From various sources including Beeton.]

SORREL SOUP. Put two ounces of butter in a saucepan, set it on the fire, and as soon as melted, put a good handful of sorrel in, stir for about one minute; then add a pint and a half of water, salt; boil two or three minutes; add again a little butter, give one boil and turn into the soup-dish in which you have *croutons*.

SOUP AND BOUILLE, Burroughs. Stew a brisket of beef with some turnips, celery, leeks and onions, all finely cut. Put the pieces of beef into the pot first, then the roots, and half a pint of beef gravy, with a few cloves. Simmer for an hour. Add more beef gravy, and boil gently for half an hour.

SOUP CRESSY, *The Jewish Manual*, Judith Cohen Montefiore, 1846. Grate six carrots, and chop some onions with a lettuce, adding a few sweet herbs, put them all into a stewpan, with enough of good broth to moisten the whole, adding occasionally the remainder; when nearly done, put in the crumb of a French roll, and when soaked, strain the whole through a sieve, and serve hot in a tureen.

SOUP DE POISSON, OR FISH SOUP, *Practical Information...*, 1846 Make a good stock, by simmering a cod's-head in water, enough to cover the fish; season it with pepper and salt, mace, celery, parsley, and a few sweet herbs, with two or three onions, when sufficiently done, strain it, and add cutlets of fish prepared in the following manner: cut very small, well-trimmed cutlets from any fish, sole or brill are perhaps best suited; stew them in equal quantities of water and wine, but not more than will cover them, with a large lump of butter, and the juice of a lemon; when they have stewed gently for about fifteen or twenty minutes, add them to the soup, which thicken with cream and flour, serve the soup with the cutlets in a tureen; force-meat balls of cod's liver are sometimes added.

SOUP LORRAIN, 1832. Boil in four quarts of water a knuckle of veal, one pound of lean beef, and one pound of mutton, a carrot, a turnip, a bunch of parsley, and a little lemon thyme, some salt and white pepper, till reduced to three, then strain the liquor; pound very finely in a marble mortar, all the white meat of a large roasted fowl, with a quarter of a pound of blanched almonds, and the yolks of four hard-boiled eggs; boil in milk the crumb of a French roll, and pound it with the other ingredients, and stir it all well into the soup; let it boil gently for ten minutes before serving.

SOUP LORRAINE, 1803. Have ready a strong veal broth that is white, and clean scummed from all then blanch a pound of almonds, beat them in a mortar, with a little water, to prevent their oiling, and the yolks of four poached eggs, fine lean part of the legs and all the white part of a roasted fowl; pound all together as fine as possible; then take three parts of the veal broth, put it into a clean stew-pan, put your ingredients in and mix them well together; chip in the crust of two French rolls well rasped; boil all together over a stove, or a clear fire. Take a French roll, cut a piece out of the top, and take out all the crumb; mince the white part of a roasted fowl very fine, season it with pepper, salt, nutmeg, and a little beaten mace; put in an ounce of butter and moisten it with two spoonfuls of your soup strained to it; set it over the stove to be thorough hot; Cut some French rolls in slices, and set them before the fire to crisp; then strain off your soup through a tammy or a lawn strainer, into another clean stew-pot; let it stew till it is as thick as cream; then have your dish ready; pout in some of your crisp bread; fill your roll with the mince, and lay on the top as close as possible; put it in the middle of the dish, and pour a ladleful of your soup over it; put in your bread first, then pour in the soup, till the dish is full. Garnish with petty patties; or make a rim for your dish, and garnish with lemon raced. If you please, you may send a chicken boned in the middle, instead of the roll; or you may send it to table with only crisp bread. [A lawn strainer is a cloth.]

SOUP MADE OF BEEF HOCK, *The Cook Not Mad*, 1831. Let the bones be well broken, boil five hours in eight quarts water, one gill rice to be added, salt sufficiently; after three hours boiling,

add twelve potatoes pared, some small carrots, and two onions; a little summer savory will make it grateful.

SOUP MEAT, *Godey's*, 1861. To make the soup very good, the meat of which there should be a large proportion, rather more than a pound into a quart of water, must remain in until it drops entirely from the bone and is boiled to rags. But none of these fragments or shreds should be found in the tureen when the soup is sent to table; they should all be kept at the bottom of the pot, pressing down the ladel hard upon them when you are dipping out the soup. If any are seen in the soup after it is taken up, let them be carefully removed with a spoon. To send the soup to table with bits of bone and shreds of meat in it is a slovenly, disgusting, and vulgar practice, and should be strictly forbidden, as some indifferent cooks will do so to save themselves the trouble of removing it. A mass of shreds left in the bottom of the tureen absorbs so much of the liquid as to diminish the quantity of the soup; and if eaten, is very unwholesome, all the nourishment being boiled out of it.

Mutton, however, need not be boiled to pieces, in the soup, which will have sufficient strength if the meat is left whole. A piece of loin of mutton that has been cooked in soup is to many persons very palatable. It is well worth sending to table.

SOUP WITHOUT MEAT, 1867. To one quart of water add three potatoes, three onions, three turnips, two carrots, a tablespoonful of rice or barley, and salt to the taste. Boil it down to one pint, then add a little parsley chopped fine about ten minutes before it is taken off the fire.

SOUP À LA FLAMANDE (Flemish), Isabella Beeton, 1861. 1 turnip, 1 small carrot, 1/2 head of celery, 6 green onions shred very fine, 1 lettuce cut small, chervil, 1/4 pint of asparagus cut small, 1/4 pint of peas, 2 oz. butter, the yolks of 4 eggs, 1/2 pint of cream, salt to taste, 1 lump of sugar, 2 quarts of stock. Put the vegetables in the butter to stew gently for an hour with a teacupful of stock; then add the remainder of the stock, and simmer for another hour. Now beat the yolks of the eggs well, mix with the cream (previously boiled), and strain through a hair sieve. Take the soup off the fire, put the eggs, &c. to it, and keep stirring it well. Bring it to a boil, but do not leave off stirring, or the eggs will curdle. Season with salt, and add the sugar.

SOUP À-LA-SAP, Eliza Rundell, 1807. Boil half a pound of grated potatoes, a pound of beef sliced thin, a pint of grey peas, an onion, and three ounces of rice, in six pints of water, to five; strain it through a colander; then pulp the peas to it, and turn it into a sauce-pan again with two heads of celery sliced. Stew it tender, and add pepper and salt; and when you serve, add also fried bread.

SOUP OF LAMB'S HEAD AND PLUCK, *The Cook Not Mad*, 1831. Put the head, heart and lights, with one pound pork into five quarts of water; after boiling one hour, add the liver, continue boiling half an hour more, which will be sufficient; potatoes, carrots, onions, parsley, summer-savory and sweet marjoram, may be added in the midst of the boiling; take half pound of butter, work it into one pound flour, also a small quantity summer-savory, pepper and two eggs, work the whole well together — drop this in small balls into the soup while hot, it is then fit for the table.

SOUPE-LORRAINE, *Royal Cookery*, 1710. Having very good Broth made of Veal and Fowl, and strain'd clean, take a Pound of Almonds, and blanch; Pound them in a Mortar very fine, putting to them a little Water to keep them from Oiling as you pound them, and the Yolks of 4 Eggs tender boil'd, and the Lean of the Legs and Breast of a roasted Pullet or two. Pound all together very fine; then take 3 Quarts of very good Veal Broth, and the Crust of 2 *French* Rolls cut in Slices; let them boil up together over a clear Fire, then put to it your beaten Almonds, let them just boil up together, strain it thro' a fine Strainer to the Thickness of a Cream, as much as will serve the Big-ness of your Dish; mince the Breasts of 2 roasted Pullets, and put them into a Loaf as big as 2 *French* Rolls, the Top cut off, and the Crum cut out; season your Hash with a little Pepper and Salt, scrape a Nutmeg, and the Bigness of an Egg of Butter, five or six Spoonfuls of your strain'd Almonds: The Bread that you put in the Bottom of your Soupe, let it be *French* Bread dry'd before the Fire, or in an Oven. So soak it with clear Broth, and a little of your strain'd Soupe; Place your Loaf in the Middle, put in your Hash warm; you may put 4 Sweetbreads, tender boil'd, about your Loaf, if you please. Let your Garnishing be a Rim, and slic'd Lemon. *So serve it.*

TO MAKE **SOPS FOR A CAPON**, *A Boke of Cokrye*, 1591. Take Tostes of Bread, Butter, Claret wine and slices of Orenges, and lay them upon the Tostes and Sinamon Sugar and Ginger.

SOUP, ROUGH AND READY, Anna Collins, 1857. Crack a shin-bone well, boil it in five or six quarts of water four hours. Take half a head of white cabbage, three carrots, two turnips, and three onions; chop them up fine, and put them into the soup with pepper and salt, and boil it two hours. Take

out the bone and gristle half an hour before serving it.

SOUP VERMISELLY, *Royal Cookery*, 1710. Take 2 Quarts of good Broth made of Veal and Fowl, put to it about Half a Quarter of a Pound of Vermiselly, a Bit of Bacon stuck with Cloves; take the Bigness of Half an Egg of Butter, and rub it together with Half a Spoonful of Flower, and disolve it in a little Broth to thicken your Soupe: Boil a Pullet or Chickens for the Middle of your Soupe. Let your Garnishing be a Rim, on the Outside of it Cut Lemon, soak your Bread in your Dish with some of the same Broth. Take the Fat off, and put your Vermiselly in your Dish. *So serve it.* You may make a Rice-Soupe the same Way, only your Rice being first boil'd tender in Water, and it must boil an Hour in strong Broth. Whereas, Vermiselly but half an Hour.

SPANISH SOUP, 1864. Take about three pounds of beef, off the leg or shin, with or without the bone — if with the bone, well crack it — a pound of knuckle of ham, or gammon. More than cover them with water, and when it boils skim it, and add a teaspoonful of pepper. The ham will probably make it sufficiently salt — if not, add a little. Let this simmer by the side of the fire until it is three parts done, which will take two hours and a half. And then well wash some cabbage plants, or small summer cabbage; cut these into small pieces, also onions cut small; a tea-cup full of rice, with a bit of eschalot; put these in the saucepan, and let it simmer a quarter of an hour or twenty minutes, until the rice is boiled enough. Then take it from the fire; separate the meat, vegetables, and rice, from the soup, and eat the soup before the meat. Separate the meat from the bones, and mix it with the vegetables. If the plants are too strong, scald them before putting them in the saucepan. In the summer, a few young peas make a great improvement. Leeks are better than onions, as you can have more in quantity of vegetables. The Spaniards use garlic. This will dine a family of seven or eight people.

SPANISH SOUP, Blot, 1869. Chop very fine two onions, one cucumber, peeled and seeded, a little pimento, two cloves of garlic, four sprigs of parsley, same of chervil, and mix the whole in a bowl with the juice of four tomatoes, and to which add two or three tablespoonfuls of bread-crumbs. Then season with oil, vinegar, salt, pepper, mustard, and water to taste and serve. The Spanish call it a cool and refreshing soup. [This is gazpacho, similar to an 1824 version.]

SPINACH SOUP, 1832. Boil in two quarts of water three sliced onions. Pick and clean as much spinach as will make two large dishes, parboil and put it in a cullender, to let the bitter water drip from it; let cold water run upon it for a minute or two, and then press out the water. Knead two ounces of fresh butter, with a table-spoonful and a half of flour, mix it with the spinach, which boil for fifteen minutes in the water and onions, then put in half a pint of cream or good milk, some salt and pepper, boil it for fifteen minutes more. In the season of green peas, a quart added with the spinach is a great improvement. It is common to boil a lamb's head and pluck with the soup, and with the peas it is quite as good without. Send them to table in the tureen. The soup is then called Lamb's Stove.

TO MAKE **SPINAGE-BROTH**, Knight, 17th century. Take strong broth, and boil a neck of Mutton, and a Marrow-bone in it, and skim it very well; then put in half a pound of French barley, and a bundle of sweet herbs, and two or three blades of Large-mace. Let these boil very well. Then mince half a peck of Spinage, and two great Onions very small, and let it boil one hour or more; season it with salt as you please, and send the Mutton and the Marrow-bone in a dish with French bread or Manchet to the Table.

SQUASH SOUP, 1867. Made as the pumpkin soup above. [Any squash would work in this soup, but winter squash would be best. See Appendix 1. Winter squash and pumpkin have been used interchangeably.]

SQUIRREL SOUP, *Kentucky Housewife*, 1839. Take two fat young squirrels, skin and clean them nicely, cut them into small pieces, rinse and season them with salt and pepper, and boil them till nearly done. Beat an egg very light, stir it into half a pint of sweet milk, add a little salt, and enough flour to make it a stiff batter, and drop it by small spoonfuls into the soup, and boil them with the squirrels till all are done. Then stir in a lump of butter, rolled in flour, a little grated nutmeg, lemon and mace; add a handful of chopped parsley and half a pint of sweet cream; stir it till it comes to a boil, and serve it up with some of the nicest pieces of the squirrels. Soup may be made in this manner of small chickens, pigeons, partridges, or pheasants.

STEW SOUP OF SALT MEAT, Beeton, 1861. Any pieces of salt beef or pork, say 2 lbs.; 4 carrots, 4 parsnips, 4 turnips, 4 potatoes, 1 cabbage, 2 oz. of oatmeal or ground rice, seasoning of salt and pepper, 2 quarts of water. Cut up the meat small, add the water, and let it simmer for 2 3/4 hours. Now add the vegetables, cut in thin small slices; season, and boil for 1 hour. Thicken with the oatmeal, and serve.

STRING-BEAN SOUP, Miss Corson, 1877. Remove the strings from a pint of beans, cut them in small pieces, wash them in cold water, and boil them in salted boiling water until they are tender enough to rub through a sieve with a potato-masher. After the beans are prepared in this way, put over the fire in a clean saucepan two table-spoonfuls each of butter and flour, and stir them until they are smoothly blended; then gradually stir in two quarts of boiling water; when the white soup thus made is boiling put in the beans, prepared as already directed; season the soup with two teaspoonfuls of salt, half a saltspoonful of white pepper, and the least dust of cayenne pepper; let it boil once.

SUMMER SOUP. Take a large neck of mutton, and hack it so as nearly to cut it apart, but not quite. Allow a small quart of water to each pound of meat, and sprinkle on a table-spoonful of salt and a very little black pepper. Put it into a soup-pot, and boil it *slowly* (skimming it well) till the meat is reduced to rags. Then strain the liquid, return it to the soup-pot, and carefully remove all the fat from the surface. Have ready half a dozen small turnips sliced thin, two young onions sliced, a table-spoonful of sweet-marjoram leaves picked from the stalks, and a quart of shelled Lima beans. Put in the vegetables, and boil them in the soup till they are thoroughly done. You may add to them two table-spoonfuls of green nasturtian seeds, either fresh or pickled. Put in also some little dumplings, (made of flour and butter) about ten minutes before the soup is done.

SWEET POTATO SOUP, 1922.

2 cupfuls baked sweet potatoes	1 quart scalded milk
2 tablespoonfuls melted butter or bacon drippings	2 tablespoonfuls flour
1 1/2 teaspoonfuls salt	1/2 cupful cooked rice, cinnamon

Bake potatoes and mash through ricer, measure two cupfuls, then put through ricer again with rice, stir hot milk slowly into mixture, return to double boiler. Brown flour, add fat, having smooth texture before adding to the hot milk mixture; do this gradually; season with salt and a dash of cinnamon.

SWISS WHITE SOUP, 19th century. Take a sufficient quantity of good broth for six people; boil it; beat up three eggs well, two spoonfuls of flour, and a cupful of milk; pour these gradually through a sieve or colander into the boiling soup;

add nutmeg, salt, and Cayenne pepper to your taste.

TOMATO SOUP, 1888. Put on a piece of beef, mutton, or lamb to boil; skim off all the fat before seasoning, then add two sliced onions, a little pepper and salt, two cloves and about a dozen tomatoes; boil three hours, then add a little thickening of flour. If the tomatoes are very sour, add a tablespoonful of sugar.

GREEN TOMATO SOUP, Rufus Estes, 1911. Chop fine five green tomatoes and boil twenty minutes in water to cover. Then add one quart hot milk, to which a teaspoonful soda has been added, let come to a boil, take from the fire and add a quarter cupful butter rubbed into four crackers rolled fine, with salt and pepper to taste.

TOMATOES AND RICE SOUP, 1867. Blanch half a dozen tomatoes, and skin them. Put them in a saucepan with a quart of broth, season with an onion sliced, three or four sprigs of parsley, one of thyme, half a dozen pepper-corns, a bay-leaf, two cloves, two cloves of garlic; salt and pepper. Boil gently till reduced to about two-thirds, when mash gently through a colander. It is understood by mashing gently, to mash so that all the liquid part shall pass through the colander, and the seeds and spices shall be retained in it and thrown away. While the tomatoes are on the fire boiling, set four ounces of rice on the fire with cold water and salt, and boil it till tender. Drain the rice, put it in a saucepan with tomato-juice after being mashed, set the saucepan on the fire, add one ounce of butter, a teaspoonful of sugar, boil, according to taste; to make the potage thin or thick, boil gently fifteen minutes, turn into the soup-dish and serve warm.

TSTCHY, Blot, 1869. Put four pounds of beef in a soup-kettle (the poorer classes always use mutton), with a chicken or a duck, half a pound of smoked pork, same of smoked sausages, four carrots, four cloves, twelve peppercorns, salt, two leeks, two onions, four stalks of parsley, and one of celery; cover the whole with fish broth, and set on a good fire. Skim off the scum carefully, and boil gently till the whole is done. As soon as either the chicken or duck, etc., is done, take it from the kettle. When the whole is cooked, drain. Put the liquor back in the kettle with a middling-sized head of cabbage cut in four, or about the same quantity of sour-krout, slices of carrots, and onions, pearl barley, *semoule*, or gruel; simmer about three hours, and it is done.

TURNIP SOUP, *New England Cookery*, 1808. Pear a bunch of Turnips (save out three or four) put them into a gallon of water, with half an ounce of white pepper, an onion stuck with cloves, three blades of mace, half a nutmeg bruised, a good bunch of sweet herbs, and a large crust of bread. Boil them an hour and a half, then pass them thro' a sieve; clean a bunch of celery, cut it small, and put it into your turnips and liquor, with two of the turnips you saved, and two young carrots cut in dice; cover it close, and let it stew; then cut two turnips and carrots in dice, flour them, and fry them brown in butter, with two large onions cut thin, and fried likewise, put them all into your soup, with some vermicelli; let it boil softly, till your celery is tender, and your soup is good. Season it with salt to your palate.

TURTLE SOUP, 1864. This recipe has been collated from the best authorities, to which is added our own experience. The day before you wish to serve up the soup it will be necessary to cut off the head of your turtle, and place it in a position to allow all the blood to be drained from it. The next morning open the turtle, being careful to do so without breaking the gall. After cutting all around the upper and lower shell, drain the water off, divide the meat in small pieces, and wash clean and carefully. Then put the shells in a large pot of boiling water, where you let them remain until you find they separate from the flesh readily; but no longer, as the softer parts must be boiled again. Keep the liquor and stew the bones thoroughly; after which it is to be used for moistening the broth. The flesh of the interior parts, and the four legs and head, must be cooked in the following manner. Mask the bottom of a large stew-pan with slices of ham, over which lay two or three knuckles of veal, according to the size of the turtle; and over the veal place the inside flesh of the turtle, covering the whole with the other parts of the turtle. Add to it about a gallon of the liquor in which the bones were stewed, and place on the fire until thoroughly done, which you must ascertain by sticking your knife into the fleshy part of the meat; and if no blood issue from it, add another gallon of the liquor. Then throw in a bunch of the stalks of sweet marjoram, lemon thyme, bay leaves, savoury, common thyme, and sweet basil; also a handful of parsley and green onions, and a large onion stuck with cloves, and a few grains of pepper. Let the whole stew until thoroughly done, say from three to four hours. The leaves of the herbs are to be used for making a sauce, to be described hereafter. When the larger portions of the turtle are done, place them aside to be used when wanted. When the flesh is also thoroughly done, drain on a dish, and make a white thickening very thin, and add to it through a tamis some portion of the liquor of the bones, and place on the fire until it boils; and, having arrived at the proper consistency, neither too thick nor too thin, set the stew-pan on the side of the stove, and skim off all the white scum and fat that arises to the surface. Then cut the softer parts — green fat and white meat — into dice of about an inch square (without any waste,) and add to the sauce, which must be allowed to simmer gently until sufficiently done, when it must be taken off, at the same time skimming it carefully. Then take the leaves of the sweet basil, sweet marjoram, lemon thyme, common thyme and winter savoury, together with a handful of parsley, some green onions, a large onion cut in four pieces, with a few leaves of mace; put the whole in a stew-pan with a quarter of a pound of butter. Let this simmer on a slow fire until melted, and add a bottle of Madeira and a small lump of sugar, and boil gently for an hour. Then rub it through a tamis, and add to your sauce, which you must boil until no white scum arises; then with a skimmer drain out all the bits of turtle, and put them into a clean stew-pan, and pass the sauce through a tamis into the stew-pan containing the turtle, and proceed as follows. Take out the fleshy part of a leg of veal, say about one pound, scrape off all the meat without leaving any of the fat or sinews in it, and soak in about the same quantity (one pound) of crumbs of bread, which, when well soaked, squeeze and put into a mortar with the veal, a small quantity of calf's udder, a little butter, the yolks of four eggs hard boiled, a little cayenne pepper, salt and spices, and pound the whole very fine. Then thicken the mixture with two whole eggs, and the yolk of a third; and, to try its consistency, put it in boiling hot water; if you find it too thin, add the yolk of another egg. When it is perfected, take one half of it, and add some chopped parsley. Cook it and roll into balls the size of the yolk of an egg; poach them in boiling water with a little salt. The other half must be made also into balls, and place the whole on a sieve to drain. Before serving your soup, squeeze the juice of two or three lemons, with a little cayenne pepper, and pour it into the soup. The fins may be served as a side dish, with a little turtle sauce. When lemon juice is used, be careful that the lemons are good; a musty lemon will spoil all the turtle, and too much will destroy its flavour.

TURTLE SOUP, 1888. Get a small live turtle weighing about twenty-five pounds, hang it by the hind legs or fins, cut off the head and let it bleed all day; then with a sharp knife part the two shells; remove the intestines; take all the meat from the shells, bones, and fins; cut each shell in four pieces and plunge, for a moment only, into boiling water to take the horny skin off.

For soup for twelve persons: Thicken three quarts of the broth with four ounces of flour browned in butter; boil half an hour, skim well; add half a pint of sherry wine, a gill of port wine, a pinch of red pepper, and enough of the turtle; boil ten minutes, skim again and serve with slices of pared lemon on a plate.

TURTLE BEAN SOUP, *Buckeye Cookery*, 1877. Soak one pint black beans over night, then put them into three quarts water with beef bones or small piece of lean salt pork, boil three or four hours, strain, season, with salt, pepper, cloves, and lemon juice. Put in a few slices of lemon, and if wished add slices of hard boiled egg. [Some turtle bean soup recipes, such as the one Jane Croly claimed to be the favorite of the Reverend Henry Ward Beecher, contained tomatoes instead of the cloves and lemon juice. Miss Corson flavored her version with dried marjoram and an onion stuck with cloves. Farmers were experimenting with turtle beans in the 1850s and they seem to have been primarily used in soup. In his 1863 treatise on field and garden vegetables Fearing Burr referred to them as soup beans. On December 13, 1855, the *Geneva Weekly Press* carried a similar recipe instructing the beans be mashed through a colander and returned to the broth with thyme, quartered boiled eggs, and lemon slices. The writer claimed few would be able to tell it from turtle soup.]

MOCK TURTLE SOUP, 1805. Take the upper from the lower part of a calf's head, and put both in a gallon of water and boil till tender. Strain the liquor, let it stand till next day, and take off the fat. Hang it over the fire three-quarters of an hour before serving it, and season it with salt, cloves, pepper, mace, and sweet herbs, tied in a bag. Add half a pint of rich gravy. Darken it with browned flour or fried sugar. Then put in the yolks of eight eggs boiled hard, the juice of two lemons, and force-meat balls. When ready to serve, add half a pint of wine.

VEAL SOUP. Skin four pounds of a knuckle of veal; break it and cut it small; put it into a stewpan with two gallons of water; when it boils skim it, and let it simmer till reduced to two quarts; strain and season it with white pepper, salt, a little mace, a dessertspoonful of lemon-juice, and thicken it with a large tablespoonful of flour, kneaded with an ounce of butter.

VEAL SOUP, *The Cook Not Mad*, 1831. Take a shoulder of veal, boil in five quarts water three hours, with two spoons rice, four onions, six potatoes, and a few carrots, sweet marjoram, parsley and summer-savory, salt and pepper sufficiently; half a pound butter worked into four spoons flour to be stirred in while hot.

VEGETABLE SOUP. To a quarter of a pound of fresh butter, boiling hot, add onions chopped very fine. When they are quite soft, throw in spinach, celery, carrots, kidney beans, etc., also chopped fine, with green peas and any other vegetables that you can collect. Stir them well in the onions and butter till they begin to dry. Have ready a teakettle of boiling water, and pour about a pint at a time over your vegetables, till you have as much as you want. Serve up with bread or toast in the bottom of the dish. Pepper and salt to your taste.

VENISON SOUP. Take four pounds of freshly-killed venison, cut off from the bones, and one pound of ham in small slices. Add an onion, minced, and black pepper to your taste. Put only as much water as will cover it, and stew it gently for an hour, keeping the pot closely covered. Skim it well, and pour in a quart of boiling water. Add a head of celery, cut small and three blades of mace. Boil it gently two hours and a half; then put in a quarter of a pound of butter, cut small and rolled in flour, and half a pint of port or Madeira. Let it boil a quarter of an hour longer, and send it to the table with the meat in it.

TO MAKE VERJUYCE, Robert May, 1685. Take crabs [crabapples] as soon as the kernels turn black, and lay them in a heap to sweat, then pick them from stalks and rottenness; and then in a long trough with stamping beetles stamp them to mash, and make a bag of course hair-cloth as square as the press; fill it with stamped crabs, and being well pressed, put it up in a clean barrel or hogs-head.

VERMICELLI SOUP, Godey's, 1861. Put into a stewpan one and a half pound of lean veal, a small slice of lean ham, a bunch of sweet herbs, a head of celery, an onion, some whole white pepper, a blade of mace, and a quarter of a pound of butter; set the pan over a clear fire, taking care the articles do not burn; then thicken two quarts of white gravy, and pour it into the pan, adding a few mushroom trimmings; when it boils, set it aside, remove the scum, and fat, and strain the soup upon some vermicelli which has been soaked a few hours in cold water, and stewed in strong broth. This soup is sometimes served with a few blanched chervil leaves in it.

VERMICELLI SOUP. Boil tender one half pound of vermicelli in a quart of rich gravy; take half of it out, and add it to more gravy; boil till the vermicelli can be pulped through a hair sieve. To both put a pint of boiling cream, a little salt and a quarter pound of Parmesan cheese. Serve with rasped bread. Add two or three eggs if you like.

BROWN VERMICELLI SOUP. It is made in the same manner [as Vermicelli Soup, above] leaving out the eggs and cream, and adding in one quart of strong beef gravy.

TO MAKE VERMICELLY SOOP, Practical House-wifry, 1764. Take a neck of beef, or any other piece; cut off some slices, and fry them with butter 'till they are very brown; wash your pan out every time with a little of the gravy; you may broil a few slices of the beef upon a grid-iron: put all together into a pot, with a large onion, a little salt, and a little whole pepper; let it stew 'till the meat is tender, and skim off the fat in the boiling; then strain it into your dish, and boil four ounces of vermicelli in a little of the gravy 'till it is soft: Add a little stew'd spinage; then put all together into a dish, with toasts of bread; laying a little vermicelli upon the toast. Garnish your dish with creed rice and boil'd spinage, or carrots slic'd thin.

WHITE SOUP. General directions for white stock have been given, but to prevent mistake, take a knuckle of veal, separated into three or four pieces, a slice of ham as lean as possible, a few onions, thyme, cloves, and mace and stew twelve or fourteen hours, until the stock is rich as the ingredients can make it; an old fowl will make it much richer if added. This soup must be made the day before it is required; when removed from the fire, after being sufficiently stewed, let it cool, and then remove the fat, add to it four ounces of pounded blanched almonds, let it boil slowly, thicken it with half a pint of cream and an egg; it should boil slowly for half an hour and then be served.

A RICH WHITE SOUP, 1845. Boil in a small quantity of water a knuckle of veal, a scrag of mutton, mace, white pepper, two or three onions and sweet herbs, the day before you want the soup. Next day take off the fat, and put the jelly into a sauce-pan, with a quarter of a pound of sweet almonds, blanched, and beaten to a paste in a mortar with a little water to prevent oiling, and put to it a piece of stale white bread, a bit of cold veal, or white chicken. Beat these all to paste, with the almond paste.

WHITE SOUP WITHOUT MEAT, 1867. Put two quarts of water into a clean saucepan, the crumb of a small baker's loaf, a bunch of sweet herbs, some whole grains of pepper, two or three cloves, an onion chopped fine and a little salt. Let it boil half an hour. Then take the white parts of celery, endive, and lettuce, cut them into pieces, boil them in the soup until quite smooth. Strain the soup, set it over the fire again, and when it begins to boil add a lump of butter rolled in a little flour; let it boil a few minutes more and serve.

Appendix III:
Some Early Cookery Books

Italy

Bartolomeo Sacchi (Platina). *De honesta voluptate* (On honest pleasure). The world's first printed cookery book. 1474. Thought to have incorporated a previous work by Martino of Como.

Cristoforo di Messisbugo. *Banchetti*. 1549.

Romoli. *La Singolare dottrina...Dell'ufficio dello Scalco*.

Bartolomeo Scappi. *Opera* (Works). 1570.

Bartolomeo Stefani. *L'Arte dib en cucinare*. 1662.

Antonio Latini. *Lo scalco alla moderna*. 1692.

Francesco Gaudencio. *Il Panunto Toscano*. Early 18th century, but not located and published until 1974.

Vincenzo Corrado. *Cuoco Galante*. 1778.

England

This Is the Boke of Cokery, and *Here Begynneth the Boke of Kervynge*. Ca. 1500. Author unknown, printed by Wynkyn de Worde.

A Proper Newe Booke of Cokerye. Ca. 1557.

Thomas Dawson. *The Good Huswifes Jewell*. 1596.

John Murrell. *A New Book of Cookerie*. 1615.

Gervase Markham. *The English Housewife*. 1615.

Robert May. *The Accomplisht Cook*. 1660.

William Rabisha. *The Whole Body of Cookery Dissected*. 1661.

Sir Kenelm Digby. *The Closet of the Eminently Learned Sir Kenelme Digbie Opened*. 1669.

Hannah Woolley. *The Cook's Guide. The Queen-Like Closet. Gentlewoman's Companion:, or, A Guide to the Female Sex*. Last published 1673.

Patrick Lamb. *Royal-Cookery: Or, The Compleat Court-Cook*. 1710.

Charles Carter. *The Complete Practical Cook: Or, A New System of the Whole Art and Mastery of Cookery*. 1730.

E. Smith. *The Compleat Housewife*. 1727.

Adam's Luxury and Eve's Cookery. 1744.

Hannah Glasse. *The Art of Cookery Made Plain and Easy*. 1747.

Martha Bradley. *The British Housewife*. 1756.

France

Le Menagier de Paris.

Chiquart. *Du Fait de Cuisine*.

Taillevent. *Le Viandier*.

Unknown. *Le Grand Cuisinier de toute cuisine*. 1540.

Lancelot de Casteau. *Ouverture de cuisine*. 1604.

François Pierre La Varenne. *Cuisinier Francois*. 1651.

Pierre de Lune. *Le Cuisinier*. 1656.

Unknown. *L'Art de Bien Traiter*. 1674.

Massialot. *Le Cuisinier roïal et bourgeois*. 1691.

Vincent La Chapelle. *Cuisinier moderne*. 1735.

Francis Marin. *Les Dons de Comus: ou L'Art de cuisine*. 1739.

Spain

Ruperto da Nola. *Libro di Cucina*. 1520 and 1525.

Diego Granado. *Libro del arte de cozina* (Book on the Art of Cooking). Ca. 1598.

Domingo Hernandez de Maceras. *Libro del Arte de Cozina*. 1607.

Francisco Martinez Montino. *Arte de Cocina, Pasteleria, Vizcocheria, y Conserveria* (Art of Cooking and Making Pastry, Biscuits, and Conserves). 1611.

Juan de Altamiras. *Nuevo arte de cocina*. 1758.

Dutch

Een Notabel Boecxhen van Cokeryen (Notable Book of Cookery). Ca. 1508.

De Verstandige Kock (The Sensible Cook). 1667.

Germanic

Koch und Kellerey, von allen Speisen unnd Getrancken (A Useful Booklet About the Nutrition of Humans, Cooking and Storage of all Foods and Drink). 1545.

Kuchenmeisterei (Mastery of the Kitchen). 1485.

Ain nützlichs buchlin von der Speis der Menschen ca. 1500.

Max Rumpolt. *Ein New Kochbuch* (A New Cookbook). 1581.

Ain sehr Künstlichs und Fürtrefflichs Kochbuck von allerlay Speysen (A Very Fancy and Excellent Cookbook of all Kinds of Foods). 1559.

Appendix IV:
Sources for Cookery Items

Thistle Dew Books
by Victoria Rumble

www.thistledewbooks.com

Victoria's Home Companion; Or, The Whole Art of Cooking is a 304-page comprehensive study of American foods and cooking techniques through 1900. See the website for reviews.

Outdoor Recreation and Leisure in 19th-Century America is 340 pages and covers all aspects of outdoor life, and the foods that accompanied them. See the website for reviews.

Heirloom foods

Rancho Gordo, www.ranchogordo.com. Heirloom beans, corn, and chilies.

Purcell Mountain Farms, www.purcellmountain farms.com. Dried heirloom beans and lentils, grains, rice, etc. Some organic.

Heirloom Seeds and Plants

Baker Creek Heirloom Seed Co. Wide selection. http://rareseeds.com

Cook's Garden. www.cooksgarden.com

J. L. Hudson, Seedsman. Box 337, La Honda, CA 94020-0037. www.jhudsonseeds.net

Excellent source of heirloom vegetables and herbs, some rare and hard-to-find varieties. JLH@JL HudsonSeeds.net

Mountain Valley Growers. 559-338-2775. www. mountainvalleygrowers.com. Herbs.

Ingredients

Verjuice. www.Igourmet.com, or www.amazon. com gourmet foods section. Igourmet has a huge selection of cheeses, oils, vinegars including must, regional foods, etc.

Barry Farm. Organic beans, spices, cereals, dried fruits and vegetables, flours, grains, etc. Large variety of hard-to-find hot cereals. www.barry-farm.com.

Historic Reproduction Utensils

Chris Henderson's Redware. Trained at Old Sturbridge Village, this potter produces numerous items though there may be a waiting list for some items. www.hendersonsredware.com

Redware by Julia Smith. Mugs, pitchers, bowls, colanders, porringers, and pots and skillets. http://www.juliasmith.com/historicpottery/redware.htm

Rick Bowman Replica Pottery. replicapottery@ msn.com. No web site. Replica Southeastern native pottery.

Tinware

Backwoods Tin. www.backwoodstin.com. Avoid stainless for use in a historic setting.

Otter Tinware. Various home and kitchen items. http://mysite.verizon.net/ottertin/octinw1.html

Carl Giordano Tinware. Various home and kitchen items including kettles. http://www.cg-tinsmith.com/catalog2.htm

Woodenware

Beaver Buckets. Basins, buckets, washboards, and more. www.beaverbuckets.com

Miscellaneous housewares

Dog River Glassworks. Sellers of crockery, crystal, and tableware. www.dogriverglassworks.com

Used Books

Abebooks.com, American Book Exchange.

Magazine

Early American Life. In addition to excellent articles they publish an annual directory of master craftspeople that can be accessed online. http://www.ealonline.com/index.php

Chapter Notes

Preface

1. Mennell, Stephen. *All Manners of Food*. 1996. The author quoted data compiled from court rolls and tenant possessions. The author is in agreement that the most common soup vegetables during this era were onions, cabbage, beans or peas, and parsley.
2. Vaultier, Roger. "La gastronomie regionale en France pendant la revolution." *Grandgousier*. 1940. Quoted by Stephen Mennell in *All Manners of Food*.

Chapter 1

1. Portuguese fable, author unknown.
2. Tylor, Edward Burnet. *Researches into the Early History of Mankind and the Development of Civilization*. London, 1865.
3. Davies, R. W. "The Roman Military Diet." *Britannia 2* (1971), pp. 122–142.
4. Smith, Eliza. *The Compleat Housewife or Accomplish'd Gentlewoman's Companion*. London, 1727.
5. Simmons, Amelia. American Cookery, or the art of dressing viands, fish, poultry, and vegetables, and the best modes of making pastes, puffs, pies, tarts, puddings, custards, and preserves, and all kinds of cakes, from the imperial plum to plain cake: Adapted to this country, and all grades of life. 1798. Reprint, Bedford, Mass.: Applewood Books, 1996.
6. Carter, Susannah. The Frugal Housewife, or, Complete Woman Cook. New York, 1803.
7. Randolph, Mary. The Virginia Housewife, or, Methodical Cook. Philadelphia: E. H. Butler and Co., 1860.
8. Lee, N. M. K. The Cook's Own Book and Housekeeper's Register. Boston, 1832.
9. Ewing, Emma P. Soup and Soup Making. Chicago and New York, 1882.
10. Brooklyn Daily Eagle, April 20, 1901.
11. Ibid.
12. Walsh, William Shepard. The Handy Book of Literary Curiosities. 1892. Reprint, Philadelphia: Lippincott, 1906.

Chapter 2

1. Goodrich, Samuel Griswold. A History of All Nations from the Earliest Periods to the Present Time. Auburn, 1851; Freeman, Edward Augustus. The Chief Periods of European History. London, 1886; Chastellux, François Jean, marquis de. An Essay on Public Happiness, Investigating the State of Human Nature, Under Each of its Particular Appearances Through the Several Periods of History. London: Printed for T. Cadell, 1774.
2. Stearns, Peter N. Encyclopedia of World History, 2001; Faiella, Graham. The Technology of Mesopotamia, 2005.
3. Brier, Bob, and Hobbs, A. Hoyt. Daily Life of the Ancient Egyptians. 1999.
4. Ibid.
5. Wilkinson, John Gardner. The Manners and Customs of the Ancient Egyptians. 1878.
6. Tannahill, Reay. Food in History, 1973; Pennell, Robert F. Ancient Greece from the Earliest Times down to 146 BC. Boston, 1893.
7. Vehling, Joseph. Apicius: Cookery and Dining in Imperial Rome, 1977, p. 6.
8. Wheeler, Edward Jewett. Current Literature. Vol. XXXI. New York, 1901.
9. Johnson, Samuel. To the Hebrides. 1773. Reprint, Edinburgh, 2007, p. 109.
10. Fowler, John Coke. William the Conqueror and the Feudal System. 1880; Howell, Thomas Bayly. A Complete Collection of State Trials and Proceedings for High Treason. London, 1817; Joyce, Patrick Weston. A Social History of Ancient Ireland. Vol. 1. New York, 1903.
11. Ibid.
12. Rumble, Victoria. Outdoor Recreation and Leisure in 19th Century America. 2007. Florence, Ala., p. 202.
13. Tannahill, p. 97.
14. Hallam, Henry. View of the State of Europe During the Middle Ages. New York: W.J. Widdleton, 1872. Reprinted 1903.
15. Fowler, John Coke. William the Conqueror and the Feudal System. 1880.
16. Ibid.; Putney, Albert H. United States Constitutional History and Law. Chicago: Illinois Book Exchange, 1908.

Chapter 3

1. Bard, Kathryn, and Shubert, Stephen Blake. Encyclopedia of Archaeology of Ancient Egypt, 1999. See also Shaw, Ian. The Oxford History of Ancient Egypt. Estimates differ greatly as to the date civilization began, but the consensus seems to put the inception of modern civilization at roughly 3100 BC.
2. Nutrition and Well-Being A to Z. http://www.faqs.org/nutrition/A-Ap/Africans-Diets-of.html

3. Southern Quarterly Review 2, no. 3 (July 1842).

4. Ibid.

5. Wilkinson, John. A Popular Account of the Ancient Egyptians. New York, 1854.

6. Bellows, Henry. The Old World in its New Face, 1867–1868. New York, 1869.

Chapter 4

1. All biblical quotations are taken from the King James Version.

2. Dalby, Andrew. Dangerous Tastes, the Story of Spices. University of California Press, 2002; Encyclopaedia Britannica, 1911.

3. Ancient Egyptian Fishing. http://www.mnsu.edu/emuseum/prehistory/egypt/dailylife/fishing_egypt.htm.

4. King James Bible.

5. Balfour, John Hutton. The Plants of the Bible, Trees, and Shrubs. London, Edinburgh, and New York, 1885.

6. Long, George, and Dunglison, Robley. An Introduction to the Study of Grecian and Roman Geography. Charlottesville, Va., 1829.

Chapter 5

1. Southern Literary Messenger 21, no. 12 (December 1855).

2. Willson, Marcius. Ancient and Modern History. New York, 1864.

3. Southern Literary Messenger 21, no. 12 (December 1855).

4. Ibid.

5. Ibid.

6. Ibid.

7. Appleton's Journal 10, no. 58 (April 1881), pp. 158, 320–325.

8. Southern Literary Messenger 21, no. 12 (December 1855).

9. Ibid.

10. Appleton's Journal 10, no. 58 (April 1881), pp. 320–325.

11. Ibid.

12. Ibid.

13. Detienne, Marcel, and Vernant, Jean Pierre. Herodotus, quoted in The Cuisine of Sacrifice Among the Greeks. Chicago, 1989.

14. Feild, Rachael. Irons in the Fire. Devon, U.K.: Marlborough, 1984.

15. O'Kelly, M. J. "Excavations and Experiments in Early Irish Cooking-Places." Journal of the Royal Society of Antiquities in Ireland, 1954, pp. 84, 105–155.

16. Tannahill, Reay. Food in History. New York: Stein and Day, 1973.

17. Solbrig, Otto T., and Solbrig, Dorothy J. So Shall You Reap: Farming and Crops in Human Affairs. Washington, D.C., 1994.

18. Ibid.

19. Vegetarians in Paradise. http://www.vegparadise.com/highestperch29.html.

20. Emerson, Ralph Waldo, and Goodwin William Watson, ed. Plutarch's Morals. Washington, 1870.

21. Adams Sentinel, July 1, 1857.

22. Hooker, Worthington, Natural History for the Use of Schools and Families. New York, 1874.

23. Plutarch, Ancient Customs of the Spartans. Harvard Classics.

Chapter 6

1. Gospel of Luke, King James Bible. Points of Truth Ministries. www.pointsoftruth.com/articles/jesusbirth.html.

2. Munsell, Joel. The Every Day Book of History and Chronology: Embracing the Anniversaries of Memorable Persons and Events, in Every Period and State of the World, from the Creation to the Present Time. New York, 1858.

3. Goodrich, Samuel Griswold. Peter Parley's Common School History. Philadelphia, 1841.

4. Lord, John. The Old Roman World. New York, 1867, p. 100.

5. Faas, p. 15.

6. Lendering, Jonas. Carthage. www.livius.org.

7. Munsell, p. 409

8. Tannahill, p. 79. Tannahill expresses the idea that much of the Romans' craze for exotic foods has been exaggerated by modern authors, though she does admit it is rooted in fact. See also Encyclopedia Americana (1851), p. 88, which states that Apicius devised a method of suffocating mullet in a pickle mixture in order that diners might observe the color changes in the fish before they died and were cooked.

9. Brooklyn Daily Eagle, April 1861.

10. Tertullian. Apologeticus and De Spectaculis. Harvard University Press.

11. Cato the Elder. De Rustica. Harvard University Press. Online at University of Liverpool, Internet Resource for Classics and Ancient History.

12. Athenaeus. Deipnosophistae. Online at www.questia.com.

13. Pliny the Elder. Naturis Historia. Online at www.perseus.tufts.edu.

14. Munsell, pp. 340, 334.

15. Ibid.

16. Josephus, Flavius. Antiquities of the Jews. Translation online at www.interhack.net.

17. Transcribed by Patrick Rousell as part of his upload of an edition of Guthrie's Pythagoras Sourcebook and Library (1920).

18. Bohn, Henry G. The Lives and Opinions of Eminent Philosophers, by Diogenes Laertius, translated by C. D. Yonge. London, 1853.

19. History of Architecture, 1850. See also "A Visit to Pompeii," Ladies' Repository, December 1875: "As to the houses and villas they differ from each other in size and elegance as their owners probably did in wealth, competence, or poverty."

20. Smith, William. A Dictionary of Greek and Roman Antiquities. New York, 1886. Potter's American Monthly, 1880, credits the origins of sausages to the Romans in the 6th century. See also Eckstein, Ernst. Quintus Claudius: A Romance of Imperial Rome. New York, 1889.

21. Fidler, Gail, and Velde, Beth. Activities, Reality and Symbol, 1999.

22. Pliny. The Natural History.

23. Ibid.

24. Appleton's Journal, April 1881.

25. Lord, John. The Old Roman World. New York, 1867. See also Godwin, Parke. Cyclaeopedia of Universal Biography. New York, 1856. The latter states that after a period of reduced financial circumstances Apicius hanged himself rather than taking poison to kill himself. A third

source, *Chambers' Information for the People*, Philadelphia, 1857, states that the equivalent of £80,000 was due him at the time of his death, an amount thought insufficient to support his appetite.

26. White, Henry. *A history of the World, on a New and Systematic Plan; from the Earliest Times to the Treaty of Vienna.* Philadelphia, 1851, p. 108.

27. Vehling. *Apicius: Cookery and Dining in Imperial Rome.*

28. Capes, W. W. *Roman History, the Early Empire.* New York, 1876, p. 189: "The citizens of Rome claimed and enjoyed one further privilege, which the franchise did not otherwise carry [with] it. This was the right to food. From early ages the government had bought up large quantities of corn to distribute freely or below cost price, or had fixed a maximum of price in harder times. C. Gracchus was the first to systematize the practice and let every household have its monthly from the state at a sum far below its value. This was to be the Roman's salary for the trouble of governing the world."

29. "The Discovery of Pompeii." *Ladies' Repository 1,* no. 4 (April 1868).

30. Monnier, Marc. *The Wonders of Pompeii.* New York: Charles Scribner & Son, 1901.

31. History of the Carrot Museum. www. carrotmuseum.co.uk.

32. Burr, Fearing. *Field and Garden Vegetables in America*, p. 158.

33. Pliny. The Natural History (XIX, 33).

34. *Appleton's Journal*, April 1881.

35. Vehling.

36. *Brooklyn Daily Eagle*, April 26, 1861.

37. Vehling.

38. *Appleton's Journal*, April 1881.

39. *Brooklyn Daily Eagle*, April 26, 1861.

40. *Appleton's Journal*, April 1881.

41. Smith, William. *A Dictionary of Greek and Roman Biography and Mythology by Various Writers.* Boston, 1867.

42. History of Turkish Cuisine, www.turkishcook.com.

43. Jefferson, John. *A Book About the Table.* London, 1875.

Chapter 7

1. Banvard, Joseph, *Plymouth and the Pilgrims; or, Incidents of Adventure in the History of the First Settlers*, 1851, Boston.

2. Skara Brae: The Discovery of the Village. www.orkneyjar.com/history/skarabrae.

3. Archaeology. http://www.archaeology.org/online/features/bog/gunhild.html.

4. Jefferson, John. *A Book About the Table.* London, 1875.

5. Martin, Martin. *A Description of the Western Islands of Scotland, ca. 1695, and A Voyage to St. Kilda.*

6. Researching Historic Buildings in Britain. www.buildinghistory.org/Buildings/Mills.htm.

7. Chambers, W., and Chambers, R., *Chambers' Information for the People*, 1864.

8. Rhind, William, *A History of the Vegetable Kingdom.* London, 1857.

9. Fluckiger, Frederich August, and Hanbury, Daniel. *Pharmocographia: A History of the Principal Drugs of Vegetable Origin.* London, 1879; Baynes, Thomas. *Encyclopaedia Britannica*, 1888.

10. *Brooklyn Daily Eagle*, April 1861.

11. Spirit Cave. www.mnsu.edu/emuseum/ archaeology/sites/asia/spiritcave.html; *The News* (Frederick, Md.), April 16, 1984; *Daily Review* (Hayward, Calif.), January 18, 1970.

12. Blencowe, Ann. *Receipt Book of Mrs. Ann Blencowe*, 1698.

13. Alexander, Mrs. *A Noble Boke of Cookry*, trans. and reprinted by Napier, 1882.

14. Jefferson.

15. Rumble, Victoria. *Outdoor Recreation &Leisure in 19th Century America.*

16. Chiquart, *On Cookery*, 1420.

17. Feild, Rachael. *Irons in the Fire.*

18. Powder fort was a spice blend usually made of long pepper, a somewhat hotter relative of black pepper.

19. A rhizome with a hot gingery flavor, commonly used in Southeast Asia.

20. Louis P. De Gouy, *The Soup Book*, 1949.

21. Plum and Prune History. http://www.pruneau.fr/ gb/fruitofasoil/index.html.

22. Archer, Thomas Andrew, and Kingsford, Charles. *The Crusades: The Story of the Latin Kingdom of Jerusalem*, 1894; Michaud, Joseph, and Robson, William. *The History of the Crusades.* London, 1881.

23. Earle, John. *Microcosmography: Or, Pieces of the World Discovered in Essays and Characters*, 1628.

24. Brenner, Barry, *Clinical Allergy and Immunology, Emergency Asthma*, 1999.

25. All About Goulash. www.budapest-tourist-guide. com/hungarian-paprika.html.

26. Hungarian Cuisine. http://recipes.wikia.com/wiki/ Hungary.

27. *Appleton's Journal 2*, no. 26 (September 25, 1869).

Chapter 8

1. Hadyn, Joseph. *Hadyn's Dictionary of Dates Relating to All Ages.* New York, 1883.

2. Blencowe, Ann. *Receipt Book of Mrs. Ann Blencowe*, 1698.

3. Dearborn, Jeremiah. *A History of the Town of Parsonfield, Maine.* Portland, Me., 1885.

4. Jefferson, John. *A Book About the Table.* London, 1875.

5. McLintock, Mrs. *Receipts for Cookery and Pastry Work*, 1736.

Chapter 9

1. *Illinois State Historical Society Report*, 1899.

2. Grant, I. F. *Highland Folk Ways.*

3. *Ibid.*

4. *Democratic State Register*, August 20, 1853.

5. *Harper's 78*, no. 466 (March 1889).

6. Keightley, Thomas. *The Illustrated History of England*, New York, 1876. Keightley noted, "In consequence of the bad faith of Peter, the prince of Wales was now deeply in debt. To raise money he imposed a hearth-tax on his subjects, which some paid with great reluctance."

7. The Hearth Tax. www.nationalarchives.gov.uk/ catalogue/RdLeaflet.asp?sLeafletID=233.

8. Baxter, Albert. *History of the City of Grand Rapids.* New York, Grand Rapids: Munsell & Co., 1891.

9. *Iowa City Press-Citizen*, June 25, 1955.

10. *Appleton's Journal 8*, no. 5 (May 1880).

11. Littell, E. *Littell's Living Age*. Vol. V. June 1845. Boston.

12. Lomax, Edward. *Encyclopedia of Architecture: A Dictionary of the Science and Practice of Architecture, Building, Carpentry, etc.*, 1850.

13. *Ibid.*

14. Littell.

15. Grant.

16. *Webster's Unabridged Dictionary*, 1856.

17. Burt, Edward. *Burt's Letters from the North of Scotland*, p. 271.

18. Scott, Sir Walter. *Fair Maid of Perth*, 1828.

19. Taylor, John. *The Pennyless Pilgrimage*. London, 1618.

20. Timbs, John. *School Days of Eminent Men*. London, 1860.

21. *The Daily Courier* (Connellsville, Pa.), October 7, 1946. *Lolo* is considered a derogatory term in China today.

22. *The Ladies' Repository*, March 1854.

23. *Ibid.*

24. Morwood, Vernon. *Our Gipsies in City, Tent, and Van*. London, 1885.

25. *Dunkirk Evening Observer* (New York), November 9, 1937.

26. *Appleton's Journal 8*, no. 5 (May 1880).

27. America As the Garden. http://xroads.virginia.edu/~hyper/hns/garden/rengarden.html.

28. *Frederick Post* (Maryland), March 15, 1995.

29. *Barlow's Report of Raleigh's First Exploration of the American Coast.*

30. *Brooklyn Daily Eagle*, August 1868.

Chapter 10

1. Celtic Journeys website. http://www.peterthestoryteller.co.uk/page14a.html.

2. Stewart, David. *Sketches of the Highlanders*, 1885.

3. Barry, Terry. *A History of Settlement in Ireland*, London: Routledge, 2000; Gostelow, Martin. *Ireland*.

4. Agnew, Andrew. *The Hereditary Sheriffs of Galloway*. Edinburgh, *1893*.

5. *Ibid.*

6. The California Academy of Sciences credits kitchen forks to the Greeks and table forks to the 7th century CE in the royal courts of the Middle East. They state forks were fairly common in wealthy Byzantium households between the 10th and 13th centuries. Although forks were known from the 11th century, they state it wasn't until the 16th century that forks became common in Italy. The fork found its way into France in 1533, brought with Catherine de Medici when she married King Henry II, but the French were slow to adopt the fork. They credit the first forks in England to Thomas Coryate who brought them home after a trip to Italy in 1608. However, it was some time afterward before they became standard.

7. Maxwell, William Hamilton. *Wild Sports of the West of Ireland*. Dublin, 1892.

8. Fitzgibbon, Theodora. *A Taste of Ireland*, 1969.

9. Evans, E. Estyn. *Irish Folk Ways*, 1957, p. 11.

10. Mahon, Brid. *Land of Milk and Honey: The Story of Traditional Irish Food and Drink*, 1991.

11. Buckley, J. *A Tour in Ireland in 1672–4*, quoted in *Journal of the Cork Historical and Archaeological Society 10*, 1904.

12. Arthur, Wollaston Hutton. *Arthur Young's Tour in Ireland 1776–1779*, London, 1892.

13. Kickham, Charles. *Knockagow, Or the Homes of Tipperary*, Dublin, 1887.

14. Johns, C. A. *Botanical Rambles*, London, 1846.

15. O Muimheneachain, Aindrias, *Stories from the Tailor*, Cork, 1978.

16. A History of Irish Cuisine. www.ravensgard.org/prdunham/irishfood.html.

17. Quoted in Wilson, *Food and Drink in Britain*, 1992.

18. Scotland's Seaweed. www.thistleandbroom.com/scotland/seaweed.htm; Use of Seaweed As Food in Ireland.seaweed.ie/uses_ireland/IrishSeaweedFood.lasso.

19. Johns.

20. *Political Anatomy of Ireland*, 1691.

21. Evans.

22. *Southern Literary Messenger 8*, no. 3 (March 1842).

23. *Ibid.*

24. *Ancient Laws of Ireland*, Vol. II.

25. *Ibid.*

26. St. Patrick's Day Feast. www.flavornotes.com/revstpatrick.html .

27. *Syracuse Herald Journal* (New York), March 12, 1974.

28. Evans.

29. History of the Potato Famine in Ireland. www.vinnysa1store.com/irishfamine.html.

30. *The Cottager's Monthly*, Vol. XXVI, London, 1856.

31. Boyle, James. *Ordnance Survey Memoirs*, 1838, quoted in *Ordnance Survey Memoirs of Ireland, Vol. 2, Parishes of Country Atrim*, Day, Angelique and McWilliams, Patrick, Dublin, 1990.

32. *Daily Herald* (Chicago), July 27, 1988.

33. *Marble Rock Weekly* (Iowa), September 21, 1899.

34. *Fort Wayne News* (Indiana), June 30, 1899.

35. *Frederick Post* (Maryland), March 15, 1995.

36. Sala, George Augustus. *Breakfast in Bed*. New York: M. Doolady, 1863.

37. Barnum, P. T. *Struggles and Triumphs; or, Forty Years' Recollections of P. T. Barnum*. Buffalo, N.Y., 1873.

Chapter 11

1. Morris, Edmund. *How to Get a Farm, and Where to Find One*. New York, 1864.

2. Chase, Benjamin. *The History of Old Chester*. Auburn, N.H., 1869.

3. Murray, Hugh. *The Encyclopedia of Geography: Comprising a Complete Description of the Earth*. Philadelphia, 1852.

4. Johnstone, Christian. *The Cook and Housewife's Manual*. 1828.

5. Alden, J. B., ed. *Notes Ambrosianae by Christopher North*. New York, 1876.

6. Celtic Journeys website, http://www.peterthestoryteller.co.uk/page14a.html.

7. *American Cyclopaedia*, D. Appleton Co., New York, 1873.

8. *Catalogue of the Cabinet of Natural History of the State of New York, and of the Historical and Antiquarian Collection Annexed Thereto*. New York State Museum, 1853.

9. Silverweed has creeping stems, yellow flowers, and pinnate leaves which are beautifully silky and silvery beneath, with an edible root tasting somewhat like that of a parsnip. Swine grub it up with avidity and it was once much esteemed as an article of food in some parts of Scotland, especially in the Hebrides where it abounds and has been a resource in times of famine. Chambers, W. R.

Chambers Encyclopedia, a Resource of Information for the People. Philadelphia, Edinburgh, 1872.

10. Martin, Martin. *A Description of the Western Islands of Scotland (ca. 1695), and A Voyage to St. Kilda*, reprint Edinburgh, 1999.

11. Miller, Hugh. *An Autobiography. My Schools and Schoolmasters; or, the Story of My Education*. Boston, 1865.

12. Goodrich, Frank B. *Man upon the Sea or a History of Maritime Adventure*, Philadelphia, 1858; Blake, William O., *The American Encyclopedia of History, Biography, and Travel*, Columbus, 1856.

13. Peterson, Hannah Mary Bouvier. *The National Cookbook*, Philadelphia, 1866.

14. White, William N. *Gardening at the South*, New York and Athens, Ga., 1856.

15. Wood, Alphonso. *Classbook of Botany*, Claremont, N.H., 1851; Buist, Robert, *The Family Kitchen Gardener*, New York, 1861. It has been considered as one of the most effectual antiscorbics when eaten as a salad with watercress.

16. Johnson, Samuel, *A Journey to the Western Isles of Scotland*, 1775.

17. Dalgairns, Mrs. *Practice of Cookery Adapted to the Business of Every-day Life*, Edinburgh, 1829.

18. "The Gipsies," *Catholic World 3*, no. 17 (August 1866).

19. *Murray's Modern Cookery Book, by a Lady*.

20. The 1867 edition of *Jamieson's Dictionary of the Scottish Language* lists two definitions of *powsowdie*: 1. Sheep's-head broth. 2. Milk and meal boiled together.

21. Colman, Henry. *European Agriculture and Rural Economy*. 1851. Boston. Quoted from a treatise published by the Royal Agricultural Society that suggested ways of economy for poor cottagers.

22. *Murray's Modern Cookery, by a Lady*.

23. Hunter, A. *Culina Famulatrix Medicinae*.

24. *Ibid.*

25. Murdoch, David. *The Dutch Dominie of the Catskills*. New York, 1861.

26. Quoted in Hazlitt, p. 31.

27. Borde, Andrew. *The First Book of the Introduction of Knowledge*, 1547.

28. Burt, Edward. *Letters from the North of Scotland.*

29. Smith, George, *The Cornhill Magazine*, Vol. XVIII (January–June 1905).

30. *Murray's Modern Cookery Book, by a Lady*.

31. *Lady Castlehill's Receipt Book*, 1976.

32. MacKenzie, Osgood. *A Hundred Years in the Highlands*.

33. *Harper's 28*, no. 168 (May 1864).

Chapter 12

1. *The What-Not, or Ladies' Handy-Book,* 1861.

2. Boorde, Andrew. *The Fyrst Boke of The Introduction of Knowledge.* 1547.

3. Rumble, Victoria. *Outdoor Recreation & Leisure in 19th Century America*, 2005.

4. Morison, Fynes. *Itenerary*, 1617.

5. Lancelot, Francis. *The Queens of England and Their Times*. New York, 1858

6. Jefferson, John. *A Book About the Table*. London, 1875.

7. Lancelott.

8. *Harper's 14*, no. 83 (April, 1857).

9. *The Century Magazine 55*, no. 1 (November 1897).

10. "A liquor obtained from grapes or apples, unfit for wine or cyder; or from sweet ones, whilst yet acid and unripe. Its chief use is in sauces, ragouts, &c." *Encyclopaedia Britannica*, 1771.

11. Newnham-Davis, Nathaniel, *The Gourmet's Guide to London*, 1914.

12. *Ibid.* Turtle soup made from West Indian green turtles became popular in England during the 18th century.

13. Jefferson.

14. Arnold, Howard Payson. *The Great Exhibition*. New York, 1868. Some sources say the soup initially got its name because it contained Windsor beans, a member of the vetch family. There was also brown Windsor soap.

15. *A Cyclopaedia of Domestic Economy*, 1857.

16. Is Chicken Soup an Essential Drug? www.cmaj.ca/cgi/content/full/161/12/1532.

17. Samuel Pepys Diary online, http://www.pepysdiary.com.

18. Russell, John. *Boke of Nurture*, ca. 1460.

19. *Times* (London), April 30, 1789.

20. *Times* (London), February 26, 1788.

21. *Brooklyn Daily Eagle*, September 8, 1868.

22. Kettner, Auguste. *Book of the Table*, 1877.

23. Cambrensis, Giraldus. The Description of Wales.

Chapter 13

1. Colman, Henry. *European Agriculture and Rural Economy*. Boston, 1851.

2. "Respectable Poverty in France." *Catholic World 27*, no. 158 (May 1878).

3. Parton, James. *The Humorous Poetry of the English Language*. New York, 1856.

4. Sorbiére, Samuel. *A Voyage to England Containing Many Things Relating to the State of Learning, Religion, and Other Curiosities of That Kingdom*.

5. Leon, Edwin Lee. "French Morals and Manners." *Appleton's Journal 6*, no. 4 (April 24, 1869).

6. *Southern Quarterly Review,* July 1846.

7. Lee, N. M. K. *The Cook's Own Book and Housekeeper's Register*. Boston, 1842.

8. "Modern and Medieval Dinners." *The Galaxy Magazine 3*, no. 7 (April 1, 1867).

9. *Ibid.*

10. *Ibid.*

11. *Ibid.*

12. *Harper's 3,* no. 15 (August 1851).

13. Inhabitants of Brittany. The region was settled ca. 500 AD by Britons driven out of their homeland.

14. "Scenes of Breton Life." *Brooklyn Daily Eagle*, October 27, 1895.

15. Dickens, Charles. *All the Year Round*, 1868; *Brooklyn Daily Eagle*, August 1868; Green, Mary Elizabeth. *Food Products of the World*. Chicago, 1892.

16. *Edinburgh Evening Courant,* September 1869.

17. Brillat Savarin. *The Physiology of Taste*, 1825.

18. Pulleyn, William. *The Treasury of Knowledge and Library Reference*, 1853.

19. *Harper's 54*, no. 324 (May 1877).

20. *The Century 35*, no. 4 (February 1888).

Chapter 14

1. *Brooklyn Daily Eagle*, April 13, 1895.

2. *Ibid.*

3. Hering, Constantine. *Analytical Therapeutics.* Vol. I. New York, 1875.

4. Keddie, Henrietta. *Musical Composers and Their Works; for the Use of Schools and Students in Music.* Boston, 1875.

5. Davidis, Henriette. *Davidis' Practical Cook Book.* Milwaukee, 1897.

6. *Das Kuchbuch der Sabrina Welserin,* 1553.

7. *Koge Bog.* Copenhagen: Salomone Sartorio, 1616.

8. *Ibid.*

9. Inntalkochbuch. 1500. Translation by Giano Balestriere. www.medievalcookery.com.

10. Recipes4us.co.uk.

11. Dembinska, Maria. Food and Drink in Medieval Poland, 1977.

12. Ibid.

13. Ibid.

Chapter 15

1. Transactions and Proceedings of the Royal Society of New Zealand 1868–1961. Vol. 18, 1885.

2. Anthon, Charles. A System of Ancient and Mediaeval Geography for the use of Schools and Colleges. New York: Harper, 1850.

3. Galton, Francis, Sir. Vacation Tourists and Notes of Travel in 1860. Cambridge and London, 1861.

4. Harper's 78, no. 465 (February 1889).

5. Greene, Charles S. "Restaurants of San Francisco." Overland Monthly 20, no. 120 (December 1892).

6. "Portuguese Superstitions." Appleton's 14, no. 334 (August 14, 1875).

7. Turner, Sharon. The Anglo-Saxons. London, 1828.

8. Herbert, Thomas, Sir. A Relation of Some Yeares Travaile Begunne Anno 1626, into Afrique and the Greater Asia. London, 1634.

9. Taylor, Bayard, Central Asia, Travels in Cashmere, Little Tibet, and Central Asia. New York, 1874.

10. Taylor, Bayard. By-Ways of Europe. New York, 1869.

11. Debow's Review, December 1851.

12. Brooklyn Daily Eagle, November 1, 1885.

13. Cushing, Caleb. Debow's Review, December 1852.

14. "Middle Class Domestic Life in Spain." Appleton's Journal 8, no. 4 (April 1880).

15. Ford, Richard. The Spaniards and Their Country. Part I. New York, 1847.

Chapter 16

1. Wood, W. W. Sketches of China. New York, 1830.

2. Hagerstown Torchlight (Maryland), October 12, 1846.

3. Wines, E. C. "China and the Chinese." Southern Quarterly Review, July 1847.

4. Indiana Progress, August 6, 1874.

5. Wines.

6. Brooklyn Daily Eagle, August 2, 1885.

7. From a poem written during the Ming dynasty, translated by Frederick Mote and quoted in Brennan, Jennifer, Cuisines of Asia: Nine Great Oriental Cuisines by Technique.

8. Beck, Louis J. New York's Chinatown: An Historical Presentation of Its People and Places. New York, 1867.

9. Shonagon Sei. The Pillow Book.

10. Remlap, L. T. The Life of General U.S. Grant: His Early Life, Military Achievements. Chicago, 1885.

11. "Japonica." Scribner's 9, no. 2 (May–February 1891).

Chapter 17

1. For particulars of any tribe see www.native-languages.org/home.htm#list or John Swanton's The Indians of the Southeastern United States. Swanton breaks wild plant food, cultivated vegetables, domesticated animals and fowl, and wild animals, fowl, fish and shellfish down to specific tribes.

2. Peck, Annie. The South American Tour. New York, 1913; Butterworth, Hezekiah, South America: A Popular Illustrated History of the South American Republics. New York, 1904; Washburn, Charles A. The History of Paraguay with Notes of Personal Observations, and Reminiscences of Diplomacy under Difficulties. New York, 1871.

3. Scribner's 18, no. 1 (May 1879).

4. Scribner's 15, no. 3 (March 1894).

5. St. James Magazine (December–March 1865).

6. The Living Age 26, no. 326 (August 17, 1850).

7. Henshaw, H. W. Indian Origin of Maple Sugar, 1890.

8. Adair, James. The History of the American Indians, London, 1775.

9. Wilson, Gilbert. Buffalo Bird Woman's Garden. 1917. Reprint, 1987, Minnesota Historical Society.

10. Beverley, Robert. The History and Present State of Virginia, London, 1705.

11. Johnson gave a detailed accounting of the preparation of dog soup from the killing of the animal to the dishing up of the finished product, "blood, brains, entrails, bones, and meat." Johnson, W. Fletcher, Life of Sitting Bull, 1891, pp. 346–347.

12. Bartram, William. "Observations on the Creek and Cherokee Indians." Transactions of the American Ethnological Society 3, 1789.

13. Romans, Bernard. A Concise History of East and West Florida. New York, 1775.

14. See also Rumble, Victoria, Victoria's Home Companion, for history of Carolina rice.

15. Pickett, Albert James. Pickett's History of Alabama, and Incidentally of Georgia and Mississippi from the Earliest Period, 1851. Regarding corn, Champlain stated it was boiled in earthenware pots and used to make bread. He discussed at length how it was grown. Champlain, The Voyages and Explorations of Samuel de Champlain, 1604–1616, 1904 version.

16. Caswell, H.S. Our Life Among the Iroquois Indians, Boston, 1892.

17. Pickett; Bossu, M. Travels through That Part of North America Formerly Called Louisiana. VI. pp. 226–278.

18. Swanton, John R. Indian Tribes of the Lower Mississippi Valley and Adjacent Coast of the Gulf of Mexico. Washington, D.C.: Government Printing Office, 1911. In order to date these feasts it is necessary to work backward through the succession of works Swanton used to compile his book. Swanton quoted heavily from Antoine Simon Le Page du Pratz' L'histoire de la Louisiane (1758); works of Bourgmont and of Charlevoix; and Dumont de Montigny's Memoires historiques sur la Louisiane (1753). Several sources indicate du Pratz' work was also used by Thomas Jefferson and Meriwether Lewis during the time of Lewis and Clark's explorations.

19. Waugh, F. W. Iroquois Foods and Food Preparation, Ottawa, 1916; Lafitau, Joseph François, Moeurs des Sauvages, Customs of the American Indians Compared with the Customs of Primitive Times, 2 vols. Toronto, 1974.

20. Burton, Richard Francis. City of the Saints. New York, 1862.

21. Johnson, Cuthbert William. The Farmer's and Planter's Encyclopedia of Rural Affairs; Embracing All the More Recent Discoveries in Agricultural Chemistry, New York, 1855. Harriot and Bartram compared this root to that of China brier. Bartram left a detailed description of its processing. It was well pounded in a wooden mortar, mixed with clean water, and strained through baskets, then the sediment was dried.

22. Riggs, Stephen. Tah-koo Wah-Kau. Boston, 1869.

23. Schele De Vere, Maximillan. Americanisms: The English of the New World, New York, 1872.

24. St. John, Horace, Mrs. Audubon the Naturalist, Boston, 1864.

25. Bond, Wesley. Minnesota and Its Resources. New York, 1853.

26. Watson, John Fanning, Annals of Philadelphia and Pennsylvania.

27. Porcher, Resources of Southern Fields and Forests, 1863.

28. Watson.

29. Ibid.

30. Ibid.

31. According to Caswell, "The dishes and spoons were also made of bark."

32. Encyclopaedia Britannica online.

33. Bond.

34. Harriot, Thomas. A Brief and True Report of the New-Found Land of Virginia, 1588.

35. See Report of Commissioner of Indian Affairs, U.S. Government Printing Office, 1873.

36. MacCauley, Clay. The Seminole Indians of Florida, 1887.

37. Rose, Peter. Foods of the Hudson, Woodstock, N.Y.: Overlook Press, 1993.

38. Drake, Samuel. Indians of North America, from Its First Discovery to 1841, Boston, 1841.

39. Waselkof, G. A., Wood, P. H., and Hatley, M. T. Powhatan's Mantl: Indians in the Colonial Southeast, University of Nebraska Press, 2006.

40. Morse, Jedediah. A Report to the Secretary of War of the United States on Indian Affairs, New Haven, Conn., 1822.

41. McLoughlin, William G. "The Cherokees in Transition: A Statistical Analysis of the Federal Cherokee Census of 1835," Journal of American History, 1977.

42. Hurt, R. Douglas. Indian Agriculture in America, Lawrence, Kan., 1987.

43. Morse, p. 206.

44. Wilson.

45. Moerman, Daniel. Native American Ethnobotany, 1998.

46. Overland Monthly, February 1896.

47. Johnston, James F. W. Notes on North America: Agricultural, Economical, and Social. Boston, 1851.

48. Hodge, Hiram C. Arizona as It Is, or, The Coming Country, New York, 1877; Foster, J. W., The Mississippi Valley: Its Physical Geography Including Sketches of the Topography, Botany, Climate, Geology, and Mineral Resources, Chicago, 1869.

49. Burton.

50. Stratton, Royal B. Captivity of the Oatman Girls, New York, 1858.

51. Powers, Stephen. "The California Indians." Overland Monthly 12, no. 6 (June 1874).

52. Ibid.

53. Swanton, John R. Early History of the Creek Indians & Their Neighbors, 1922.

54. Timberlake, Henry. Memoirs of Lieut. Henry Timberlake, London, 1765.

55. The Living Age 35, no. 447 (December 11, 1852).

56. Indian Fishing and Hunting, Fort Raleigh National Historic Site website.

57. Beckwith, Thomas. The Indian or Mound Builder, Cape Girardeau, Mo., 1911.

58. Webster's (1857) defined alewife as "The Indian name of a fish. See Winthrop on the culture of maize in America. ... It resembles the herring."

59. Harriot.

60. Beverley, Robert, The History and Present State of Virginia in 4 parts, London, 1705. See also Rumble, Victoria, Outdoor Recreation and Leisure in 19th Century America for a list of fish and the names by which they were known in early America.

61. McClintock, Walter, The Old North Trail, 1910.

62. Lawson, John. A New Voyage to Carolina; Containing the Exact Description and Natural History of That Country: Together with the Present State Thereof. And a Journal of a Thousand Miles, Travel'd Thro' Several Nations of Indians. Giving a Particular Account of Their Customs, Manners, &c. 1714.

63. Lawson.

64. Shea, John G. Discovery and Exploration of the Mississippi Valley, with the Original Narratives of Marquette, Allouez, Member, Hennepin, and Anastase Douay. Chilton Hill, N.Y., 1852.

65. Ibid.; see also Waugh.

66. Riggs.

67. A refuse pit, either a single use pit left by nomadic peoples, or, as in this case, pits that were used for dumping refuse for a long period of time.

68. From Desperate Crossing: The Untold Story of the Mayflower, a History Channel documentary.

69. O'Callaghan, E. B. History of New Netherland. New York, 1855.

70. Brooklyn Daily Eagle, May 30, 1854.

71. Ibid.

72. King, Richard. Narrative of a Journal to the Shores of the Arctic Ocean in 1833, 1836.

73. Catlin, George. North American Indians, London, 1848.

74. Ibid, p. 54.

75. Charlevoix, Pierre F. X. de. Histoire et description générale de la Nouvelle France, Paris, 1744.

76. Schoolcraft, H. R. Historical and Statistical Information Respecting the History, etc. of the Indian Tribes of the U.S., Philadelphia, 1851.

77. Dellenbaugh, Frederick Samuel. The North Americans of Yesterday, G.P. Putnam's Sons, 1900.

78. Bates, H. W. The River Amazon, The Naturalist. Vol. II. London, 1863.

79. Kalm, Peter. Travels in North America, 1750.

80. Caswell.

81. Sage, Rufus. Rocky Mountain Life: or, Startling Scenes and Perilous Adventures in the Far West During an Expedition of Three Years. Boston, 1859.

82. Pike, Zebulon. An Important Visit, 1805. (Waugh gives several similar recipes in Iroquois Foods and Food Preparation.)

83. Williams, Roger. A Key into the Language of America. Collections of the Rhode Island Historical Society, Providence, 1827.

84. Caswell.
85. Pringle, Catherine Sager. "Across the Plains in 1844." Oregon Trail website, www.isu.edu/~trin-mich/00.ar.sager1.html.
86. Abbott, Jacob. American History. New York, 1860.
87. French, B. F. Historical Collections from Louisiana and Florida. New York, 1869. Also described in Thwaite's Jesuit Relations (1897) and Sagard's Le grand voyage (1865). Sagard said it was made from corn, "which they cook plain, with a little meat or fish, if they have such" and squashes. Allen compared sagamite to mush or the Italian polenta. Allen, F. Sturges, Allen's Synonyms and Antonyms, New York, 1921.
88. Williams.
89. Lafitau.
90. Sagard.
91. Bartram.
92. Champlain, Samuel de. The Voyages of Samuel de Champlain. Project Gutenberg online.
93. Swanton.
94. The American Society of Naturalists, The American Naturalist, Philadelphia, 1878.
95. Account of James Smith, Captives Among the Indians, Nelson Doubleday, 1915.
96. Ibid.
97. Ibid.
98. Ibid.
99. Ibid.
100. The American Society of Naturalists, The American Naturalist, Philadelphia, 1878.
101. Heckewelder, John. History, Manners and Customs of the Indian Nations.
102. Beach, 1877.
103. Ibid.
104. Stratton.
105. Ibid.
106. Condition of the Indian Tribes, 1867.
107. Ibid.

Chapter 18

1. Kalm, Peter. Travels in North America. 1770, translated from the Swedish, 1937.
2. Freeman, Frederick. The History of Cape Cod. Boston, 1860; "Foods of Early New England." Journal of Home Economics, 1920.
3. Hollister, G. H. The History of Connecticut. Hartford, 1857.
4. Furman, Gabriel. Antiquities of Long Island. New York, 1874.
5. Tusser, Thomas. Five Hundred Points of Good Husbandry, 1557.
6. Penn, Gulielma. Penn Family Recipes. Ed. Benson, Evelyn Abraham, 1966.
7. Harriot, Thomas. A Briefe and True Report of the New Found Land of Virginia. London, 1584. Harriot's work was undertaken at the direction of Sir Walter Raleigh.
8. Hollister.
9. Dampier, William. Dampier's Voyage (1679–1701). Ed. Masefield, John. New York, 1906.
10. Johnston, James F. W. Notes on North America, Agricultural, Economical, and Social. Boston, 1851.
11. Brooklyn Daily Eagle, October 28, 1895.
12. Ibid.
13. Digby, Kenelme, Sir. The Closet of the Eminently

Learned Sir Kenelme Digby, Kt. Opened 1669. Devon: Prospect Books, 1997.
14. Davis, William T. Plymouth Memories of an Octogenarian. 1906. See www.thistledewbooks.com.
15. Donnel, William M. Pioneers of Marion County, Des Moines, 1872.
16. Schele De Vere, Maximilian. Americanisms; the English of the New World. New York, 1872.
17. This passage was quoted in multiple magazines, including Putnam's Monthly (April 1854). None gave an explanation of what chequits were, but they were clearly fish. Discussions with other foodways historians indicate it is the English version of the Mohegan-Pequoit spoken term for fish. The spelling in America is also found squeteague. It is apparently the fish known today as weakfish, or sea trout.
18. Murray, Amelia. Letters from the United States, Cuba, and Canada, 1856.
19. Herbert, William Henry.
20. De Gouy, Louis P. The Soup Book, Ontario, 1949.
21. Independent American (Platteville, Wis.), July 24, 1857.
22. King, Elijah. The Waif of Elm Island. Boston, 1869.
23. Field, Maunsell Bradhurst. Memories of Many Men and Some Women. New York, 1874.
24. Lewis, Alonzo, and Newhall, James. History of Lynn, Essex County, Massachusetts: Including Lynnfield, Saugus, Swampscott, and Nahant. Boston, 1865.
25. Putnam's Monthly, 1857.
26. Cothren, William. History of Ancient Woodbury, Conn. Waterbury, Conn., 1854.

Chapter 19

1. Bartram, William. Travels. 1791. Reprint, New York: Penguin, 1988.
2. Thwaites, Reuben Gold. France in America. New York: Harper & Bros., 1905.
3. Father Claude Allouez wrote in 1677 that the Indians of Illinois utilized 14 kinds of roots in their diet. He had partaken of some of them and found them agreeable. One, macopine, was likely the yellow pond lily.
4. John Swanton spoke of the Alabama Creek performing the bison dance after settling in East Texas where there were known to be no bison. This led him to believe they brought this dance with them from Alabama. Brewer, Willis. Alabama: Her History. Birmingham, Ala., 1872. "The bison, which only two centuries ago came east to the Alleghanies and south to Alabama, has become extinct south of latitude 55°, except where preserved in the National Park," according to Self Culture, A Magazine of Knowledge. Vol. VIII. 1898. Accounts exist in the journals of Cabeza de Vaca, Thevet (1558) and Coronado in 1540. Parkman, Francis. Pioneers of France in the New World. Boston, 1918.
5. Allen, Joel. History of the American Bison. 1877.
6. Munro, William. Crusaders of New France: Chronicles of Fleur-de-lis in the Wilderness. Toronto, 1921. Champlain, Samuel de. Voyages and Explorations of Samuel de Champlain.
7. Machar, Agnes. Stories of New France. Boston, 1890.
8. Baxter, James. The Pioneers of New France in New England. Albany, 1894; Crowley, Mary. A Daughter of New France. Boston, 1903.
9. Rose, Peter G. The Sensible Cook: Dutch Foodways in the Old and New World, and interview August 2007.

10. Turner, Sharon. *The Anglo-Saxons.* London, 1828.

11. Kalm, Peter. *Travels in North America.* Vol. I and II. 1770. Edited from the original Swedish by Benson, Adolph B. New York: Dover Publications, 1937.

12. Holm, Thomas. *Description of the Province of New Sweden.* Philadelphia, 1834.

Chapter 20

1. The Journals of the Lewis and Clark Expedition. http://lewisandclarkjournals.unl.edu; *Sgt. Ordway's Journal.* Collections of the State Historical Society of Wisconsin, 1916.

2. Baking and Books: A Collection of Pastimes. www.bakingandbooks.com.

3. *Eclipse of the Crescent Moon.* 1533, trans. 1901.

4. Allen, Alfred Henry. *Allen's Commercial Organic Analysis.* Vol. III. 1913. Philadelphia.

5. Portlock, Nathaniel. *A Voyage Around the World; but More Particularly the Northwest Coast of America.* 1789. London.

Chapter 21

1. *The Cottager's Monthly,* Vol. XXVI, London, 1846.

2. Robinson, Solon. *How to Live, Saving or Wasting, or Domestic Economy Illustrated.* New York, 1860.

3. Froissart, John. *Chronicles of England, France, Spain, and Adjoining Countries.*

4. *The Homemaker, An Illustrated Monthly Magazine.* Vol. 2. (April–September 1889).

5. *Pictures from the Life of Napoleon.* Part VII, Vol. 23, no. 12 (December 1863), p. 741.

6. Cunningham, A. *Anecdotes of Napoleon Bonaparte and His Times.* Philadelphia, 1855.

7. La Bédoyère, Charles Angélique François Huchet, comte de. *Memoirs of the Public and Private Life of Napoleon Bonaparte.* London: G. Virtue, 1827.

8. Kalm, Peter. *Travels in North America.* 1750. Reprint, New York: Dover, 1937.

9. Kingsford, William. *History of Canada.* Vol. III. Toronto, 1880; Hamilton, Peter. *The Colonization of the South.* London, 1904; McMullen, John. *The History of Canada: From Its First Discovery to the Present.* 1855; Machar, Agnes. *Stories of New France.* Boston, 1890.

10. Cassidy, Frederick, and Hall, Joan. *Dictionary of American Regional English,* 2003; *The Gentleman's Magazine,* 1893; Beckford, William. *A Descriptive Account of the Island of Jamaica,* 1790; Dunlap, William. *History of the Rise and Progress of the Arts of Design in the United States.* New York, 1834.

11. Schenone, Laura. *A Taste of Philadelphia* website. See also her *A Thousand Years Over a Hot Stove,* 2003.

12. Conference Notes prepared for the Quartermaster School for the Quartermaster General, January 1949. www.qmfound.com.

13. *Ibid.*

14. *Southern Literary Messenger,* March 1835.

15. *The Soldier's Friend,* 1798.

16. *Ibid.*

17. Rifkind, H. R. *Fresh Foods for the Army, 1775–1950.* Quartermaster Corps, United States Army.

18. Cook, Joel. *The Siege of Richmond.* Philadelphia, 1862.

19. *Harper's 29,* no. 171 (August 1864).

20. Conference Notes prepared for the Quartermaster School for the Quartermaster General, January 1949. www.qmfound.com.

21. Lossing, Benson J. *Pictorial Field Book of the War of 1812,* 1869.

22. Dunlop, William, and Colquhoun, Arthur. *Recollections of the American War 1812–1814,* Toronto, 1905.

23. Buckham, E. W. *Personal Narrative of Adventures in the Peninsula During the War in 1812–1813.* London, 1827. Spain, Portugal, and the United Kingdom opposed the French on the Iberian Peninsula during the Napoleonic Wars.

24. *Rough Notes by an Old Soldier During Fifty Years' Service.* London, 1867.

25. Ballentine, George. *The Mexican War by an English Soldier in the United States Army.* New York, 1860.

26. McMillan, W. Diary edited by Keith Hingle.

27. Columbia Detachment Rations. http://www.royalengineers.ca/CDRats.html.

28. *Galveston Daily News,* November 23, 1869.

29. Barber, John Warner. *All the Western States and Territories, from the Alleghanies to the Pacific, and from the Lakes to the Gulf, Containing Their History from the Earliest Times.* Cincinnati, 1867.

30. Letterman, Jonathan. Official Records 1861–1865. Series I, Vol. II, part III. Washington, D.C.: Government Printing Office, 1884.

31. Carey, Henry. *The Past, the Present, and the Future.* Philadelphia, 1872.

32. Erckmann-Chatrian. "The Veterans of Yesterday." *Appleton's Journal 10,* no. 55 (January 1881).

33. Abbott, John S. C. *Christopher Carson; Familiarly Known as Kit Carson.* New York, 1874.

34. Bond, J. Wesley. *Minnesota and Its Resources: To Which Are Appended Camp-fire Sketches, or, Notes of a Trip from St. Paul to Pembina and Selkirk Settlement on the Red River of the North.* New York, 1853.

35. Van Tramp, John C. *Prairie and Rocky Mountain Adventures; or, Life in the West.* Columbus, Ohio, 1870.

36. *Ibid. Yampah* has a nutlike flavor and a fragrance similar to caraway. The root can be cooked or eaten raw, or dried for storage and used in preparing porridge or soup. The seeds were parched and used like caraway seed. The tender leaves were also eaten, either raw or cooked. Indians and mountain men alike ate it often.

37. Mullaly, John. *The Laying of the Cable.* New York, 1858.

38. Mullaly.

39. Colton, Walter. *Deck and Port; Or, Incidents of a Cruise in the United States Frigate* Congress *to California.* New York, 1850.

40. Mullaly.

41. Smollett, Tobias. *Select Works of Tobias Smollett.* Philadelphia, 1851, p. 83.

42. Kephart, Horace. *Camping and Woodcraft.* 1916.

43. McElroy, John. *Andersonville: A Story of Rebel Military Prisons.* Toledo, Ohio, 1879.

44. Diary published in installments in the *Reedsburg Free Press* (Wisconsin) on September 20 and September 27, 1872. This prison was designed to hold 2,000 men, but at its peak between 1861 and 1865 actually had 10,000 prisoners.

45. *Janesville Weekly Gazette* (Wisconsin), February 16, 1865.

46. Donnel, *Pioneers of Marion County.* Des Moines, 1872.

47. Livermore, Mary. *My Story of the War.* Hartford, Conn., 1896.

48. Ames, Mary Clemmer. *Ten Years in Washington.* Hartford, Conn., 1874.

49. *Daily Herald,* August 3, 1898.

50. *Brooklyn Daily Eagle,* March 23, 1863.

51. *Marion Weekly Star* (Ohio), July 24, 1886.

52. *Daily Constitutionalist* (Augusta, Ga.), November 9, 1861.

53. Tripler, Charles S., and Blackman, George C. *Handbook for the Military Surgeon.* Cincinnati, 1861.

54. Hamilton, Frank Hastings. *A Treatise on Military Surgery and Hygiene.* New York, 1865.

55. Bradburn, J. *Battle-Fields of the South.* New York, 1864.

56. *Ibid.*

57. *Ibid.*

58. *Ibid.*

59. Zimmer, Anne Carter. *Robert E. Lee Family Cooking and Housekeeping Book.* Chapel Hill: University of North Carolina Press, 1997.

60. *Oakland Tribune,* December 12, 1898.

61. *Brooklyn Daily Eagle,* July 22, 1881.

62. *Brooklyn Daily Eagle,* August 14, 1900.

63. *Brooklyn Daily Eagle,* September 13, 1898.

64. *Army Manual Cookery Book.* 1896.

65. *Wisconsin Daily Palladium,* July 31, 1852. Scott (1786–1866) fought in the War of 1812, the Mexican-American War, the Blackhawk War, the Second Seminole War, and the American Civil War.

Chapter 22

1. Marcy, Randolph B. *Prairie Traveler,* 1859.

2. "Camp and Travel in Colorado." *Overland Monthly 15,* no. 89 (May 1890).

3. *Missouri Gazette,* March 19, 1847.

4. Kelly, Fanny. *Narrative of My Captivity Among the Sioux Indians.* Hartford, Conn., 1871.

5. *California as I Saw It: First Person Narratives 1849–1900,* Library of Congress Digital Files, http://memory.loc.gov/ammem/cbhtml/cbhome.html.

6. Cole, Gilbert. *In the Early Days Along the Overland Trail in Nebraska Territory in 1852.* Kansas City, Mo.: Franklin Hudson, 1905.

7. Baynes, Thomas. *Encyclopaedia Britannica,* 1888.

8. *Elvira Evening Telegram* (Ohio), October 9, 1913.

9. Ball, John. *Across the Plains to Oregon 1832,* Grand Rapids, Mich., 1925.

10. Bonniwell, George. *The Goldrush Diary of George Bonniwell.* May 1850. Online at http://www.emigrantroad.com/gold01.html.

11. *Wisconsin Patriot,* July 2, 1859.

12. "California in '49." *Overland Monthly 34,* no. 202 (October 1899).

13. "California Culinary Experiences." *Overland Monthly 2,* no. 6 (June 1869).

14. *Ibid.*

15. "California Cereals." *Overland Monthly 2,* no. 7 (July 7, 1883).

16. "California Mission Fruits." *Overland Monthly 11,* no. 65 (May 1888).

2. University of Kentucky Libraries, Notable Kentucky African-American Database. http://www.uky.edu/Libraries/NKAA; Bower, Anne. *African American Foodways.* After being granted his freedom James Hemmings committed suicide while in his 30s. He and Peter were brothers of Sally Hemmings, who many believe bore several children fathered by Thomas Jefferson. Information on Hercules and the Hemmings brothers may be found at: http://findarticles.com/p/articles/mi_m1546/is_n1_v10/ai_16769688/pg_1 and www.neh.gov/news/humanities/2004-11/upstairsdownstairs.html.

3. Whitcomb, John and Claire. *Real Life at the White House.* New York, 2002.

4. *Harper's 13,* no. 74 (July 1856). The Kru were an ethnic group who lived in the Independent State of Maryland (Liberia) on the west coast of Africa. The Kru were known to fiercely resist capture and transport into slavery by Europeans. Liberia was established in 1822 by freed African-American slaves.

5. DeBow, J. D. B. *Industrial Resources of the Southern and Western States, Returns of the Census of 1850.* 1852. New Orleans.

6. Goodell, William. *The American Slave Code in Theory and Practice.* New York, 1853; Clarke, Lewis, *Interesting Memoirs and Documents Relating to American Slavery and Making for Emancipation.* London, 1846.

7. Love, Nat. The Life and Adventures of Nat Love Better Known in the Cattle Country as "Deadwood Dick" by Himself. Electronic Edition. http://docsouth.unc.edu/neh/natlove/menu.html.

8. *Southern Quarterly Review,* January 1852.

9. Lewis, Edna. *The Taste of Country Cooking.* New York: Knopf, 1976.

10. Ball, Charles. *A Narrative of the Life and Adventures of Charles Ball, a Black Man, Who Lived Forty Years in Maryland, South Carolina, and Georgia as a Slave.* Pittsburgh, 1854.

11. Born in Slavery: Slave Narratives from the Federal Writers' Project, 1936-1938 contains more than 2,300 first-person accounts of slavery and 500 black-and-white photographs of former slaves. These narratives were collected in the 1930s as part of the Federal Writers' Project of the Works Progress Administration (WPA) and assembled and microfilmed in 1941 as the seventeen-volume Slave Narratives: A Folk History of Slavery in the United States from Interviews with Former Slaves. This online collection is a joint presentation of the Manuscript and Prints and Photographs Divisions of the Library of Congress and includes more than 200 photographs from the Prints and Photographs Division.

12. Ibid.

13. Calhoun, Arthur Wallace. A Social History of the American Family from Colonial Times to the Present. Vol. I. Cleveland, 1917.

14. Ball.

15. Mackie, Milton. From Cape Cod to Dixie and the Tropics. New York, 1864.

16. Slave Narratives.

17. Ibid.

18. Ibid.

19. "Negro Slavery at the South. Part II." Debow's Review 7, no. 5 (November 1849).

Chapter 23

1. Lossing, Benjamin. *Recollections and Private Memoirs of the Life and Character of Washington.* 1860. NY.

Chapter 24

1. Earle, Alice. Stage-Coach and Tavern Days. 1900, p. 196.

2. Ibid, p. 39.

3. Ibid, page 40.

4. Ibid.; Shea, John, The Historical Magazine and Notes and Queries. 1873.

5. Boston Illustrated, 1872.

6. Calkins, Raymond. Substitutes for the Saloon. 1901.

Chapter 25

1. Steiner, Edward Alfred. On the Trail of the Immigrant. New York, 1906.

2. The Jewish Manual; or, Practical Information in Jewish and Modern Cookery with a Collection of Valuable Recipes and Hints Relating to the Toilet. Edited by a Lady. 1846. Reprint, New York: Nightingale Books, 1983.

3. Levy, Esther. The Jewish Cookery Book Founded on Principles of Economy Adapted for Jewish Housekeepers.

4. Interview with Rabbi Ken Wolf, Temple B'nai Israel, Florence, AL, June 2008.

5. Kraft, Irma. The Power of Purim and Other Plays. The Jewish Publication Society of America. Philadelphia, 1915.

Chapter 26

1. Brooklyn Daily Eagle, September 14, 1868.

2. Ibid.

3. Johnstone, Christian. The Cook and Housekeeper's Manual, 1828.

4. Ortolans are tiny birds found in Europe. In North America they are known as rice birds or bobolinks. Ortolans were captured live by netting them in vast numbers, then fattened on oatmeal and millet and artfully roasted, after which they were consumed bones and all because of their delicate size. Rumble, Victoria, Outdoor Recreation and Leisure in 19th Century America, 2006, Florence, AL.

5. Soyer, Alexis. The Modern Housewife or Menagére Comprising Nearly One Thousand Receipts for the Economic and Judicious Preparations of Every Meal of the Day.... New York, 1866.

6. Hooker, Margaret. The Gentlewoman's Housewifery. New York: Dodd, Mead, 1896.

7. Beeton, Isabella. Beeton's Book of Household Management. London, 1863.

8. Escoffier, A. Le Guide Culinaire. 1907. Trans. Cracknell, H. L., and Kaufmann, R. J.

9. Gouffé, Jules. The Royal Cookery Book. London: Low & Marston, 1869.

10. Cassell. Cassell's Dictionary of Cookery. London: Cassell, Petter, Galpin & Co., 1875.

11. Lathrop, C. M., Mrs. Riverside Recipe Book. New York: Press of W. R. Jenkins, 1890.

12. Storke, Elliot G. Domestic and Rural Affairs. 1859. New York.

13. Star and Banner (Gettysburg, Pa.), March 2, 1849.

14. Brooklyn Daily Eagle, October 21, 1902.

15. Glasse, Hannah. The Art of Cookery Made Plain and Easy. London: Printed for the Author, 1747.

16. Sala, George Augustus. Breakfast in Bed. New York, 1863.

17. Optic, Oliver. Northern Lands, or, Young America in Russia and Prussia. Boston, 1874.

18. Wisconsin Patriot, September 17, 1859, and various other newspapers.

19. Bushick, Frank. Frontier Times, July 1927.

20. San Antonio Light, September 12, 1937.

21. For a full history of chili, see Linda Stradley's What's Cooking America website.

22. Frontier Times. July 1927; Bushick, Frank. Glamorous Days. 1934.

23. North Adams (MA) Transcript, March 8, 1999.

24. Johnstone, Christian. The Cook and Housewife's Manual.

25. Robinson, Solon. How to Live: Saving and Wasting. New York, 1860.

26. Murdoch, David. The Dutch Dominie of the Catskills. New York, 1861.

27. Overland Monthly, July 1891.

28. "In a Mining Kitchen." Overland Monthly 9, no. 53 (May 1887).

29. Johnston, James F. W. Notes on North America: Agricultural, Economical, and Social. Edinburgh: William Blackwood & Sons, 1851.

30. Livermore, Mary. The Story of My Life. Hartford, Conn.: A.D. Worthington, 1897.

31. Norway Heritage.com

32. De Vere, Sir Stephen. Letter of steerage passenger, November 30, 1847. www.wesleyjohnson.com/users/Ireland/past/famine/emigration.html.

33. Milwaukee Semi-Weekly Gazette, December 3, 1845.

34. Scribner's 10, no. 6 (December 1891).

35. Beyond the Mississippi from the Great River to the Great Ocean. Hartford, Conn., 1867.

36. Debow's Review, October 1855.

37. Ladies' Repository, July 1865.

Chapter 27

1. Hearn, Lafcadio. La Cuisine Creole. New Orleans, 1885.

2. Bremer, Fredrika. The Homes of the New World, Impressions of America. New York, 1853.

3. Johnson, Cuthbert William. The Farmer's and Planter's Encyclopedia of Rural Affairs. New York, 1855.

4. Reports of the United States Commissioners to the Paris Universal Exposition 1867. Washington, D.C.: Government Printing Office, 1870.

5. Ibid.

6. Castellanos, Henry. New Orleans as It Was: Episodes of Louisiana Life. New Orleans, 1895.

7. Robinson, Solon. The American Agriculturalist, March 25, 1849.

Chapter 28

1. Berkey, William. The Money Question. Grand Rapids, Mich., 1876.

2. Congressional Record, 1854–1904. Extract from speech given by the Hon. James E. Watson of Indiana, November 23, 1903.

3. Ibid.

4. Margoshes, Samuel, and Jewish Community of New York City. Jewish Communal Register of New York, 1918.

5. Ibid, p. 56.

6. Congressional Record, 1854–1904.

7. Hanes, Richard C., and Hanes, Sharon M. "Food 1929–1941." Historic Events for Students: The Great Depression. Vol. 2. Detroit: Gale, 2002.

8. Ibid.

Chapter 29

1. The Reports of the Society for Bettering the Condition and Increasing the Comforts of the Poor. Vol. 1. 1798, p. 28; Hillyer, William. Extract from an account of a London soup shop. January 24, 1798, pp. 205–212.

2. Cedar Rapids Times (Iowa), February 22, 1872.

3. Journal of the Statistical Society of London. Vol. I. London, 1839.

4. Smith, John Frederick, and Howitt, William. John Cassell's Illustrated History of England. Vol. II. London and New York, 1862.

5. Martineau, Harriet. History of the Peace: Being a History of England from 1816 to 1854. Boston: Walker, Wise and Company, 1865.

6. Hawthorne, Nathaniel. The Complete Works of Nathaniel Hawthorne. Vol. I. Boston, 1883.

7. Brooklyn Daily Eagle, September 2, 1900.

8. Annual Report. Correctional Association of New York. Albany, 1865.

9. Clarke, Lewis Garrard. Interesting Memoirs and Documents Relating to American Slavery and Emancipation. London, 1847.

10. Brooklyn Daily Eagle, April 10, 1855.

11. Edinburgh Advertiser, March 2, 1798.

12. Ibid., May 13, 1800.

13. Ibid., July 1, 1800.

Chapter 30

1. Food That Can Win the War, and How to Cook It, 1918.

2. New York Times, June 10, 1941.

3. Ibid., November 7, 1943.

4. Ibid., April 22, 1943.

Chapter 31

1. Rumble, Victoria. Outdoor Recreation and Leisure in 19th Century America.

2. Laba, R. P. Jean Baptiste. Nouveau Voyage aux îles de l'Amerique. Paris. 1742. quoted in Price, Caribbean Fishing and Fishermen.

3. Sears, George Washington. Woodcraft. New York: Forest and Stream Pub. Co., 1920.

4. Rumble.

5. "Good Eating." Southern Literary Messenger 37, no. 5 (May 1863).

6. "Essay on the Slow Progress of Mankind." Southern Literary Messenger 18, no. 7 (July 1852).

7. Overland Monthly, April 1900.

Chapter 32

1. The Old Foodie website. Used with permission.

2. Brooklyn Daily Eagle, November 1858.

3. The National Magazine, May 1858.

Bibliography

Books

A.W. *A Book of Cookrye*. 1591. London. Online. Transcribed by Mark and Jane Waks.

Abbott, Jacob. *American History by Jacob Abbott*. New York, 1860.

Abbott, John S. C. *Christopher Carson: Familiarly Known as Kit Carson*. New York, 1874.

Abel, Mary Hinman. *Practical and Economic Cooking Adapted to Persons of Moderate and Small Means*. American Public Health Association, 1890.

Abell, L.G. *A Mother's Book of Traditional Household Skills*. 1852. Reprint, New York: Lyon Press, 2001.

Abercrombie, John. *The Complete Kitchen Gardener, and Hot-Bed Forcer*. London, 1789.

An Account of a Meat and Soup Charity Established in the Metropolis, in the Year 1797, by a Magistrate. London, 1797.

Acton, Eliza. *Modern Cookery, In All Its Branches; Reduced to a System of Easy Practice, for the Use of Private Families*. Philadelphia, 1852.

Adair, James. *The History of the American Indians*. London, 1775.

Adam's Luxury and Eve's Cookery. London, 1744.

Agnew, Andrew. *The Hereditary Sheriffs of Galloway*. Edinburgh: D. Douglas, 1893.

Alcock, L. *Economy, Society, and Warfare Among the Britons and Saxons*. Cardiff: University of Wales Press, 1987.

Alcott, William A. *The Young Housekeeper or Thoughts on Food and Cookery*. Boston, 1838.

Alden, J. B. *Notes Ambrosianae by Christopher North*. New York, 1876.

Alexander, Mrs. *A Noble Boke of Cookry*. Trans. and reprinted by Napier, 1882.

Allen, A. B., and R. L. Allen. *The American Agriculturist*. New York, 1843.

Allen, Alfred Henry. Allen's Commercial Organic Analysis. Vol. III. Philadelphia, 1913.

Allen, Ann. *The Housekeeper's Assistant*. Boston, 1845.

Allen, F. Sturges. *Allen's Synonyms and Antonyms*. New York: Harper & Brothers, 1921.

Allen, Joel. *History of the American Bison*. Washington, D.C.: U.S. Government Printing Office, 1877.

Allinson, T. R. *Dr. Allinson's Cookery Book*, 1915.

Alsop, Richard. *The Universal Receipt Book or Complete Family Direction by a Society of Gentlemen in New York*. New York, 1814.

American Cyclopedia. New York, 1873.

The American Housewife, by an Experienced Lady. New York, 1841.

American Society of Naturalists. *The American Naturalist*. Philadelphia, 1878.

Ames, Mary Clemmer. *Ten Years in Washington: Life and Scenes in the National Capital, as a Woman Sees Them*. Hartford, Conn., 1874.

Ancient Laws of Ireland. Vol. II.

Annals of the Cleikum Club. From Margaret Dods' Manual. 1826.

Anthon, Charles. *A System of Ancient and Mediaeval Geography for the Use of Schools and Colleges*. New York: Harper, 1850.

Apicius. *The Roman Cookery Book*. Barbara Flower, Elisabeth Rosenbaum, trans. London: Harrap, 1958.

Archer, Thomas Andrew, and Charles Kingsford. *The Crusades: The Story of the Latin Kingdom of Jerusalem*. 1894.

Archestratus. *The Life of Luxury*. John Wilkins and Shaun Hill, trans. Devon, U.K.: Prospect Books, 1994.

Argyll, Duke of. *Crofts and Farms in the Hebrides*. Edinburgh: D. Douglas, 1883.

Army Manual Cookbook. 1896.

Arnold, Howard Payson. *The Great Exhibition*. New York: Hurd and Houghton, 1868.

Arthur, Wollaston Hutton. *Arthur Young's Tour in Ireland, 1776–1779*. London and New York: G. Bell & Sons, 1892.

Aston, M. *Medieval Fish, Fisheries and Fishponds in England*. Oxford, U.K.: B.A.R., 1988.

Athenaeus. *Deiphnosophistae*. Trans. Gulick, Charles Burton. Cambridge: Harvard University Press, 1927.

Baillie, Grisell. *The Household Book of Lady Grisell Baillie, 1692–1733*. Edinburgh: Printed at the University Press by T. and A. Constable for the Scottish History Society, 1911.

Balfour, John Hutton. *The Plants of the Bible, Trees, and Shrubs*. London, Edinburgh, and New York, 1885.

Ball, Charles. *A Narrative of the Life and Adventures of Charles Ball, a Black Man, Who Lived Forty Years in Maryland, South Carolina, and Georgia as a Slave*. Pittsburgh, 1854.

Ball, John. *Across the Plains to Oregon 1832*. Grand Rapids, Mich., 1925.

Ballentine, George. *The Mexican War by an English Soldier in the United States Army*. New York, 1860.

Banvard, Joseph. *Plymouth and the Pilgrims; or, Incidents of Adventure in the History of the First Settlers*. Boston, 1851.

Barber, John Warner. *All the Western States and Territories, from the Alleghanies to the Pacific, and from the Lakes to the Gulf, Containing Their History from the Earliest Times*. Cincinnati, 1867.

Bard, Kathryn, and Stephen Blake Shubert. *Encyclopedia of Archaeology of Ancient Egypt*. New York: Routledge, 1999.

Barlow's Report of Raleigh's First Exploration of the American Coast.

Barnum, P. T. *Struggles and Triumphs; or, Forty Years' Recollections of P. T. Barnum*. Buffalo, N.Y.: Johnson, 1873.

Barry, Terry. *A History of Settlement in Ireland*. London: Routledge, 2000.

Bartram, John. *Observations Made in His Journey from Pennsylvania to Onondago, Oswego and the Lake Ontario of Canada*. London, 1751.

Bartram, William. *Travels of William Bartram*, 1792.

_____. *Travels through North and South Carolina, East and West Florida*. 1791. Reprint, New York: Penguin Books, 1988.

Baskerville, G. *English Monks and Suppression of the Monasteries*. Midland, MI: Mackaye Press, 2008. Originally published 1937.

Baxter, Albert. *History of the City of Grand Rapids, Michigan*. New York, Grand Rapids: Munsell, 1891.

Baxter, James. *The Pioneers of New France in New England*. Albany: J. Munsell's Sons, 1894.

Baynes, Thomas. *Encyclopaedia Britannica*. 1888.

Beck, Louis J. *New York's Chinatown: An Historical Presentation of Its People and Places*. New York, 1867.

Beckford, William. *A Descriptive Account of the Island of Jamaica*. London: Printed for T. and J. Egleton, 1790.

Beckmann, Johann. *History of Inventions, Discoveries and Origins*, 1846.

Beckwith, Thomas. *The Indian, Or Mound Builder*. Cape Girardeau, Mo.: Naeter Bros., 1911.

Beecher, Catherine. *Mrs. Beecher's Domestic Receipt Book*. New York, 1850.

Beecher, Catherine E. *A Treatise on Domestic Econ-

omy, for the Use of Young Ladies at Home and at School*. Boston, 1842.

Beeton, Isabella. *Beeton's Book of Household Management*. London, 1861.

Begué, Mme. *Mme Begué and Her Recipes: Old Creole Cookery*. San Francisco: Southern Pacific Sunset Route, 1900.

Bell, Agrippa Nelson. *A Knowledge of Living Things, with the Laws of their Existence*. New York: Bailliere, 1860.

Bell, Hugh. *Recollections of Hunting in Kentucky 1790–1791*. Draper Manuscripts: Draper's Notes, 30 S 257–264, Wisconsin Historical Society.

Bellows, Albert J. *Philosophy of Eating*. New York, 1867.

Bellows, Henry. *The Old World in Its New Face, 1867–1868*. New York, 1869.

Benko, Stephen. *Pagan Rome and the Early Christians*. Bloomington: Indiana University Press, 1985.

Bennett, R., and J. Elton. *History of Corn Milling*. London, 1899.

Berkey, William. *The Money Question*. Grand Rapids, Mich., 1876.

Bernan, Walter. *On the History of Art of Warming and Ventilating Rooms and Buildings ...* London: Bell, 1845.

Beverley, Robert. *The History and Present State of Virginia in 4 parts*. London, 1705.

Blair, William. *The Soldier's Friend; or, The Means of Preserving Health of Military Men, Addressed to the Officers of the British Army*. London, 1798.

Blake, William O. *The American Encyclopedia of History, Biography, and Travel*. Columbus, 1856.

Blencowe, Ann. *Receipt Book of Mrs. Ann Blencowe*. 1698.

Blot, Pierre. *Hand-Book of Practical Cookery*. New York: D. Appleton, 1868.

Bohn, Henry G. *The Lives and Opinions of Eminent Philosophers, by Diogenes Laertius*, translated by C. D. Yonge. London, 1853.

Bond, John Wesley. *Minnesota and Its Resources: To Which Are Appended Camp-fire Sketches, or, Notes of a Trip from St. Paul to Pembina and Selkirk Settlement on the Red River of the North*. Minnesota, 1853.

Boorde, Andrew. *Dyetary of Helth*. 1584. Reprint, London, 1870.

_____. *The First Boke of the Introduction of Knowledge*. 1547.

Bossu, M. *Travels Through That Part of North America Formerly Called Louisiana*. VI. 1771.

Boston Illustrated. Boston. 1872.

Boswell, James. *A Journal of a Tour to the Hebrides*. 1786.

Bothmer, Marie. *German Home Life*, 1876.

Bourne, Edward, ed. *Narratives of the Career of Hernando De Soto*. New York, 1914.

Bower, Anne. *African American Foodways*. Urbana: University of Illinois Press, 2007.

Bowles, John. *Henry VIII.*

Boyle, James. *Ordnance Survey Memoirs.* Quoted in *Ordnance Survey Memoirs of Ireland.* Vol. 2. 1838.

Brace, Charles Loring. *Home Life in Germany.* New York, 1853.

Bradburn, J. *Battle-Fields of the South.* New York, 1864.

Bremer, Fredrika. *The Homes of the New World, Impressions of America.* New York, 1853.

Brennan, Jennifer. *Cuisines of Asia: Nine Great Oriental Cuisines by Technique.* New York: St. Martin's/Marek, 1984.

Brenner, Barry. *Clinical Allergy and Immunology, Emergency Asthma.* New York: M. Dekker, 1999.

Brewer, Ebeneezer Cobham. *Dictionary of Phrase and Fable.* Philadelphia, 1898.

Brier, Bob, and A. Hoyt Hobbs. *Daily Life of the Ancient Egyptians.* Westport, Conn.: Greenwood Press, 1999.

Briggs, Richard. *The English Art of Cookery.* London, 1794.

_____. *The New Art of Cookery.* Philadelphia, 1792.

Brillat Savarin, Jean Anthelme. *The Physiology of Taste.* 1825.

Brown, Catherine. *Scottish Cookery.* Glasgow: Drew, 1990.

Brown, Charles E. *The New England Cook Book. The Latest and the Best Methods for Economy and Luxury at Home. Containing Nearly a Thousand of the Best Up-to-date Receipts for Every Conceivable Need in Kitchen and Other Departments of Housekeeping.* Boston: Charles E. Brown, 1905.

Brown, Harry Collins. *In the Golden Nineties.* Hastings-on-Hudson, N.Y.: Valentine's Manual, Inc., 1928.

Brown, P. Hume. *Early Travelers in Scotland.* 1891.

Brownell, Charles, and Joel Taylor Headley. *The Indian Races of North and South America.* Hartford, Conn., Hurlbut, Scranton & Co.; Chicago, E.B. & R.C. Treat, 1864.

Bryan, Lettice. *The Kentucky Housewife.* Cincinnati, Ohio: Shepard & Stearns, 1839.

Buckham, E. W. *Personal Narrative of Adventures in the Peninsula During the War in 1812–1813.* London, 1827.

Buckeye Cookery and Practical Housekeeping: Compiled from Original Receipts. Minneapolis, Minn., 1877.

Buckley, J. *A Tour in Ireland in 1672–4.* Quoted in *Journal of the Cork Historical and Archaeological Society.* Vol. 10. 1904.

Buist, Robert. *The Family Kitchen Gardener.* New York: Saxton, Barker, 1861.

Burke, Edmund. *The Annual Register.* London, 1831.

Burns, Robert. *The Complete Works of Robert Burns.* Boston, 1859.

Burr, Fearing. *Field and Garden Vegetables of America.* Boston: Crosby and Nichols, 1863.

Burt, Edward. *Burt's Letters from the North of Scotland.* Edinburgh, 1754.

Burton, Richard Francis. *The City of the Saints, and Across the Rocky Mountains to California.* New York, 1862.

Bushick, Frank. *Glamorous Days.* San Antonio, Tx.: Naylor, 1934.

Butterworth, Hezekiah. *South America: A Popular Illustrated History of the South American Republics.* New York: Doubleday, Page, 1904.

Cadogan, William. *An Essay upon Nursing and the Management of Children from Birth to Three Years of Age.* London, 1748.

Caesar, Julius. *Conquest of Gaul.*

Calhoun, Arthur Wallace. *A Social History of the American Family from Colonial Times to the Present.* Vol. I. Cleveland: Arthur H. Clark, 1917.

Calkins, Raymond. *Substitutes for the Saloon.* Boston: Houghton Mifflin, 1901.

Cambrensis, Giraldus. *The Description of Wales.*

Campbell, Lord Colin. *The Crofter in History: By Dulriad.* Edinburgh: William Brown, 1885.

Campbell, Helen. *The Easiest Way in Housekeeping and Cooking.* Boston, 1893.

Capes, W. W. *Roman History: The Early Empire.* 1879.

Carême. *French Cookery.*

Carey, Henry. *The Past, the Present, and the Future.* Philadelphia, 1872.

The Carolina Housewife, by a Lady of Charleston. Charleston, 1847.

Carter, Anne Zimmer. *The Robert E. Lee Family Cookbook.* Chapel Hill: University of North Carolina Press, 1997.

Carter, Charles. *The Compleat City and Country Cook: Or, Accomplish'd Housewife.* London, 1732.

Carter, Susannah. *The Frugal Housewife, or, Complete Woman Cook.* New York, 1803.

Cassell. *Cassell's Dictionary of Cookery.* London: Cassell, Petter, Galpin, 1875.

Cassidy, Frederick, and Joan Hall. *Dictionary of American Regional English.* Cambridge, Mass.: Belknap Press of Harvard University Press, 1985–2002.

Castellanos, Henry. *New Orleans as It Was: Episodes of Louisiana Life.* New Orleans, 1895.

Caswell, H. S. *Our Life Among the Iroquois Indians.* Boston, 1892.

Catalogue of the Cabinet of Natural History of the State of New York, and of the Historical and Antiquarian Collection Annexed Thereto. New York State Museum, 1853.

Catlin, George. *Letters and Notes on the Manners, Customs, and Condition of the North American Indians.* New York, 1844.

Chambers, Robert. *Chambers's Information for the People.* Philadelphia: J. B. Lippincott, 1867.

Chambers, W., and R. Chambers. *Chambers Information for the People.* 1864.

_____. *Chambers' Encyclopedia, A Resource of Information for the People.* Edinburgh, 1872.

_____. *Chambers' Journal of Popular Literature Science and Arts.* London, 1861.

Champlain, Samuel de. Edited by Slafter, Edmund. *Voyages of Samuel de Champlain*. Project Gutenberg. http://www.gutenberg.org/etext/6653.

Chan, Shiu Wong. *The Chinese Cookbook*. New York: Stokes, 1917.

Chapman, Billies. *The American Frugal Housewife*. Boston, 1833.

Chapman, Lucretia. *The Trial of Lucretia Chapman*. Philadelphia, 1882.

Charlevoix, Pierre F. X. de. *Histoire et description générale de la Nouvelle France*. Paris, 1744.

_____. *Journal of a Voyage to North America*. 2 vols. London, 1761.

Chase, Benjamin. *The History of Old Chester*. Auburn, N.H.: The author, 1869.

Chastellux, François Jean, marquis de. *An Essay on Public Happiness, Investigating the State of Human Nature, Under Each of its Particular Appearances Through the Several Periods of History*. London: Printed for T. Cadell, 1774.

Chaucer, G. *Canterbury Tales*.

Child, Lydia Maria. *The Frugal Housewife*. Boston, 1829, 1832.

Chiquart. *On Cookery. (Du Fait de Cuisine)*. 1420. Trans. Terence Scully. New York: Lang, 1986.

Christison, Robert. *A Treatise on Poisons*. Edinburgh, 1836.

Clarke, Lewis Garrard. *Interesting Memoirs and Documents Relating to American Slavery and Making for Emancipation*. London: Chapman Bros., 1846.

Clelland, Elizabeth. *A New and Easy Method of Cookery*. Edinburgh, 1759.

Cockayne, Oswald. *Leechdoms, Wortcunning, and Starcraft*. 1851. Reprint, London: Holland Press, 1961.

Cole, Gilbert. *In the Early Days Along the Overland Trail in Nebraska Territory in 1852*. Kansas City, Mo.: Franklin Hudson, 1905.

Cole, Mrs. Mary. *The Lady's Complete Guide*. London, 1789.

Collingwood, Francis, and John Woollams. *The Universal Cook and City and Country Housekeeper*. London, 1792.

Collins, Angelina Maria. *The Great Western Cookbook*. New York: A.S. Barnes, 1857.

Colman, Henry. *European Agriculture and Rural Economy*. Boston: Phillips, Sampson, 1851.

Colton, Walter. *Deck and Port; Or, Incidents of a Cruise in the United States Frigate* Congress *to California*. New York: A.S. Barnes, 1850.

A Compleat Body of Husbandry. London, 1756.

Constable, G. *Monastic Tithes from Their Origins to the Twelfth Century*. Cambridge, U.K.: Cambridge University Press, 1964.

Cook, Joel. *The Siege of Richmond*. Philadelphia, 1862.

Correctional Association of New York. *Annual Report*. Albany, 1865.

Cothren, William. *History of Ancient Woodbury, Conn*. Waterbury, Conn., 1854.

Cronon, William. *Changes in the Land: Indians, Colonists, and the Ecology of New England*. New York: Hill and Wang, 1983.

Crossley-Holland, Nicole. *Living and Dining in Medieval Paris: The Household of a Fourteenth-Century Knight*. Cardiff: University of Wales Press, 2007.

Crowley, Mary. *A Daughter of New France*. Boston: Little, Brown, 1901.

Culpepper, Nicholas. *The Complete Herbal*.

Cunningham, A. *Anecdotes of Napoleon Bonaparte and His Times*. Philadelphia, 1855.

Curtis, Isabel Gordon. *Good Housekeeping Everyday Cook Book*. New York: Phelps, 1903.

Cushing, Caleb. *Debow's Review*, December 1852.

A Cyclopaedia of Domestic Economy. 1857.

D. Appleton and Co. *The American Cyclopaedia*. New York, 1873.

The Daily News Cookbook. Chicago, 1896.

Dalby, Andrew. *Dangerous Tastes: The Story of Spices*. Berkeley: University of California Press, 2002.

Dalgairns, Mrs. *The Practice of Cookery*. Edinburgh: Printed for Cadell, 1829.

Dampier, William. *Dampier's Voyages (1679–1701)*. Edited by John Masefield. New York: E.P. Dutton, 1906.

Danachair, C. *Bread*. Ulster Folklore, 1958.

Danaher, K. *Fires, Fireplaces, and Cooking Biatas*. Dublin, 1992.

Davidis, Henriette. *Davidis' Practical Cook Book*. Milwaukee, 1897.

Davis, William T. *Plymouth Memories of an Octogenarian*. Plymouth, Mass.: Printed by the Memorial Press, 1906.

Day, Angelique, and Patrick McWilliams. *Parishes of Country Antrim*. Dublin, 1990.

Dearborn, Jeremiah. *A History of the Town of Parsonfield, Maine*. Portland, Maine, 1885.

DeBow, J. B. D. *Industrial Resources of the Southern and Western States, Returns of the Census of 1850*. New Orleans, 1852.

Defoe, Daniel. *Tour Through the Island of Great Britain*. 1724.

De Gouy, Louis. *The Soup Book*. 1949. Reprint, New York: Dover, 1974.

Dellenbaugh, Frederick Samuel. *The North Americans of Yesterday*. New York: Putnam's, 1900.

Dembinska, Maria. *Food and Drink in Medieval Poland*. Philadelphia: University of Pennsylvania Press, 1999.

Description of the Various Wheel-carriages; Preservation of Health; Domestic Medicines, andc., andc. New York, 1845.

Detienne, Marcel, and Jean Pierre Vernant. Herodotus, quoted in *The Cuisine of Sacrifice Among the Greeks*. Chicago: University of Chicago Press, 1989.

Dick and Fitzgerald. *Inquire Within, or Over 3700 Facts for the People*. 1858.

_____. *The Corner Cupboard; or Facts for Everybody*.

Complete Encyclopedia of Useful Knowledge. New York, 1859.

Dickens, Charles. *All the Year Round.* London, 1881.

_____. *Our Mutual Friend.* 1864. Reprint, New York: Signet Books, 1964.

Digby, Sir Kenelme. *The Closet of the Eminently Learned Sir Kenelme Digby, Kt. Opened 1669.* Devon: Prospect Books, 1997.

Diodorus Siculus. *History.*

Dods, Margaret. *The Cook and Housewife's Manual.* 1826.

Donnel, William M. *Pioneers of Marion County.* Des Moines, 1872.

Drake, Samuel. *Indians of North America, from Its First Discovery to 1841.* Boston, 1841.

Driver, Christopher. *John Evelyn, Cook. The Manuscript Receipt Book of John Evelyn.* Devon, U.K.: Prospect Books, 1997.

Dunbar, Seymour. *A History of Travel in America.* Indianapolis: Bobbs Merrill, 1915.

Dunlap, William. *History of the Rise and Progress of the Arts of Design in the United States.* New York: George P. Scott, 1834.

_____, and Arthur Colquhoun. *Recollections of the American War 1812–1814.* Toronto: Historical Publications, 1908.

Earle, Alice. *Stagecoach and Tavern Days.* New York: Macmillan, 1900.

Earle, John. *Microcosmography, Or a Piece of the World Discovered In Essays and Characters.* 1628. Reprint, London: Tutorial Press, 1933.

Eckstein, Ernst. *Quintus Claudius: A Romance of Imperial Rome.* New York, 1889.

Eclipse of the Crescent Moon. 1533, trans. 1901.

Edgeworth, Mary. *The Southern Gardener and Receipt Book.* Philadelphia, 1860.

Edwards, John. *The Roman Cookery of Apicius.* Vancouver: Hartley and Marks, 1984.

Ellis, William. *The Country Housewife's Family Companion, or Profitable Directions for Whatever Relates to the Management and Good Economy of the Domestick Concerns of a Country Life.* London, 1750.

Emerson, Lucy. *The New England Cookery.* Montpelier, Vt., 1808.

Emerson, Ralph Waldo, and William Watson Goodwin, ed. *Plutarch's Morals.* Washington, 1870.

Encyclopaedia Britannica, 1911 edition.

Encyclopedia Americana. Boston, 1851.

Escoffier, A. *Le Guide Culinaire.* 1907. Trans. H. L. Cracknell and R. J. Kaufmann.

Eustis, Celestine. *Cooking in Old Creole Days.* New York: R.H. Russell, 1904.

Evans, E. Estyn. *Irish Folk Ways.* London: Routledge & Paul, 1957.

Evans, G. G., editor. *Life of Col. David Crockett, written by himself.* Philadelphia, 1860.

Evelyn, John. *Acetaria.* 1699.

Ewing, Emma P. *Soup and Soup Making.* Chicago and New York, 1882.

The Experienced English Housekeeper. 1818.

Faiella, Graham. *The Technology of Mesopotamia.* New York: Rosen, 2006.

The Family Receipt Book, Containing Eight Hundred Truly Valuable Receipts in Various Branches of Domestic Economy, Selected from the Works of British and Foreign Writers of Unquestionable Authority and Experience, and from the Attested Communications of Scientific Friends. Philadelphia: Collins and Croft, 1818.

Feild, Rachael. *Irons in the Fire.* Marlborough, U.K.: Crowood House, 1984.

Fidler, Gail, and Beth Velde. *Activities: Reality and Symbol.* Thorofare, N.J.: Slack, 1999.

Field, Maunsell Bradhurst. *Memories of Many Men and of Some Women: Being Personal Recollections of Emperors, Kings, Queens, Princes, Presidents, Statesmen, Authors, and Artists, at Home and Abroad, During the Last Thirty Years.*

Fisher, Abby. *What Mrs. Fisher Knows About Old Southern Cooking.* San Francisco, 1881.

Fitzgibbon, Theodora. *A Taste of Ireland.* Boston: Houghton Mifflin, 1969.

Fletcher, Banister. *A History of Architecture.* Oxford: Architectural Press, 1996.

Fleury, Claude, and Adam Clarke. *Manners of the Ancient Israelites.* New York, 1825.

Fluckiger, Frederich August, and Daniel Hanbury. *Pharmocographia: A History of the Principal Drugs of Vegetable Origin.* London, 1879.

Food That Can Win the War and How to Cook It. 1918.

Ford, Richard. *The Spaniards and Their Country.* Part I. 1847. New York.

Forsyth, William. *The Novels and Novelists of the Eighteenth Century, in Illustration of the Manners and Morals of the Age.* New York, 1871.

Foster, J. W. *The Mississippi Valley: Its Physical Geography Included Sketches of the Topography, Botany, Climate, Geology, and Mineral Resources.* Chicago, 1869.

Fowler, John Coke. *William the Conqueror and the Feudal System.* 1880.

Frazer, Mrs. *The Practice of Cookery.* 1791.

Freeman, Edward Augustus. *The Chief Periods of European History.* London, 1886.

Freeman, Frederick. *The History of Cape Cod.* Boston, 1860.

French, B. F. *Historical Collections from Louisiana and Florida.* New York, 1859.

Froissart, John. *Chronicles of England, France, Spain, and Adjoining Countries.*

Fryer, John. *A New Account of East India and Persia 1672–1681.* London: Printed for the Hakluyt Society, 1909.

Furman, Gabriel. *Antiquities of Long Island by Gabriel Furman.* New York, 1874.

Galton, Francis, Sir. *Vacation Tourists and Notes of Travel in 1860.* Cambridge, London, 1861.

Geddes, Olive. *The Laird's Kitchen.* Edinburgh: H.M.S.O., National Library of Scotland, 1994.

Gerard, John. *The Herball.*

Gibbon, E. *The Decline and Fall of the Roman Empire*, Vol. V. New York: Peter Fenelon Collier & Son, 1901.

Gibson, Jeremy. *The Hearth Tax, Other Later Stuart Tax Lists, and the Association Oath Rolls*. Plymouth, U.K.: Federation of Family History Societies, 1985.

Gies, Joseph, and Frances Gies. *Life in a Medieval Castle*. New York: Harper & Row, 1979.

Gillette, Mrs. F. L. *The White House Cookbook*, 1887.

Glasse, Hannah. *The Art of Cookery Made Plain and Easy*. London: Printed for the Author, 1747; Printed for the author, 1758; Printed for Alexander Donaldson, 1774.

Glen, James, and George Milligan. *Colonial South Carolina: Two Contemporary Descriptions*. Columbia: University of South Carolina Press, 1951.

Godwin, Parke. *Cyclopaedia of Universal Biography*. New York, 1856.

Goethe, J. W. von. *Italian Journey: 1786–1788*. Trans. Auden, W. H., and Mayer, Elizabeth. San Francisco: North Point Press, 1982.

Goldsmith, Oliver. *A History of the Earth and Animated Nature*. London, 1825.

Good Housekeeping. *Good Housekeeping Book of Menus, Recipes, and Household Discoveries*. New York: Good Housekeeping, 1922.

Goodell, William. *The American Slave Code in Theory and Practice*. New York, 1853.

Goodfellow, Mrs. *Mrs. Goodfellow's Cookery as It Should Be*. New York, 1872.

Goodrich, Frank B. *Man Upon the Sea or a History of Maritime Adventure*. Philadelphia: Lippincott, 1858.

Goodrich, Samuel Griswold. *A History of All Nations from the Earliest Periods to the Present Time*. Auburn, 1851.

_____. *Peter Parley's Common School History*. Philadelphia, 1841.

Gosse, Philip Henry. *The Ocean*. Philadelphia: Parry & McMillan, 1856.

Gostelow, Martin. *Ireland*. Lausanne: JPM Publications, 2002.

Gouffé, Jules. *The Royal Cookery Book*. London: Low & Marston, 1869

Graham, Henry Grey. *Social Life of Scotland in the Eighteenth Century*. London: Black, 1906.

Grant, Elizabeth, of Rothiemurchus. *Memoirs of a Highland Lady*. 1797–1827.

Grant, I. F. *Highland Folk Ways*. 1961. Reprint, Edinburgh: Birlinn, 1995.

Granville, Augustus Bozzi. *The Spas of Germany*. London, 1838.

Green, Mary Elizabeth. *Food Products of the World*. Chicago: The Hotel World, 1902.

Grey, C. *The Early Years of His Royal Highness, the Prince Consort. Compiled under the Directions of Her Majesty the Queen*. New York: Harper & Brothers, 1867.

Grinnell, George Bird. *The Cheyenne Indians, Their History and Ways of Life*. New Haven, Conn.: Yale University Press, 1923.

Griswold, Rufus. *The Republican Court; or, American Society in the Days of Washington*. New York, 1856.

Grocock, Christopher, and Sally Grainger. *Apicius: A Critical Edition with an Introduction and an English Translation*, Devon: Prospect Books, 2006.

Gulick, Charles. *The Life of the Ancient Greeks*. New York, 1902.

Gunnis, Rupert. *Historic Cyprus: A Guide to its Towns and Villages, Monasteries and Castles*. London: Methuen, 1936.

Gutzlaff, Rev. Charles. *A Sketch of Chinese History; Ancient and Modern*. Vol. I. New York, 1834.

Hadyn, Joseph. *Hadyn's Dictionary of Dates Relating to All Ages*. New York, 1883.

Hakluyt, Richard. *The Voyages of the English Nation to America Before the Year 1600*. Vol. II. Edinburgh, 1889.

Hale, Sarah J. *Early American Cookery, The Good Housekeeper*. 1841. Reprint, Garden City, N.Y.: Dover, 1996.

Hale, Sarah Josepha. *The Ladies New Book of Cookery*. New York, 1852.

Hale, Thomas. *Barkham Burroughs' Encyclopedia of Astounding Facts and Useful Information*. 1889.

Hallam, Henry. *View of the State of Europe During the Middle Ages*. New York: W.J. Widdleton, 1872. Reprinted 1903.

Hamilton, Frank Hastings. *A Treatise on Military Surgery and Hygiene*. New York, 1865.

Hamilton, Peter. *The Colonization of the South*. Philadelphia: Printed for subscribers only by G. Barrie, 1904.

Hanes, Richard C., and Sharon M. Hanes. "Food 1929–1941." *Historic Events for Students: The Great Depression*. Vol. 2. Detroit: Gale, 2002.

Harland, Marion. *Common Sense in the Household: A Manual of Practical Housewifery*.

Harriot, Thomas. *A Brief and True Report of the New Found Land of Virginia*. London, 1584. New York. J. Sabin and Sons, 1871.

Harrison, Sarah. *The House-Keeper's Pocket-book*. London, 1755.

Hartley, Dorothy. *Food in England*. London: McDonald and Jane's, 1975.

_____. *The Land of England*. London: Macdonald, 1979.

Hassall, Arthur. *Periods of European History*. London: Rivingtons, 1899.

Hawkes, J. G. *The Diversity of Crop Plants*. Cambridge, Mass.: Harvard University Press, 1983.

Hawthorne, Nathaniel. *The Complete Works of Nathaniel Hawthorne*. Vol. I. Boston, 1883.

Hearn, Lafcadio. *La Cuisine Creole*. New Orleans, 1885.

Heckewelder, John. *History, Manners, and Customs of the Indian Nations*. Philadelphia: Historical Society of Pennsylvania, 1876.

_____. *A Narrative of the Missions of the United Brethren among the Delaware and Mohegan Indians from Its Commencement in the Year 1740 to the Close of the Year 1808.* Edited by William Elsey Connelly. Cleveland: Burrows Brothers, 1907.

Henderson, Mary. *Practical Cooking and Dinner Giving.* New York: Harper and Bros., 1877.

Henshaw, H. W. *Indian Origin of Maple Sugar.* 1890.

Herbert, Thomas, Sir. *A Relation of Some Yeares Travaile Begunne Anno 1626 into Afrique and the Greater Asia.* London, 1634.

Hering, Constantine. *Analytical Therapeutics.* Vol. I. New York, 1875.

Herrick, Cheesman. *History of Commerce and Industry.* New York: Macmillan, 1917.

Hess, Karen. *The Carolina Rice Kitchen.* Columbia: University of South Carolina Press, 1992.

Hewes, Fletcher, and William McKinley, Jr. *What Are the Facts— Protection and Reciprocity.* New York: H.F. Clark, 1892.

Hieatt, Constance B., and Sharon Butler, trans. *Curye on Inglysch: English Culinary Manuscripts of the 14th Century.* Oxford, U.K.: Oxford University Press, 1985.

Higginson, Francis. *New England's Plantation.* 1630. Quoted in Mass. Historical Society 62:311.

Hill, Janet McKenzie. *Practical Cooking and Serving. A Complete Manual of How to Select, Prepare, and Serve Food.* New York, 1915.

Hill, John. *A History of Plantes.* London, 1751.

History of Architecture. 1850.

Hodge, Hiram C. *Arizona as It Is, or, The Coming Country.* New York, 1877.

Hollister, G. H. *The History of Connecticut, from the First Settlement of the Colony to the Present Constitution.* Hartford, 1857.

Holm, Thomas. *Description of the Province of New Sweden.* Philadelphia, 1834.

Homespun, Priscilla. *The Universal Receipt Book; Being a Compendious Repository of Practical Information. Cookery, Preserving, Pickling, Distilling, and All the Branches of Domestic Economy. To Which Is Added Some Advice to Farmers.* Philadelphia, 1818.

Hooker, Margaret. *Ye Gentlewoman's Housewifery.* New York: Dodd, Mead, 1896. Reprinted as *Early American Cooking,* Scotia, N.Y.: Americana Review, 1981.

Hooker, Worthington. *Natural History for the Use of Schools and Families.* New York, 1874.

Hooper, Edward James. *The Practical Farmer, Gardener, and Housewife.* Cincinnati, 1839.

Houlston and Sons. *Enquire Within.* 1894.

Howell, Thomas Bayly. *A Complete Collection of State Trials and Proceedings for High Treason.* London, 1817.

Howitt, William. *Rural and Domestic Life of Germany.* London, 1842.

Howland, E. A. *The American Economical Housekeeper and Family Receipt Book.* Worcester, 1894.

Hunt, Leigh. *The Autobiography of Leigh Hunt.* New York, 1850.

Hunter, A. *Culina Famulatrix Medicinae; Or, Receipts in Modern Cookery.* York, 1806.

Hurt, R. Douglas. *Indian Agriculture in America.* Lawrence, Kan.: University Press of Kansas, 1987.

Illinois State Historical Society Report. Springfield, 1899.

Irving, Washington. *The Works of Washington Irving.* New York, 1860.

James, Edwin. *Account of an Expedition from Pittsburgh to the Rocky Mountains, Performed in the Years 1819, 1820.* 3 volumes. London: Printed for Longman, Hurst, Rees, Orme, and Brown, 1823.

Jamieson, John. *Jamieson's Dictionary of the Scottish Language.* 1867.

Jefferson, John. *A Book About the Table.* London, 1875.

Jenks, James. *The Complete Cook.* London, 1768.

Jennings, Walter Wilson. *Introduction to American Economic History.* New York: Thomas Y. Crowell, 1928.

The Jewish Manual; or, Practical Information in Jewish and Modern Cookery with a Collection of Valuable Recipes and Hints Relating to the Toilet. Edited by a Lady. 1846. Reprint, New York: Nightingale Books, 1983.

Johns, C. A., Rev. *Botanical Rambles.* London: Printed for the Society for Promoting Christian Knowledge, 1846.

Johnson, Cuthbert William. *The Farmer's and Planter's Encyclopedia of Rural Affairs; Embracing All the More Recent Discoveries in Agricultural Chemistry.* New York, 1855.

Johnson, James. *The Medico-Chirurgical Review and Journal of Practical Medicine.* London, 1843.

Johnson, Samuel. *A Journey to the Western Isles of Scotland.* 1775.

_____. *To the Hebrides.* 1773. Reprint, Edinburgh: Birlinn, 2007.

_____. *The Works of the English Poets from Chaucer to Cowper.* 1810.

Johnson, W. Fletcher. *Life of Sitting Bull.* 1891.

Johnston, James F. W. *Notes on North America: Agricultural, Economical, and Social.* Edinburgh: William Blackwood & Sons, 1851.

Johnston, Thomas. *A History of the Working Class of Scotland.* Glasgow: Forward Publishing, 1920.

Johnstone, Christian. *The Cook and Housewife's Manual.* 1828.

Journal of Horticulture and Cottage Gardener and Home Farmer. 1875.

Journal of the Statistical Society of London. Vol. I. London, 1839.

Joyce, Patrick Weston. *A Social History of Ancient Ireland.* Vol. I. New York, 1903.

Kalm, Peter. *Travels in North America.* Vol. I and II. 1770. Edited from the original Swedish by Benson, Adolph B. New York: Dover Publications, 1937.

Keddie, Henrietta. *Musical Composers and Their Works*. Boston, 1875.

Keightley, Thomas. *The Illustrated History of England*. New York: World Pub. House, 1876.

Kelly, Fanny. *Narrative of My Captivity Among the Sioux Indians*. Hartford, Conn., 1871.

Kephart, Horace. *Camping and Woodcraft*. New York: Outing Publishing, 1916–17.

Kettilby, Mary. *A Collection of Above Three Hundred Receipts in Cookery...* London, 1734.

Kettner, Auguste. *Book of the Table*. 1877.

Kickham, Charles. *Knockagow, or, the Homes of Tipperary*. Dublin: James Duffy, 1887.

Kidder, Ed. *Receipts of Pastry and Cookery for the Use of his Scholars*. 18th century.

King, Elijah. *The Waif of Elm Island*. Boston, 1869.

King, Richard. *Narrative of a Journal to the Shores of the Arctic Ocean in 1833*. 1836.

Kingsford, William. *History of Canada*. Vol. III. Toronto: Roswell & Hutchinson, 1887–1898.

Kitchiner, William. *The Cook's Oracle; and Housekeeper's Manual. Containing Receipts for Cookery, and Directions for Carving. A Complete System of Cookery for Catholic Families*. New York: J. & J. Harper, 1833.

Koge Bog. Copenhagen: Salomone Sartorio, 1616.

Kraft, Irma. *The Power of Purim and Other Plays*. Philadelphia: The Jewish Publication Society of America, 1915.

Das Kuchbuch der Sabrina Welserin, 1533.

La Bédoyère, Charles Angélique François Huchet, comte de. *Memoirs of the Public and Private Life of Napoleon Bonaparte*. London: G. Virtue, 1827.

Ladd, Paul R. *Early American Fireplaces*. New York: Hastings House, 1977.

Ladies of Presbyterian Church. *Housekeeping in the Blue Grass. A New and Practical Cook Book: Containing Nearly a Thousand Recipes*. Paris, Ky., 1879.

Lafitau, Joseph François. *Moeurs des sauvages. Customs of the American Indians Compared with the Customs of Primitive Times*. 2 vols. Trans. William Fenton and Elizabeth Moore. Toronto: Champlain Society, 1974.

Lancelott, Francis. *The Queens of England and Their Times*. New York: Appleton, 1858.

Lane, Edward William. *The Manners and Customs of the Modern Egyptians*. New York: E.P. Dutton, 1908.

Lanman, Charles. *Adventures in the Wilds of the United States and British American Provinces: by Charles Lanman. Illustrated by the author and Oscar Bessau, with an Appendix by Lieutenant Campbell Hardy*. Philadelphia, 1856.

Lathrop, Mrs. C. M. *Riverside Recipe Book*. New York: Press of W. R. Jenkins, 1890.

Latini, Antonio. *Lo scalco alla moderna*. Naples, Italy, 1692.

La Varenne, François Pierre. *The French Cook*, translated into English in 1653 by I.D.G., with an introduction by Philip and Mary Hyman. East Sussex, U.K.: Southover Press, 2001.

Lawson, John. *A New Voyage to Carolina; Containing the Exact Description and Natural History of That Country: Together with the Present State Thereof. And A Journal of a Thousand Miles, Travel'd Thro' Several Nations of Indians. Giving a Particular Account of Their Customs, Manners, andc.* 1714.

Le Clerque, Chrestien. *New Relation of Gaspesia*. Trans and edited by Ganong, William F. Toronto: Champlain Society, 1910.

Lee, Guy Carleton, and Francis Newton Thorpe. *History of North America: The Growth of the Nation 1809–1837*. Philadelphia: Printed for subscribers only by G. Barrie & Sons, 1905.

Lee, N. M. K. *The Cook's Own Book and Housekeeper's Register*. Boston, 1842.

LeMoyne, Jacques. *Narrative of Le Moyne, an Artist Who Accompanied the French Expedition to Florida under Laudonniere*. Trans. De Bry. London, 1564.

Leslie, Eliza. *The Lady's Receipt-book*. Philadelphia, 1847.

_____. *Miss Leslie's Directions for Cookery*. 1851. Reprint, Mineola, N.Y.: Dover, 1999.

Letterman, Jonathan. *Official Records, 1861–1865*. Series I, Vol. II, Part III. Washington, D.C.: U.S. Government Printing Office, 1884.

Leucke, Barbara K. *Feeding the Frontier Army, 1775–1865*. Eagan, Minn.: Grenadier Publications, 1990.

Levy, Esther. *The Jewish Cookery Book Founded on Principles of Economy Adapted for Jewish Housekeepers*. Philadelphia: W.S. Turner, 1871.

Lewis, Alonzo, and James Newhall. *History of Lynn, Essex County, Massachusetts: Including Lynnfield, Saugus, Swampscott, and Nahant*. Boston, 1865.

Lewis, Edna. *The Taste of Country Cooking*. New York: Knopf, 1976.

Lewis, Meriwether, and William Clark. *Original Journals of the Lewis and Clark Expedition, 1804–1806*. Volumes 1–7. New York: Dodd, Mead, 1904–1905.

Lincoln, Mrs. A. D. *Boston Cooking School Cook Book*. 1884. Reprint, Garden City, N.Y.: Dover, 1996.

Littell, E. *Littell's Living Age*. Vol. V, June 1845. Boston.

Livermore, Mary. *My Story of the War*. Hartford, Conn., 1896.

_____. *The Story of My Life*. Hartford, Conn.: A.D. Worthington, 1897.

Livingston, Edward. *A System of Penal Law for the State of Louisiana*. Philadelphia, 1833.

Lockhart, Martha. *Lady Castlehill's Receipt Book*. Glasgow: Molendinar Press, 1976.

Lomax, Edward. *Encyclopedia of Architecture. A Dictionary of the Science and Practice of Architecture, Building, Carpentry, etc.* New York: Martin and Johnson, 1850.

Long, Edward. *The History of Jamaica. Or, General Survey of the Ancient and Modern State of That Island*. London, 1774.

Long, George, and Robley Dunglison. *An Introduction to the Study of Grecian and Roman Geography*. Charlottesville, Va., 1829.

Lord, John. *The Old Roman World: the Grandeur and Failure of Its Civilization*. New York, 1867.

Lossing, Benjamin. *Recollections and Private Memoirs of the Life and Character of Washington*. New York, 1860.

Lossing, Benson J. *Pictorial Field Book of the War of 1812*. 1869.

Lowell, James R. *The Bookman: A Review of Books and Life*. New York, 1913.

Luard, Elisabeth. *The Old World Kitchen*. New York: Bantam Books, 1987.

Lucas, A. T. *Irish Food Before the Potato*. Cork: Munster Express, 1991.

Lynde, Benjamin. *The Diaries of Benjamin Lynde and Benjamin Lynde, Jr*. Boston, 1880.

MacCauley, Clay. *The Seminole Indians of Florida*. 1887.

MacGavock, Randal. *A Tennessean Abroad; or Letters from Europe, Africa and Asia*. New York, 1854.

Machar, Agnes. *Stories of New France*. Boston, 1890.

Mackenzie, Alexander Slidell. *A Year in Spain*, 1829.

MacKenzie, Colin. *Five Thousand Receipts in All the Useful and Domestic Arts, Constituting a Complete and Universal Practical Library, and Operative Cyclopaedia*. Philadelphia, 1827.

MacKenzie, Osgood. *A Hundred Years in the Highlands (1800–1900)*. London: E. Arnold, 1921.

Mackie, Milton. *From Cape Cod to Dixie and the Tropics*. New York, 1864.

Mahon, Brid. *Land of Milk and Honey: The Story of Traditional Irish Food and Drink*. Dublin: Poolbeg, 1991.

Malek, Leona Alford. *Prudence Penny's Cookbook*. New York: Prentice-Hall, 1939.

Marcy, Randolph. *Prairie Traveler*. 1859.

Margoshes, Samuel, and Jewish Community of New York City. *Jewish Communal Register of New York City, 1917–1918*. New York: Kehillah (Jewish Community) of New York City, 1918.

Markham, Gervase. *The English House-wife*. 1649. Reprint, Falconwood Press, 1998.

Marshall, Josiah. *The Farmer's and Emigrant's Hand-Book: Being a Full and Complete Guide for the Farmer and the Emigrant*. New York, 1845.

Marshall, William Humphrey. *The Rural Economy of the West of England*. London, 1805.

Martin, Martin. *A Description of the Western Isles of Scotland Ca. 1695; and, A Voyage to St. Kilda*. Edinburgh: Birlinn, 1999.

Martineau, Harriet. *History of the Peace: Being a History of England from 1816 to 1854*. Boston: Walker, Wise, 1865.

Matteson, David Maydole. *The American Nation: A History*. New York and London: Harper, 1908.

Matthews, Washington. *Ethnography of the Hidatsa Indians*. Ann Arbor, Mich., 1877.

Maxwell, William Hamilton. *Wild Sports of the West of Ireland*. Dublin, 1892.

May, Robert. *The Accomplisht Cook, or The Art and Mystery of Cookery*. 1678. Reprint, Falconwood Press, 1999.

McClintock, Walter. *The Old North Trail, or, Life, Legends, and Religion of the Blackfeet Indians*. 1910.

McDonald, Colin. *Croft and Ceilidh*. Edinburgh: Moray Press, 1947.

McElroy, John. *Andersonville: A Story of Rebel Military Prisons*. Toledo, Ohio, 1879.

McIver, Mrs. *Cookery and Pastry as Taught and Practiced by Mrs. McIver*. Edinburgh.

McKenna, Theobald. *A Review of Some Interesting Periods of Irish History*. London, 1786.

McLean, John. *Canadian Savage Folk: Tribes of Canada*. 1896.

McLintock, Mrs. *Receipts for Cookery and Pastry Work*. 1736.

McMullen, John. *The History of Canada: From Its First Discovery to the Present*. 1855.

McNeill, F. Marian. *The Scots Kitchen, Its Lore and Recipes*. London: Blackie & Son, 1971.

Melville, Herman. *Moby Dick*. 1851. Reprint, New York: Dodd, Mead, 1942.

Mennell, Stephen. *All Manners of Food*. Oxford: Basil Blackwell, 1985.

Mereness, Newton D. *Travels in the American Colonies, Ed. Under the Auspices of the National Society of the Colonial Dames of America*. New York: Macmillan, 1916.

Michaud, Joseph, and William Robson. *The History of the Crusades*. London, 1881.

Michigan State Geologist. *State Geologist Survey*. Lansing, 1861.

Miller, Hugh. *An Autobiography. My Schools and Schoolmasters; or, The Story of My Education*. Boston: Gould and Lincoln, 1865.

Miller, T. *Old English Version of Bede's Ecclesiastical History*. Vols. I and II. London: N. Truebner, 1890.

Mitchell, John. *Treatise on the Falsifications of Food*. London, 1848.

Moerman, Daniel. *Native American Ethnobotany*. Portland, Ore.: Timber Press, 1988.

Molokhovets, Elena. *Classic Russian Cooking: Elena Molokhovets' A Gift to Young Housewives*. Translated and introduced by Joyce Toomre. 1861. Reprint, Bloomington: Indiana University Press, 1992.

Monnier, Marc. *The Wonders of Pompeii*. New York: Scribner's, 1871.

Mooney, James. *Myths of the Cherokees* and *Sacred Formulas of the Cherokees*, 1891, 1900.

Moore, Isabella. *The Useful and Entertaining Family Miscellany: Containing the Complete English Housekeeper's Companion*. London, 1766.

Morris, Edmund. *How to Get a Farm, and Where to Find One*. New York: J. Miller, 1864.

Morris, Richard, trans. *Liber cure Cocorum*. Ca. 1420–1440. Berlin: Printed for the Philological Society by A. Asher, 1862.

Morrison, Mary Gray. *The Last Three. Overland Monthly and Out West Magazine*. New York, 1850.

Morse, Jedediah. *A Report to the Secretary of War of the United States on Indian Affairs*. New Haven, Conn., 1822.

Morwood, Vernon. *Our Gipsies in City, Tent, and Van*. London: S. Low, Marston, Searle & Rivington, 1885.

Moryson, Fynes. *An Itenerary*. 1617. Reprint, Glasgow, 1907.

Moxon, Elizabeth. *The English Housewifry*. 1764.

Mrs. McLintock's Receipts for Cookery and Pastry Work. Scotland, 1736.

Mullaly, John. *The laying of the cable, or the ocean telegraph; being a complete and authentic narrative...* New York, 1858.

Munro, William. *Crusaders of New France: Chronicles of Fleur-de-lis in the Wilderness*. New Haven, Conn.: Yale University Press, 1921.

Munsell, Joel. *The Every Day Book of History and Chronology: Embracing the Anniversaries of Memorable Persons and Events, in Every Period and State of the World, from the creation to the present time*. New York: Appleton, 1858.

Murdoch, David D. D. *The Dutch Dominie of the Catskills; or, The Times of the "Bloody Brandt."* New York, 1861.

Murdoch, David. *The Dutch Dominie of the Catskills*. New York, 1861.

Murphy, Margot. *Wartime Meals*. New York: Greenberg, 1942.

Murray, Amelia N. *Letters from the United States, Cuba, and Canada*. 1856.

Murray, Hugh. *The Encyclopedia of Geography: Comprising a Complete Description of the Earth*. Philadelphia: Blanchard and Lea, 1852.

Murray, Janet. *Traditional Scots Recipes*. New York: Bramhall House, 1972.

Murray, John. *Murray's Modern Cookery Book, by a Lady*. London, 1851.

Murrell, John. *A Delightful Daily Exercise for Ladies and Gentlemen*.

Napier, Mrs. Alexander. *A Noble Boke of Cookery*.

Neil, Edna. *The A&P Everyday Cook and Recipe Book*. New York: The Great Atlantic & Pacific Tea Co., 190?.

New American Cookery or Female Companion, Containing Full and Ample Directions for Roasting, Broiling, Stewing, Hashing, Boiling, Preserving, Pickling, Potting, Fricasees, Soups, Puff-pastes, Puddings, Custards, Pies, Tarts, andc. Also, The Making of Wines and Cheese. By An American Lady. New York, 1805.

Newnham-Davis, Nathaniel. *The Gourmet's Guide to London*. New York: Brentano's, 1914.

Nicholson, Elizabeth. *The Home Manual*. Philadelphia, 1865.

Nicholson, Peter. *The Encyclopedia of Architecture: A Dictionary of the Science and Practice of Architecture, Building, Carpentry, Etc*. New York, 185?

Notes on the Floridian Peninsula, Its Literary History, Indian Tribes, and Antiquities. Philadelphia, 1859.

O Muimheneachain, Aindrias. *Stories from the Tailor*. Cork, 1978.

O'Brien Education. *Life in Ireland*. Dublin, 1972.

O'Callaghan, E. B. *The History of New Netherland*. New York, 1855.

Ogilvie, R. M. *The Romans and Their Gods*. London: Hogarth Press, 1986.

Ohio Annals. Dayton, Ohio, 1876.

Ojakangas, Beatrice. *Scandinavian Feasts*. Minneapolis: University of Minnesota Press, 2001.

O'Kelly, M. *Harvests and Hardships*. 1954.

Olmstead, Frederick. *A Journey Through Texas; or, A saddle-trip on the Southwestern Frontier; with a Statistical Appendix*. New York, 1857.

Omond, George William Thomson. *The Arniston Memoirs 1571–1838: Three Generations of a Scottish House*. 1887.

Optic, Oliver. *Northern Lands, or Young America in Russia and Prussia*. Boston: Lee and Shephard, 1874.

Ordway, Sgt. *Sgt. Ordway's Journal Kept on the Expedition of Western Exploration 1803–1806*. Vol. 22. Collections of the State Historical Society of Wisconsin, 1916.

Oswald, Ella. *German Cookery for the English Kitchen*. London: A. Siegle, 1906.

Ovid. *Fasti*. Harvard University Press.

Owen, David Dale. *Second Report of a Geological Reconnaissance of the Middle and Southern Counties of Arkansas, Made During the Years 1859 and 1860*. Philadelphia, 1860.

Parke, Godwin. *Cyclopaedia of Universal Biography*. New York, 1856.

Parker, Samuel. *Journal of an Exploring Tour Beyond the Rocky Mountains*. Ithaca, New York, 1840.

Parkman, Francis. *France and England in North America*. Boston, 1867.

_____. *Oregon Trail: Sketches of Prairie and Rocky Mountain Life*. Scott, 1919.

_____. *Pioneers of France in the New World*. Boston: Little, Brown, 1918.

Parloa, Maria. *Miss Parloa's Young Housekeeper. Designed Especially to Aid Beginners. Economical Receipts for Those Who Are Cooking for Two or Three*. Boston, 1893.

Parton, James. *The Humorous Poetry of the English Language*. 1856. New York.

Parzen, Jeremy, trans. Maestro Martino. *The Art of Cooking, the First Modern Cookbook*. 15th century. Berkeley: University of California Press, 2005.

Payne, A. G. *Cassell's Vegetarian Cookery*, 1891.

Peck, Annie. *The South American Tour*. New York: George H. Doran, 1913.

Pegge, Samuel. *The Forme of Cury*.

Penn, Gulielma. *Penn Family Recipes*. Edited by Benson, Evelyn Abraham. York, Pa.: Shumway, 1966.

Pennant, Thomas. *A Tour of Scotland*. London, 1774.

Pennell, Robert F. *Ancient Greece from the Earliest Times Down to 146 BC*. Boston, 1893.

Perry, William, Sir. *Tracts Chiefly Relating to Ireland*. Report Dublin, 1769.

Peterson, Hannah Mary Bouvier. *The National Cook Book. By a Lady of Philadelphia. A Practical Housewife; and Author of the "Family Save-All."* Philadelphia: T.B. Peterson and Brothers, ca. 1866.

Phillips, Henry. *History of Cultivated Vegetables*. London, 1822.

The Picayune's Creole Cook Book. New Orleans: Picayune, 1901.

Pichon, Jerome. *Le Menagier de Paris*. 1846. Reprinted Geneva, 1970.

Pickett, Albert. *Pickett's History of Alabama and Incidentally of Georgia and Mississippi from the Earliest Period*. Charleston, 1851.

Pierce, Anne. *Home Canning for Victory*. New York: M. Barrows, 1942.

Pike, Zebulon. *An Account of Expeditions to the Sources of the Mississippi, and Through the Western Parts of Louisiana, to the Sources of the Arkansas, Kans, La Platte, and Pierre Jaun, Rivers*. Philadelphia: Published by C. and A. Conrad; Somervell and Conrad; Bonsal, Conrad; and Fielding Lucas, Jr., 1810.

_____. *An Important Visit*. 1806.

Pinkerton, John. *Modern Geography; a Description of the Empire, Kingdoms, States, and ...* Vol. 1. Philadelphia: J. Conrad, 1804.

Platt, Sir Hugh. *Delightes for Ladies, to Adorne Their Persons, Tables, Closets and Distillatories*. London, 1609.

_____. *The Jewell House of Art and Nature*.

Plutarch. *Ancient Customs of the Spartans*. Harvard Classics.

_____. *Moralia*. Harvard University Press.

Poirteir, C. *The Great Irish Famine*. Cork: Munster Express, 1995.

Political Anatomy of Ireland. 1691.

Porcher, Francis P. *Resources of Southern Fields and Forests, Medical, Economical, and Agricultural*. 1863.

Portlock, Nathaniel. *Voyage Round the World; But More Particularly to the Northwest Coast of America*. London: John Stockdale and George Goulding, 1789.

Power, Eileen Edna. *Le Menagier de Paris* [The Goodman of Paris]. 1393. Reprint, London: G. Routledge, 1928.

The Present State of Ireland, London Report. 1673.

Priestley, J. B. *The Edwardians*. London: Heinemann, 1964.

Prisch, Betty Coit. *Aspects of Change in Seneca Iroquois Ladles A.D. 1600–1900*. Rochester, N.Y.: Research Division, Rochester Museum and Science Center, 1982.

Pulleyn, William. *The Treasury of Knowledge and Library Reference*. London, 1853.

Putnam's Tales and Sketches for the Fireside by the Best American Authors. New York, 1857.

Putney, Albert H. *United States Constitutional History and Law*. Chicago: Illinois Book Exchange, 1908.

Quennell, Marjorie. *A History of Everyday Things in England*. London: Batsford, 1961.

Raffield, Elizabeth. *The Experienced English Housekeeper*. London, 1808.

Randall, Henry S. *The Life of Thomas Jefferson*. New York, 1858.

Randolph, Mary. *The Virginia Housewife, or, Methodical Cook*. Philadelphia: E. H. Butler, 1860.

Read, Mrs. George. Manuscript cookbook, 1813. Holcomb Collection, Historical Society of Delaware, Wilmington, Delaware.

Redon, Odile, Francoise Sabban, and Silvano Serventi. *The Medieval Kitchen: Recipes from France and Italy*. Trans. Schneider, Edward. Chicago: University of Chicago Press, 1998.

Reese, Richard. *The Gazette of Health*. 1820.

Reid, John. *The Scots Gard'ner together with The Gard'ners Kalendar*. 1683. Reprint, London, Edinburgh: T.N. Foulis, 1907.

Remlap, L. T. *The Life of General U.S. Grant: His Early Life, Military Achievements*. Chicago. 1885.

Report of Commissioner of Indian Affairs. U.S. Government Printing Office, 1873.

Report of General Board of Health. Dublin, 1822.

The Reports of the Society for Bettering the Condition and Increasing the Comforts of the Poor. Vol. 1, 1798.

Reports of the United States Commissioners to the Paris Universal Exposition 1867. Washington, D.C.: U.S. Government Printing Office, 1870.

Rhind, William. *A History of the Vegetable Kingdom*. London, 1857.

Richardson, Albert Deane. *Beyond the Mississippi from the Great River to the Great Ocean*. Hartford, Conn.: American Pub., 1867.

Rifkind, H. R. *Fresh Foods for the Army 1775–1950*. Quartermaster Corps, U.S. Army.

Riggs, Stephen Return. *Tah-koo wah-kan: or, The Gospel Among the Dakotas*. Boston, 1869.

Robertson, William. *The history of Scotland, during the reign of Queen Mary and King James VI Till His Accession to the Crown of England*. New York, 1856.

Robinson, James. *The Whole Art of Curing, Pickling, and Smoked Meat and Fish*. London, 1847.

Robinson, Solon. *Facts for Farmers; also the Family Circle A Variety of Rich Materials for all land-owners about Domestic Animals and Domestic Economy, ...* New York, 1867.

_____. *How to Live, Saving or Wasting, or Domestic Economy Illustrated*. New York, 1860.

Rochefort, Charles de. *Histoire naturelle et morale des îles Antilles de l'Amerique*.

Romans, Bernard. *A Concise History of East and West Florida*. New York, 1775.

Rorer, Sarah Tyson Herston. *Mrs. Rorer's Vegetable Cookery and Meat Substitutions*. Philadelphia: Arnold, 1909.

Rose, Peter. *Foods of the Hudson*. Woodstock, N.Y.: Overlook Press, 1993.

Rose, Peter G. *The Sensible Cook*. 1683. Reprint, Syracuse, N.Y.: Syracuse University Press, 1989.

Ross, John. *History of Corea [sic], Ancient and Modern*. London: E. Stock, 1891.

Rough Notes by an Old Soldier During Fifty Years' Service. London, 1867.

Rountree, Helen C. "Powhatan Indian Women: The People Captain John Smith Barely Saw," *Ethnohistory 45*, no. 1 (1998).

Rumble, Victoria. *Outdoor Recreation and Leisure in 19th Century America*. Florence, Ala.: Thistle Dew Books, 2007.

Rumpolt, Marx, trans. *Ein New Kochbuch*. Ca. 1581.

Rundell, Maria Eliza. *A New System of Domestic Cookery*. Boston, 1807.

Russell, John. *Boke of Nurture*. Ca. 1460. Edited by Samuel Pegge, 1785.

Russell, John. *A Tour in Germany*. Edinburgh, 1820.

Ruttenber, Edward Manning. *History of the Indian Tribes of Hudson's River: Their Origin, Manners, and Customs*. Albany, 1872.

Sagard, Gabriel. *Le Grand Voyage*. Paris: Libraries Tross, 1865.

Sage, Rufus. *Rocky Mountain Life: Or, Startling Scenes and Perilous Adventures in the Far West During an Expedition of Three Years*. Boston, 1859.

St. John, Horace. *Audubon the Naturalist*. Boston, 1864.

Sala, George Augustus. *Breakfast in Bed*. New York: M. Doolady, 1863.

Salmon, William. *Botanologia. The English Herbal or, History of Plants*, 1710.

Sanderson, J. M. *Complete Cook*. Philadelphia, 1864.

Sargent, Epes. *Arctic Adventures by Sea and Land*. Boston, 1857.

Schaw, Janet. *Journal of a Lady of Quality, Being a Narrative of a Journey from Scotland to the West Indies, North Carolina, and Portugal in the years 1774–1776*. New Haven, Conn.: Yale University Press, 1939.

Schele De Vere, Maximilian. *Americanisms; the English of the New World*. New York, 1872.

Schoolcraft, H. R. *Historical and Statistical Information Respecting the History, etc. of the Indian Tribes of the U.S.* Philadelphia, 1851.

Schultz, James Willard. *My Life as an Indian*. New York: Doubleday, Page, 1907.

Schwanitz, Franz. *The Origin of Cultivated Plants*. Harvard University Press, 1967.

Schwartz-Nobel, Loretta. *Starving in the Shadow of Plenty*. New York: Putnam's, 1981.

Scott, Col. H. L. *Military Dictionary: Comprising Technical Definitions: Information on Raising and Keeping Troops; actual service, including makeshifts and improved material*. New York, 1861.

Scott, Sir Walter. *The Antiquary*. http://www.walterscott.lib.ed.ac.uk/etexts/etexts/antiquary1.htm.
_____. *Fair Maid of Perth*. 1828.
_____. *Scotland*. 1899.
_____. *The Waverly Novels*. Philadelphia. 1855.

Scully, Terence. *The Art of Cooking in the Middle Ages*. Woodbridge, U.K.; Rochester, N.Y., Boydell Press, 1995.

_____, trans. *The Vivendier: A 15th-Century French Cookery Manuscript*. Devon, U.K.: Prospect Books, 1997.

Sears, George Washington. *Woodcraft*. New York: Forest and Stream Pub., 1920.

Sedgwick, Catherine. *Letters from Abroad to Kindred at Home*. New York: Harper, 1841.

Sereni, Emilio. *History of the Italian Agricultural Landscape*. Litchfield, R. Burr, trans. Princeton, N.J.: Princeton University Press, 1997.

Sexton, R. *A Little History of Irish Food*. London: Kyle Cathie Ltd., 1998.

Shackelford, Ann. *The Modern Art of Cooking*. London, 1767.

Shadburn, Don L. *Cherokee Planters in Georgia*. Vol. 2. Roswell, Ga.: W.H. Wolfe Associates, 1989.

Shaw, Ian. *The Oxford History of Ancient Egypt*. Oxford: Oxford University Press, 2000.

Shea, John. *The Historical Magazine and Notes and Queries*. 1873.

Shea, John G. *Discovery and Exploration of the Mississippi Valley, with the Original Narratives of Marquette, Allouez, Hennepin, and Anastase Douay*. Chilton Hill, New York, 1852.

Shonagon, Sei. *The Pillow Book*.

Shuman, Carrie V. *A Columbian Autograph Souvenir Cookery Book*. Chicago, 1893.

Simmonds, Peter. *Commercial Products of the Sea*. London, 1883.

Simmons, Amelia. *American Cookery, or the art of dressing viands, fish, poultry, and vegetables, and the best modes of making pastes, puffs, pies, tarts, puddings, custards, and preserves, and all kinds of cakes, from the imperial plum to plain cake: Adapted to this country, and all grades of life*. 1798. Reprint, Bedford, Mass.: Applewood Books, 1996.

Singleton, Arthur. *Letters from the South and West*. Boston, 1824.

Skeat, W. W. *Aelfric's Lives of the Saints*. 1881.

Smallzried, Kathleen Ann. *The Everlasting Pleasure: Influences on America's Kitchens, Cooks and Cookery, from 1565 to the Year 2000*. New York: Appleton-Century-Crofts, 1956.

Smith, Eliza. *The Complete Housewife or Accomplish'd Gentlewoman's Companion*. London, 1727.

Smith, James. *Captives Among the Indians*. Oyster Bay, N.Y.: Nelson Doubleday, 1915.

Smith, John. *Narratives of Early Virginia 1606–1625*. Ed. Tyler, Lyon Gardiner. New York, 1907.

Smith, John Frederick, and William Howlitt. *John Cassell's Illustrated History of England*. Vol. II. London and New York: 1862.

Smith, William. *A Dictionary of Greek and Roman Biography and Mythology by Various Writers.* Boston, 1867.

Smollett, Tobias. *Selected Works of Tobias Smollett.* Philadelphia, 1851.

Solbrig, Otto T., and Dorothy J. Solbrig. *So Shall You Reap: Farming and Crops in Human Affairs.* Washington, D.C.: Island Press, 1994.

The Soldier's Friend. 1789.

Sorbière, Samuel. *A Voyage to England Containing Many Things Relating to the State of Learning, Religion, and Other Curiosities of That Kingdom.* London: J. Woodward, 1709.

Soyer, Alexis. *The Modern Housewife or Menagére Comprising Nearly One Thousand Receipts for the Economic and Judicious Preparations of Every Meal of the Day....* New York, 1866.

_____. *A Shilling Cookery for the People.*

Stanhope, Philip Henry. *History of England, from the Peace of Utrecht to the Peace of Versailles, 1713–1783.* Boston, 1853.

Starkey, Thomas. *England in the Reign of Henry VIII.*

Stearns, Peter N. *Encyclopedia of World History,* Boston: Houghton Mifflin, 2001.

Steiner, Edward Alfred. *On the Trail of the Immigrant.* New York: Revell, 1906.

Stewart, David. *Sketches of the Highlanders.* 1885.

Storke, Elliot G. *Domestic and Rural Affairs.* New York, 1859.

Stowe, Harriet Beecher. *Sunny Memories of Sunny Lands.* London, 1854

Stratton, Royal B. *Captivity of the Oatman Girls.* New York, 1858.

Sturtevant, E. Lewis. *Sturtevant's Notes on Edible Plants.* Albany, N.Y.: Department of Agriculture, 1919.

Swanton, John. *Early History of the Creek Indians and Their Neighbors.* Washington, D.C.: U.S. Government Printing Office, 1922.

_____. *Indian Tribes of the Lower Mississippi Valley and Adjacent Coast of the Gulf of Mexico.* Washington, D.C.: U.S. Government Printing Office, 1911.

_____. *The Indians of the Southeastern United States.* 2 vols. Washington, D.C.: U.S. Government Printing Office, 1946.

Sweet Home Family Soap. Sweet Home Cook Book. Buffalo, N.Y., 1888.

Taillevent. *Le Viandier de Guillaume Tirel dit Taillevent.*

Tannahill, Reay. *Food in History.* New York: Stein and Day, 1973.

Tanty, Francois. *La Cuisine Française.* Chicago, 1893.

Tarbell, John Adams. *Sources of Health and Prevention of Disease.* Boston, 1850.

Taylor, Alfred S. *On Poisons in Relation to Medical Jurisprudence and Medicine.* Philadelphia, 1859.

Taylor, Bayard. *By-Ways of Europe.* New York, 1869.

_____. *Central Asia, Travels in Cashmere, Little Tibet, and Central Asia.* New York, 1874.

Taylor, John. *The Pennyless Pilgrimage.* London, 1618.

Taylor's Guide to Vegetables and Herbs. Boston. Houghton Mifflin, 1961.

The Terrific Register; or, Record of Crimes, Judgments, Provinces, Etc. Vol. II. London, 1825.

Tertullian. *Apologeticus and De Spectaculis.* Harvard University Library Press.

Thomas, Austin. *Two fifteenth-century cookery-books.*

Thompson, C. J. S. *Quacks of Old London.* 1928. Reprint, New York: Barnes & Noble, 1993.

Thompson, Francis. *Crofting Years.* Ayrshire, U.K.: Luath Press, 1984.

Thwaites, Reuben Gold. *An American Nation. A History of France in America.* New York: Harper & Bros., 1905.

_____. *Jesuit Relations.* Cleveland, 1897.

Timberlake, Henry. *Memoirs of Lieut. Henry Timberlake.* London, 1765.

Timbs, John. *School Days of Eminent Men.* London 1860.

Traditional Food from Scotland. London: Thomas Nelson and Sons, 1932.

Transactions and Proceedings of the Royal Society of New Zealand 1868–1961. Vol. 18. 1885.

Tripler, Charles S., and George C. Blackman. *Handbook for the Military Surgeon.* Cincinnati, 1861.

Tschirky, Oscar. *Cookbook by Oscar of the Waldorf.* Chicago, 1896.

Tuckerman, Henry T. *America and Her Commentators, with a Critical Sketch of Travel in the U.S.* New York, 1864.

Turabi, Efendi. *Turkish Cookery Book: A Collection of Receipts.* 1862. Reprint, Rottingdean: Cooks, 1987.

Turner, Sharon. *The Anglo-Saxons.* London, 1828.

Turner, Elle V. *Holland's Cook Book.* Dallas: Texas Farm and Ranch Publishing, 1923.

Tusser, Thomas. *Five Hundred Pointes of Good Husbandrie.* Payne, William, ed. 1557, 1580. Reprint, London: Truebner, 1878.

Tylor, Edward Burnet. *Researches into the Early History of Mankind and the Development of Civilization.* London, 1865.

Ude, Louis Eustache. *The French Cook.* London, 1813.

United States. Bureau of Indian Affairs. Annual Report of the Commissioner of Indian Affairs to the Secretary of the Interior, 1873.

_____. Congress. Report of the Joint Special Committee, Appointed under Joint Resolution on March 3, 1865. No. 2. Condition of the Indian Tribes. 1867.

Usher, Abbott Payson. *The History of the Grain Trade in France 1400–1710.* Cambridge, Mass.: Harvard University Press, 1913.

Van Tramp, John C. *Prairie and Rocky Mountain Adventures; or, Life in the West.* Columbus, Ohio, 1870.

Vaultier, Roger. "La gastronomie regionale en France pendant la revolution." Grandgousier, 1940.

Vehling, Joseph. *Apicius: Cookery and Dining in Imperial Rome.* Garden City, N.Y.: Dover, 1977.

Verral, William. *A Complete System of Cookery.* London, 1759.

Wailes, Benjamin L. C. *Report on the Agriculture and Geology of Mississippi: Embracing a Sketch of the Social and Natural History of the State.* E. Barksdale, 1854.

Waley, Arthur. *The Book of Songs.* New York: Houghton Mifflin, 1937.

Walsh, William Shepard. *The Handy-Book of Literary Curiosities.* 1892. Reprint, Philadelphia: Lippincott, 1906.

Walton, Izaak. *The Complete Angler.*

Ward, Edward. *Five Travel Scripts.* London, 1698.

Waselkof, G. A., P. H. Wood, and M. T. Hatley. *Powhatan's Mantle: Indians in the Colonial Southeast.* Lincoln: University of Nebraska Press, 2006.

Washburn, Charles A. *The History of Paraguay with Notes of Personal Observations, and Reminiscences of Diplomacy Under Difficulties.* New York, 1871.

Watkins, T. H. *The Hungry Years: A Narrative History of the Great Depression in America.* New York: Henry Holt, 1999.

Watson, Henry Clay. *The Camp-fires of Napoleon: Comprising the Most Brilliant Achievements of the Emperor and His Marshals.* Philadelphia, 1854.

Watson, John Fanning. *Annals of Philadelphia and Pennsylvania, in the Olden Time; ....* Ottawa: Government Printing Bureau, 1916.

Weber, Georg. *Outlines of Universal History, from the Creation of the World to the Present Time.* Boston, 1859.

Webster, Mrs. A. L. *Book of Receipts with Engravings.* Boston, 1855.

Webster, Thomas. *Encyclopedia of Domestic Economy.* New York: Harper & Bros., 1845.

Webster, William Clarence. *A General History of Commerce.* Boston: Ginn, 1903.

The What-Not; or, Ladies' Handy Book. London, 1861.

Wheeler, Edward Jewett. *Current Literature.* Vol. XXXI. New York, 1901.

Whitcomb, John, and Claire Whitcomb. *Real Life at the White House.* New York: Routledge, 2002.

White, Henry. *A History of the World, on a New and Systematic Plan; from the Earliest Times to the Treaty of Vienna.* Philadelphia, 1851.

White, William N. *Gardening at the South.* New York and Athens, Ga., 1856

Whitehead, Charles E. *The Camp-Fires of the Everglades.* Edinburgh, 1891.

Wilhide, Elizabeth. *The Fireplace: A Guide to Period Style.* Boston: Little, Brown, 1994.

Wilkinson, John Gardner. *The Manners and Customs of the Ancient Egyptians.* 1878.

_____. *A Popular Account of the Ancient Egyptians.* New York, 1854.

Williams, Roger. *A Key into the Language of America.* Providence, 1827.

Williams, Samuel Wells, and John Orr. *The Middle Kingdom.* Vol. II. New York and London, 1848.

Williams, T. *The Accomplished Housekeeper, and Universal Cook.* London, 1797.

Willis, Brewer. *Alabama: Her History.* Montgomery, Ala.: Barrett & Brown, 1872.

Willis, N. Parker. *The Convalescent.* New York, 1859.

Willson, Marcius. *Ancient and Modern History.* New York, 1864.

_____. *Outlines of History.* New York, 1864.

Wilson, Anne. *Food and Drink in Britain.* Stirling, 1934.

_____. *Two Fifteenth Century Cookbooks.*

Wilson, C. Anne. *Food and Drink in Britain.* Chicago: Academy Chicago Publishers, 1991.

Wilson, Gilbert. *Buffalo Bird Woman's Garden.* 1917. Reprint, St. Paul: Minnesota Historical Society, 1987.

Winslow, Susan. *Brother, Can You Spare a Dime? America from the Wall Street Crash to Pearl Harbor, An Illustrated Documentary.* New York: Paddington Press, 1976.

Wolley, Hannah. *The Cook's Guide.*

_____. *The Gentlewoman's Companion.*

_____. *The Queen-Like Closet or Rich Cabinet.* London, 1672.

Wood, Alphonso. *Classbook of Botany.* Claremont, N.H., 1851.

Wood, W. W. *Sketches of China.* New York, 1830.

Wood, William. *New England's Prospect.* 1635. Reprint, Amherst: University of Massachusetts Press, 1977.

Woolman, John. *The Journal of John Woolman.* Collier, 1909.

Wordsworth, Dorothy. *Recollections of a Tour Made in Scotland.* 1803.

Works Project Administration. *Louisiana: A Guide to the State.* Baton Rouge, 1941.

Wortley, Lady Emmeline Stuart. *Travels in the U.S. Etc. during 1849 and 1850.* New York, 1851.

The Young Lady's Companion. London, 1734.

Young, Arthur. *A Tour of Ireland.* London, 1780.

Zimmer, Anne Carter. *The Robert E. Lee Family Cooking and Housekeeping Book.* Chapel Hill: University of North Carolina Press, 1997.

Zimmerman, Wilhelm. *A Popular History of Germany: From the Earliest Period to Present Day.* Vol. II. New York, 1878.

Periodicals

Adams Sentinel (Gettysburg, Pa.). July 1, 1857.

Appleton's Journal 10, no. 58 (April 1881).

Appleton's Journal 2, no. 26 (September 25, 1869).

Appleton's Journal 8, no. 5 (May 1880).

Appleton's. November 13, 1869.

Arthur's Magazine. January–December 1866.

Bartram, William. "Observations on the Creek and Cherokee Indians." *Transactions of the American Ethnological Society 3*, 1789.

Bates, H. W. "The River Amazon." *The Naturalist.* Vol. II. London, 1863.

Blackwood's Edinburgh Magazine, 1844.

Brooklyn Daily Eagle, April 21, 1853.

Brooklyn Daily Eagle, October 5, 1853.

Brooklyn Daily Eagle, May 30, 1854.

Brooklyn Daily Eagle, April 10, 1855.

Brooklyn Daily Eagle, August 31, 1858.

Brooklyn Daily Eagle, November 1858.

Brooklyn Daily Eagle, April 26, 1861.

Brooklyn Daily Eagle, March 23, 1863.

Brooklyn Daily Eagle, March 31, 1864.

Brooklyn Daily Eagle, August 12, 1868.

Brooklyn Daily Eagle, August 29, 1868.

Brooklyn Daily Eagle, September 8, 1868.

Brooklyn Daily Eagle, September 14, 1868.

Brooklyn Daily Eagle, December 7, 1868.

Brooklyn Daily Eagle, November 13, 1869.

Brooklyn Daily Eagle, May 28, 1872.

Brooklyn Daily Eagle, August 19, 1877.

Brooklyn Daily Eagle, November 20, 1877.

Brooklyn Daily Eagle, September 22, 1878.

Brooklyn Daily Eagle, July 26, 1880.

Brooklyn Daily Eagle, July 22, 1881.

Brooklyn Daily Eagle, April 13, 1895.

Brooklyn Daily Eagle, October 28, 1895.

Brooklyn Daily Eagle, September 13, 1898.

Brooklyn Daily Eagle, August 14, 1900.

Brooklyn Daily Eagle, September 2, 1900.

Brooklyn Daily Eagle, April 20, 1901.

Brooklyn Daily Eagle, October 21, 1902.

Brooklyn Eagle, August 17, 1844.

Brooklyn Eagle, October 1, 1849.

Bushick, Frank. *Frontier Times*, July 1927.

"California Cereals." *Overland Monthly 2*, no. 7 (July 7, 1883).

"California Culinary Experiences." *Overland Monthly 2*, no. 6 (June 1869).

"California in '49." *Overland Monthly 34*, no. 202 (October 1899).

"California Mission Fruits." *Overland Monthly 11*, no. 65 (May 1888).

"Camp and Travel in Colorado." *Overland Monthly 15*, no. 89 (May 1890).

Carlyle, Thomas. *Frazier's Magazine for Town and Country* (July–December 1853). London.

Cedar Rapids Times (Iowa), February 22, 1872.

The Century 35, no. 4 (February 1888).

The Century Magazine 55, no. 1 (November 1897). New York.

Chidsey, Charles E. "First Settlements in Louisiana." *Old Spanish Trail Magazine* (December 1920).

The Cottager's Monthly. Vol. XXVI. 1846. London.

Croly, Jane Cunningham. *The Homemaker Illustrated Monthly Magazine 2* (April–September 1889).

Cullen, L. "Irish History without the Potato." *Past and Present 40* (July 1968), pp. 72–83.

The Daily Constitutionalist (Augusta, Ga.). November 9, 1861.

The Daily Courier (Connellsville, Pa.). October 7, 1946.

Daily Herald (Chicago). July 27, 1988.

The Daily Herald. August 3, 1898.

Daily Review (Hayward, Ca.). January 18, 1970.

Davies, R. W. "The Roman Military Diet." *Britannia 2* (1971).

Debow's Review 9, no. 6 (December 1850).

Debow's Review (December 1851).

Democratic State Register. August 20, 1853.

"Discovery of Pompeii." *Ladies' Repository 1*, no. 4 (April 1868).

Douglas Jerrold's Shilling Magazine, 1846.

Dunkirk Evening Observer (New York). November 9, 1937.

The Eclectic Magazine of Foreign Literature, 1843.

Edinburgh Advertiser, July 1, 1800.

Edinburgh Advertiser, March 2, 1798.

Edinburgh Advertiser, May 13, 1800.

Edinburgh Evening Courant, September 1869.

Edinburgh Medical and Surgical Journal. 1844.

Elvira Evening Telegram (Ohio). October 9, 1913.

Erckmann-Chatrian. "The Veterans of Yesterday." *Appleton's Journal 10*, no. 55 (January 1881).

"Essay on the Slow Progress of Mankind." *Southern Literary Messenger 18*, no. 7 (July 1852).

Field and Fireside, various issues, 1860s.

"Foods of Early New England." *Journal of Home Economics*. 1920.

Fort Wayne News (Indiana). June 30, 1899.

Frederick Post (Maryland). March 15, 1995.

"French Soups." *Medical Times and Gazette*. 1885.

The Galaxy. April 1867.

The Galaxy. February 1868.

The Galaxy. March 1869.

The Galaxy. May 1869.

The Galaxy. July 1869.

Galveston Daily News. November 23, 1869.

Galveston News (Texas). October 17, 1869.

"Gastronomy and Gastronomers." *London Quarterly Review*, 1835.

Gentleman's Magazine, 1753.

The Gentleman's Magazine, January 1843.

The Gentleman's Magazine, 1893.

"The Gipsies." *Catholic World 3*, no. 17 (August 1866), pp. 702–715.

"Good Eating." *Southern Literary Messenger 37*, no. 5 (May 1863).

Greene, Charles. "Restaurants of San Francisco." *Overland Monthly 20*, no. 120 (December 1892).

Griffiths, Ralph. *The Monthly Review*. 1807.

Griffiths, Ralph. *The Monthly Review*. Vol. XV. 1830. London.

Hagerstown Torchlight (Maryland). October 12, 1846.

Harcum, Cornelia G. "Roman Cooking Utensils in the Royal Ontario Museum of Archaeology." *American Journal of Archaeology 25*, no. 1 (January–March 1921).

Harper's, 1853.

Harper's 13, no. 74 (July 1856).

Harper's 14, no. 83 (April 1857).

Harper's 28, no. 168 (May 1864).

Harper's 29, no. 171 (August 1864).

Harper's 54, no. 324 (May 1877).

Harper's 78, no. 465 (February 1889).

Harper's 78, no. 466 (March 1889).

"Historical and Statistical Collections of Louisiana." *Debow's Review*, 1851.

History of Irish Cuisine. http://www.ravensgard. org/prdunham/irishfood.html.

History of the Carrot Museum. www.carrotmuse um.co.uk.

History of the Potato Famine in Ireland. http://www. vinnysa1store.com/irishfamine.html.

History of Turkish Cuisine. www.turkishcook.com.

The Homemaker, An Illustrated Monthly Magazine 2 (April–September 1889).

Independent American (Platteville, Wisc.). July 24, 1857.

Indiana Progress (Indiana, Pa.). June 11, 1871.

Indiana Progress (Indiana, Pa.). February 19, 1874.

Indiana Progress. August 6, 1874.

Iowa City Press-Citizen. June 25, 1955.

Janesville Weekly Gazette (Wisconsin). February 16, 1865.

Janesville Weekly Gazette (Wisconsin). May 24, 1879.

"Japonica." *Scribner's 9*, no. 2 (1891).

Laba, R. P. Jean Baptiste. *Nouveau Voyage aux îles de l'Amerique*. Paris, 1742. Quoted in Richard Price. "Caribbean Fishing and Fishermen: A Historical Sketch." *American Anthropologist* (1966), Anthropological Society of Washington, D.C.

The Ladies' Repository. March 1854.

The Ladies' Repository, July 1865.

Leon, Edwin Lee. "French Morals and Manners." *Appleton's Journal 1*, no. 4 (April 24, 1869).

The Living Age 26, no. 326 (August 17, 1850).

The Living Age 35, no. 447 (December 11, 1852).

Marble Rock Weekly (Iowa). September 21, 1899.

Marion Weekly Star (Ohio), July 24, 1886.

McLoughlin, William G. "The Cherokees in Transition: A Statistical Analysis of the Federal Cherokee Census of 1835." *Journal of American History*, 1977.

The Metropolitan Magazine. 1835.

"Middle Class Domestic Life in Spain." *Appleton's 8*, no. 4 (April 1880).

Milwaukee Semi-Weekly Gazette. December 3, 1845.

Missouri Gazette. March 19, 1847.

"Modern and Medieval Dinners." *The Galaxy Magazine 3*, no. 7 (April 1, 1867). New York.

National Magazine, May 1858.

"Negro Slavery at the South, Part II." *Debow's Review 7*, no. 5 (November 1849).

New York Times. June 10, 1941.

New York Times. April 22, 1943.

New York Times. November 7, 1943.

The News (Frederick, Md.). April 16, 1984.

North Adams Transcript (Mass.). March 18, 1899.

Oakland Tribune. December 12, 1898.

Ohio Repository (Canton, Ohio). January 10, 1855.

O'Kelly, M. J. "Excavations and Experiments in Early Irish Cooking-Places." *Journal of the Royal Society of Antiquities in Ireland*. 1954.

Out West Magazine. August 1900.

Overland Monthly. July 1891.

Overland Monthly. February 1896.

Overland Monthly. April 1900.

Parsons, James. "Sea Turtles and Their Eggs." *Cambridge World History of Food*. Eds. Kenneth Kiple and Kriemhild Ornelas. Vol. 1. Cambridge, United Kingdom: Cambridge, 2000. 567–574. 2 vols. *Gale Virtual Reference Library*. Thomson Gale.

"A Peep into the Kitchens of the Ancients," *Brooklyn Daily Eagle*, April 26, 1861.

"The Philosophy of Drawing Rooms." *Appleton's Journal*, May 1880.

Pictures from the Life of Napoleon. Part VII, Vol. 23, no. 12 (December 1863).

Platina. *On the Right Pleasure and Good Health*. Critical edition and translation by Mary Ella Milham. (Medieval and Renaissance Texts and Studies, Vol. 168), 1998.

"Portuguese Superstitions." *Appleton's 14*, no. 334 (August. 14, 1875).

Potter's American Monthly. 1880.

Powers, Stephen. "The California Indians." *Overland Monthly 12*, no. 6 (June 1874).

The Quarterly Review. February 1836. London.

"The Queen's Closet Opened." *Atlantic Monthly*, August 1891.

Reedsburg Free Press (Wisconsin). Diary published in installments. September 20, September 27, 1872.

"Reminiscences of Cuba." *Debow's Review*, October 1855.

The Republican Compiler (Gettysburg, Pa.). October 21, 1850.

"Respectable Poverty in France." *Catholic World 27*, no. 158 (May 1878).

Robinson, Solon. *The American Agriculturist*. February 1846.

_____. *The American Agriculturist*. March 25, 1849.

_____. *The American Agriculturist*. May 1849.

Ross, A. A. "The Wrongs of the Cherokees." *Ladies' Repository* (June 1845).

Rotterdam, 1665. Quoted in Richard Price. "Caribbean Fishing and Fishermen: A Historical Sketch." *American Anthropologist* (1966), Anthropological Society of Washington, D.C.

The Saint James Magazine. December–March 1865. London.

San Antonio Light. September 12, 1937.

"Scenes of Breton Life." *Brooklyn Daily Eagle*. October 27, 1895.

Scribner's 10, no. 6 (December 1891).

Scribner's 15, no. 3 (May 1879).

Scribner's 18, no. 1 (March 1894).

Self Culture: A Magazine of Knowledge. Vol. VIII (1898). Akron.

Smith, George. *The Cornhill Magazine.* Vol. XVIII (January to June1905). London.

Southern Literary Messenger (March 1835).

Southern Literary Messenger 7, no. 9 (September 1841).

Southern Literary Messenger 8, no. 3 (March 1842).

Southern Literary Messenger 21, no. 12 (December 1855).

Southern Quarterly Review 2, no. 3 (July 1842).

Southern Quarterly Review (July 1846).

Southern Quarterly Review (January 1852).

Star and Banner (Gettysburg, Pa.). March 2, 1849.

Stradley, Linda. What's Cooking America? http://whatscookingamerica.net.

Syracuse Herald Journal (New York). March 12, 1974.

The Times (London). February 26, 1788.

The Times (London). April 30, 1789.

Wines, E. C. "China and the Chinese." *Southern Quarterly Review*, July 1847.

Wisconsin Daily Palladium. July 31, 1852.

Wisconsin Patriot (Madison). July 2, 1859.

Interviews, Lectures and Speeches

Chisholm, Rachel, director Highland Folk Museum, Kingusee, Scotland. Personal interview. July 2006.

Congressional Record, 1854–1904. Extract from speech given by the Hon. James E. Watson of Indiana, November 23, 1903.

Furnas, Robert S. Lecture. International Congress of Millers, held at Paris. August, 1889.

He Who Stands Firm. Interview. Mt. Tremper, New York, November, 19, 2007.

Hillyer, William. Extract from an account of a London soup shop. January 24, 1798.

Leucke, Barbara K. Interview, December 2007.

Matuck, Archie. Interview, December 2007.

McMillan, W. Diary, edited by Keith Hingle.

Rose, Peter G. Interview, June 7, 2007.

Wolf, Rabbi Ken. Interview. June 2008. Temple B'nai Israel, Florence, Ala.

Websites

All About Hungarian Goulash. http://www.budapest-tourist-guide.com/hungarian-goulash.html

America As the Garden During the Renaissance. http://xroads.virginia.edu/~hyper/hns/garden/rengarden.html.

Archaeology. http://www.archaeology.org/online/features/bog/gunhild.html.

Baking and Books: A Collection of Pastimes. http://www.bakingandbooks.com.

Bonniwell, George. *The Goldrush Diary of George Bonniwell.* May 1850. Online at http://www.emigrantroad.com/gold01.html.

"California as I Saw It." First-Person Narratives of California's Early Years, 1849–1900. Library of Congress Digital Files. http://memory.loc.gov/ammem/cbhtml/cbhome.html.

Cato, Marcus Porcius. *De Rustica.* Harvard University Press. Online at University of Liverpool Internet Resource for Classics and Ancient History.

Celtic Journeys website. http://www.peterthestoryteller.co.uk/page14a.html.

Champlain, Samuel de. Edited by Slafter, Edmund. *Voyages of Samuel de Champlain.* Project Gutenberg. http://www.gutenberg.org/etext/6653.

Columbia Detachment Rations. http://www.royalengineers.ca/CDRats.html.

Daniels, Chuck. Ancient Egyptian Fishing. Available online: www.mnsu.edu/emuseum/prehistory/egypt/dailylife/fishing_egypt.htm. Retrieved September 18, 2008.

De Vere, Sir Stephen. Letter of steerage passenger, November 30, 1847. www.wesleyjohnson.com/users/Ireland/past/famine/emigration.html.

Effects of the Famine: Emigration. www.wesleyjohnston.com/users/ireland/past/famine/emigration.html.

The Hearth Tax. http://www.nationalarchives.gov.uk/catalogue/RdLeaflet.asp?sLeafletID=233.

Hungarian Cuisine. http://recipes.wikia.com/wiki/Hungary.

Indian Fishing and Hunting. Fort Raleigh National Historic Site. http://www.nps.gov/fora/forteachers/indian-fishing-and-hunting.htm.

"Inntalkochbuch." 1500. Trans. Giano Balestriere. www.medievalcookery.com.

Is Chicken Soup an Essential Drug? http://www.cmaj.ca/cgi/content/full/161/12/1532.

Josephus, Flavius. Antiquities of the Jews. Translation online at www.interhack.net.

The Journals of the Lewis and Clark Expedition. http://lewisandclarkjournals.unl.edu.

Lendering, Jona. Carthage. www.livius.org.

Love, Nat. The Life and Adventures of Nat Love Better Known in the Cattle Country as "Deadwood Dick" by Himself. Electronic Edition. http://docsouth.unc.edu/neh/natlove/menu.html.

Martin, Martin. *A Description of the Western Islands of Scotland.* 1695. Online at www.appins.org/martin.htm.

Norway Heritage: Hands across the Sea. http://norwayheritage.com.

Notable Kentucky African-Americans Database. University of Kentucky Libraries. http://www.uky.edu/Libraries/NKAA.

Nutrition and Well-Being A to Z. Africans, Diets of. http://www.faqs.org/nutrition/A-Ap/Africans-Diets-of.html.

Pepys, Samuel. *Diaries.* www.pepysdiary.com.

A Plate of Hungarian History — Goulash. http://www.cookbook.hu/angol_receptek/GoulashE.html

Pliny the Elder. The Natural History. Online at http://www.perseus.tufts.edu/cgi-bin/ptext?doc=Perseus%3Atext%3A1999.02.0137.

Plum and Prune History. http://www.pruneau.fr/gb/fruitofasoil/index.html.

Pringle, Catherine Sager. Across the Plains in 1844. Oregon Trail website. www.isu.edu/~trinmich/00.ar.sager1.html.

Quartermaster General. Conference Notes prepared for the Quartermaster School. January 1949. www.qmfound.com.

Researching Historic Buildings in Britain. www.buildinghistory.org/buildings/Mills.htm.

"Rock Tripe." *Encyclopaedia Britannica* online.

Rumble, Victoria. *Victoria's Home Companion; Or, The Whole Art of Cooking. A History of 19th Century Food.* www.geocities.com/thistledewbooks.

St. Patrick's Day Feast. http://www.flavornotes.com/revstpatrick.html.

Schenone, Laura. *A Taste of Philadelphia* website.

Scotland's Seaweed. http://www.thistleandbroom.com/scotland/seaweed.htm.

Scott, Sir Walter. *The Antiquary.* http://www.walterscott.lib.ed.ac.uk/etexts/etexts/antiquary1.htm.

Skara Brae: The Discovery of the Village. http://www.orkneyjar.com/history/skarabrae.

Soup As a Weapon. The Old Foodie, December 2006. http://theoldfoodie.blogspot.com/2006/12/soup-as-weapon.html.

Spanish Cooking. http://www.ctspanish.com/Cooking.htm.

Spirit Cave. http://www.mnsu.edu/emuseum/archaeology/sites/asia/spiritcave.html.

Use of Seaweed As Food in Ireland. http://www.seaweed.ie/uses_ireland/IrishSeaweedFood.lasso.

Vegetarians in Paradise. www.vegparadise.com/highestperch29.html.

Le Viandier de Taillevent. Online translation.

Warren Ledger (Warren, Pa.). March 11, 1875.

Welserin, Sabina. Medieval Cookbooks. http://www.daviddfriedman.com/Medieval/Cookbooks/Sabrina_Welserin.html.

Index